Transformations of Capitalism

Economy, Society and the State in Modern Times

Edited by

Harry F. Dahms
Associate Professor of Sociology
Florida State University
Tallahassee

First published 2000 by
MACMILLAN PRESS LTD
Houndmills, Basingstoke, Hampshire RG21 6XS
and London
Companies and representatives
throughout the world

ISBN 0–333–67420–0 hardcover
ISBN 0–333–67426–X paperback

A catalogue record for this book is available
from the British Library.

This book is printed on paper suitable for recycling and
made from fully managed and sustained forest sources.

10 9 8 7 6 5 4 3 2 1
09 08 07 06 05 04 03 02 01 00

Printed and bound in Great Britain by
Antony Rowe Ltd, Chippenham, Wiltshire

Contents

Series Preface

Main Trends of the Modern World is a series of books analyzing the main trends and the social psychology of our times. Each volume in the series brings together readings from social analysts who first identified a decisive institutional trend and from writers who explore its social and psychological effects in contemporary society.

The series works in the classical tradition of social theory. In this view, theory is the historically informed framing of intellectual problems about concrete social issues and the resolution of those problems through the analysis of empirical data. Theory is not, therefore, the study of the history of ideas about society, nor the abstract, ahistorical modeling of social realities, nor, as in some quarters, pure speculation often of an ideological sort unchecked by empirical reality. Theory is meaningful only when it illuminates the specific features, origins, and animating impetus of particular institutions, showing how these institutions shape experience and are linked to the social order as a whole.

Social analysts such as Karl Marx, Max Weber, Émile Durkheim, Sigmund Freud, Georg Simmel, Thorstein Veblen, and George Herbet Mead, whose works we now consider classics, never consciously set out to construct paradigms, models, or abstract theories of society. Instead they investigated concrete social phenomena such as the decline of feudal society and the emergence of industrial capitalism, the growth of bureaucracy, the consequences of the accelerating specialization of labor, the significance of religion in a scientific and secular age, the formation of self and the moral foundations of modern society, and the on-going rationalization of modern life. The continuing resonance of their ideas suggests the firmness of their grasp of deep-rooted structural trends in Western industrial society.

Later European and American social thinkers, deeply indebted though they were to the intellectual frameworks produced by the remarkable men who preceded them, faced a social order marked by increasing disarray, one that required fresh intellectual approaches. The social, cultural, and intellectual watershed was, of course, the Great War and its aftermath. The world's first total war ravaged a whole generation of youth. In Europe, it sowed the seeds of revolution, militarism, totalitarianism, fascism, and state socialism; in both Europe and America it signaled the age of mass propaganda. On both continents the aftermath of the war brought economic and political turmoil, cultural frenzies, widespread disenchantment and disillusionment, and social movements of every hue and description that led eventually to the convulsions of the Second World War. These later social thinkers grappled with issues such as:

- The deepening bureaucratization of all social spheres and the ascendance of the new middle classes.
- The collapse of old religious theodicies that once gave meaning to life and the emergence of complex social psychologies of individuals and masses in a rationalized world.
- The riddles posed by modern art and culture.
- The emergence of mass communications and propaganda as well as the manufacture of cultural dreamworlds of various sorts.
- War, militarism, and the advent of totalitarianism, fascism, and state socialism.
- The deepening irrational consequences and moral implications of the thoroughgoing rationalization of all life spheres.

Emil Lederer, Hans Speier, Joseph Schumpeter, Kenneth Burke, Robert MacIver, Harold Lasswell, Walter Lippmann, Robert Park, W. I. Thomas, Florian Znaniecki, George Orwell, Hannah Arendt, Herbert Blumer, and Hans H. Gerth are only a few of the men and women who carried forward the theoretical attitude of the great classical thinkers in the course of working on the pressing issues of their own day. In this tradition, social theory means confronting head-on the social realities of one's own times, trying to explain both the main structural drift of institutions as well as the social psychologies of individuals, groups, and classes.

What then are the major structural trends and individual experiences of our own epoch? Four major trends come immediately to mind, each with profound ramifications for individuals. We pose these as groups of research problems.

BUREAUCRACY AS THE ORGANIZATIONAL FORM OF MODERNITY

- What are the social and psychological consequences of living and working in a society dominated by mass bureaucratic structures? How do these structures affect the private lives of the men and women exposed to their influences?

- What is the structure and meaning of work in a bureaucratic society? In particular, how does bureaucracy shape moral consciousness? What are the organizational roots of the collapse of traditional notions of accountability in our society?
- What is the relationship between leaders and followers in a society dominated by a bureaucratic ethos? What are the changing roles of intellectuals, whether in the academy or in public life, in defining, legitimating, challenging, or serving the social order?

THE TECHNOLOGIES OF MASS COMMUNICATION AND THE MANAGEMENT OF MASS SOCIETY

- What role do public relations, advertising, and bureaucratized social research play in shaping the public opinions and private attitudes of the masses?
- What is the relationship between individuals' direct life experiences (with, for example, family, friends, occupations, sex, and marriage) and the definitions that the mass media suggest for these individual experiences? What illusions and myths now sustain the social order? What are the ascendant forms of this-worldly salvation in our time?
- What are the different origins, dynamics, and consequences of modern political, social, and cultural mass movements with their alternative visions of justice and morality?
- What social, economic, and cultural trends have made many great metropolises, once the epitomes of civilization and still the centers and symbols of modern life, into new wildernesses?

THE ON-GOING SOCIAL TRANSFORMATION OF CAPITALISM

- What are the prospects for a transformed capitalism in a post-Marxist, post-Keynesian era?
- How has the emergence of large bureaucratic organizations in every sector of the social order transformed the middle classes? What is the social and political psychology of these new middle classes?
- What transformations of the class and status structure have been precipitated by America's changing industrial order?
- What are the social, cultural, and historical roots of the pervasive criminal violence in contemporary American society? What social factors have fostered the breakdown of traditional mechanisms of social control and the emergence of violence as a primary means for effecting individual or group goals?

THE CLASH BETWEEN WORLDVIEWS AND VALUES, OLD AND NEW

- How has science, particularly in its bureaucratized form, transformed the liberal doctrines of natural rights, individual rights, and concomitant conceptions of the human person, including notions of life and death?
- How have the old middle classes come to terms with mass bureaucratic institutions and the subsequent emergence of new classes and status groups? What social forces continue to prompt the framing of complicated social issues in terms of primal antagonisms of kith, kin, blood, color, soil, gender, and sexual orientation?
- What are the roots of the pervasive irrationalities evident at virtually every level of our society, despite our Enlightenment legacy of reason and rationality and our embrace of at least functional rationality in our organizational apparatus? To what extent is individual and mass irrationality generated precisely by formally rational bureaucratic structures?

In short, the modern epoch is undergoing social transformations every bit as dramatic as the transition from feudalism to industrial capitalism. The very complexity of the contemporary world impedes fixed social scientific understanding. Moreover we may lack the language and concepts necessary to provide coherent analyses of some emerging features of our social order. Nonetheless this series tries to identify and analyze the major trends of modern times. With a historical awareness of the great intellectual work of the past and with a dispassionate attitude toward contemporary social realities, the series fashions grounded, specific images of our world in the hope that future thinkers will find these more useful than speculation or prophecy.

Each volume in this series addresses one major trend. The book in hand analyzes the underlying patterns of the transformation of capitalism in the last century. It also delineates the emergence of distinctively different systems of capitalism, even in the midst of economic globalization.

ROBERT JACKALL
ARTHUR J. VIDICH

Introduction*

Harry F. Dahms

Over the course of the twentieth century, both the organization of the capitalist economic process and the relationship between business, labor, and government underwent several transformations. These transformations include the rise of big business, the decline of economic policies inspired by laissez-faire, the emergence of the regulatory state, the continuous restructuring of corporate control that accompanied the shift from manufacturing to services, and the creation of an infrastructure conducive to the formation of a global economy. In different ways and to varying degrees, these transformations have changed the face and functioning of capitalism.

As we move into the twenty-first century, we need to do so with a clear understanding of the actual depth and scope of these transformations, and their implications for future social, economic, and political change. Did these transformations fundamentally alter the "nature and logic" of the capitalist process?[1] In what ways, and in whose interest, did the transformations enhance or inhibit economic development and social change in capitalist societies? Is the capitalist economy at the turn from the twentieth to the twenty-first century more transparent, stable, and reliable than in 1900? Is the capitalist economy of today more or less central to modern society and culture? Finally, are the economically most advanced nations in a better position than at the beginning of the twentieth century to confront and solve the most pressing social, political, and environmental problems and challenges?

Changes in both the economic process and the constellation between business, labor, and government comprised both major transformations

---

*   Written for this volume.

that redefined the rules governing social, political and economic decision-making processes, and minor modulations that were necessitated by changing social, political, and environmental circumstances, emerging technological possibilities, and shifting priorities and perceptions within corporate leadership. Since major transformations may not be discernable directly, the simultaneity of major and minor changes requires that we differentiate between types of change. Technological adjustments and organizational modifications are endemic to capitalism as a dynamic socioeconomic system. Though often presumed to constitute profound reconfigurations of the capitalist system, most of these adjustments and modifications do not alter the overall functioning and structure of the capitalist economy.[2] In fact, *qualitative* transformations that alter the structural foundations and the primary social, cultural, and political features of capitalist society, appear to be rather extraneous to this social order. The purpose of this volume, then, is to identify and examine transformations of the latter type, and to determine how they engendered qualitative changes in the operation of capitalism – economically, politically, and socially.

Capitalist society is both multidimensional and contradictory: a multiplicity of trends, forces, imperatives and necessities push and pull institutions, organizations, and social groups in directions that cannot be reconciled according to any one guiding principle. Though the role of the economy is more central to capitalism than to other forms of social organization, we must guard against the temptation to reduce the complexity of the latter to the supposed simplicity of the former. As will become apparent, attempts to identify the underlying patterns of all the transformations of capitalism within one single theoretical framework, or with the means of one social scientific discipline, are bound to remain inadequate. Yet the question remains: were there any underlying patterns of the transformations of capitalism during the twentieth century, and how can we identify them?

The issue of underlying patterns may be more urgent now than at any other point during the last two centuries. Once again, advanced societies find themselves at a historical juncture where the question arises as to who and what should and will determine future developments. Should the latter be the result of conscious social, political and economic decision-making and priorities? Or should the future follow mechanisms such as the self-regulating market economy which purportedly guide us in ways conscious and "rational" decision-makers never could? Once again, the question arises: should "we" delegate the responsibility to make crucial decisions, to the inferred logic of one or several more or less clearly understood mechanisms that promise to lead us toward prosperity and progress for all?

By most accounts, the transformation currently under way, "globalization," points toward the ever-more sophisticated utilization and exploitation of modern and traditional forms of social, cultural, and political assets (in addition to natural resources and scientific and technological innovations), for purposes of increasing competitiveness and enhancing profit opportunities.[3] The challenge of analyzing the logic and direction of globalization appears to be even more daunting than the analysis of transformations that prepared it. Clearly, penetrating analyses of globalization are essential to understanding the likely and possible futures of capitalist societies in the twenty-first century. Yet without an adequate assessment of the transformations of the twentieth century, we cannot hope to begin examining globalization and its possible implications for the future of different societies at varying stages of economic and political development.

In different national contexts, globalization will have profound consequences for the relationship between the economy, the state, and society, and for existing and future constellations of business, labor, and government. At the same time, it is necessary to caution that globalization may be a trend that is contingent on economic expansion and strength in the leading nations; and that this transformation may come to an abrupt halt once the most important industrial economies experience another recession. (Should these economies succeed at reducing further the threat of recessionary conditions, on the other hand, the implications would be far-reaching indeed.) In this light, the purpose of this collection of contributions by economic sociologists and political economists is to provide appraisals of what arguably were the five main transformations that shaped and reshaped capitalist societies over the course of the twentieth century.

Capitalism, control, and organization

Since the early twentieth century, political and social developments became ever more closely tied to changes in the organization of capitalist economies. Considering the breadth and depth of the study of "capitalism," the vastness of the literature, and the diversity of analytical approaches, the purpose of this Introduction is to determine whether there is a common denominator to the analyses compiled in this volume – beyond their concern with twentieth-century transformations. Since most conceptualizations of capitalism are based on economic categories that are either very broad, or very narrow and specific, their analytical value today first needs to be reassessed. Paradoxically, the common theme that appears to emerge in these analyses is not economic in nature, but sociological.

Analyses of capitalism on the basis of concepts like "free market," "private enterprise," or "innovative entrepreneurship," tend to engender working definitions that are increasingly problematic in light of the transformations of advanced capitalism at issue in this volume. What if these transformations have reshaped the "inner logic" of the capitalist market mechanism to such a degree that the descriptive and analytical value of the above concepts is in doubt? This question also applies to the laws that govern how business, labor, and government fulfill their respective tasks in society, and how they relate to each other. In what sense was the mechanism that regulated the production and distribution of goods and services at the end of the twentieth century, a "market," and in what sense is the latter "free"? Considering that many of the largest corporations today have hundreds of thousands of employees, and are owned by thousands of stockholders – is it appropriate to think of the currently dominant form of capitalist economic organization, in terms of "private enterprise"? Finally, how does "innovative entrepreneurship," for instance, describe the *modus operandi* of businesses whose strategies for bringing about and implementing innovations has been rationalized to the point of genuine planning?[4] In short, many conceptualizations of capitalism – especially with regard to public policies – tend to derive from nineteenth-century economic thinking, when small and medium-sized businesses were the dominant forms of economic organization, instead of large corporations, and when the economic role of governments was far less conspicuous than today?

Many critical analyses of capitalism in the tradition of Karl Marx's critique of political economy in important respects also remained bound to categories that applied to the liberal phase of capitalism in the nineteenth century.[5] Marx's theory did predict the rise of ever-larger units of economic organization as a necessary outcome of the process of capital accumulation (culminating at the imperialist stage of "finance capitalism" – as analyzed by Rudolf Hilferding[6]). Yet his critique of political economy rested on foundations that were quintessentially economic; it had not been designed to recognize the consequences resulting from the shift from the industrial enterprise converting natural resources into commodities, to the bureaucratic logic of managerial hierarchies that emerged around 1900 in the United States. Though Marx's critique of political economy was designed to identify the "inner logic"[7] of capital accumulation, most critiques of capitalism inspired by his work neglected the growing relevance of bureaucratic forms of organization which Max Weber analyzed in terms of his sociological theory of rationalization in modern society[8] – along with the growing importance of a finance sector that pointed beyond industrial capitalism centered around manufacturing.

In sociology, theories of capitalism and modern society tend to polarize around one of two concepts: structure at one end, culture at the other. In addition, for much of the century, theoretical sociologists endeavored to lay the foundations for their science on either of two related perspectives: the *macro-theoretical* assumption that existing and evolving societal structures shape the actions, ideas and motivations of individual actors; or the *micro-theoretical* supposition that structures are expressions rather than the basis of the normative and cultural patterns basic to all social groups. Yet neither of these perspectives succeeded at establishing the kind of unifying theoretical foundation for sociology as a social science that would convince most sociologists.

In recent years, an increasing number of theorists and sociologists have acknowledged the need to establish bridges between micro and macro analyses,[9] and between structure and culture. Among the solutions proposed, two motifs prevail. Theorists either define the challenge as the need to develop a theoretical paradigm designed to comprise both micro and macro, or structure and culture (in addition to such core categories as agency – as in Giddens' theory of structuration[10]). Or they attempt to link the opposing paradigms toward the formulation of fundamental principles that can be observed empirically; the chosen duality may not be deemed desirable, albeit necessary for analytical purposes (e.g. structure/culture, structure/agency, or – as in Habermas' theory of communicative action – system/lifeworld[11]).

Many social scientists have abandoned an interest in structural analyses oriented toward economic issues, and their implications for social life, in favor of more culturally oriented concerns and categories.[12] Poststructuralists and postmodernists tend to analyze social reality and its cultural manifestations either as independent of their economic foundations, or as specific economic foundations being a manifestation of social and cultural factors. Instead of abandoning structural analyses altogether, in favor of a more culturalist orientation, however, a third alternative might be more feasible: to link structural and cultural analysis on the level of organization.

For the purposes of theoretically informed, concrete social analyses of socio-historically specific social formations and phenomena, abstract theoretical categories as such may occlude rather than reveal the defining features of twentieth-century capitalism. Though most of the analyses of the five transformations compiled here are explicitly concerned with economic matters, as will become apparent, their explanatory rigor more or less openly centers around two sociological concepts: *organization* and *control*. Early modern thinkers, including Niccolò Machiavelli, Thomas Hobbes, and John Locke, were among the first to recognize the importance of social and political stability for enduring trade relations, economic activity and expansion. From different angles, the contributions in this volume describe how economic and political decision-makers continue to struggle with devising mechanisms designed to sustain profit opportunities under conditions that threaten socio-political stability, economic growth, and development, in economies where economic organizations operate at ever higher levels of societal complexity.

In principle, capitalism as a social system does not rest on a stable economic system, and it does not constitute a secure social order. Instead, capitalism is a potentially volatile social formation that is highly contingent on the faith in its continued existence and viability among those involved in it – the more or less well-to-do and even the most disadvantaged. The large corporations that emerged at the beginning of the twentieth century learned that while there could not be any profitability without productivity and efficiency, there also could not be any control over economic factors and processes without control over the social, political, and cultural environments. Limiting the threat of competition, reducing perils for economic growth and monetary stability, securing gains made, and preparing future profit opportunities – these are the principal challenges faced by economic organizations.

Understanding the specific forms of organization prevalent during a certain time period may be more important for the social analysis of capitalism than the apparatus of economic concepts, or such general categories as structure and culture. To see how structure and culture are related in capitalist societies, we must examine the economic organizations that mediate between the large-scale requirements of integrated, complex mass societies, and the motivational needs of individuals in terms of incentives and the construction of meaningful life histories. The analyses compiled in this volume confirm basic tenets put forth by new institutionalism in economics and sociology.[13]

This volume also confirms a basic thesis about sociology put forth by Jack Gibbs: that *control* has the potential of being "sociology's central notion."[14] Gibbs does not situate his claim historically, nor does he relate the utility of this notion to the predominance of specific forms of organization. He argues that "control" has the potential of serving as the core concept of sociological theory, far beyond the study of what is commonly known as "social control," and independently of the stage of social development. His claim that "control" is a useful tool for analyzing all forms of social organization in history is certainly compelling; yet his thesis appears to apply especially well in and for the sociology of American capitalism in the twentieth century. During this century, the degree of control garnered by new forms of organization reached qualitatively new levels.[15]

"Control" and "organization" thus constitute the vantage points required for the critical and systematic analysis of the transformations of twentieth-century capitalism. They constitute the foundation *par excellence* for sociological analyses of the modern economy, and of the political economy of the twentieth century. Focusing on the structural shifts in advanced political economies, this volume brings to light the fundamental trends that operate "below" the surface of economic activity, conveying the central importance of organization and control. Since these trends constitute crucial aspects of economic decision-making processes in bureaucratic capitalism, they commonly are implicitly presumed, and rarely become the explicit subject of economic analysis and theory in the narrow, disciplinary sense. As will become apparent, organization and control also provide the means to illustrate effectively the affinity between economic decisions made by large corporations and political decisions made by the governments of mass-democratic nation-states. In different ways, the chapters illustrate how organization and control must be recognized as integral elements of the transformations examined below. They also provide a glimpse of the likely trajectories of future social, political, and economic change resulting from the transformations of capitalism in the twentieth century.

Five transformations of capitalism: a sketch of the twentieth century

Among societies that are centered around economic activity, capitalist societies have historically been the most dynamic and revolutionary form of social order. At the same time, this capacity to undergo change without collapsing appears to be limited to certain areas of social life and order, at the expense of others. Over the course of the last two centuries, capitalism has undergone a multitude of transformations. Througout the nineteenth century, economists and social and political thinkers tried to come to terms with the newly emerging economic system, and its corresponding social formation. During its early, "liberal" phase, capitalism underwent transformations that were oriented toward stabilizing the emerging social and political order as an environment conducive to increasing efficiency and continuous competition, conditioning a disciplined work force, and the satisfaction of emerging markets – toward the enhancement of profit opportunities. During this liberal phase, a network of expanding and proliferating local economies and markets took shape that culminated in the formation of national markets in Europe and North America at the end of the nineteenth century. In emerging national economies, businesses and industries laid the foundations for the economic competition between nations.

At the turn to the nineteenth century, the industrial revolution had been taking hold in Britain, laying the foundation for "competitive capitalism": an increasingly predictable and reliable production process based on the work discipline of industrial laborers, facilitating growing control over the extraction and transportation of known (and not-yet-known) natural resources, the security and comfort resulting from rising prosperity in society, and sustained competition between industrial economic enterprises, many of which were privately owned. By the turn to the twentieth century, a profound transformation of the organization of the economic production was underway, most visibly so in America: the shift from liberal, competitive capitalism to the new world of "corporate capitalism."

During the nineteenth century, the prevailing values and ambitions in American society were those of independent, self-reliant farmers and small businessmen. Until the end of the Civil War in 1865, most of America's growing population remained insulated from, and unaffected by the social, political and cultural turmoil that forced British society to adapt its aristocratic values to the new order of liberal capitalism.[16] America's industrialization on the large scale was contingent on the victory of the industrializing Northern Union, over the agrarian Confederate South. During the decades of Reconstruction following the Civil War, farmers and small businessmen began to sense that the emergence of the industrial economic order in America threatened their most cherished values of individual self-determination, independence and self-reliance.[17] In America, the new economic order of increasingly concentrated and bureaucratic managerial capitalism proved too productive and too powerful to contain, and the principles of scientific management quickly were applied in other capitalist countries as well.

In the United States, the tension between the values of farmers and small business owners, on the one hand, and the ongoing concentration of American business during the twentieth century, on the other, was never resolved. In other countries like Germany and Japan, however, big business capitalism was more compatible with existing traditions and preconceived notions about organizations, and its spread occurred with less friction.[18]

The present state of affairs in the world economy is the result of transformations that have shaped the functioning of the economic process during the twentieth century. These transformations also have contributed to our perceptions of social, political, and economic problems, the necessary strategies for tackling these problems, and possibilities for their solution. While each of these transformations appears to have originated in and emanated from the economic process, they illustrate how closely economic institutions and processes are entwined with social, political, and cultural changes in modern western societies. The relationship between economic imperatives and the direction of societal change has been one of social scientists' chief concerns for more than a century. Continuously emerging profit opportunities, prevailing patterns of employing factors of production (natural resources, capital, human labor power, etc.), and the allocation of scarce resources impact directly on social order and change in society.

By and large, the twentieth century can be divided into five distinct time periods characterized by major changes in the relationship between the economy, society, and the state. In the United States, these phases correspond especially well with the five transformations analyzed in this volume. Since America was shaken by fewer social and political convulsions than most other advanced capitalist countries, the transformations manifested themselves more distinctly and clearly.[19] In other western societies, which will receive ample attention in this volume also, the concept as well as the reality of capitalism has been tempered to a greater extent than in the United States by political, social, and cultural factors and preconceived notions that imposed limits on the importance of the economy and its role in society. Since the late nineteenth century, the United States may well have been the most capitalistic society.[20] For all of these reasons, we may gain a better sense of things to come by paying special attention to capitalism in America.

Toward the end of the nineteenth century, most manufacturing enterprises (which formed the center of industrial capitalism) in America were still run by the entrepreneurs who had created them, or were being organized according to principles that conformed to the model of the privately owned firm, with personal relationships between employers and employees.[21] During the 1890s, however, the "robber barons" – entrepreneurs like Andrew Carnegie, Rockefeller, Jay Gould, and others who had built and personally owned vast economic empires – brought about the transition from the entrepreneurial firm as the dominant form of economic organization, to corporations with ever more complex and intricate managerial hierarchies.[22] The 1890s saw the first major "merger wave," which continued well into the early twentieth century.

The initial phase of capitalism in the twentieth century lasted from the closing decade of the nineteenth century to the end of the 1920s. By then, large corporations had become the newly dominant form of economic organization in America. In the economically most developed European countries, the organizational reconstruction of capitalism that reached its early successes in America during the first two decades of the century began to make itself felt after the First World War, partly as the result of the economic imperatives that came with the war effort, and partly as a consequence of the need and opportunity to reconstruct the more or less ravaged industrial infrastructures. During the 1920s, the principles of Frederick Taylor's scientific management[23] were applied in the United States, during Germany's reconstruction after the First World War, and in Japan and other European countries, especially Britain and France – generating competitive advantages of different types in different countries.[24] During the "golden" 1920s, with the sphere of influence of corporations, trusts, and conglomerates growing steadily, the new economic organizations seemed to guarantee economic prosperity in all advanced capitalist societies, to the benefit of a continuously growing faction of their populations.

As the large industrial corporation emerged on the economic stage, investment banks began to move toward the center of industrial society.[25] Yet while the rise of big business coincided with the birth of "finance capitalism," these trends pointed in slightly different directions, as they were characterized by slightly different logics of decision-making. In America, in particular, the rise of big business was brought about in part by the need to establish an infrastructure for long-distance transportation and distribution at the national scale, which occurred in manufacturing above all (see Chandler, Chapter 1 in this volume, pp. 33–50).

The rise of the large corporation in the "key industries" (in Veblen's use, they are responsible for the extraction and supply of natural resources, see Chapter 2 in this volume, pp. 51–65), as they were controlled by banks, forced manufacturing enterprises to follow the banks' financial orientation, toward expanding profit margins for the sake of profits, and no longer for the sake of increasing the production levels of products deemed socially desirable. The rise of big business entailed both the emergence of large-scale economic organizations *and* the move of finance capitalism from the margins of manufacturing-based industrial capitalism to the center. As Thorstein Veblen never tired to point out, big business capitalism is dominated by "absentee owners" oriented first and foremost toward quarterly dividends, and not toward increasing an economy's (or an enterprise's) overall productivity and competitiveness. With the rise of big business, managerial hierarchies became the dominant form of economic organization in advanced capitalism, accompanied by an increasing orientation toward profit-making as a purpose in and of itself: finance capitalism as big *business*. Since then, finance capitalism has continually expanded its influence over all other sectors of the economy (see Fligstein, Chapter 16 in this volume, pp. 296–314).

By the late 1920s, however, the perilous side-effects of this new economic order became apparent, as the US economy, the most productive economy of all, began to show clear signs first of a slowdown, and then of a downturn, during 1929.[26] The new economic order, as it was based increasingly on large corporations, brought with it changes in the process of production and distribution, and the conditions of profit-making. These changes put the new economy at great risk, without providing any clear mechanism as to how to counterbalance the threatening tendencies, at a time when the state in the United States still conceived of itself, and was regarded by the business community, as a passive regulator of business interests in general, of the market in terms of sustaining conditions for competition, and of trends toward the ever greater concentration of assets and power. Yet the Great Depression would not have occurred without the internationalization of finance, the growing entwinement of domestic economies and international markets, that accompanied the rise of big business. After Britain vacated the position of the world's leading economy – and of guarantor of international economic stability – during the 1920s, the US government was not ready to take on this responsibility (see

Kindleberger, Chapter 6 in this volume, pp. 121–36). Instead, the American government functioned as the far more active controller of labor unions and the guarantor of social and political stability – thus solidifying the infrastructure of the national economy. At the time, neither government nor business considered the possibility that in the new economic order of the early twentieth century, the state would have to take responsibility for protecting big business against its own strategies for profit-making.

The second phase of twentieth-century capitalism began in 1929, rung in by the stock market crash in October of that year. Though the specific role that the crash played in causing the relative collapse of the American economy and the world-wide Great Depression remains unclear, the latter forced the American government to ponder whether to stay the course and uphold the philosophy of laissez-faire, or to endow the state with responsibility for *economic* stability, in addition to maintaining social and political order.

The Great Depression signaled that the organizational changes that had occurred in the advanced economies since the late 1890s called for a different relationship between the economy and the state, forcing democratic governments to manage economic crises and to reduce the likelihood of future economic crises. The downside of the changes that brought about the new world of large-scale corporations was that an economy dominated by such organizations operated according to laws that did not directly correspond to those espoused by Adam Smith in the founding text of modern neoclassical economics, *The Wealth of Nations*. In fact, some argued, the Great Depression was ample proof that the laws governing corporate capitalism, the interaction between corporations and other social and political institutions, effectively undermined the "self-healing forces" of the market. As a result, the claim to social and economic superiority of capitalist economies over other forms of economic organization itself was thrown into question (see Polanyi, Chapter 7 in this volume, pp. 137–50).

The Great Depression began in America, and quickly spread throughout the capitalist world. In different countries, social and political responses to the economic crisis of the 1930s differed profoundly. While all governments were caught by surprise by the economic crisis, governments of advanced capitalist societies reacted quite differently, some drawing on existing national traditions that were more conducive to government intervention than they were in the United States, others turning to more fundamental "solutions", as in Germany with National Socialism.

In order to protect the capitalist socio–economic order, western governments had to respond to what turned out to be the worst economic crisis of the twentieth century with drastic measures, taking definitive steps toward strong government involvement in the economic process. To a certain extent, government had to protect big business capitalism against its own self-destructive tendencies – that is, economic decision-making that followed the principles of nineteenth-century liberal capitalism, rather than recognizing the basics of corporate capitalist economics.[27] For all *practical* purposes, the dogma of laissez-faire had to be replaced as the basis for economic policies by a doctrine that reflected the need of active government involvement in economic matters (see Keynes, Chapter 5 in this volume, pp. 101–20). While Keynes' argument – that in advanced capitalist economies, government had to generate demand for employees, products, and services, to intervene at times of economic downturn (recessions or depressions), and to alleviate the extent of unavoidable downturns to begin with – was presented in explicitly systematic terms, it was by no means the only instance of this post-laissez-faire doctrine. As Robert A. Brady put it in the early 1940s:

> Since [1931, the] dual process of expanding business organization and business-government interpenetration has been greatly speeded up. Within ... major capitalistic countries the fusion between private enterprise and political authority has been extended far enough for the habit of regarding politics and economics as but two facets of a single thing to become the rule and not the exception.[28]

While from today's perspective, it is difficult to say whether the Second World War would have occurred without the Great Depression having preceded it, there is no doubt that without the War and the heightened need for rapid and large-scale armament production, pushing further the growth of large-scale economic organizations, the capitalist world would not have emerged from the Depression as quickly, if at all. During the years immediately following the end of the Second World War in 1945, the organizational foundations for a new period of prosperity in the advanced capitalist countries were laid, in different ways, with different effects, and in part sustained by the US economy's support of the American government's determination to win the Cold War with the Soviet Union and its centrally planned economic system (see Schumpeter, Chapter 8 in this volume, pp. 151–63). The growing importance and proliferation of social, political and economic control-enhancing forms of organization was common to all industrial societies, whether capitalist or socialist (see Aron, Chapter 4 in this volume, pp. 86–97).

This third period of twentieth-century capitalism has been referred to as the "golden age of capitalism," or the initial phase of the "American century." During this period, which lasted from the late 1940s to the early 1970s, the principles of cooperation between government and large-scale business organizations that had formed during the Second World War, were refined further during decades of competition with Soviet Communism. Economic growth and prosperity, technological progress, and continuous productivity increases resulted that had never before been seen on Earth. The Bretton Woods system, established in 1944, provided the framework for an international monetary order that lasted into the early 1970s.[29] While large businesses had enabled American society to generate the resources and equipment to emerge victoriously from the War, the claim first made during the 1930s, that large corporations were becoming the dominant form of social organization in America (see Berle and Means, Chapter 3 in this volume, pp. 66–85), was fulfilled beyond doubt during the 1950s and 1960s. Though small businesses continued to exist and play an important role, their ability to influence national policy decisions, the role of government, and the direction of social change, was eroding quickly.[30] The new alliance between government and large corporations formed a "technostructure" that enhanced advanced economies' productivity, insured social and political stability, and enabled governments to directly pursue political challenges by delegating the nation's economic planning function to large corporations (see Galbraith, Chapter 9 in this volume, pp. 167–83). The economic theory put forward by Keynes in 1935 as the only viable solution to the economic crisis of the time, became the dominant economic doctrine for almost three decades after the end of the Second World War.[31]

During the Cold War, Keynesianism enabled governments to facilitate continuous economic growth, and to generate fiscal stability by means of taxation imposed on businesses and the population at large. In many instances, government did not just cooperate with large corporations. Many corporations were created by the government, or established at the request or with the active support of government agencies (see Adams, Chapter 10 in this volume, pp. 184–200). Whether the challenge was to finance the military build-up required to confront the perceived Soviet threat, to compete with socialism and the claim that "actually existing socialism" is a viable alternative to the social system of advanced capitalism, or the need to rebuild the industrial infrastructures in countries where they had been destroyed or severely damaged during the Second World War – democratic governments had to be able to confidently face any large-scale economic problem. At the same time, Keynesianism provided a "peace formula" to arrest the danger of social and political instability through the establishment and expansion of welfare state policies directed at alleviating poverty and unemployment. Keynesianism held sway into the 1970s, when the advanced western economies experienced economic slowdown, downturn, stagnation, and "stagflation" – economic stagnation combined with inflation (see Offe, Chapter 12 in this volume, pp. 222–36).

During the late 1960s and the early 1970s, it became apparent that the period of prosperity would not last forever. Western societies were undergoing major political and cultural changes, amplified in the United States by the Vietnam War, and the "baby boom" generation, which had experienced continuous and growing economic prosperity as well as growing political freedoms and rights, and was not to be satisfied by the traditional norms, values, and the outlook of their parents and grandparents. Economically, the third phase came to a close with the end of the Bretton Woods system – terminating the system that tied the value of the US dollar to the value of gold – and the first severe post-Second World War economic crisis, foreshadowed by the oil crisis of 1973–4 (see Block, Chapter 17 in this volume, pp. 317–41). The later 1970s were characterized by a period of high inflation and high unemployment, and low economic growth. What followed was a turn away from Keynesianism, and an incremental return to supply-side economics, which culminated with the election of Margaret Thatcher in 1979, and of Ronald Reagan in 1980 (see Bensman and Vidich, Chapter 18 in this volume, pp. 342–63).

Since the 1980s, when neoclassical economics replaced Keynesianism as the dominant paradigm of both economic theory and economic policy, there has been a renaissance of ideas related to laissez-faire, and to innovative entrepreneurship as conceived of by Joseph Schumpeter, the other great economic theorist of the first half of the twentieth century and, in many ways, Keynes's nemesis. To foster innovation and entrepreneurship became one of the staple objectives of economic policy since the early 1980s. However, this revival of laissez-faire and entrepreneurship occurred under conditions that could not have been more different from those that prevailed before the rise of big business at the beginning of the twentieth century. The 1980s' return to laissez-faire principles did not bring about a slowdown in the growth of large corporations, despite different types of restructuring strategies that decreased the size of operating units, accelerated the decline in union membership, and reduced the size of the industrial workforce (see Bluestone and Harrison, Chapter 13 in this volume, pp. 239–56 and Kolko, Chapter 15 in this volume, pp. 274–95) – a shift from concentration with centralization to "concentration without centralization."[32] The US government's policy orientation, for instance, also was rather mixed: a combination of entrepreneurial and competition-oriented ideas (see Cohen and Zysman, Chapter 14 in this volume, pp. 257–73), with a vast expansion in state-subsidized military spending, generating the largest national debt of any country in history – and with it, the tremendous growth of related firms and corporations, an increase in planning and cooperation between government and the largest corporations (see Jordan, Chapter 11 in this volume, pp. 201–21). The liberalization policies of the 1980s, designed to reduce the regulatory power of the government, also facilitated a boom in financial speculation, bringing about a wave of hostile take-overs and leveraged buyouts – thus revealing the continued and growing importance of the "finance conception" of corporate control in the American economy (see Fligstein, Chapter 16 in this volume, pp. 296–314) – and the stock market crash in October 1987.[33]

The end of the Cold War alleviated the pressures to compete with an "actually existing" alternative socio-economic system on the *social* level. The demise of East European communism cleared the way for the continuous reduction of the size of the welfare state in many countries, without causing social unrest, and the spread of ideas and practices oriented toward globalization. A growing number of individual companies have been replaced by complex relationships between the economy, the state, and different types of corporations operating in different spheres and markets – national, multinational, and transnational. During this fourth period of twentieth-century capitalism, the multinational corporation became the dominant form of economic organization (see Gilpin, Chapter 19 in this volume, pp. 364–84). No longer dominated by industrial production, but centered around computer-based service jobs, capitalist economies have successfully integrated the remnants of the industrial working class into the moral order of capitalist society.

After the election of Bill Clinton as US President in 1992, America experienced a period of continuous economic growth, continued corporate downsizing, an acceleration in the frequency and scope of mergers within and between most sectors of the industry, and a decline in the official unemployment rate. At the same time, America's main economic competitors, Japan and Germany, found themselves in severely weakened positions, for reasons that could not be explained exclusively in economic terms (including in Germany, the economic consequences of unification, and in Japan, the long-term effects of the collapse of the real estate market). This fifth period at the close of the twentieth century returned America to the position of the leading economy in the world. The 1990s established the structural and ideological foundations for the move toward globalization, and entailed a limited return to principles of Keynesian economic policies (see Helleiner, Chapter 20 in this volume, pp. 385–97). The economic and fiscal policies of the Clinton Administration in particular successfully integrated elements of demand-side and supply-side economics. As network-based transnational corporations began to dominate the international economy, nation-states and national economies integrated further, under the umbrella of industrial alliances growing in size and number. As the overall importance of the nation-state appears to continue to decline, the relative importance of geographical regions dominated by one or two national economies is on the rise, with increasing opportunities for the conditions of international competition being organized within and between these blocks (see Stallings and Streeck, Chapter 21 in this volume, pp. 398–415).

Economy, society, and the state in modern times: sociology of business, labor, and government

Capitalist society is above all an economic society, and every aspect of this society has an economic dimension. Considering this centrality of the economic dimension to the study of all spheres of life in capitalist society, the relative neglect of the shaping power of the prevailing mode of economic production and the dominant form of economic organization in modern society by the mainstream social sciences is surprising. The relationship between capitalism and sociology is most instructive, as the emergence of the latter is directly tied to the historical entrenchment of the former.

During the nineteenth century, the social sciences emerged as attempts to identify the uniqueness, achievements, functioning, and promise of the capitalist market economy, the nation-state, and the labor movement, as genuinely modern phenomena – the three societal dimensions of what came to be called "modern society." As Jürgen Habermas put it, sociology emerged as the social science designed to reflect upon the impact of two specific historical developments that began during the late eighteenth century, solidified during the nineteenth century, and became the respective subject matters of economics and political science: the formation of the modern, self-regulating market economy, and the rise of the nation-state.[34] Sociology was the academic response to these developments, and the effects they engendered on politics, culture, and society. As a discipline, sociology developed as a set of theories and a catalogue of methodological and conceptual tools designed to determine how modern societies differ from premodern societies, and to identify the defining features of modern society.[35] To conceive of sociology as a social science independently of these two developments would be to abstract from the historical conditions that were necessary for sociology to emerge. In response to the perceived need for a new science of this new society, sociology began as the science of modern capitalist society in relation to its most important pillars: the self-regulating market economy and the administrative nation-state.

Many of the theoretical frameworks that economists and social scientists employed toward grasping the nature and logic of capitalism in the twentieth century derived from theories designed to analyze capitalism in its "liberal" phase, along with its various problems, concerns, and categories. To determine how well designed their theories were for purposes of analyzing twentieth-century capitalism is one of the tasks of this volume. To fulfill it, we must examine how well their respective frameworks enabled social scientists to determine the importance and scope of the transformations of capitalism, and their implications. Did the nineteenth-century theorists predetermine subsequent analyses to the point where the social analysts were not able to distinguish between different types of transformations? Did they enhance their successors' ability to distinguish qualitative from quantitative transformations, and structural from superficial transformations? How do we have to read and apply the liberal theories to fit the changes that occurred during the twentieth century?

For purposes of this volume, I will conceive of "sociology" as the social science of capitalist society, the science of a society where economic activity proliferates, under the umbrella of increasing bureaucratization. Sociology in this sense also is always the sociology of business, labor, and government. To analyze sociologically the features of capitalism is to analyze specific constellations of business, labor, and government. To determine how exactly a modern society is a capitalist society, we need to be able to determine precisely how business, labor, and government relate to each other, practically and ideologically, and how they have related to each other, in specific instances, historically.

Modern capitalism is by no means monolithic; the differences among American, British, German, French, Italian, Japanese and Korean capitalisms at times are so dramatic that application of "capitalism" to a specific society may occlude rather than expose specific constellations of business, labor, and government prevalent in a particular country.[36] As a result, it is necessary to apply a comparative perspective to different economic systems under the general category of capitalism, as well as different forms of organization within each of those economic systems. In addition, the emergence of distinctive global centers of capitalism in Europe (the European Union), North America (the North American Free Trade Agreement – NAFTA), and in the Pacific Rim, has subverted the idea of a global economy as a unified and homogeneous system. Still, modern society is characterized by a qualitatively unique constellation of economy, society and the state.

The extent of economic performance constitutes the material foundation of modern societies and provides the fiscal basis for the administrative state in those societies, with more or less immediate implications for the overall stability of society and for the operation of all the different subsystems and their institutional ability to fulfill the multifarious tasks that are integral to the functioning of a highly integrated and complex society. Though the superiority of the capitalist economic system over other economic systems is likely to be based mostly in its greater economic power, its legitimacy derives from the claim that society's overall benefits deriving from capitalist economic principles and institutions by far outweigh any other known forms of economic organization at the local and national level. By providing democratic government with the tax-income required for it to pursue policies that are in the general interest of society, capitalist market economies effectively enhance the quality of life in society.

The state is both dependent on, and responsible for, the conditions that are necessary for continuous economic growth and economic development. Without the growing tax revenue that results from expanding production and distribution, the state would not be able to fulfill that function which economic organizations, however well coordinated, are not able to fulfill directly: the maintenance (and, if necessary, the reestablishment) of social and political stability. This fundamental affinity between the respective functions of the market economy (making profits by increasing productivity) and the administrative state (sustaining order to facilitate economic growth) makes it difficult at times to carefully distinguish between the interests of the economy and the interests of the state, and to determine the degree of relative autonomy of the economy from the state, and vice versa. Whenever we examine the relationship between "the economy" and "the state" in a particular society at a particular time, we must ask: how (in)dependent are economic actors from state regulators; how independent are politicians, civil servants and government administrators from economic decision-makers?

"Society," finally, is the *critical* factor in relation to economy and administrative state, mostly in two ways. Society is both critical *to*, and at times critical *of*, economic organizations and the values that are basic to capitalist market economies and capitalist societies. Society is critical to capitalist market economics in the sense that it provides the moral, normative, and institutional foundation of a functioning market economy. Capitalist economic activity is contingent on a favorable social and cultural environment that provides the kind of institutional ties and forms of organization that are essential to the functioning of the spectrum of types of economic organizations, ranging from family-owned small businesses to large national and multinational corporations. Irrespective of whether these organizations take the form of such basic units as the nuclear family, of national and multinational corporations, or the all-embracing nation-state, they instill in the members of capitalist societies from early childhood onward values and norms that induce an interest in, or tolerance for, a business-oriented, economic outlook on life. However, rather than being based on openly economic values, the business orientation that is central to capitalist societies derives from norms and values that are social and cultural at root, that date back to precapitalist times, that are religious in origin and nature, or that explicitly contradict the individualistic, self-interested orientation of capitalist economic activity.

On the basis of these precapitalist or anti-capitalist norms and values, segments of "society" (as embodied in social groups of different sizes) may be critical *of* the economic orientation basic to capitalism. As was evidenced for most of the twentieth century by the labor movements of different countries, various church organizations, and more recently, by various environmentalist movements, the proliferation of civil, political and social rights[37] that is so essential to modern society, both supports and threatens the smooth functioning of economic production, and the centrality of economic organizations in all societies at the turn to the twenty-first century. To maximize the support and to minimize the threat, large-scale economic organizations (at times in concert with government agencies) have taken it upon themselves to intervene, more or less openly, on behalf of "society's" interest in economic growth. To control, educate, subdue, and shape potential criticism of globalizing capitalism has become one of the political functions that the largest corporations have taken on. As a result, large corporations appear to have expanded the realm of modern society they deem necessary to control to include social and cultural institutions, groups and movements.

Economic thinkers since Adam Smith have reminded us that the interests of economic actors are never necessarily those of the general public. Recall, for instance, the warning Smith formulated in *The Wealth of Nations* when, within the context of his synoptical class theory, he wrote about the "three original orders of society": "those who live by rent" of land, "those who live by wages" of labor, and "those who live by profits" of stock.[38] Smith endeavored to determine the nature of the relationship between the economic interests of each of these orders, and "the general interest of the society." Proprietors of land, he wrote, as well as laborers, cannot deceive the public, and their fate is directly tied to the general interest and economic situation of society. If society is doing well economically speaking, land owners and laborers are doing well also. Smith's specific concern, however, was with the relationship between the interests of the "third order" of society – of employers, merchants, master manufacturers, dealers – and the general interest of society. He wrote:

> [The] employers constitute the third order, that of those who live by profit. It is the stock that is employed for the sake of profit, which puts into motion the greater part of the useful labour of every society. The plans and projects of the employers of stock regulate and direct all the most important operations of labour, and profit is the end proposed by all those plans and profits [and continued] But the rate of profits does not, like rent and wages, rise with the prosperity, and fall with the declension, of the society. On the contrary, it is naturally low in rich, and high in poor countries, and it is always highest in the countries which are going fastest to ruin ... The interest of the dealers ... in any particular branch of trade or manufactures, is always in some respects different from, and even opposite to, that of the public. To widen the market and to narrow the competition, is always the interest of the dealers. To widen the market may frequently be agreeable enough to the interest of the

public; but to narrow the competition must always be against it, and can serve only to enable the dealers, by raising their profits above what naturally would be, to levy, for their own benefit, an absurd tax upon the rest of their fellow-citizens (*The Wealth of Nations*, pp. 249–50).

As the most prominent advocate of free market capitalism, Smith's emphasis on the need to sustain competition is not surprising; his contention that it is in the interest of employers, master manufacturers, merchants and dealers to eliminate competition, however, is all too often forgotten. We also would be well-advised to keep in mind the closing passage of Smith's theory of the "three orders of society" ibid.:

The proposal of any new law or regulation of commerce which comes from [the third] order, ought always to be listened to with great precaution, and ought never to be adopted till after having been long and carefully examined, not only with the most scrupulous, but also with the most suspicious attention. It comes from an order of men, whose interest is never exactly the same with that of the public, who have generally an interest to deceive and even to oppress the public, and who accordingly have, upon many occasions, both deceived and oppressed it.

Extrapolating from this conclusion, we might surmise that in an increasingly globalized world economy operating according to principles of profit-making under conditions of more or less global competition, more and more businesses will be forced to treat society and its cultural, political, and social dimensions as an assemblage of resources to be utilized for purposes of profit-making at best, or sheer survival in the market place at worst. From the perspective of businesses, society has to be malleable for economic purposes, especially since society has the capacity to resist. The more powerful the dominant form of economic organization, the stronger its position to break the resistance, ideally before it emerges. This is not to say, however, that because the scale and scope of economic organizations and their activities reached ever-new heights, contemporary political economies are more monopolistic now than at any earlier point during the 20th century, and that the largest corporations are in the position to pursue a multiplicity of objectives and strategies without concern about competitive pressure. Under conditions of global competition, even the most powerful corporations are not likely to reach the position of monopoly, or to remain in such a position for an extended period of time. In fact, it would not be in the interest of large corporations to attain the position of monopoly, since it would make them vulnerable to the kind of social and political criticism that will be silenced as long as the market is dominated by a few, competing oligopolistic corporations. All the more reason for corporations to reduce the non-economic impediments to business success that do not result from competition, such as social, political and cultural counter-trends.

On the other hand, the state is not in the position either to direct economic affairs without mediation and the cooperation – if tenuous – of business leaders. Instead, while the state has to administer society so as to "best" fulfill its economic responsibilities, the state is at the same time the extension of economic interests in this sense. Smith's "class theory" should serve as a reminder that despite economic rationalization and modernization, the growing influence the largest businesses exert in a globalizing economy may effectively inhibit the rational solution of many social, political and economic problems at the local, national and international levels.

Toward a social theory of modern capitalism

The endeavor to analyze capitalism in its complexity is at the same time an endeavor to analyze the complex nature of modern society. The two are so strongly entwined that it is impossible to analyze one without the other.[39] In addition, given the specific "logics" of economic processes and decision-making, those social sciences that were not specifically designed to analyze them will not be capable of confronting the challenge. This is not to say, however, that only those sciences specifically designed to analyze, say, the logic of economic decision-making within the capitalist firm have contributions to make to their understanding. Quite the opposite: whenever we contend that only the specialized sciences should be allowed to make definite determinations as to what is the truth about this relationship, that condition, yet another phenomenon, etc. – we must endeavor to *integrate* all the approaches that have important contributions to make. The challenge of analyzing capitalism is precisely to resist the trend to categorize and eliminate that which does not belong, to draw definite distinctions, to isolate pertinent approaches to crucial questions. At the same time, there is no "royal path" to doing so: the search of an adequate economics as well as of an adequate sociology of modern capitalist society will continue as long as we are not capable of integrating all the pertinent tributaries to the understanding of complex phenomena. Though every individual approach within the social sciences will have to reduce the complexity of the whole to make intelligible statements that stand up to scrutiny, the individual contributions also will remain deficient as long as they continue to be disconnected from each other.

This collection is intended to provide the kind of perimeter that will enable those willing to engage in the endeavor to link together the often seemingly incompatible, disjointed, and openly contradictory contributions to the understanding of modern capitalism. Though such incompatibility is distressing to many, it should not be so to the point where desperation is the only feasible response. Since the contributions assembled here start out from often very different presuppositions, pursuing diverse objectives based on diverging theoretical presumptions, the selection is designed to illustrate how despite apparent incompatibility and contradiction, it is possible to arrive at an intelligible narrative of the transformations of capitalism in the twentieth century. Many of the authors who provided the analyses collected here start out from conflicting assumptions; many of them have written important work on issues covered by others included. The central theme providing the organizing principle is: what do these analyses tell us about what happened in the twentieth century, and how can we learn from them toward coping with (or responding well to) the challenges of the twenty-first?

By focusing on what arguably are the five most important transformations of capitalism, we will be in a better position to go about addressing this question. We must carefully distinguish between those features that have not changed or changed very little, and those that may have changed to a far greater extent. Only if we make this distinction will we be in the position to ask whether, despite the apparent evidence to the contrary, is it possible that over the course of the twentieth century, capitalism did not become more diffuse, disorganized, and less discernable, but instead, more crystalline, and its features more transparent.

If changes in the mode of production, in the market, in what constitutes the central factor of production, in the role of technological change, etc. do not engender a transformation in the definition of organizational control, the changes may remain superficial. The nature of *decision-making processes* needs to change, along with the kind of *interactions* among business organizations, and between the latter and labor organizations and government. Unless such a change indeed has occurred, we have to assume that while the transformation at hand may have affected a specific area of economic action, it may leave unaffected the operation of the economy as a whole. Accordingly, studies that endeavor to demonstrate that major changes have resulted from a recent trend must be able to show that a change in the production process, the central mode of production, the core factor of production, or the dominant new technology, will bring with it a qualitative transformation that *translates into organizational change.*[40] Such organizational change must occur within and/or between the dominant forms of economic organization, labor organizations, and government. Accordingly, the definitive criteria for determining whether there has been qualitative change in capitalism is whether it has brought with it a qualitative transformation of the dominant form of economic organization, and the prevailing definition of organizational control. This criterion applies both in terms of positive and negative changes, desirable and destructive transformations. Whether a transformation of capitalism has occurred can be established if we are able to identify a transformation in the prevailing culture of economic organizations, which engenders a different definition of control within and between the basic social, political, and economic organizations in modern society. Changes in the central factor of production, the dominant mode of production, and in the organization of economic production, distribution and employment which do not bring about a new organizational culture, or type of constellation between business, labor, and government, do not constitute transformations of capitalism.

None of the contributions included here argues from a narrow and clearly specifiable theoretical position. Instead, they combine insights gained in several social sciences. In this sense, this volume is a set of examples for interdisciplinary social science over the course of the 20th century, crossing borders between economics, sociology, political science, and organizational studies. Though the diagnoses the chapters present may lead to conclusions about what is to be done that appear (or in fact are) incompatible, suggest that there may not be a necessary relationship between the diagnoses and the conclusions that ought to be drawn – except in the narrow sense and for the specific set of questions addressed in each single piece.[41] This collection ought to be understood as an attempt to *prepare* the kind of comprehensive perspective without which we cannot hope to address effectively any issues pertaining to capitalism in general, to the nature of the relationship between economy, state, and society, and to constellations of business, labor, and government. This is, after all, the promise of modern times: that we can move beyond the narrow definitions of "reality" (whether political, economic, ideological, religious, or theoretical), to arrive at a better sense of the whole by means of unimpeded intellectual and practical exchange. The kind of answers that must be considered by societies cannot be arrived at on the basis of any individual interpretation, approach, or science, however much we may try. To provide the foundation for a forum where all those involved and concerned can strive for the formulation of feasible and viable strategies is the task of social scientists and scholars. The best "solutions" cannot be forced, they must evolve. If they do not, any attempt to impose them likely will not succeed, as they are contingent on the agreement, even if tenuous, of those affected – unless success can be achieved by raising the level of control applied, and the complexity of organization implemented. While this may be disheartening to those who conceive of solutions for, and the resolution of, structural problems as forceful implementations of "correct" strategies, it may serve as a reminder that desirable solutions should be compelling to those involved and affected.

Notes and References

1. Robert L. Heilbroner, *The Nature and Logic of Capitalism* (New York: W. W. Norton, 1985).
2. Temporary periods of success or failure in different countries, or shifts in the relative economic position of one country as opposed to its main competitors (especially, between the United States, Germany and Japan), frequently form the basis for extrapolations regarding the viability of various models. For instructive examples, see Lester Thurow, *Head to Head. The Coming Economic Battle Among Japan, Europe, and America* (New York: Warner Books, 1992), Michel Albert, *Capitalism vs. Capitalism. How America's Obsession with Individual Achievement and Short-term Profit has Led It to the Brink of Collapse* (New York: Four Wall Eight Windows, 1993); also Mortimer Zuckerman, "A Second American Century," *Foreign Affairs*, 77 (3) (May–June 1998), pp. 18–31. On this issue in general, see Paul Krugman, "America the Boastful," *Foreign Affairs*, 77 (3) (May–June 1998), pp. 32–45.
3. Ulrich Beck, *Was ist Globalisierung? Irrtümer des Globalismus – Antworten auf Globalisierung* (Frankfurt/M.: Suhrkamp, 1997).
4. See Joseph A. Schumpeter, *Capitalism, Socialism, and Democracy* (New York: Harper & Row, 1942); also Harry F. Dahms, *Schumpeter's Dynamic Theory of Capitalism: The Rise and Fall of the Entrepreneur* (Minneapolis: University of Minnesota Press, forthcoming).
5. Though Marx's theory comprises both economic and sociological analyses, among others, he did not anticipate the implications of full-scale bureaucratization of all spheres of life. On the need to distinguish between those

elements in Marx's theory designed to analyze and critique liberal capitalism, and those that were designed for capitalism and modern society in general, see Moishe Postone, *Time, Labor, and Social Domination. A Reinterpretation of Marx's Critical Theory* (Cambridge: Cambridge University Press, 1993).

6. Rudolf Hilferding, *Finance Capital. A Study of the Latest Phase of Capitalist Development* [1910] (London: Routledge & Kegan Paul, 1981). See also Jonas Zoninsein, *Monopoly Capital Theory. Hilferding and Twentieth Century Capitalism* (New York: Greenwood Press, 1990); Wilfried Gottschalch, *Strukturveränderungen der Gesellschaft und politisches Handeln in der Lehre von Rudolph Hilferding* (Berlin: Duncker & Humblot, 1962); and also Harry F. Dahms, "The Early Frankfurt School Critique of Capitalism: Critical Theory Between Pollock's 'State Capitalism' and the Critique of Instrumental Reason," *The Theory of Capitalism in the German Economic Tradition*, ed. Peter Koslowski (Berlin: Springer, 2000).

7. For a reassessment of Weber's concept, see Harry F. Dahms, "Theory in Weberian Marxism: Patterns of Critical Social Theory in Lukács and Habermas," *Sociological Theory* 15 (3) (1997), pp. 181–214.

8. Max Weber, *Economy and Society. An Outline of Interpretive Sociology* [1922], trans. E. Fischoff *et al.*; ed. Guenther Roth and Claus Wittich (Berkeley: University of California Press, 1978); also Henry Jacoby, *The Bureaucratization of the World* (Berkeley: University of California Press, 1973).

9. See Jeffrey Alexander and Bernhard Giesen (eds), *The Micro–Macro Link* (Berkeley: University of California Press, 1987).

10. Anthony Giddens, *The Constitution of Society* (Berkeley: University of California Press, 1984); see also Ira J. Cohen, *Structuration Theory: Anthony Giddens and the Constitution of Social Life* (Basingstoke: Macmillan, 1989).

11. Dichotomies of this type are expressive of the degree to which theoretical sociology itself has adapted to the continued division of labor that prevails in, and continually transforms, all aspects of life in modern capitalist society. For the sake of clarity, I consider the type of theory that is oriented toward the development of generally valid, formal categories intended to apply to a multiplicity of social groups at different stages of development, and to ground sociology as a social sciences, as *sociological theory*. By contrast, the purpose of this volume is to contribute to the *social theory* of twentieth-century capitalism – a project that requires theoretical concepts and tools targeted toward the analysis of a concrete socio–historical formation. See, for example, Nicos Mouzelis, *Sociological Theory: What Went Wrong? Diagnoses and Remedies* (London: Routledge, 1995), pp. 3–8.

12. At the beginning of this century, as well as during the Great Depression, heated debates about the desirability (and lack thereof) of market economies operating according to capitalist principles were commonplace. By the end of the century, however, as globalization was well underway, scholars and political activists equally abstained from considering the possibility of viable modifications of and alternatives to capitalist market economies. See Richard Rorty, *Achieving Our Country. Leftist Thought in Twentieth-Century America* (Cambridge, Mass.: Harvard University Press, 1998).

13. See, for example, the collection of analyses edited by Walter W. Powell and Paul J. DiMaggio, *The New Institutionalism in Organizational Analysis* (Chicago: University of Chicago Press, 1991).

14. Jack P. Gibbs, *Control: Sociology's Central Notion* (Urbana: University of Illinois Press, 1989); also *A Theory about Control* (Boulder: Westview Press, 1994).

15. A similarly curious example for using "control" toward grounding the sociological analysis of contemporary phenomena is Harrison C. White's *Identity and Control. A Structural Theory of Social Action* (Princeton: Princeton University Press, 1992). White presents his work as a theory of social action that is independent of the specific macro-conditions of social life. Yet when viewed within the context of the transformations of twentieth-century capitalism, it could well be read as a *specific* theory of forms of social action under conditions of life emerging in network-based, transnational capitalism (though White does not suggest such a reading).

16. Charles G. Sellers, *The Market Revolution: Jacksonian America, 1815–1846* (New York: Oxford University Press, 1991).

17. Martin L. Sklar, *The Corporate Reconstruction of American Capitalism. The Market, the Law, and Politics* (New York: Cambridge University Press, 1988).

18. In *Socializing Capital. The Rise of the Large Industrial Corporation in America* (Princeton: Princeton University Press, 1997, pp. 272–3), William G. Roy put it as follows:

> The large American corporation arose during a period sometimes called the organizational revolution, when many areas of social life were becoming socialized ... The emergent system of professions was for the first time socializing the control that occupational groups had over their work and embarking on campaigns of collective social mobility ... Workers were organizing to socialize the sale of labor power, defensively pitting a united labor force against a united capitalist class. Philanthropists were creating foundations to combine sources of the wealthy into more rational and sustained programs. And governments were forming a new type of organization, different from executive, judicial, and legislative bodies that had previously governed: 'independent' regulatory agencies that were socializing the monitoring of food production, transportation, commerce, and the production of social statistics. Individualism was increasingly a hollow, albeit still formidable, ideology beckoning more toward a past that never really existed than affirming the present. Thus socialized activities are more than networks; they are organized in institutions.

19. Consider, for instance, the political response to the Great Depression in Germany, and its national and geopolitical implications.

20. See, for instance, Seymour Martin Lipset, *American Exceptionalism: A Double-Edged Sword* (New York: W. W. Norton, 1996).

21. Mark Casson, *The Entrepreneur: An Economic Theory* (Totowa, NJ: Barnes & Noble, 1982); and *The Firm and the Market: Studies on Multinational Enterprise and the Scope of the Firm* (Cambridge, Mass.: MIT Press, 1987).

22. Matthew Josephson, *The Robber Barons. The Great American Capitalists 1861–1901* (New York: Harcourt, Brace & Co., 1934); Jonathan Hughes, *The*

Vital Few. The Entrepreneur and American Economic Progress (New York: Oxford University Press, 1986; expanded edn). On the new forms of organization, see Alfred D. Chandler, Jr., and Herman Daems (eds), *Managerial Hierarchies. Comparative Perspectives on the Rise of Modern Enterprise* (Cambridge, Mass.: Harvard University Press, 1980).

23. Frederick Winslow Taylor, *The Principles of Scientific Management* (New York: W. W. Norton, 1947).

24. On the general issue of competitive advantage, see Michael E. Porter, *The Competitive Advantage of Nations* (New York: Free Press, 1990).

25. See William G. Roy, *Socializing Capital. The Rise of the Large Industrial Corporation in America* (Princeton: Princeton University Press, 1997), esp. Chapter 5.

26. John Kenneth Galbraith, *The Great Crash, 1929* (Boston: Houghton Mifflin, 1979).

27. See Hans H. Gerth, "A Marx for Managers," in Joseph Bensman, Arthur Vidich and Nobuko Gerth (eds), *Politics, Character and Culture: Perspectives from Hans Gerth* (Westport, Conn.: Greenwood Press, 1982).

28. Robert A. Brady, *Business as a System of Power* (New York: Columbia University Press, 1943), p. 295.

29. Georg Schild, *Bretton Woods and Dumbarton Oaks: American Economic and Political Post-war Planning in the Summer of 1944* (New York: St Martin's Press, 1995). See also A. L. K. Acheson, J. F. Chant and M. F. J. Prachowny (eds), *Bretton Woods Revisited. Evaluations of the International Monetary Fund and the International Bank for Reconstruction and Development* (Toronto: University of Toronto Press, 1972) – the collection of reevaluations of the Bretton Woods system that were delivered at a conference in 1969, two years before President Nixon suspended the convertibility of the dollar, plunging "the international monetary system into its gravest crisis since Bretton Woods" (p. xxiii).

30. Kim McQuaid, *Uneasy Partners: Big Business in American Politics 1945–1990* (Baltimore: Johns Hopkins University Press, 1994).

31. John Maynard Keynes, *The General Theory of Employment, Interest and Money* (San Diego: Harcourt, Brace & Jovanovich, 1936).

32. See Bennett Harrison, *Lean and Mean. The Changing Landscape of Corporate Power in the Age of Flexibility* 2nd ed. (New York: Guilford Press, 1997).

33. See, for example, Ruben J. Dunn and John Morris, *The Crash Put Simply. October 1987* (New York: Praeger, 1988).

34. "[S]ociology originated as the discipline responsible for the problems that politics and economics pushed to one side on their way to becoming specialized sciences. Its theme was the changes in social integration brought about within the structure of old-European societies by the rise of the modern system of [nation] states and by the differentiation of market-regulated economy. Sociology became the science of crisis par excellence; it concerned itself above all with the anomic aspects of the dissolution of traditional social systems and the development of modern ones."

(Jürgen Habermas, *The Theory of Communicative Action*, Boston: Beacon Press, 1984, vol. 1, p. 4)

35. Harry F. Dahms, "Beyond the Carousel of Reification: Critical Social Theory After Lukács, Adorno, and Habermas," *Current Perspectives in Social Theory* 18 (1998), pp. 3–62.
36. See David J. Hickson (ed.), *Management in Western Europe. Society, Culture and Organization in 12 Nations* (Berlin: Walter de Gruyter, 1993).
37. According to T. H. Marshall, the last three centuries can be understood in terms of the successive establishment of civil rights, political rights, and social rights. In *Citizenship and Social Class, and Other Essays* (Cambridge: Cambridge University Press, 1950).
38. Adam Smith, *An Inquiry into the Nature and Causes of the Wealth of Nations* (New York: The Modern Library, 1937), p. 248
39. See Stuart Hall, David Held, Don Hubert and Kenneth Thompson (eds), *Modernity. An Introduction to Modern Societies* (Malden: Blackwell, 1996); esp. Vivienne Brown, "The Emergence of the Economy," pp. 90–121, and Anthony McGrew, "A Global Society?", pp. 466–503.
40. See, for example, Manuel Castells, *The Rise of Network Society*, Vol. 1 of *The Information Age: Economy, Society and Culture* (Malden, Mass.: Blackwell, 1996); David Harvey, *The Condition of Postmodernity. An Enquiry into the Origins of Cultural Change* (Cambridge, Mass.: Blackwell, 1990), on post-Fordism, esp. pp. 119–197; Peter F. Drucker, *Post-Capitalist Society* (New York: Harper Business, 1993), on the rise of the knowledge society; and, for an earlier example, Daniel Bell, *The Coming of Post-Industrial Society: A Venture in Social Forecasting* (New York: Basic Books, 1973).
41. See, for instance, Claus Offe, "Ungovernability: On the Renaissance of Conservative Theories of Crisis," in Jürgen Habermas (ed.), *Observations on "The Spiritual Situation of the Age." Contemporary German Perspectives*, trans Andrew Buchwalter (Cambridge, Mass.: MIT Press, 1985).

Part I

The Rise of "Big Business": Industrial Society between Economic Concentration and Finance Capitalism

1

The Role of Business in the United States: A Historical Survey (1972)*

Alfred D. Chandler, Jr.

For a paper on the historical role of business in America to provide a solid foundation for discussions of the present and future, it must examine a number of questions: Who were the American businessmen? How did they come to go into business? How were they trained? How broad was their outlook? And, of even more importance, what did they do? How did they carry out the basic economic functions of production, distribution, transportation, and finance? How was the work of these businessmen coordinated so that the American economic system operated as an integrated whole? Finally, how did these men and the system within which they worked adapt to fundamental changes in population, to the opening of new lands, resources, and markets, and to technological developments that transformed markets, sources of supply, and means of production and distribution? The answers to these questions, as limited as they may be, should help to make more understandable the present activities and future capabilities of American business.

The colonial merchant

The merchant dominated the simple rural economy of the colonial period. By the eighteenth century he considered himself and was considered by others to be a businessman. His economic functions differentiated him from the farmers who produced crops and the artisans

* From Eli Goldston, Herbert C. Morton and G. Neal Ryland (eds), *The American Business Corporation. New Perspectives on Profit and Purpose* (Cambridge, Mass.: MIT Press, 1972), pp. 39–56. This article is an outline of a study of the history of American business that the author is undertaking with generous support from the Alfred P. Sloan, Jr. Foundation.

who made goods. Although the farmers and artisans occasionally carried on business transactions, they spent most of their time working on the land or in the shop. The merchant, on the other hand, spent nearly all his time in handling transactions involved in carrying goods through the process of production and distribution, including their transportation and finance.

The colonial merchant was an all-purpose, non-specialized man of business. He was a wholesaler and a retailer, an importer and an exporter. In association with other merchants he built and owned the ships that carried goods to and from his town. He financed and insured the transportation and distribution of these goods. At the same time, he provided the funds needed by the planter and the artisan to finance the production of crops and goods. The merchant, operating on local, inter-regional, and international levels, adapted the economy to the relatively small population and technological changes of the day and to shifts in supply and demand resulting from international tensions.

These men of business tended to recruit their successors from their own family and kinship group. Family loyalties were important, indeed essential, in carrying on business in distant areas during a period when communication between ports was so slow and uncertain. Able young clerks or sea captains might be brought into the family firm, but sons and sons-in-law were preferred. Trading internationally as well as locally, the merchants acquired broader horizons than the farmer, artisan, and day laborer. Only a few of the great landowners and leading lawyers knew the larger world. It was the colonial merchants who, allied with lawyers from the seaport towns and with the Virginia planters, encouraged the Revolution, brought about the ratification of the Constitution, and then set up the new government in the last decade of the eighteenth century.

The rise of the wholesaler, 1800–1850

During the first half of the nineteenth century, although the American economy remained primarily agrarian and commercial, it grew vigorously. The scope of the economy expanded as the nation moved westward into the rich Mississippi Valley, and as increasing migration from Europe still further enlarged its population. Even more important to American economic expansion were the technological innovations that occurred in manufacturing in Great Britain. Without the new machines of the Industrial Revolution, the westward movement in the

United States and the migration to its shores would have been slower. These innovations reshaped the British textile industry, creating a new demand for cotton from the United States. Before the invention of the water frame, the spinning jenny, the mule, and then the power loom, cotton bad never been grown commercially in the United States, but by 1800 it had become the country's major export. The new plantations in turn provided markets for food grown on the smaller farms in both the Northwest and Southwest. The growth of eastern commercial cities and the development of the textile industry in New England and the middle states enlarged that market still further. The titanic struggle between Great Britain and Napoleon obscured the significance of these economic developments, but shortly after 1815 the economy's new orientation became clear.

The merchants who continued to act as economic integrators had the largest hand in building this new high-volume, regionally specialized, agrarian–commercial system. The merchants of Philadelphia, Baltimore, and New York took over the task of exporting cotton, lumber, and foodstuffs and of importing textiles, hardware, drugs, and other goods from Great Britain and the Continent. Those in the southern coastal and river ports played the same role in exporting cotton and importing finished goods to and from the eastern entrepôts; those in the growing western towns sent out local crops and brought in manufactured goods in a similar way. At first the western trade went via rivers of the Mississippi Valley and New Orleans. Later it began to be transported east and west through the Erie Canal and along the Great Lakes. To meet the needs of the expanding trade, the merchants, particularly those of the larger eastern cities, developed new forms of commercial banking to finance the movement of crops, set up packet lines on "the Atlantic Shuttle" between New York and Liverpool to speed the movement of news and imports, founded specialized insurance companies, and helped to organize and finance the new canals and turnpikes that improved transportation between them and their customers.

These innovations enabled the merchants to handle still more business, and the high-volume trade in turn forced the merchants to alter their functions and, indeed, their whole way of life. They began to specialize, becoming primarily wholesalers or retailers, importers or exporters. They came to concentrate on a single line of goods – dry goods, wet goods, hardware, iron, drugs, groceries or cotton, wheat or produce. Some became specialists in banking and insurance and spent their time acting as managers for these new financial corporations.

Of the new specialists, the wholesalers played the most influential role, taking the place of the colonial merchants as the primary integrators and adaptors of the economy. More than the farmers or the retailers, the wholesalers were responsible for directing the flow of cotton, corn, wheat, and lumber from the West to the East and to Europe. More than the manufacturers, they handled the marketing of finished goods that went from eastern and European industrial centers to the southern and western states.

Moreover, the wholesalers financed the long-term growth of the economy. Enthusiastic promoters of canals, turnpikes, and then railroads, they provided most of the local capital for these undertakings. They pressured the state and municipal legislatures and councils (on which they or their legally trained associates often sat) to issue bonds or to guarantee bonds of private corporations building transportation enterprises. At times they even persuaded the state to build and operate transport facilities.

The wholesalers also encouraged the adoption of the new technology in manufacturing. In Boston, the Appletons, the Jacksons, and the Cabots financed the new textile mills of Lowell and Lawrence. In New York, the Phelps and the Dodges started the brass industry in the Connecticut Valley, while in Philadelphia and Baltimore wholesalers like Nathan Trotter and Enoch Pratt financed the growing Pennsylvania iron industry. They not only raised the funds for plants and machinery, but also supplied a large amount of the cash and credit that the new manufacturers needed as working capital to pay for supplies and labor.

Although the wholesalers made important contributions to early nineteenth-century economic life, they played a less dominant role in the economy than had the colonial merchant of the eighteenth century. The economic system had become too complex – involving too many units of production, distribution, transportation, and finance – for one group to supervise local, inter-regional, and international flows. Nonetheless, the wholesalers had more influence in setting prices, managing the flow of goods, and determining the amount and direction of investment than had other groups – the farmers, manufacturers, retailers, and bankers.

As the economy expanded, the recruitment of businessmen became more open than it had been in the colonial period. At the same time, the outlook of even the most broad-gauged businessmen grew narrower. Family and family ties became less essential, although they could still be a useful source of capital. Businessmen began to place more value on personal qualities, such as aggressiveness, drive, and self-reliance. Nor did one need any lengthy training or education to set up a shop as a wholesaler. Because of their increasing functional specialization, this new breed of wholesalers rarely had the international outlook of the colonial merchants. Not surprisingly, they and the lawyers and politicians who represented them saw their needs in sectional rather than national terms – as did so many Americans in the years immediately prior to the Civil War.

The rise of the manufacturer before 1900

By mid-century the American agrarian and commercial economy had begun to be transformed into the most productive industrial system in the world. The migration of Americans into cities became more significant in this transformation than the final settling of the western frontier. Immigration from Europe reached new heights, with most of the new arrivals staying in the cities of the East and the old Northwest. By 1900, therefore, the rate of growth of the rural areas had leveled off. From then on, the nation's population growth would come almost wholly in its cities.

The second half of the nineteenth century was a time of great technological change – the age of steam and iron, the factory and the railroad. The steam railroad and the steamship came quickly to dominate transportation. In 1849 the United States had only 6,000 miles of railroad and even fewer miles of canals, but by 1884 its railroad corporations operated 202,000 miles of track, or 43 per cent of the total mileage in the world. In 1850 the factory – with its power-driven machinery and its permanent working force – was a rarity outside the textile and iron industries, but by 1880 the Bureau of the Census reported that 80 per cent of the three million workers in mechanized industry labored in factories. And nearly all these new plants were powered by steam rather than by water.

America's factories made a vital contribution to the nation's economic growth. By 1894 the value of the output of American industry equalled that of the combined output of the United Kingdom, France, and Germany. In the next twenty years American production tripled, and by the outbreak of the First World War the United States was producing more than a third of the world's industrial goods.

As manufacturing expanded, the wholesaler continued for many years to play a significant role in the economy. The period up to 1873 was one of increasing demand and rising prices. The manufacturers, concentrating on building or expanding their new factories, were more than happy to have the wholesalers supply them with their raw and semifinished materials and to market their finished goods. In addition, wholesalers continued to provide manufacturers with capital for building plants, purchasing equipment and supplies, and paying wages.

After the recession of 1873, however, the manufacturer began to replace the wholesaler as the man who had the most to say about coordinating the flow of goods through the economy and about adapting the economy to population and technological changes. The shift came for three reasons. First, the existing wholesale network of hundreds of thousands of small firms had difficulty in handling efficiently the growing output of the factories. Secondly, the manufacturer no longer needed the wholesaler as a source of capital. After a generation of production, he was able to finance plant and equipment out of retained profits. Moreover, until 1850 the commercial banking system had been almost wholly involved in financing the movement of agricultural products, but about mid-century it began to provide working capital for the industrialist. Commercial banks also began to provide funds for plant and equipment, particularly to new manufacturing enterprises.

The third and most pervasive reason why the manufacturer came to a position of dominance resulted from the nature of factory production itself. This much more efficient form of manufacturing so swiftly increased the output of goods that supply soon outran demand. From the mid-1870s to the mid-1890s, prices fell sharply. Moreover, the large investment required to build a factory made it costly to shut down and even more expensive to move into other forms of business activity. As prices fell, the manufacturers organized to control prices and the flow of goods within their industries. If the wholesalers would and could help them in achieving such control, the manufacturers welcomed their cooperation. If not, they did it themselves. In most cases, the industrialist came to play a larger role than the wholesalers in integrating the economy.

The wholesaler was pushed aside in transportation before he was in manufacturing. Railroad construction costs were high, and after 1849 when railroad expansion began on a large scale, the local merchants simply could not supply the necessary capital. Modern Wall Street came into being during the 1850s to meet the need for funds. By 1860 the investment banker had replaced the wholesaler as the primary supplier of funds to American railroads.

In the 1850s and 1860s the railroads also captured many of the merchant's functions. They took over freight forwarding in large towns and eliminated the merchant by handling through traffic in many commercial centers along the main routes west and south. Indeed, during the 1860s the railroads had absorbed most of the fast freight and express companies developed earlier by the wholesalers in order to use the new rail transportation. By the 1870s the coordination of the flow of most inter-regional transportation in the United States had come under the direction of the traffic departments of a few large railroads.

The first manufacturers to move into the wholesalers' domain were those who found that the wholesaler could not meet their special needs. These were of two types. The makers of new technologically complex and relatively expensive durable products quickly realized that wholesalers were unable to handle the initial demonstration to the consumer, provide consumer credit, or ensure the repair and servicing of the products sold. Thus manufacturers of agricultural implements, sewing machines, typewriters, cash registers, carriages, bicycles, or, most important of all, electrical machinery and equipment created national and even international marketing organizations well before the turn of the century. So did the second type, the processors of perishable goods requiring refrigeration, quick transportation, and careful storage for their distribution – fresh meat, beer, bananas, and cigarettes.

Once the pioneers of both types of enterprises – the McCormicks, the Remingtons, George Westinghouse and Charles Coffin, the Swifts and Armours, the Pabsts and Schlitzes, Andrew Preston and James B. Duke – had created their widespread distribution networks, they began again to eliminate the wholesaler by doing their own purchasing. They could not run the risk of stopping complex fabrication, or assembling processes because they lacked critical parts or materials. Some integrated backwards even further, doing their own purchasing by building or buying factories to manufacture parts, controlling their own iron, steel, or lumber, or obtaining their own refrigerated cars and ships.

The manufacturers who produced standard commodities that might be distributed easily through the existing wholesaler network were slower to move into wholesaling. Even though the pioneering firms were demonstrating the economies resulting from a combination of mass production and mass distribution, most manufacturers had to be pushed rather than enticed into a strategy of vertical integration. They did so only after they failed to meet the oppressive pressure of falling prices by the more obvious methods of price controls through trade associations, cartels, and other loose combinations.

The railroads pioneered in developing ways to control prices in the face of excess capacity and heavy fixed costs. During the 1870s, the railroads formed regional associations, of which the Eastern Trunk Line Association was the most powerful. By the 1880s, however, the railroad presidents and traffic managers admitted defeat. The associations could only be effective if their rulings were enforced in courts of law, but their pleas for legalized pooling went unheard. Indeed, the Interstate Commerce Act of 1887 specifically declared pooling illegal. As a result, the American railroad network became consolidated into large "self-sustaining," centrally managed regional systems. By 1900 most of American land transportation was handled by about twenty-five great systems informally allied in six groupings.

Where the railroads had hoped for legalized pooling, the manufacturers sought other ways of obtaining firmer legal control over the factories in their industries. They began personally to purchase stock in one another's companies. After 1882 when the Standard Oil Company devised the trust as a way of acquiring legal control of an industry, companies began to adopt that device. The holding company quickly superseded the trust as a more effective and inexpensive way of controlling price and production after 1889, when New Jersey passed a general incorporation law that permitted one company to hold stock in many others. The Supreme Court's interpretations of the Sherman Antitrust Act (1890) encouraged further consolidation in manufacturing. Court decisions discouraged loose combinations of manufacturers (or railroads) in any form, but (at least until 1911) appeared to permit consolidation of competing firms through a holding company if that company came to administer its activities under a single centralized management.

In many cases these new consolidations embarked on a strategy of vertical integration. Where the railroads formed "self-sustaining" systems to assure control of traffic over primary commercial routes, the manufacturers attempted to assure the uninterrupted flow of goods into and out of their production and processing plants. John D. Rockefeller and his associates at Standard Oil were the first of the combinations to adopt this strategy. The Standard Oil Trust had been formed after associations in the petroleum industry had proven to be, in Rockefeller's words, "ropes of sand." Legal control of the industry was followed by administrative consolidation of its refineries under a single centralized management. In the mid-1880s, the trust began to build its own distribution network of tank farms and wholesaling offices. Finally, after enlarging its buying organization, it moved in the late-1880s into the taking of crude oil out of the ground.

The examples of Standard Oil, the Swifts, the McCormicks, and others who had by-passed the wholesaler, the rulings of the Supreme Court, the memories of twenty years of declining prices resulted between 1898 and 1902 in the greatest merger movement in American history. Combinations, usually in the form of holding companies, occurred in nearly all major American industries. Holding companies then were often transformed into operating companies. After manufacturing facilities were centralized under a single management, the new consolidated enterprise integrated forwards and backwards.

At the same time, retailers who began to appreciate the potential of mass markets and economies of scale also moved to eliminate the wholesalers – although they did so in a more restricted way than the manufacturers. The mail order houses (Sears, Roebuck, and Montgomery Ward), which turned to the rural markets, and the department and chain stores, which looked to the growing cities, began to buy directly from the manufacturers. By the turn of the century, some large retailers had even bought into manufacturing firms. As a result, wholesalers' decisions were of less significance to the operation of the economy than they had been fifty years earlier. Far more important were the decisions of the manufacturers who had combined, consolidated, and integrated their operations and the few giant retailers who had adopted somewhat the same strategy.

As manufacturers replaced wholesalers as key coordinators in the national economy, they became the popular symbol of American business enterprise. The industrialists and the railroad leaders were indeed the reality as well as the symbol of business power in the Gilded Age. The recruitment of this new dominant business group remained open, at least for a generation. As had been true earlier for the wholesaler, aggressiveness, drive, and access to capital or credit were prerequisites for success. Lineage or specialized training were less important, but some technological know-how was an advantage. Although the manufacturers' horizons were more national and less regional than the wholesalers', they came to view the national scene from the perspective of their particular industry. They and their representatives in Washington tended to take positions on the major issues of the day – tariff, currency, immigration, and the regulation of business – from an industrial rather than a sectional or regional viewpoint.

It was not long, however, before the needs of the manufacturers and their response to these needs altered the recruitment and training of the nation's most powerful businessmen. The increasingly high investment required for large-scale production made the entry of new men and firms more difficult. The emergence of the vertically integrated enterprise limited opportunities still further. By 1900 it was becoming easier to rise to positions of business influence by moving through the new centralized managements than by starting a business enterprise of one's own. This pattern was already clear in the railroads, the nation's first modern business bureaucracies.

The dominance of the manager since 1900

Although the twentieth century was to become the age of the manager, the growing significance of the manager's role in the operation of the American economy was not immediately apparent. Until the 1920s manufacturers and their assistants concentrated on rounding out their integrated enterprises, creating the internal structures and methods necessary to operate these business empires, and employing the managers necessary to staff them.

At first, external conditions did not seriously challenge the new enterprises. Population trends continued, and heavy migration from abroad sustained urban growth until the outbreak of the First World War. During the war, migration from the rural areas to the cities increased. At the same time, impressive technological innovations, particularly those involved with the generating of power by electricity and the internal combustion engine created new industries and helped transform older ones. The continuing growth of the city, the expansion of the whole electrical sector, and the coming of the automobile and auxiliary industries made the first decades of the twentieth century ones of increasing demand and rapid economic growth.

The initial task of the men who fashioned the first integrated giants at the beginning of this century was to build internal organizational structures that would assure the efficient coordination of the flow of goods through their enterprises and permit the rational allocation of the financial, human, and technological resources at their command. First came the formation of functional departments–sales, production, purchasing, finance, engineering, and research and development. At the same time, central offices were organized, usually in the form of an executive committee consisting of the heads of the functional departments. These offices supervised, appraised, and coordinated the work of the departments and planned long-term expenditures.

By the late-1920s the pioneer organization-builders at du Pont, General Motors, General Electric, Standard Oil of New Jersey, and Sears, Roebuck had developed new and sophisticated techniques to perform the vital coordinating and adaptive activities. They based both long- and short-term coordination and planning on a forecast of market conditions. On the basis of annual forecasts, revised monthly and adjusted every ten days, the companies set production schedules, purchases of supplies and semifinished products, employment and wage rolls, working capital requirements, and prices. Prices were determined by costs, which in turn closely reflected estimated volume of output. The annual forecasts took into consideration estimates of national income, the business cycle, seasonal fluctuations, and the company's normal share of the market. Long-term allocations were based on still broader estimates of demand. After 1920, the managers of many large corporations began to include in these allocations the funds and personnel needed to develop new products and processes through technological innovation. From that time on, the integrated firm began to diversify. The Depression and the Second World War helped to spread these methods, so that by mid-century most of the key industries in the United States were dominated by a few giant firms administered in much the same way.

Their managers considered themselves leaders in the business community and were so considered by others. Yet they differed greatly from the older types of dominant businessmen – the merchants, the wholesalers, and the manufacturers: They were not owners; they held only a tiny portion of their company's stock; they neither founded the enterprise nor were born into it; and most of them had worked their way up the new bureaucratic ladders.

Even to get on a ladder they were expected to have attended college. Studies of business executives in large corporations show that by 1950 the large majority had been to college – an advantage that was shared by few Americans of their age group. Like most of those who did receive higher education, these managers came primarily from white Anglo-Saxon Protestant stock. Once the college man with his WASP background started up the managerial ladder, he usually remained in one industry and more often than not in a single company. That company became his career, his way of life.

As he rose up the ranks, his horizon broadened to national and international levels. Where his firm diversified, his interests and concerns spread over several industries. Indeed, in some ways his perspectives were wider in the 1950s than those of most Americans; nevertheless, because of his specialized training, he had little opportunity to become aware of the values, ideas, ambitions, and goals of other groups of Americans. He had even fewer direct contacts with farmers, workers, and other types of businessmen than had the wholesaler and the manufacturer.

The dominance of the large integrated enterprise did not, of course, mean the disappearance of the older types of businessmen. Small business remained a basic and essential part of the American economy. The small non-integrated manufacturer, the wholesaler, and retailer have all continued to be active throughout the twentieth century. The number of small businesses has continued to grow with the rapid expansion of the service industries (such as laundries and dry cleaners, service and repair shops not directly tied to the large firm); with the spread of real-estate dealers, insurance agencies, and stock brokerage firms; and with this continuing expansion of the building and construction industries. Throughout the century small businessmen have greatly outnumbered the managers of big business. The former were, therefore, often more politically powerful, particularly in ... local politics, than the latter. Economically, however, the managers of the large integrated and often diversified enterprises remained the dominant decision-makers in the urban, industrial, and technologically sophisticated economy of the twentieth century. Their critically significant position has been repeatedly and properly pointed out by economists ever since Adolph A. Berle and Gardiner C. Means wrote the first analysis of the role and functions of the modern corporation in 1932 [see Chapter 3 in this volume].

In many ways, the managers were more of an elite than the earlier businessmen had been. Even though this elite was based on performance rather than birth and played a critically constructive role in building and operating the world's most productive economy, its existence seemed to violate basic American democratic values. At the same time, its control of the central sector of the American economy challenged powerful economic concepts about the efficacy of a free market. After 1930, the managers came to share some of their economic power with others, particularly the federal government. Nevertheless, they were forced to do so not because of ideological reasons, but because they failed by themselves to assure the coordination and growth of the economy, the basic activities they had undertaken after 1900.

Until the Depression, the government had played a trivial part in the management of the American economy. The merchants had used the government to assist in financing internal improvements that they found too costly or risky to undertake themselves, and the manufacturers had called upon the government to protect them from foreign competition. Small businessmen – wholesalers and retailers – had joined farmers and workers to use the government to regulate the large corporation, but such regulation did not deter the growth of big business nor significantly alter the activities of the managers. Before the Depression, the government had developed few means to influence consciously the over-all performance of the American economy, the major exception being the creation of a central banking system in 1913.

The Depression clearly demonstrated that the corporation managers alone were unable to provide the coordination and adaptation necessary to sustain a complex, highly differentiated, mass production, mass-distribution economy. The coming of the Depression itself reflected population and technological developments. Legislation in the 1920s cut immigration from abroad to a tiny flow. After the First World War, migration from country to city slowed. Meanwhile, new industries, particularly the electric and automobile industries, reached the limit of demand for their output permitted by the existing size and distribution of the national income. At the same time, improved machinery as well as the more efficient management of production and distribution meant that in still other industries potential supply was becoming greater than existing demand. By the mid-1920s prices had begun to decline. Only the existence of credit helped maintain the economy's momentum until 1929.

Corporate giants, like General Motors, General Electric, and du Pont, fully realized that ... demand was leveling off in the 1920s, but they could do little more than maintain production at the existing rate or even cut back a bit. When the 1929 crash dried up credit and reduced demand, they could only roll with the punch. As demand fell, they cut production, laid off men, and canceled orders for supplies and materials. Such actions further reduced purchasing power and demand and led to more cuts in production and more layoffs. The downward pressure continued relentlessly. In less than four years, the national income was slashed in half. The forecasts at General Motors and General Electric for 1932 indicated that, at best, the firms would operate at about 25 per cent capacity.

The only institution capable of stopping this economic descent appeared to be the federal government. During the 1930s it undertook this role, but with great reluctance. Until the recession of 1937, Franklin D. Roosevelt and his Secretary of the Treasury still expected to balance the budget and to bring the end to government intervention in the economy. Roosevelt and his Cabinet considered large-scale government spending and employment only temporary. When Roosevelt decided in 1936 that the Depression was over despite high unemployment, he sharply reduced government expenditures. National income, production, and demand immediately plummeted in 1937. The nation then began to understand more clearly the relationship between government spending and the level of economic activity, although acceptance of the government's role in maintaining economic growth and stability was a decade away.

The Second World War taught other lessons. The government spent far more than the most enthusiastic New Dealer had ever proposed. Most of the output of these expenditures was destroyed or left on the battlefields of Europe and Asia. But the resulting increased demand sent the nation into a period of prosperity the like of which had never before been seen. Moreover, the supplying of huge armies and navies fighting the most massive war of all time required a tight, centralized control of the national economy. This effort brought corporate managers to Washington to carry out one of the most complex pieces of economic planning in history. That experience lessened the ideological fears over the government's role in stabilizing the economy. This new attitude, embodied in legislation by the Employment Act of 1946, continued to be endorsed by Eisenhower's Republican Administration in the 1950s.

The federal government is now committed to ensuring the revival of investment and demand if, and only if, private enterprise is unable to maintain full employment. In 1949 and again in 1953, 1957, and 1960, the government carried out this role by adjusting its monetary and fiscal policies, building roads, and shifting defense contracts. The continuing Cold War made the task relatively easy by assuring the government ample funds. The new role has been defined so that it meets the needs of the corporate managers. The federal government takes action only if the managers are unable to maintain a high level of aggregate demand; it has not replaced the managers as the major coordinators in the economy, but acts only as a coordinator of last resort.

The Depression helped bring the federal government into the economy in another way. During the late-nineteenth and twentieth centuries, workers, farmers, and (to some extent) retailers, wholesalers, and other small businessmen had formed organizations to help them share in making the economic decisions that most intimately affected their well-being. During the 1930s, when the managers were having difficulties in maintaining economic stability, these numerically larger and more politically influential groups were able to get the federal and state governments to support their claims. Through government intervention many workers acquired a say in determining policies in wages, hours, working rules, promotions, and layoffs; farmers gained control over the prices of several basic commodities; and retailers and wholesalers increased their voice in the pricing of certain goods they sold. Nevertheless, the Wagner Act, the Agricultural Adjustment Acts, the Robinson–Patman Act, and the "fair trading" laws did not seriously infringe on the manager's ability to determine current output and to allocate resources for present and future economic activities.

The growth of organized labor during the twentieth century indicates much about the economic power of the large corporation, for this politically powerful group has been able to impress its will on the decisions of corporate managers only in a limited way. Until the Depression, labor unions had little success in organizing key industries dominated by large, managerially operated enterprises. Even during its first major period of growth at the turn of the century, the American Federation of Labor [AF of L] was not successful in the manufacturing industries. From the start, organized labor's strength lay in mining, transportation, and the building and construction trades. In the manufacturing sector, the Federation's gains came not in factory but small-shop industries, such as cigar, garment, hat and stove-making, and ship-building. During the first quarter of the twentieth century, organized labor acquired its members in those industries where skilled workers achieved their goals by bargaining with many small employers. (The railroads were the exception.) The geographically oriented operating structure developed by the American Federation of Labor unions was admirably suited to this purpose.

Precisely because the craft union had grown up in industries where the factory and the large integrated enterprise had never been dominant, the American Federation of Labor found itself in the 1930s unable to organize, even with strong government support, the mass-production, mass-distribution industries so basic to the operation of the modern economy. To unionize these industries required the creation of a structure to parallel the structure of the large integrated enterprise and a program that appealed to semiskilled rather than skilled workers. The AF of L failed to meet this challenge. Only after "a civil war" within the ranks of labor and the creation of a new national labor organization, the CIO[1], did the automobile, iron and steel, nonferrous metal, rubber, electrical machinery, and other key industries become fully unionized.

During the great organizing drives of the late-1930s and immediately after the Second World War, union leaders rarely, if ever, sought to gain more than a voice in the determination of wages and hours, working rules, and hiring as well as promotion and layoff policies. Even when they asked (unsuccessfully) for an opportunity "to look at the company's books," union spokesmen did so primarily with the hope of assuring themselves that they were obtaining what they considered a fair share of the income generated by the firm. The critical issue over which management and labor fought in the years immediately following the Second World War was whether the managers or the union would control the hiring of workers. The unions almost never asked to take part in decisions about output, pricing, or resources allocation. With the passage of the Taft–Hartley Act of 1947, the managers obtained a control over hiring which has never been seriously challenged. Nor have any further inroads into "management's prerogatives" been seriously proposed.

Since 1950, business managers have continued to make the decisions that most vitally affect the coordination of the economy and the pace of its growth. They have also continued to have a major say in how the economy adapts to external forces generated by population movements and technological change.

Population movements in the 1960s present a different challenge than they did before the 1930s. Migration from abroad has remained only a trickle and that from the country to the city has continued to drop. The move to the suburbs, the most significant post-Depression development, has expanded the urban sprawl and undermined the viability of the central city. The resulting problems are, however, more political and social than economic. Whether government officials are better trained than corporate managers to handle these new problems is open to question. If the business managers fail to meet these new challenges, the government will obviously have to do so.

Meanwhile, technological change has maintained a revolutionary pace. Through their concentration on research and development of new products and new methods of production and distribution, corporate managers have been trained to handle the processes and procedures of technological innovation. The large corporation has so "internalized" the process of innovation that this type of change is no longer simply an outside force to which businessmen and others in the economy adjust. Here the expertise of the business manager covers a broader field than that of governmental or military managers. In most of the costly government programs involving a complex technology, the development and production of new products have been turned over to the large corporations through the contracting process. The federal government does, however, supply the largest share of funds for research and development. Thus, even though the business manager continues to play a critical part in adapting the economy to technological change, government officials are in a position to determine the direction and the areas in which research and development will be concentrated.

This brief history of the role of business in the operation of the American economy suggests several tentative conclusions. From the beginning, it seems, businessmen have run the American economy. They can take the credit and the blame for many of its achievements and failures. They, more than any other group in the economy, have managed the production, transportation, and distribution of goods and services. No other group – farmers, blue-collar workers, or white-collar workers – has ever had much to do with the over-all coordination of the economic system or its adaptation to basic changes in population and technology.

Over the two centuries, however, the businessman who ran the economy has changed radically. Dominance has passed from the merchant to the wholesaler, from the wholesaler to the manufacturer, and from the manufacturer to the manager. In the last generation, businessmen have had to share their authority with others, largely with the federal government. Even so, the government's peace-time role still remains essentially a supplementary one, as coordinator of last resort and as a supplier of funds for technological innovation.

In the past, businessmen have devoted their energies to economic affairs, giving far less attention to cultural, social, or even political matters. Precisely because they have created an enormously productive economy and the most affluent society in the world, the non-economic challenges are now becoming more critical than the economic ones. There is little in the recruitment, training, and experience of the present business leaders – the corporate managers – to prepare them for handling the difficult new problems, but unless they do learn to cope with this new situation, they may lose their dominant position in the economy. As was not true of the merchant, wholesaler, or manufacturer, the corporate managers could be replaced by men who are not businessmen. To suggest how and in what way the managers will respond to the current challenges is, fortunately, not the task of the historian. Such analyses are properly left to social scientists and businessmen.

Note

1. *Editor's Note:* The Committee of Industrial Organizations was founded in 1935, later to be called the Congress of Industrial Organizations.

2

The Industrial System of the New Order: Business vs. Manufacturing (1923)*

Thorstein Veblen

That new order of things which has been coming to a head since the close of the century is especially plain to be seen in the conduct of business. Business runs on something of a new footing. But it is a new order of material conditions that has enabled this new dispensation in business to come on and go into action. It runs on an altered state of the industrial arts, coupled with a continual growth of population. And the new dispensation in business has arisen out of the endeavors of the business men to profit by the enlarged opportunities which these altered material conditions have offered them. It has been their work to turn the new industrial situation to account for their own gain while working under rules of the game of business that have come down from the old order.

This has involved a progressive change. It has taken time and experiment as well as the help of legal counsel to discover and work out suitable expedients of business procedure and to get into the habit of them. At the same time the underlying industrial situation has been subject to a continued, cumulative, alteration; an advance in mass and extension, in the scale and range of operations, as well as in the complexity, balance, and precision of details. Therefore the new order of business procedure has gone into action in a progressive and tentative fashion. And for the same reason it has never reached the end of its development; nor, indeed, is there any promise of its reaching anything like a final state of stability and finished growth in the calculable future; for the reason that the state of the industrial arts which under-

* From *Absentee Ownership and Business Enterprise in Recent Times* (New York: B. W. Huebsch, 1923), pp. 229–50.

lies it is forever unstable. And just now the industrial arts are in a state of unexampled instability. And the business men who aim to benefit by the use and control of these industrial arts will have to take them as they come, and it is the habitual procedure of these business men that determines what the methods and organization of business will be.

There is little that can be said in the way of confident forecast as touches the future of the industrial arts or as regards any final outcome of this continued advance in technology and in the consequent sweep and scale and articulation of the industrial system; and the business community will have to face these new exigencies as they arise. Yet in one respect, at least, the course of things in the recent past may be taken to indicate the nature of the situation which the business management will have to deal with as time goes on. As it stands now the industrial system is inordinarily productive. Its productive capacity per unit of the factors engaged – the coefficient of productive capacity – has in recent times continually been increasing at a continually accelerated rate, and the situation holds a clear promise of a still more inordinate productive capacity in the course of further time and change. The technicians are forever occupied with contriving new ways and means designed to compass that end.[1]

In so speaking of a "New Order of Things" there is no intention to imply that the new is divided from the old by a catastrophic break of continuity. To use a geologic figure of speech, there has been no faulting of the strata. No sudden thrust has upset the orderly advance of technological knowledge and practice. There has been an orderly cumulative advance which has gone forward without serious interruption and at a constantly increasing rate of advance. It is an instance of cumulative growth, which has now passed a critical point of such a nature as to give rise to a new situation which differs effectually from what went before.

In the case of America this cumulative growth of the industrial arts and of the industrial system has been particularly notable since about the middle of the nineteenth century. Coupled with this advancing industrial situation and conditioned upon it, there has at the same time gone forward a sweeping progressive reorganization of the business community, which has placed the country's business affairs on a footing of credit and corporate ownership. With the result that toward the close of the century the financial community, who command the country's solvency and dispense the country's credit, found themselves in a position to take over the control and the usufruct of the country's industrial system by taking over the ownership of those strategically dominant members of the industrial system that are known as the "Key Industries." Since then the key industries have been progressively taken over into the absentee ownership of the country's credit institutions, and this absentee ownership has progressively been consolidated and arranged in manageable shape. The arrangement has now been brought to a passable degree of balance and stability, although the work has not been brought to a neatly finished conclusion; nor need it be. Nor is there any present likelihood that this working arrangement will be rounded out into a statistically all-inclusive block of absentee ownership in the hands of a formally consolidated, going concern of investment-bankers.

Irrepressible new technological advances are forever running out new ramifications of industry, which are forever requiring further attention at the hands of these captains of ownership. So that the work of taking things over is an endless task, at the same time that something less than universal ownership will serve the purpose quite handsomely. All that is needed for the purpose of an effectual usufruct of the country's work and output is a strategically effectual control of the country's industrial system as a going concern, and that much is now an accomplished fact. The several branches and strata of the industrial system overlap and interlock in such a way as to vest a strategically effectual control of the whole in the hands of those who command the standard natural resources and control the key industries. All that remains needful to be done is to bring the several absentee concerns who control the key industries to a settled and facile footing of collusion, and much has been accomplished along that line these last few years.

In America, as an outcome of the nineteenth century, the industrial work of the community has fallen into the shape of a three-fold division or stratification of industries which work together in a balanced whole, a moving equilibrium of interlocking processes of production: (a) the primary, initial, or key industries, so called, which command the greater natural resources of the country and turn out the prime staple necessaries of the mechanical industry in the way of power, transportation, fuel, and structural material; (b) the secondary or continuation industries, manufactures, which turn these crude supplies and services into consumable goods and distribute them; (c) agriculture.

This may seem a gratuitous and illogical classification, particularly as regards agriculture. It is quite evident, of course, that agriculture has to do with the greatest and most essential of the country's natural resources, at the same time that it is the indispensable source of supply for a wide and varied range of staple industries. So it is as usual as it is unquestionably proper to class agriculture with the "extractive industries," and not unusual to give it the first place in that class; and there is no fault to be found with that arrangement. The conventional scheme would be: (a) extractive industries; (b) manufactures; (c) distribution. Which would be a sound logical plan and classification of productive industry, in the absence of business considerations.

On the other hand the three-fold division which is spoken for above is drawn in view of those business considerations that are decisive for the conduct of industry here and now. It is not intended to violate or set aside the grouping of industries that has been usual in the theoretical speculation of the economists, but is made only for present convenience. What is aimed at is a convenient definition of the facts for the present argument, which has to do with the relations between business and industry in America in the twentieth century; and the three-fold division spoken for above answers this purpose. Each of these three industrial groups or strata occupies a peculiar place in the industrial system, in respect of ownership and business connections. There are at the same time no sharp lines of division between the three groups. They overlap, interlock and blend; and each group will show doubtful and marginal cases; but in the large, as component factors in the framework of the industrial system, each group stands out by itself, typically distinct from the rest, particularly in respect of the business considerations by which each is bound or actuated.

At the same time it is also not to be overlooked that these three strata of productive industry are marked by characteristic differences on the technological side, as well as in respect of the business considerations that govern them. They each stand on a somewhat special and distinctive footing in the industrial arts; all the while that they all move within the framework of the modern industrial system and are, each in its degree, dominated by that mechanical industry that gives its distinctive character to the system as a whole and as contrasted with what has gone before. But the three groups or departments of industry do not share alike or in the same degree in that characteristic shift to a mechanical footing that has resulted from the industrial revolution of the past one hundred and fifty years.

As it runs now, the industrial system centers in quantity production of goods and services by use of inanimate energies engaged in mechanical work, or engaged in chemical processes that are of a mechanical nature and effect. Typically, the standard processes of this modern industry engage inanimate forces and materials; or materials and forces which can effectually be applied on a mechanical plan. In this respect the current state of the industrial arts differs notably from its own past as well as from the industrial systems that still prevail among outlying and backward people – backward, that is, in respect of the mechanical technology. In the main and typically, this state of the industrial arts is a technology of physics and chemistry; having to do with inanimate ways and means, and carrying on its most characteristic work by use of inorganic processes and materials.

But all the while it remains true, of course, that this mechanistic state of the industrial arts has come out of a past phase in which workmanship ran on another plan; a past in which the industrial arts were dominated by a different range of conceptions. Through some ninety-nine per cent., at least, of this past period of experience and growth the industrial arts have been, in the main and typically, a technology of animate (human) energies, workmanlike manipulation, and organic processes of fecundity, growth and nurture; and there are many holdovers out of the organic technology of the past that still make up a very substantial part of the industrial system.

Agriculture, e.g. still rests on a body of such old-fashioned holdovers, much of it of unknown antiquity and out of touch with the logic of the mechanical industry. Yet in the main and as contrasted with what has gone before, and allowing for extensive holdovers, the industrial system that engages the civilized nations runs on a technology of physics and chemistry, and its work converges on quantity production of mechanically standardized goods and services. Therefore manufactures are the focus of the industrial system. It is a technology of manufacture, of mechanical standardization and quantity production; and the same technical principles and procedures are all the while reaching out into the outlying fields of agriculture and back into the other extractive industries that have to do with the primary supply of power, fuel, and raw and structural materials.

As the case now stands the manufacturing industries are able and ready to meet all current needs of the market by the use of the existing equipment and man-power, and the technicians and workmen are ready at any time to extend, amplify and intensify the available equipment and industrial processes to take care of any new growth in the demand for goods. The manufacturing industries, where mechanical power and quantity production rule the case, are inordinately productive, in the sense that they are ready at any time to cover a demand for goods greatly in excess of their ordinary output.

It is one of the features of the current situation that there is always an available slack which can be taken up in case of need, a margin of unemployed equipment and man-power ready to go to work, and a fringe of technical knowledge which has not yet been turned to account but which is fit to speed up the quantity production of staple goods at any point where an additional output may be called for. In effect, the work and output of the manufacturing industries are not now limited by the productive capacity of their equipment, workmen, or technical processes. But they are subject to limitation on the one side by the available supply of power and materials, and on the other side by the market for their output; and the available supply of power and essential materials is limited, in the main and decisively, by the current output of the key industries which command the country's staple resources; which output in turn is limited by consideration of what the traffic will bear, at the hands of the absentee owners of the staple resources and their business agents. On both sides, therefore, the output of staple goods in the manufacturing industries is limited, not by productive capacity or by capacity for consumption, but by business considerations. And the business considerations which chiefly decide what the volume of output of manufactured goods shall be are the considerations which govern the key industries and their output of power, fuel, and raw and structural materials.

It follows that the manufacturing industries as a class are dependent immediately on the key industries and on the terms which the management of the key industries may choose to offer them, somewhat arbitrarily. From which it follows also that the manufacturers as a class necessarily conduct their enterprise on a short-term plan; governed by the visible supply and the orders outstanding; since the management of the sovereign key industries, like other business men, keep their own counsel as to what they will do about their own business – when and how and how far they may see fit to alter the terms on which they are willing to supply the necessary materials of industry. So the manufacturers must hold themselves ready to slack off or to speed up, to widen or narrow the margin of unemployment, with a vigilant eye to the main chance and waiting watchfully for any adroit maneuvers in the key industries.

So also it follows that the manufacturing industries as a class are on a competitive footing; competing for the available supply of power and primary materials, but more particularly competitors for custom in the market. This competition has been taking on a special character during the past two or three decades, not contemplated in the manuals of economic theory, and ... it is in some degree a novel development due to a complication of circumstances ...

The place and nature of the key industries in the industrial system scarcely require elaborate discussion here. They are such as the name, "key industries," implies. And they are key industries because they command the main run of the country's staple resources. Technologically the key industries come into the same class with manufactures, and some of the best work of applied chemistry and physics is to be found here; as, e.g. in metallurgy and the refining of petroleum. But as business concerns the key industries stand in a special relation to the industrial system. They hold the initiative by virtue of their hold on the staple natural resources; and by active collusion or by routine which has been settled on lines of collusion they have during the last few decades come to exercise a decisive control over the industrial system at large, so that the country's industry will now speed up, slack off, or shut down, very much as the massive concerns in the background among these key industries may decide; and their decision in these matters is, of course, guided not by consideration of serviceability to industry at large or to the livelihood of the underlying population but by pursuit of the largest obtainable net gain for themselves.

Of course, there is in this respect no difference in principle between the business management of the key industries and business-as-usual anywhere else. It is only that the business of the key industries is in a peculiarly fortunate position, such a position of virtual monopoly and free initiative as all business men in all lines of enterprise aim to achieve if they can. It should be added that this strangle-hold of the key industries upon the country's industry at large has been gaining in breadth, rigor, and security, and that the present outlook is for further gains of the same nature.[2]

In practice there is no sharp line to be drawn between the key industries and the common run of manufactures. They all belong together within the lines of the machine industry, and the business interests which control them make no account of any technical distinction between the two groups of industrial enterprises. In coal, oil, steel, and transportation, e.g. the business concerns interested have been reaching out among the manufacturing industries which draw on them for service and materials, and have been acquiring an interest also in the business of distribution. And many manufacturing concerns have on occasion, for security and despatch, reached back among the key industries and secured a hold on some needed line of staple resources. As an illustrative instance, corporate interests whose business centers in the extraction, refining, and transportation of petroleum and its products have gone largely into merchandising business as distributors of their own output, wholesale and retail, and at the same time they are also to be found intimately interested in a business way in linseed oil and the manufacture of paints and pigments, as, e.g. white-lead, as well as in soaps, candles, unguents, medicines, and cosmetics. So also there are industrial business concerns that have to do with manufacturing and that would have to be classed as manufactures in the technological respect, at the same time that they occupy a strategical position of much the same character as the key industries. Such are, e.g. the meat-packers and the flour-millers; and there are other concerns interested in sugar, gas, electricity, telephones, trolley lines, and the like, that fall more or less patently in the same doubtful or ambiguous class.

Among all these, that group of business concerns of which the packers and millers are the type-form occupies a special position, peculiarly difficult to classify. On the formal face of things they are manufacturers, but in effect they command those natural resources from which their raw materials are drawn. In effect their command of the tributary agricultural resources is so unqualified that it will scarcely be an over-statement to say that they hold these natural resources of the farming region in usufruct, with power of use and abuse. It is also quite safe to say that this usufruct of the farm resources has been capitalized and included among the assets of these corporations so as to count in a substantial way in the current market value of their outstanding corporate securities. Of course it does not follow, nor need one entertain a suspicion, that the corporate interests in question have ever abused the power which their virtual monopoly of the country's resources is in meat and grain so vests in them. The point of interest here is rather that the cleavage between the key industries and the common run of manufactures is by no means neatly observed in business practice, although the technical distinction between the two is fairly obvious. The trail of the net gain will cross technological frontiers as readily as national frontiers.[3]

The third of these contrasted industrial groups, or strata, in the three-fold division spoken for above, the farm community, is more sharply set off from the rest of the industrial system, both technologically and in respect of the business relations by which it is governed. In both respects farming is on a footing different from the rest; and the reason for its different business footing is its different technological character.

Outside of farming, the main body of the industrial system has undergone a revolutionary experience during the past one-hundred-fifty years. The industrial system at large, outside of farming, has been reshaped by the machine industry and that standardized quantity-production which the machine industry has brought into action. The industrial system at large is dominated by the technology of physics and chemistry; it is essentially a system of mechanical power, inanimate materials, and inorganic processes. On the other hand agriculture still rests on a body of industrial arts that are older than the Industrial Revolution, – older even than that handicraft system which the technology of physics and chemistry has been displacing. In farming, these mechanical appliances and applications of mechanical power are still "labor-saving devices," and they still come into the case only as accessory ways and means which "facilitate and abridge" the manual operations of the husbandman. All these things have hitherto touched agriculture only in a superficial way. They do not make the output; they only help along in the manipulation and distribution of it.

The agriculture from which the civilized peoples draw their livelihood and on which civilized life depends is a system of "mixed farming" which does not differ, in its elements, from the mixed farming of neolithic Europe some ten or twelve thousand years ago. It is mixed farming. That is to say it makes use of a certain equipment of domestic animals and crop-plants; and the equipment as well as the methods and purposes of it all are still, in their elements, the same as ruled the case in the husbandry of neolithic Europe. The industry still continues to turn out essentially the same output of grain, milk, butter, cheese, eggs, meat, wool, and hides; and it turns out these necessaries of civilized life by recourse to the same technology of breeding and nurture, fortified by a variety of mechanical helps.

But these mechanical helps and expedients do not make the output and "are not of the essence of this contract." Farm produce is still an output of those processes of growth and nurture that date back for their technological character to the domestication of plants and animals in prehistoric times. And the mixed farming of the civilized nations still rests on the technological foundations that were laid for it when the crop-plants and domestic animals found their way into neolithic Europe. Improvements in methods and appliances have been many and various, but those improvements and advances that have cut at all deeply into the substance of husbandry have been advances in breeding and tillage; that is to say, they have continued the work of domestication which the neolithic husbandmen already had taken in hand some ten or twelve thousand years ago. The methods of breeding and nurture as well as the equipment of livestock and crop plants have been improved and extended, and farmers' work has been "facilitated and abridged" here and there by the use of many mechanical contrivances, as well as by the introduction of more productive contrivances in the way of crop-plants unknown to neolithic Europe, as, e.g. corn (maize) and potatoes and cotton; but all the while it remains true that those technological improvements and advances which have counted substantially toward an enhanced output of farm produce have continued to be something in the nature of elaboration and refinement on the same old procedure of breeding and nurture that supplied the necessaries of life in neolithic times.

There is no call to undervalue the service which the machine industry and industrial chemistry have rendered, but when all has been said and allowed for it remains true that these agencies of the Industrial Revolution have not made farming over in their own image, and that husbandry is after all a matter of the skilled breeding and nurture of animals and crop-plants; and the conditioning circumstances which govern these elemental processes of breeding and nurture are still the ancient circumstances of space, air, rainfall, sunshine, soil, and seasons. These conditioning circumstances still govern the farm industry and the life of the farm population. The American husbandry, mixed farming, is necessarily spread abroad over the face of the land. Livestock and crops live and multiply only in that way, and the farm population under whose skilled care they live and multiply will have to live with them. That is the neolithic way.

Quantity-production and the large-scale process come into this mixed farming mainly by way of a figure of speech. It is true, the farm unit has been growing larger gradually during the past half or three quarters century, both on an average and in the typical case; and that such has been the drift of things during this interval is due to mechanical improvements, to the use of mechanical power and the like applications of the technology of physics and chemistry; but it also remains true that husbandry is not built upon these inanimate factors, and that, in the large, the scale and pace of things in farming still wait on the processes of breeding and nurture, not on the massing of inanimate forces and the concatenation of inanimate chemical reactions.

The farm population is still given over to a workday surveillance of these processes of breeding and nurture. Farm life is still a neighborhood life of homely detail and seasonal fortuities; and the inveterate habituation to which the farm population is subject still makes for the good spirit of parochialism and personalities, of neighborhood gossip and petty intrigue. The organization of the work necessarily runs to small-scale parcelment and isolation; relatively small work units which are necessarily masterless and self-directing in their processes of work, however greatly they may be tied-up, hampered and retarded by pecuniary obligations to absentee owners out-side.

Because of this necessary parcelment, and because of the intimately personal character of the farmer's technical knowledge and proficiency, he is still the "independent farmer" in respect of the day's work. Only in a slight, external, and essentially inconsequential way, are the farm population subject to that wide-sweeping, impersonal, mechanistic discipline of standardization and mass movement that gives its character to the industrial system at large. The abiding and pervasive factors of habituation for the husbandman and his folks are still the homely movements of human nature working in collusion with the animate forces of plant and animal life, settled habits of thought that have to do with breeding and nurture. With the result, among other things, that the rural community is still shot through with prehistoric animism in a degree that passes the comprehension of any person whose habits of thought have been shaped by the technology of physics and chemistry. So it has come about that the rural community is still the repository of timeworn superstitions, magical, religious, and political, such as would do credit to the best credulity of neolithic man.[4]

Technologically speaking, and seen in the light of the latterday industrial arts, agriculture is grounded in a system of holdovers that have come down from remote antiquity and embody habits of thought that are suited to the institutional structure of those good old days; days which antedate not only the machine industry and Big Business, but the era of handicraft as well. By technical necessity the farming industry is still conducted on a plan of dispersion, discontinuous parcelment, and individual responsibility, so far as regards the day's work. But in point of business relations the farmer is caught in the net of the system at large; which is a system of absentee ownership and works out in a network of credit, markets, organized salesmanship, corporate capitalization, and Big Business managed on the principle of what the traffic will bear. To the farmer and his folks all these things are external circumstances over which he has no control, but to which he and his folks are required to conform on pain of "getting left." He is within the system but not of it. He and the work of his hands are in it as a bone of contention; something for adroit salesmen to buy cheap and sell dear, and something to which absentee title is to be acquired by a tactical use of credit.

Reluctantly but as a matter of course the farmer and all his work and ways are involved in the all-pervading system of credit, for more or less. It is a business system, and business runs on credit, and the Big Business which dominates the system begins and ends its work within the convolutions of credit. In the rural community, on the other hand, the rule still runs that indebtedness is an "incumbrance" to be got away from as fast and far as may be. That is to say, the farmer is a victim of the credit system, not a manipulator of it. His property is not assets to be employed as collateral by use of which to swell his capitalization, but "production goods," visible means of support to be jealously kept clear of the money-lender, if such a thing were possible.[5]

The farmer and his folks and work are bound by the run of the market, but he does not create or control the run of the market by any exercise of deliberation or discretion on his part. It is not his market, except in the sense that he is dependent on it. Perhaps he "ought" to control his market, and make the terms on which he will buy and sell; but in practical fact his choice in the matter goes no farther than to take or leave the terms that are offered him. The run of the market is made for him and he can take it or leave it, but mostly take it lest a worse thing befall him. The run of the market is made up on the principle of what the traffic will bear for Big Business, by those massive business interests that move obscurely in the background, – railway interests, ware-house interests, jobbing interests, packing interests, milling interests, farm-implement interests, coal interests, oil interests, steel interests, cordage interests, and the like.

And every once in a while the farmers make a broad gesture of collusive strategy and concerted action. Every once in a while there springs up a hope, born of desperation, that the massive interests which move in the background of the market are to be set at naught by the farmers' taking thought together in a business way; or they are to be confounded by some intelligent alignment of rural political forces. And always this collusive strategy of the rural communities disintegrates into a parcelment of self-seeking detail and mutual sharp practice, and always the political class-action of the independent farmers runs out in a dust-heap of parochial chicanery. And the rural community remains an inalienable domain of that business enterprise that buys cheap and sells dear.

In respect of industrial articulation, as regards technical interdependence and mutual support among the members or strata of the existing system, the case stands somewhat as follows. The industrial arts, the employment of this technology of physics and chemistry, come to a head in the manufacturing industries, dominated by standard mechanical processes and quantity production. This industrial system owes its unexampled productivity to the mechanistic technology of the manufacturing industries, and the apex of technological growth is in that field. These industries draw on farming and the key industries for mechanical power, man-power and materials, at the same time that they supply ways and means that are indispensable to the work in farming and the key industries. The whole constitutes a balanced system of work, a moving equilibrium of interlocking processes, in which the efficiency of any given part is conditioned on the due working of all the rest. No part of the system can do its share of the work in isolation or in severalty, and any degree of failure or curtailment at any point, in rate, volume or quality of output, entails a degree of curtailment and inefficiency throughout the system. The dominant factor in this moving equilibrium of work, technologically speaking, is the manufacturing industry, and it is on the output of this industry that the efficiency of the industrial system converges.

Such is the technical character of the system as an industrial organization, and such would be its working balance and articulation in the absence of other incentives and considerations than the production of useful goods. But under the existing system of ownership that consideration is not decisive. The incentive of business is not to produce goods but to make money, and business considerations are decisive in the control and management of the industrial system. And the articulation and balance of the industrial system as it is organized for business purposes is accordingly a different one. Technologically the apex of the system is the manufacturing industry, but in the business organization of it the key industries are at the apex; and they hold this dominant position by owning the right to retard or curtail the supply of necessary power and materials that goes to the manufacturing industries. Industrially the country's farming is the primary source of its livelihood, and therefore of its available man-power, but in the business organization the farm community serves as ways and means of that commercial enterprise that handles the country's manufactured products, which in turn is subject to such businesslike curtailment and retardation as the pursuit of profits in the key industries may entail.

What has just been said about the industrial system describes the situation in America. And what is true of America will hold true with all inconsequential change of words for the industrial system more at large, to include the civilized nations, in about the same measure in which they are civilized; or a more guarded statement would be, in the same measure in which they are included in the framework of the modern European civilization. In many of the characteristic features of the case America may be taken as an exemplar of the civilized world, particularly as regards the civilized world's present status in industry and business.

The civilized nations, in the degree in which they are civilized, are all unavoidably bound together in a single working system of industry, and they are now similarly bound up in a comprehensive system of business enterprise; although the articulations of business run on lines somewhat different from those technological lines of specialization and mutual support that bind the civilized peoples in an inclusive organization of industry. In the industrial respect, as determined by the state of the industrial arts, the civilized peoples are held in a network of interlocking processes of work, so close-knit and so far-reaching as to make them a single going concern working together toward a maximum quantity production of staple goods by use of the world's known resources of mechanical power, raw materials and man-power. All this is quite obvious, and it is coming to be quite familiar, at large and in detail, to the technical men within whose horizon these matters lie.

But in respect of their business interests, or rather in respect of the strategy of their business men, the civilized nations are not similarly bound together in a cooperative commonwealth. Business enterprise, being competitive, runs at cross purposes. And it is these cross purposes of business enterprise that chiefly obstruct the due articulation of industrial undertakings and so act to derange and curtail the work in hand, both in the industrial system at large and in the detail conduct of industrial undertakings within any given national frontiers. As the matter stands now the division between nations is a division of business interests, and national policies are chiefly occupied with the competitive cross purposes of vested interests which do business under one flag and another. This, too, is quite obvious, and it is a familiar matter of course, at large and in detail, to the absentee owners and statesmen who have to take care of these matters.

Notes

1. As has been remarked in an earlier passage, "inordinate" is here employed in something of a technical sense, as meaning excessively and unguardedly productive, beyond the ordinary needs of business in ordinary times. That is to

say, if the available resources in the way of materials, equipment and man-power were to be employed under competent technical management with a view to maximum production, the output of industry would be greatly in excess of what the traffic will bear, considered as a business proposition. Not that the output would exceed the consumptive capacity of the underlying population, but only that it would be too large to yield the maximum net gain in terms of price to the business concerns of the country. "Inordinate" refers to the needs of business, not to livelihood.

2. The past three or four years (1920–1923) have shown how these matters stand. The country's industry has hung in a state of suspended animation while the business concerns that take care of coal, iron and transportation have been engaged – no doubt righteously and legally – in bringing the man-power employed in those industries to profitable terms by a campaign of protracted unemployment and privation.

3. The underlying principle of it all was formulated in another connection by Jacob Fugger back in the 16th century: "er wäre kleinmütig wollte verdienen dieweil er konnte." – Quoted by Sombart, *Moderne Kapitalismus* (1st edn, vol. I, p. 396).

4. To this pervasive animistic credulity of the rural community the salesman-like folks of the country town have to "play up," in their unremitting pursuit of profitable customers. So that by force of salesmanlike pusillanimity the country towns are driven to underbid the lowest survivals of neolithic animism in a competitive endeavor to conform to all holdovers of supersti-tion that may conceivably have a commercial value; ... .

5. Right lately, the farmers and their delegates among the nation's official per-sonnel have been much occupied with contrivances for facilitating and amplifying "farm credits," designed to bring agriculture and the farm popu-lation within the pale of the credit-system and enable them to turn their assets to account as collateral on which to expand their effective capitalisa-tion. Of course, as seen from another angle, the whole project may also look like a contrivance to induce the farm population to increase their liabilities and overhead charges beyond what their earning-capacity will bear.

3

The Concentration of Economic Power (1932)*

Adolph A. Berle, Jr. and Gardiner C. Means

The corporate system has done more than evolve a norm by which business is carried on. Within it there exists a centripetal attraction which draws wealth together into aggregations of constantly increasing size, at the same time throwing control into the hands of fewer and fewer men. The trend is apparent; and no limit is as yet in sight. Were it possible to say that circumstances had established the concentration, but that there was no basis to form an opinion as to whether the process would continue, the whole problem might be simplified. But this is not the case. So far as can be seen, every element which favored concentration still exists, and the only apparent factor which may end the tendency is the limit in the ability of a few human beings effectively to handle the aggregates of property brought under their control.

The size of the modern giant corporation is difficult to grasp. Many people would consider large a corporation having assets of a million dollars or an income of $50,000. Measured by the average corporation this idea would be justified. In 1927 two-thirds of all corporations reporting net incomes earned "less than $5,000 each."[1] The average non-banking corporation in that year had an income of only $22,000,[2] and gross assets of but $570,000.[3] In comparison with the average corporation the million dollar company would be large. But in comparison to the great modern corporation both are pygmies. On the basis of assets, the American Telephone and Telegraph Company would be equivalent to over 8,000 average sized corporations, and both the United States Steel Corporation and the Pennsylvania Railroad Company to over 4,000. A hundred million dollar company would be

---

* From *The Modern Corporation and Private Property* (New York: Macmillan, 1932), pp. 18–19, 24–7, 28–33, 35, 40–6, 356–7.

equivalent in assets to nearly 200 average corporations. Clearly such great organisms are not to be thought of in the same terms as the average company. Already the Telephone Company controls more wealth than is contained within the borders of twenty-one of the states in the country.

The great extent to which economic activity is today carried on by such large enterprises is clearly indicated by ... [a] list of the two hundred largest[4] non-banking corporations, compiled as of January 1, 1930.[5] Nearly all of these companies had assets of over one hundred million dollars, and fifteen had assets of over a billion dollars. Their combined assets amounted to eighty-one billions of dollars or, as we shall see, nearly half of all corporate wealth in the United States.

These great companies form the very framework of American industry. The individual must come in contact with them almost constantly. He may own an interest in one or more of them, he may be employed by one of them, but above all he is continually accepting their service. If he travels any distance he is almost certain to ride on one of the great railroad systems. The engine which draws him has probably been constructed by the American Locomotive Company or the Baldwin Locomotive Works; the car in which he rides is likely to have been made by the American Car and Foundry Company or one of its subsidiaries, unless he is enjoying the services of the Pullman Company. The rails have almost certainly been supplied by one of the eleven steel companies on the list; and coal may well have come from one of the four coal companies, if not from a mine owned by the railroad itself. Perhaps the individual travels by automobile – in a car manufactured by the Ford, General Motors, Studebaker, or Chrysler Companies, on tires supplied by Firestone, Goodrich, Goodyear or the United States Rubber Company. He may choose among the brands of gas furnished by one of the twenty petroleum companies all actively seeking his trade. Should he pause to send a telegram or to telephone, one of the listed companies would be sure to fill his need.

Perhaps, on the other hand, the individual stays in his own home in comparative isolation and privacy. What do the two hundred largest companies mean to him there? His electricity and gas are almost sure to be furnished by one of these public utility companies: the aluminum of his kitchen utensils by the Aluminum Co. of America. His electric refrigerator may be the product of General Motors Co., or of one of the two great electric equipment companies, General Electric and Westinghouse Electric. The chances are that the Crane Company has supplied his plumbing fixtures, the American Radiator and

Standard Sanitary Corp. his heating equipment. He probably buys at least some of his groceries from the Great Atlantic and Pacific Tea Co. – a company that expected to sell one-eighth of all the groceries in the country in 1930[6] – and he secures some of his drugs, directly or indirectly, from the United Drug Company. The cans which contain his groceries may well have been made by the American Can Company; his sugar has been refined by one of the major companies, his meat has probably been prepared by Swift, Armour, or Wilson, his crackers put up by the National Biscuit Company. The newspaper which comes to his door may be printed on International Paper Company paper or on that of the Crown Zellerbach Corporation; his shoes may be one of the International Shoe Company's makes; and although his suit may not be made of American Woolen Company cloth, it has doubtless been stitched on a Singer sewing machine.

If he seeks amusement through a radio he will almost of necessity use a set made under a license of the Radio Corporation of America. When he steps out to the movies he will probably see a Paramount, Fox, or Warner Brothers' picture (taken on Eastman Kodak film) at a theater controlled by one of these producing groups. No matter which of the alluring cigarette advertisements he succumbs to he is almost sure to find himself smoking one of the many brands put out by the "big four" tobacco companies, and he probably stops to buy them at the United Cigar store on the corner.

Even where the individual does not come in direct contact, he cannot escape indirect contact with these companies, so ubiquitous have they become. There are few articles of consumption to whose production one of the big companies has not to some extent contributed. The International Harvester Company and the Deere Company, plow-makers, have aided in the production of most of the bread that the American eats, to much of the cotton he wears and to many of the other agricultural products he consumes. It is almost impossible to obtain electric power from a local utility without receiving service from generating equipment supplied by one of the two big electric equipment companies. Few industrial products are made without the aid at some point in the process of steel derived from one of the big companies. And nearly every article involves transportation by one of the big railroads, either in the state of a raw material or that of a finished product.

While these companies play an integral part in the business of the country, their dominant position becomes apparent only when we seek to examine their importance in relation to the whole of the

American economy. Here we must turn to the tool of statistics for only thus can we grasp the picture of our economic life as a whole. To make a statistical comparison of the relative importance of the large corporations, it is first necessary to decide upon a measure of importance. Since this study is primarily concerned with property, we have taken wealth, the economic equivalent of property, as the criterion of "importance" and have further assumed that the gross assets[7] controlled by a corporation are roughly proportional to its wealth. Wherever possible, however, the results obtained have been checked by the use of a second measure of importance – net earnings.[8]

In seeking to present a picture of the relative positions of these large corporations, four economic areas will be examined: (1) the New York stock market; (2) all corporate wealth; (3) all business wealth; and (4) the national wealth.

In the New York stock market there can be no question of the dominant position of the large corporation. Taking the list of stocks published weekly by the "Commercial and Financial Chronicle" and covering all but the most inactive stocks traded on the New York Stock Exchange in a normal week, 130 out of the 573 independent American corporations represented can be classed as huge companies, each reporting assets of over one hundred million dollars.[9] These 130 companies controlled more than 80 per cent of all the companies represented. In [Table 3.1], these corporations are grouped by size showing the total assets held by each group and the per cent which this represents of the assets of all the corporations covered.[10]

Besides showing the overwhelming importance of the huge corporation, this table shows what is perhaps of even greater significance, the relative unimportance of the medium-sized corporation having assets between $50,000,000 and $100,000,000 and as a group controlling less than 8 per cent of the total assets represented. The small corporations –

Table 3.1   The US Corporation

Size measured by gross assets	Number of companies	Gross assets held by group	Per cent of total assets represented
Under $50,000,000	372	$7,325,000,000	10.9
$50–$100,000,000	71	4,950,000,000	7.4
Over $100,000,000	130	54,714,000,000	81.7
Total	573	$66,989,000,000	100.0

and in this day of industrial giants the reader must not be shocked by the reference to all corporations with assets less than $50,000,000 as small – though numerous, do not hold an important position. It is noteworthy, however, that practically half the corporations included had less than $30,000,000 assets and as a group controlled less than 6 per cent of the total.

When we compare the combined assets of the two hundred largest non-banking corporations with the assets of all non-banking corporations, their dominant role is further emphasized. These companies, 42 railroads, 52 public utilities, and 106 industrials, each with assets over ninety million dollars, had combined assets at the beginning of 1930 of $81,074,000,000.[11] According to an estimate based on Income Tax figures, the total assets of all non-banking corporations at the beginning of 1930 amounted to $165,000,000,000.[12] Thus the two hundred big companies controlled 49.2 per cent or nearly half of all non-banking corporate wealth, while the remaining half was owned by the more than 300,000 smaller companies.

The same dominant position of the large companies is shown when we compare the net income of the largest companies with the net income of all corporations. In 1929, the most recent year for which Income Tax statistics have been published, the largest two hundred non-banking corporations, each with an income of over $5,000,000, received 43.2 per cent of the income of all non-banking corporations.

Even this figure, however, tends to minimize the importance of the big companies. To a very considerable extent the Income Tax statistics, on which it is based, fail to include as part of the income of a big company all the income derived from property under its control. In compiling the figures of income the Treasury Department has tabulated as separate corporations all companies filing separate Income Tax returns, even when they were actually controlled by other companies. Since any subsidiary company controlled through ownership of less than 95 per cent of its stock (or of the voting stock) was required to file a separate return[13] – and any subsidiary could file a separate return if it so desired – many companies are included as separate when actually they were controlled by other companies and for the present purpose should have their earnings consolidated with the latter.

For instance, the American Telephone and Telegraph Company was presumably represented in Income Tax returns as at least four companies, the parent company with assets over $3,000 million in 1928, the

Pacific Telephone and Telegraph Company with assets over $379 million, the New England Telephone and Telegraph Company with $268 million assets and the Mountain States Telephone and Telegraph Company with $80 million assets.[14] Even dividends received from these subsidiaries were not included in the statutory net income of the parent. Many other large corporations were in the same situation. For this reason the earned incomes reported by the large companies are frequently less than the earnings of property under their control.

A second factor tending to minimize the apparent importance of the large corporation, is the greater proportion of its income which is paid out as interest and therefore is not included as "statutory net income." It is fairly certain that large companies, particularly railroad and public utilities, tend to have a larger indebtedness in proportion to their size than small companies. If the net income of all subsidiary corporations had been included in the net income of parents, and if income had included income represented by amounts paid out as interest, it is probable that the two hundred largest would have received well over 45 per cent of the net income of all corporations. This figure would therefore tend to give support to the figure derived on the basis of gross assets.

The income figures also indicated that the medium-sized corporation is not a particularly important factor. The 800 non-financial corporations next in size (according to net income) after the largest 200, received only 19.3 per cent of the net income of all corporations. This figure covers all corporations reporting income of over one million dollars and less than four and one-half million dollars, incomes representing assets ranging roughly from 18 to 80 million dollars. If all corporations had filed consolidated income accounts, the 800 corporations would have reported a still smaller proportion of corporate income since that of many important corporations would have been shifted into the higher group and only a slight balancing would come through addition from below.

In contrast to the medium-sized, the small corporation, reporting an income under one million dollars, makes an important showing. Such corporations accounted for 37.5 per cent of all corporate income, due, in large measure, to the sheer weight of numbers among the smallest units. This would seem to indicate that the bulk of corporate wealth was represented either by huge units having assets running into the hundreds of millions or by relatively small corporations having assets under four million dollars.

When we seek to compare the wealth of the big companies with that of all industry we get into difficulty since there appears to be no adequate basis for estimating the total business wealth in the country. A very rough estimate,[15] however, indicates that at least 78 per cent and probably a larger proportion of American business wealth is corporate wealth. Since the two hundred largest corporations controlled approximately 49 per cent of all corporate wealth, the rough calculation would indicate that they controlled 38 per cent or more of all business wealth.

When we come to national wealth, we are necessarily dealing with estimates which can at best be only most approximate. The National Industrial Conference Board has estimated that the national wealth at the end of 1928 amounted to $360,062,000,000.[16] If we assume an increase equal to the average of the previous six years we should have $367,000,000,000 as the national wealth in 1929. Since the total assets of the two hundred big companies in that year amounted to $81,077,000,000,[17] they controlled roughly 22 per cent of the total wealth of the country. The lower relative importance of the large corporation in comparison to the national wealth is in large measure due to the importance of agricultural land and improvements, residential real estate, personal property including automobiles, and the large volume of government property.

To recapitulate, [Table 3.2] gives the results of the foregoing analysis:

Table 3.2   **Relative importance of large corporations**
(on or about January 1, 1930)

	Results obtained by actual computation (%)	Probable limits (%)
Proportion of corporate wealth (other than banking) controlled by the 200 largest corporations	49.2	45–53
Proportion of business wealth (other than banking) controlled by the 200 largest corporations	38.0*	35–45
Proportion of national wealth controlled by the 200 largest corporations	22.0	15–25

* Unadjusted for unconsolidated income tax returns.

It is apparent from these figures that a very considerable portion of the industrial wealth of the country has been concentrated under the control of a relatively few huge units. There were over 300,000 non-financial corporations in the country in 1929. Yet 200 of these, or less than seven-hundredth of one per cent, control nearly half the corporate wealth.

It must further be remembered that the influence of one of these huge companies extends far beyond the assets under its direct control. Smaller companies which sell to or buy from the larger companies are likely to be influenced by them to a vastly greater extent than by other smaller companies with which they might deal. In many cases the continued prosperity of the smaller company depends on the favor of the larger and almost inevitably the interests of the latter become the interests of the former. The influence of the larger company on prices is often greatly increased by its mere size, even though it does not begin to approach a monopoly. Its political influence may be tremendous. Therefore, if roughly half of corporate wealth is controlled by two hundred large corporations and half by smaller companies it is fair to assume that very much more than half of industry is dominated by these great units. This concentration is made even more significant when it is recalled that as a result of it, approximately 2,000 individuals out of a population of one hundred and twenty-five million are in a position to control and direct half of industry.

The actual extent to which the concentration of power has progressed is striking enough. More striking still, however, is the pace at which it is proceeding. In 1909, the assets of the 200 then largest non-banking corporations amounted to only $26.0 billion. By 1919 they had reached $43.7 billion, an increase of 68 per cent in ten years. In the next ten years from 1919 to 1929 they increased to $81.1 billion, an increase of 85 per cent.

The assets of 44 identical railroads increased from $18 billion in 1919 to $23 billion in 1928 or 24 per cent; 71 identical industrial corporations increased from $14 billion to $23 billion in the same period, a growth of approximately 58 per cent in nine years. In the public utility field, as is well known, the rate has been vastly more rapid. In the same nine years the assets of 35 identical utilities grew from $6 billion to $18 billion, or nearly three times. The more rapid growth of the utilities approximately compensates for the slow growth of the railroads, and the total for the 150 corporations shows a growth from $39 billion to $63 billion, or an increase of practically 63 per cent.

Though the growth of the large corporations shown in these tables is rapid, it is truly significant only if it has been more rapid than the growth of all industrial wealth. We have already discussed the difficulty in estimating the total industrial wealth for each year; but, as we have seen, more accurate material is available with reference to the wealth of corporations. Here again the distinction between banking and non-banking corporations is necessary, especially in view of the rapid growth of investment trusts which have been included, for the present purpose, with banks. Where industrial activity is concerned, there is reason to exclude such companies from consideration. In examining the growth of the 200 largest corporations, the increase in their gross assets has been accepted as a reasonable measure of growth. In measuring the growth of all non-financial corporations, no accurate figures for gross assets are available. For certain years, notably 1921, 1924, and 1926 to 1929, a figure which the Federal Trade Commission has designated as "wealth used in corporate business" can, however, be employed as a satisfactory measure of growth. This item includes only cash, inventory, land, buildings and equipment. In each of these years the figure is based upon the data supplied from tax returns, and, to make the data for the different years comparable, certain adjustments have been necessary. With these adjustments, the figures for different years become reasonably comparable and should indicate with a fair degree of accuracy the rate of increase of all corporate wealth exclusive of that of banking corporations. For the year 1909 less satisfactory material is available; but an estimate, involving a very much larger margin of error, has been made for that year.

When the rates of growth of the wealth of all nonfinancial corporations and of the assets of the 200 largest corporations are thus compared, they show the large corporations as a group to be growing very much more rapidly than all corporations. For the period from 1909 to 1928 their annual rate of growth has been 5.4 per cent, while that of all corporations (assuming the estimates are reliable) has amounted to only 3.6 per cent, and for corporations other than the largest 200 only 2.0 per cent. The large corporations would thus appear to be increasing in wealth over 50 per cent faster than all corporations or over two and one-half times as fast as smaller corporations. From 1921 to 1928 the annual rate of growth of the large corporations has been 6.1 per cent compared with 4.4 per cent for all corporations or 3.1 per cent for the smaller companies. From 1924 to 1928, a period of most rapid growth, the annual rates were respectively 7.7 per cent for the large, 4.9 per cent for all, and only 2.6 per cent for corporations other than the largest 200, indicating that the large corporations were growing more than half again as fast as all corporations and three times as fast as smaller corporations.

This very much more rapid rate of growth of the big companies in comparison to other companies is equally evident when we examine the proportion of the income of all non-banking corporations which has been reported each year by the 200 companies reporting the largest incomes. For 1921 the results are misleading as in that year, the year of depression, the net income of all corporations was extremely low, and on purely statistical grounds, one would expect the proportion received by the corporations reporting the largest income to be very much greater than normal. In the remaining years, however, there is no reason to think that the figures are not reasonably comparable for different years. The results run roughly parallel to those obtained when the growth in assets was examined. Thus, while the years from 1924 to 1929 show no noticeable growth in the proportion of net income received by the 200 largest, from 1924 to 1929 there is a very marked increase in the proportion of all corporate income going to the 200 largest, increasing from 33.4 per cent in 1920 to 43.2 per cent in 1929 or from an average of 33.5 per cent in the years 1920–1923 to an average of 40.4 in the years 1926–1929.

This increase in the proportion received by the large companies could theoretically be explained on two grounds other than the actual growth of the large corporations. If they had obtained an increasing rate of return on their capital in comparison with the smaller companies, the increase in the proportion of income could be explained. It could likewise be explained on the ground that for a large number of subsidiary corporations the net income was not consolidated with the parent in the earlier years and was so consolidated in the later years. This latter explanation, however, could at most account for only a very small part of the increase, since approximately the same proportion of all non-financial corporate dividends were reported as received by non-financial corporations in 1927 as in 1922,[18] indicating that subsidiaries were reported as separate corporations to approximately the same extent throughout the period.

It is quite conceivable that an important part of the increase is explained by the greater profitableness of large corporations; but the fact that the change coincides roughly with the change shown for corporate wealth tends to strengthen the conclusion that the large corporations have increased greatly both their proportion of the wealth and their proportion of the income of all corporations.

Though it is not possible to obtain figures for the growth of industrial wealth, we have already seen that the corporation has become increasingly important in industry after industry. Presumably a constantly increasing proportion of all industrial wealth has come under corporate sway.[19] If that be the fact, the proportion of industrial wealth controlled by the 200 corporations has been increasing at a rate even more rapid than their proportion of all corporate wealth.

The relative growth of the wealth of the large corporations and the national wealth can only be very roughly calculated. As we have indicated, national wealth is a difficult concept to define, and all estimates of national wealth must be, at best, approximate; so that too much reliance should not be placed on any comparison of the growth of corporate wealth with that of national wealth. Between 1922 and 1928 the estimates by the National Industrial Conference Board[20] indicate a growth in national wealth of 12.5 per cent compared with the growth in assets[21] of the 200 largest corporations of 45.6 per cent, or annual rates of growth of 2.0 per cent and 6.3 percent *respectively*.[22] While the estimates based on the 1930 census figures may be considerably higher than those of the Conference Board, the estimates of the latter for 1928 would have to be increased by over 30 per cent to make the rate of increase in the national wealth equal to that of the 200 corporations. There can, therefore, be little doubt that the wealth of the large corporations has been increasing at a very much more rapid rate than the total national wealth.

To summarize the conclusions with relation to growth:

(1) On the basis of gross assets, the large corporations appear to have been growing between two and three times as fast as all other non-financial corporations.
(2) This conclusion is supported by the figures of corporate income.
(3) Since an increased proportion of industrial wealth presumably continues to come under corporate sway, the proportion of industrial wealth controlled by the large corporations has been increasing at a rate even faster than the proportion of corporate wealth controlled by them.
(4) Since estimates of national wealth are extremely approximate it is not possible to determine the growth in the proportion of national wealth controlled by the large corporations, but there can be little question that the proportion has been increasing at a rapid rate.

Just what does this rapid growth of the big companies promise for the future? Let us project the trend of the growth of recent years. If the wealth of the large corporations and that of all corporations should each continue to increase for the next twenty years at its average annual rate for the twenty years from 1909 to 1929, 70 per cent of all corporate activity would be carried on by 200 corporations by 1950.[23] If the more rapid rates of growth from 1924 to 1929 were maintained for the next twenty years 85 per cent of corporate wealth would be held by two hundred huge units. It would take only over forty years at the 1909–1929 rates or only thirty years at the 1924–1929 rates for all corporate activity and practically all industrial activity to be absorbed by two hundred giant companies. If the indicated growth of the large corporations and of the national wealth were to be effective from now until 1950, half of the national wealth would be under the control of big companies at the end of that period.

Whether the future will see any such complete absorption of economic activity into a few great enterprises it is not possible to predict. ... [T]he rate of growth has not been uniform. The years from 1921 through 1923 showed little more growth by the large corporations than by all, though this slackening may reflect only a breathing spell after the excessive growth of the war years. One would expect, moreover, that the rate of concentration would slacken as a larger and larger proportion of industry became absorbed and less remained to be added. The trend of the recent past indicates, however, that the great corporation, already of tremendous importance today, will become increasingly important in the future.

This conclusion is still further confirmed when we examine the ways in which the growth of the large companies takes place and compare their growth by each method with that of other companies. A given corporation can increase the wealth under its control in three major ways: by reinvesting its earnings, by raising new capital through the sale of securities in the public markets, and by acquiring control of other corporations by either purchase or exchange of securities. While there are numerous other ways by which an increase could take place, such as private sale of securities to individuals, these three so far outweigh other methods that they alone need to be considered.

A comparison of the savings of large corporations with those of all corporations indicates that the big companies as a group save a larger proportion of their net income. In the six-year period from 1922 to

1927 inclusive, 108 corporations (all of the 200 largest for which consolidated statements could be obtained for each year) saved 38.5 per cent of their net income available for dividends. In the same period, all corporations combined saved only 29.4 per cent of their net income.[24] Since the earnings of the large corporations are included as an important proportion in the earnings of all corporations and since these large companies saved a larger than average percentage of earnings, the remaining corporations, mainly smaller companies, must have saved a proportion very much smaller than average, probably less than 25 per cent of their earnings. The importance of this method of growth is indicated by the fact that roughly a quarter of the growth of the large corporations was derived from earnings between 1922 and 1927.

Of much greater importance as a source of relative expansion has been the second method – the raising of new capital in the public markets. Over 55 per cent of the growth of the large companies has been made possible by the public offering of additional securities, a fact which particularly concerns us here since these offerings are all made to the public investor, and since the dependence of these corporations on new capital is undoubtedly one of the strongest factors determining the relation between those who control the corporations and their investing stockholders. Here again the large corporation increases the wealth under its control by this means of expansion to a much greater extent than the smaller companies. From 1922 to 1927 inclusive, a sample study indicated that two-thirds of all public offerings of new securities (as reported by the "Commercial and Financial Chronicle" – excluding banking companies) were made by the two hundred largest companies or their subsidiaries.

The third and more spectacular method of growth of the large corporations is by consolidation or merger. Within the eleven years, 1919 through 1929, no less than 49 corporations recorded among the largest two hundred at one time or another during the period have disappeared by merging with other large companies on the list. It would be an extensive task to chronicle all the smaller companies which the companies on our list have absorbed. Roughly twenty per cent of the growth of the largest companies which we have been observing can be attributed to additions through merger, a growth which effects a reduction in the corporate wealth lying outside the control of the largest group.

The growth in the assets of the two hundred largest corporations in the six-year period from 1922 to 1927 inclusive is given below, as well as estimates of the manner of growth.

	$	per cent
Estimated savings out of earnings	5,748,000,000	2.5
Estimated new capital from sale of securities	11,813,000,000	5.0
Estimated growth as a result of mergers	4,000,000,000	18.5
	21,561,000,000	100.0
Estimated reduction from reappraisals, etc., and error in estimates	2,000,000,000	
Net growth in assets, 1922–1927, inclusive	19,561,000,000	

One question yet remains – are these companies likely to survive? It is sometimes said that consolidations of great magnitude sooner or later, more often sooner, go into a period of decline, – that beyond a certain point the organization breaks down, and the whole falls of its own weight. There appears, however, to be little foundation for such a suggestion. Examination of the condition in 1928 of the two hundred companies which were largest in 1919 shows the following:[25]

Of the 200 largest corporations in 1919: –
23 merged with larger companies.
154 were included in list of largest 200 corporations in 1928.
21 remained large and active concerns though 7 of them went through reorganization.
2 liquidated or the equivalent.
200

This table shows 25 companies actually disappearing in nine years, or a rate of disappearance of 1.4 per cent a year. If this were the normal rate of disappearance it would indicate an average expectancy of over 70 years of further life. At the same time the disappearance of a corporation through merger does not indicate that its organization has broken down and that it is about to fall into dissolution; it passes, but does not die. If we regard the two liquidated companies as the only ones which actually disappeared, we would have a dissolution rate of 1 per cent in nine years or an average expectancy of 900 years of life, either as an independent concern or as an integral part of a larger enterprise. On the other hand if we apply the rates of merger and of dissolution simultaneously they indicate that at the end of 360 years sixteen of the two hundred companies would have disappeared through dissolution and all the remaining companies would have merged into a single corporation having a life expectancy of over 1,000 years. Furthermore, if the changes in the nine years are a promise of the future, half of the companies included in the 1919 list of 200 companies will also be represented in a list of the largest two hundred compiled a century hence, ten directly and ninety as absorbed units in these ten.

These figures are, of course, an unwarranted extension into the future of the trend of the nine years from 1919 to 1928. They serve, however, to indicate that there is little in the history of the two hundred companies in the nine-year period considered to suggest that the large corporation has a short life cycle ending in dissolution.

In conclusion, then, the huge corporation, the corporation with $90,000,000 of assets or more, has come to dominate most major industries if not all industry in the United States. A rapidly increasing proportion of industry is carried on under this form of organization. There is apparently no immediate limit to its increase. It is coming more and more to be the industrial unit with which American economic, social, and political life must deal. The implications of this fact challenge many of the basic assumptions of current thought.

(1) Most fundamental of all, it is now necessary to think, to a very important extent, in terms of these huge units rather than in terms of the multitude of small competing elements of private enterprise. The emphasis must be shifted to that very great proportion of industry in the hands of a relatively few units, units which can be studied individually and concretely. Such studies will reveal the operation of half of industry and what is more important, that half which is likely to be more typical of the industry of the future.[26]

(2) Competition has changed in character and the principles applicable to present conditions are radically different from those which apply when the dominant competing units are smaller and more numerous. The principles of duopoly have become more important than these of free competition.

(3) An increasing proportion of production is carried on for use and not for sale. With the increase in the large companies, a larger proportion of goods are consumed by the producing organization in the process of making further goods. To this extent the calculus of cost versus quality would presumably be solved in the interest of

producing a product which would yield the maximum use per unit of cost rather than the maximum profit per unit of investment. Under the latter incentive the consumer is only incidentally offered the product which will give him the most use per unit of cost unless he himself is easily able to measure usefulness. Adulteration, shoddy goods, and goods of lower quality than would be economically desirable are frequent under the incentive for profit. To the extent that production is for use by the producing organization there is no such incentive.[27]

(4) The nature of capital has changed. To an increasing extent it is composed not of tangible goods, but of organizations built in the past and available to function in the future. Even the value of tangible goods tends to become increasingly dependent upon their organized relationship to other tangible goods composing the property of one of these great units.

(5) Finally, a society in which production is governed by blind economic forces is being replaced by one in which production is carried on under the ultimate control of a handful of individuals.[28] The economic power in the hands of the few persons who control a giant corporation is a tremendous force which can harm or benefit a multitude of individuals, affect whole districts, shift the currents of trade, bring ruin to one community and prosperity to another. The organizations which they control have passed far beyond the realm of private enterprise – they have become more nearly social institutions.

Such is the character of the corporate system – dynamic, constantly building itself into greater aggregates, and thereby changing the basic conditions which the thinking of the past has assumed.

The new concept of the corporation

In still larger view, the modern corporation may be regarded not simply as one form of social organization but potentially (if not yet actually) as the dominant institution of the modern world. In every age, the major concentration of power has been based upon the dominant interest of that age. The strong man has, in his time, striven to be cardinal or pope, prince or cabinet minister, bank president or partner in the House of Morgan. During the Middle Ages, the Church, exercising spiritual power, dominated Europe and gave to it a unity at a time when both political and economic power were diffused.

With the rise of the modern state, political power, concentrated into a few large units, challenged the spiritual interest as the strongest bond of human society. Out of the long struggle between church and state which followed, the state emerged victorious; nationalist politics superseded religion as the basis of the major unifying organization of the western world. Economic power still remained diffused.

The rise of the modern corporation has brought a concentration of economic power which can compete on equal terms with the modern state – economic power versus political power, each strong in its own field. The state seeks in some aspects to regulate the corporation, while the corporation, steadily becoming more powerful, makes every effort to avoid such regulation. Where its own interests are concerned, it even attempts to dominate the state. The future may see the economic organism, now typified by the corporation, not only on an equal plane with the state, but possibly even superseding it as the dominant form of social organization. The law of corporations, accordingly, might well be considered as a potential constitutional law for the new economic state, while business practice is increasingly assuming the aspect of economic statesmanship.

Notes

1. Statistics of Income (1927), p. 19.
2. Ibid. pp. 16 and 17. "Non-banking" is here used to exclude banks, insurance companies, and investment trusts.
3. Ibid. pp. 371, 372.
4. Largest according to gross assets less depreciation, as reported in Moody's Railroad, Public Utility, and Industrial Manuals. In the cases where a consolidated balance sheet was not given in Moody's, an estimate as made based on the assets of subsidiaries and the assets of the parent corporation *minus* its investments in affiliated companies. These estimates, while they cannot be perfectly accurate, are sufficiently so for the present purpose. In two cases, no balance sheet of the parent was given but a very rough estimate of the assets controlled was made, based on the bonds and stocks of the parent company and the assets of certain of its subsidiaries. No company is included in the list, a majority of whose voting stock was known to be owned by another corporation.
5. *Editor's Note*: The original chapter, published in *The Modern Corporation and Private Property*, contained a series of tables, statistics and appendices regarding the composition and size of big corporations. From today's perspective, these data are of little interest, and have not been reproduced here, along with references in the text and footnotes to related tables and appendices. Interested readers may consult the original version of Berle and Means' book, or later editions thereof.
6. Wall Street Journal (November 25, 1929).

7. Gross assets *less* depreciation. In some balance sheets depreciation is subtracted from assets and in others it is included as a liability. Both practices are legitimate, but the latter results in a larger figure for gross assets. An adjustment has, therefore, been made where necessary to obtain gross assets exclusive of depreciation.

8. Statutory net income as compiled by the Treasury Department. This consists of the untaxed net income derived by a corporation directly from its business operations.

9. The stocks of 678 corporations were included in the list published by the "Commercial and Financial Chronicle" in the issue selected, that of the typical week of March 9, 1929. Of these, 76 were subsidiaries of other corporations on the list, 21 were foreign corporations and 8 were financial corporations. When a corporation listed on the exchange was a subsidiary of a corporation not listed, the parent was regarded as represented on the exchange. The assets of the listed corporations were obtained in Moody's Manuals for 1928 and 1929.

10. A similar study was made for the independent companies listed on the New York Curb Exchange, using the curb transaction list from the same issue of the "Commercial and Financial Chronicle." Unfortunately, the study was first made for a different purpose which involved only the companies in existence in 1927 and a compilation of assets as of that date. For this reason it does not include many companies which should be added. As the correction would probably not make a radical difference in the set of percentages, the uncorrected results are given below:

Size measured by gross assets	Number of companies	Gross assets held by group	Per cent of total assets represented
Under $ 50,000,000	371	$3,731,000,000	24.3
$50–$100,000,000	31	2,308,000,000	15.0
Over $100,000,000	37	9,338,000,000	60.7
Total	439	$15,377,000,000	100.0

11. In the 26 cases where a consolidated balance sheet was not given in Moody's an estimate was made based on the assets of subsidiaries and the assets of the parent corporation *minus* its investments in affiliated companies. These estimates, while they cannot be perfectly accurate, are sufficiently so for the present purpose. In two cases, no balance sheet of the parent was given but a very rough estimate of the assets controlled was made, based on the bonds and stocks of the parent company and the assets of certain of its subsidiaries.

12. This estimate was arrived at by making an estimate of the gross assets of all non-banking corporations on December 31, 1929, according to the method described in "The Large Corporation in American Economic Life," *American Economic Review*, 21 (March, 1931), pp. 15, 16.

13. Revenue Act of 1926, Section 240 (a), (c) and (d). In case 95 per cent or more of the stock or of the voting stock of each of two or more corporations was owned by "the same interests" the corporations could file a consolidated return and would, therefore, appear as a single corporation in the statistics of income. Such a situation arises so infrequently that it need not be regarded here.

14. Subsidiaries of the American Telephone and Telegraph Company presumably filing income tax returns separate from parent in 1928 (i.e., less than 95 per cent owned). Derived from "Bell Telephone Securities – Reference Tables and Descriptions" (1929), published by the Bell Telephone Securities Company, a subsidiary of the American Telephone and Telegraph Company. Figures as of December 31, 1928:

Gross assets in millions ($)	Name	Per cent stock owned by A T & T Co.
80.1	Mountain States Tel. & Tel. Co	72.82
268.6	New England Tel. & Tel. Co	61.98
379.6	Pacific Tel. & Tel. Co.	82.00

15. The method employed is described in "The Large Corporation in American Economic Life" [see n. 12] pp. 19, 20.

16. National Industrial Conference Board, *Conference Board Bulletin*, No. 38 (February 25, 1930), p. 303 (National Industrial Conference Board, New York).

17. The error due to including bills receivable in gross assets is not sufficiently large in comparison to the probable error in the estimate of national wealth to warrant making an adjustment.

18. 20.3 per cent in 922 and 20.5 per cent in 1927. Derived from Statistics of Income, 1922, pp. 18, 19 and 22, and *ibid.*, 1927, pp. 312 and 315.

19. The 1899 census reported 66.7 per cent of all manufactured products are made by corporations, as against 87.0 per cent in 1919. An extension of trend based on the log of the figure for the per cent of manufactured products not made by corporations according to the census figures of 1899, 1909, and 1919 indicates that in 1929 approximately 94 per cent of all manufactured products were made by corporations. Basic figures obtained from 14th Census of the United States, vol. viii, pp. 14, 108.

20. National Industrial Conference Board, *Conference Board Bulletin*, No. 38 (February 25, 1930), p. 303.

21. The use of the gross assets of corporations rather than their tangible wealth is reasonable, since the comparison is primarily for noting changes in relationship rather than an absolute relationship.

22. Compounded annually.

23. Assuming 49.2 per cent of non-banking corporate wealth was held by the largest 200 in 1927-9.

24. This difference in rate of saving is probably not an indication of greater liberality in paying dividends on the part of the small corporations but an

indication of their greater liability to loss. For both groups, the net income for the group included the net income of those making a profit minus the losses suffered by the remainder.

25. A study of the present status of the two hundred companies included as the largest in the list for 1910 yield percentage results per unit of time almost identical with those for the 1919 list.

26. For instance, it seems likely that a study of the directors and senior officers of the 200 largest companies, their training, social background, and other characteristics, would reveal more of vital importance to the community than a study of those at the head of thousands of smaller companies. The same would be true of the ownership of the large companies, their labor policies, their price policies, their promotion practices, etc. This is not to suggest that the practices of the large companies would be typical of the smaller companies, but rather that they would be factually more important.

27. For instance, it is to the advantage of the American Telephone and Telegraph Company to have its subsidiary, the Western Electric Company, make the best possible vacuum tubes for the innumerable repeater sets in use on its long distance lines. On the other hand, it might be to the advantage of a corporation making tubes for sale to the public to make second-grade tubes which would wear out quickly and allow a second sale at a second profit to be made.

28. Approximately 2,000 men were directors of the 200 largest corporations in 1930. Since an important number of these are inactive, the ultimate control of nearly half of industry was actually in the hands of a few hundred men.

4

Industrial Society: On the Convergence of Capitalism and Socialism (1961)*

Raymond Aron

An industrial society might be simply defined as a society in which large-scale industry, such as is found in Renault or Citroën enterprises, is the characteristic form of production. From this definition a number of other features of an industrial economy might be inferred. First, the enterprise is completely separated from the family. The separation of work place and family circle is by no means universal, even in our own society, as is shown by many artisan and peasant enterprises.

Secondly, an industrial firm introduces a new form of the division of labor, which not only involves the division which has existed in every society between the various sections of the economy, peasants, merchants and craftsmen, but a technological division of labor within the firm, which is one of the characteristics of modern industrial societies.

Thirdly, an industrial enterprise implies an accumulation of capital. Each workman must use a substantial amount of capital, which must be constantly renewed. The idea of a progressive economy develops from the idea of industrial society; hence Marx's famous phrase, "Accumulate, accumulate, this is the law and the prophets," which he used to describe capitalist society. We know from contemporary historical experience that the accumulation of capital is not characteristic only of capitalist societies, but of all industrial societies. No doubt, Stalin would have applied Marx's formula to his own society.

Fourthly, as soon as the worker requires a large amount of capital in a process of expansion the idea of rational calculation is introduced. In a

---

*   From *18 Lectures on Industrial Society* (London: Weidenfeld & Nicolson, 1961), pp. 73–84.

big enterprise, such as Renault or Citroën, it is necessary to make continuous calculations in order to achieve the lowest cost price and to renew and increase the capital. No modern industrial society can avoid what both bourgeois and Marxist economists alike call the economic calculus. We shall see how this varies in different régimes, but at the outset it can be said that every industrial society implies rigorous economic calculation. Without it there would be enormous losses of wealth and energy.

I have said economic and not technical calculation. These must be distinguished. For example, the French railways are technically miraculous, but they are in a permanent state of financial disequilibrium. I am not saying that this disequilibrium is a consequence of the technical perfection, only that technical improvements ought to be subject to economic calculation. One must know whether it is profitable to replace a rail which is not the latest model by a more highly perfected one. And as the question arises of whether to replace a machine within a single enterprise such as the railways, so it arises for the transport system as a whole. How should resources be allocated between rail and road transport systems? And in an even wider sphere, how should the total resources of a community be allocated among the different uses? In an industrial economy it is never possible to produce everything that is technologically feasible at a given time ... [T]here is not the slightest chance of using all the most advanced techniques at any time, for this would require unlimited capital resources. There will always be time lags in certain sectors in relation to the technical possibilities. In order to decide which techniques should be introduced an economic calculation must be made.

The fifth feature of industrial enterprise is the concentration of labor in the work place. Here the question of the ownership of the means of production arises. There is concentration of labor in every industrial society whatever the system of ownership of the means of production. But naturally, when there are hundreds or thousands of workers on one side and a small number of owners on the other, the problem of the relations between owners and workers is bound to arise. In all industrial societies there will be some organisation of the workers and a challenge to the individual ownership of the means of production. The idea of common ownership is as old as civilisation. There have always been men who protested against the inequality resulting from private property, and who dreamed of a system of common ownership which would put an end to inequalities. But it would be absurd to confuse this centuries-old socialist dream with the problem of socialism in industrial society; for this is the first time that these great concentrations of workers have occurred, that the means of production have grown beyond the capacity of individual ownership and consequently have posed the question of who should own them.

Certain features of our industrial societies can thus be inferred from the preliminary definition of industrial society. Nevertheless, this analysis seems superficial and I should like to try to go deeper by considering from various points of view the characteristics of an economic system. This will facilitate a more rigorous examination of capitalism as a type of industrial society.

The very notion of *economic* is difficult to define. There are two types of definition. First, one may refer to the needs of individuals, and term economic the activity which tends to satisfy these needs. But this definition is not very satisfactory. First, there are needs, such as sex, which cannot be said to involve economic activity as such; furthermore, it has proved impossible to define human needs precisely. It seems paradoxical, but is really trite to say that man is an animal whose apparently non-essential needs are as urgent as those which are acknowledged as essential. As soon as the basic needs for food, shelter, etc. are satisfied, there arise others of a social nature, such as the need for recognition, prestige, and power, so that it is impossible to say that certain needs are economic while others are not.

The second kind of definition refers to the meaning of economic activity, or to use the terminology of Max Weber, to the meaning which men give to the economy in their behavior. In this sense, economics is concerned with the administration of scarce resources, or with the relation between means and ends when means are scarce and have alternative uses.

This way of defining economic by a meaningful characteristic behaviour is satisfactory for developed societies, where the goals of individuals are numerous and explicit. Needs and desires continually increase; the means of satisfying them are numerous and have alternative uses. In particular, the use of money and the generally accepted monetary valuation of goods introduces choice, alternative ways of spending resources and a multiplicity of goals. Money is a kind of universal method of achieving the goals that each man sets himself.

The difficulty of this definition of economic activity as the administration of scarce resources is that in small or primitive societies it is almost impossible to isolate the activity which would constitute a rational choice of means to achieve chosen ends. In the simplest societies the means are not subject to calculations of alternative uses, the needs and goals are largely determined once and for all by custom or religious beliefs. It would be difficult to isolate economic calculations or a rational consideration of the use of scarce resources. In primitive societies, the economic sector is not separated from the rest of society. Men's economic behaviour cannot be isolated because ends and means alike are determined by beliefs which seem to us to be outside the economic sphere.

The difficulties involved in both these definitions can be overcome if we remember that supra-historical concepts are bound to be formal in character and that to understand particular historical situations we have to give these concepts a specific content. It is obvious that man must satisfy certain elementary animal needs in order to survive. As soon as men began to live in society they experienced other non-biological needs, which are just as urgent and demanding as the elementary ones. All societies are poor and must solve what we call an economic problem. But this does not mean that all societies are conscious of it, that is, of the rational use of scarce resources. All societies have an economy and solve economic problems, but they do not always pose them in explicit economic terms.

In societies where economic activity is not distinct one is tempted to identify it with the satisfaction of elementary needs. But this is only a convention. At all events, every economy, even in a primitive society, comprises production, exchange and consumption.

Production, which is the work of gathering the products of the earth or transforming raw materials, has existed ever since man left the Garden of Eden. The condition of man is such that he can only survive by satisfying his needs and to do this he must work. Work can be considered from three points of view:

1 Technological: what tools are available to the individual or the society which is being studied?
2 Legal: who owns the tools and, especially, the land?
3 How is social labor organized and administered?

... This distinction is fundamental, as we shall see, for it is impossible to understand the economic problems of our time without distinguishing between what is common to all production, the technological aspect, and the legal variations which arise from the ownership of the instruments of production, as well as the differences in organisation which may or may not result from the legal differences.

The problem of exchange arises from the fact that even in the simplest societies there is some social or collective production. There is no society in which everyone keeps what he has produced; there is always a minimum of exchange and from this arises a problem of trade and distribution. We have to study an economic system from the point of view of the method of exchange, the monetary system which enables the exchanges to take place, and from the point of view of the distribution of goods, or the degree of equality or inequality in consumption. The aim of every economy is the satisfaction of desires and needs: the final goal is consumption. To study an economy in relation to consumption, one must first consider what the society wishes to consume, i.e. what are its goals, what are the goods it values and wishes to obtain. In a complex society, to study consumption is to determine the level of consumption of the whole society, of a certain class or of certain individuals, and also to try to see how, with given resources, individuals decide what to consume in order to satisfy their desires. This leads to the distinction between the standard of life, which is a quantitative idea, and the way of life which is a qualitative notion.

An economic unit may be considered from several points of view:

1 The extent and type of the division of labor.
2 The motive force of its economic activity. Here I must make a commonplace but necessary distinction: one can produce to satisfy one's own desires, or one can produce for the market, that is, for profit. Every French peasant produces partly for his own needs and partly for the market. These two motives may apply to a part of an economy or to the whole. Some societies produce mainly for personal needs, some mainly for the market, for profit.
3 The type of regulation or organisation of the economic system. In every economy it is necessary to decide on the goals, to distribute resources and to strike a balance between what is produced and what is purchased outside. There are at least two simple ways of regulating an economy – by central planning or by the mechanism of the market. These are abstractions. A big industrial enterprise, such as the Renault factories, is directed from the center, and plans production for a year and possibly for several years, but these plans are subject to revision because the sales of Renault cars cannot be planned, since they depend on the desires of consumers. All economic units have a mixture of central planning and regulation according to supply and demand.

The ideal type of a planned economy is one in which planners would decide at the beginning of the year the total amount to be produced and the total income to be allocated to each individual and in which, as a result of decisions taken by the central planning office, there would be a balance between production and demand. Needless to say, a totally planned economy has never existed and could not exist. But there are great differences in the degree of planning and in the free operation of market mechanisms. The differences between industrial societies do not consist mainly in a clear opposition between a market economy and planning, but in the relative importance of the roles played by each.

4 The relative importance of the state and of individuals in the economic system.

I do not like the contrast between privately controlled and state controlled economies because it is ambiguous. Does it refer to the ownership of the instruments of production, individual or collective, or to the method of regulating the economy?

It is necessary to distinguish in the conception of the role of the state, as it is commonly used, a number of different elements. What are the most important of these different points of view from which an economic unit may be studied? I shall not attempt to outline a general theory of the types of economy, but shall try to show the problematical character of most of the distinctions which have been made so far.

In the fields of pre-history and early history, historians, anthropologists and archaeologists usually adopt what I have called the technological point of view. In fact, for primitive man it was the quality and quantity of tools which determined, if not the total way of life, the limits within which human life could vary. The complex societies studied by Spengler and Toynbee in their histories of civilization or culture have included as a minimum animal husbandry and agriculture. A strictly technological point of view is inadequate, because different forms of ownership of the means of production and class relations grow out of the same technology. In the history of the development of societies it is impossible to relate every change to a change in technology. The use of the technological criterion only allows us to make very broad and vague assertions. Suppose, for example, that in the USA 7 per cent of the working population are employed in agriculture, 45 per cent in industry and the rest in the tertiary sector. This distribution requires a productive force, to use a Marxist expression, which did not exist before the modern period. The energy available in societies determines the limits within which they can vary but not their detailed organisation. Modern societies seem to belong to a completely new type, precisely because of their energy potential. A commonly used notion is that of the mechanical slave, that is the approximate energy represented by a man working normally for eight hours a day for 300 days. In 1938 French society had at its disposal 15 mechanical slaves per worker, Great Britain had 36, the USA 55. If these figures are multiplied by 10, one can imagine a type of society which is unique by comparison with all past societies.

Societies have been classified by reference to one or other of the viewpoints I have listed. One of the best known classifications is that of Karl Bücher, a German economist who considered that economic history could be reduced to a series of three stages: closed domestic economy, urban economy and national economy. A classification of this kind is based on the sphere of exchange and asserts that an economy can be characterized according to the extent of the area within which products circulate. A number of historical examples of this can be found, but there is not a strict succession of these three types. Moreover, these types may be applied both to sectors within society and to whole societies.

There are other classifications in terms of the methods of economic calculation and of exchange: natural economy, monetary economy and credit economy. One of the most famous classifications is that of Marx, set out in the preface to his *Contribution to the Critique of Political Economy*. Marx suggests that several modes of production can be distinguished: the Asiatic, the ancient mode founded on slavery, the feudal mode based upon serfdom, and finally the capitalist mode of production based upon wage labor. The central point of Marx's classification is a historical analysis of the relations of men within the productive process. Many, but not all, the characteristics of the ancient, medieval and modern economies may be illuminated by these concepts of slavery, serfdom and wage labor.

My aim in setting out these criteria is chiefly to show that in order to understand an economic unit one must examine it from several points of view. In the present state of knowledge it cannot be claimed that any one criterion predominates or by itself determines the type of economy. A wage economy, in which there is a distinction between employers and employees, may be a feature of present-day India as much as of the USA, but to say that in both cases the economy is based upon wage labor is of limited interest; for the two countries are so different that it is not so much the fact that both have wage labor as the difference in the form of wages that claims our attention. With any particular criterion one must try to determine the degree of variations.

Suppose that, in accordance with the Marxist method, we were to say: modern capitalist economies are based upon wage labor. The worker is therefore separated from the instruments of production which belong to an entrepreneur or capitalist. The worker possesses nothing but his labor power. The scientific problem is as follows: what are the features to be found in any economy where there is this separation between the entrepreneur and the employees and what are the limits of variation in such economies?

To repeat what was said earlier about all industrial economies: the enterprise is separated from the family and this results in a new type of production, a technical division of labor, an accumulation of capital and a progressive economy; the economic calculus becomes inevitable and a concentration of workers takes place. Now that we have reviewed all the various possible criteria, we can pose this question. These five features are to be found in a Soviet economy as well as in a capitalist one. What are the differences between these varieties of industrial society? Essentially, the difference concerns two points:

1 The ownership of the instruments of production: in a capitalist economy they belong to private individuals and not to the state.
2 The methods of regulation. In one system the distribution of resources is determined centrally by the planning authority, and in the other it is determined by the decisions of individuals in the market; or in other words, the balance between supply and demand is achieved in one case by planning and in the other by guesswork in the market.

If we look for the consequences of these fundamental differences we shall find other minor points of contrast. To what extent do the relations between workers and directors differ in a system of private property and in a system of public ownership? How far do the motives of economic activity vary according to the regulating method adopted? Or again, does the profit motive play the same role in both systems, and if not, precisely what is the difference?

By combining the various criteria I enumerated above, the capitalist régime may be characterised as follows:

1. The means of production are privately owned.
2. The regulation of the economy is decentralized, that is, the balance between production and consumption is not established once for all by planned decision, but piecemeal and pragmatically in the market.

3 Employers and employees are separate from each other, so that the latter possess only their labor power while the former own the instruments of production. This is the origin of the wage-earning class.
4 The profit motive predominates.
5 Since the distribution of resources is not determined by planning, supply and demand cause prices to fluctuate in each part of the market and even in the economy as a whole. This is called polemically capitalist anarchy. These oscillations of prices result inevitably from excessive or inadequate total demand in relation to total supply and from time to time they produce crises which may or may not show regularities. But in fact, no capitalist society is completely capitalist. In present-day France, for example, a considerable part of industry is publicly owned. Equally, it is not true that in a capitalist system all economic subjects are animated only by the desire for profit. We are only trying to pick out the most basic features of a purely capitalist régime.

Why does capitalism seem to some people to be evil incarnate? So far I have made no value judgement, but I shall now compare this régime with other possible methods of regulation, and systems of ownership and production. What are the fundamental criticisms to be made of a capitalist economy? Intellectual fashion plays some part in this matter. A hundred years ago the anti-capitalist created a scandal; today it would more probably be those who do not call themselves anti-capitalist who would seem scandalous in certain intellectual milieus. I am neither the one nor the other, but in order to take a closer look at the capitalist régime, I should like to examine the principal charges against it.

The chief complaints seem to be that it involves the exploitation of the worker, that it is immoral in so far as it is based on the desire for profit; that it results in extreme inequality of incomes; and that it is anarchic, that is, that it is not planned, that it does not allocate resources and incomes in a calculated way, and so entails a permanent danger of crises. A final argument which I shall examine later is that capitalism is self-destructive.

I shall now consider briefly the first of these arguments. Without going into detail, I shall refer to Marx's classic argument in *Capital* – the theory of surplus value, from which the general idea of exploitation is derived. Not all the present-day theorists of exploitation have read *Capital* but ... once an idea has become popular, there is no need to refer to the original text. If it is claimed that exploitation exists wherever there is inequality of distribution, then it goes without saying that the organisation of large capitalist firms implies exploitation, since the inequality of incomes is obvious there. It might even be said, without undue pessimism, that incomes tend to be higher the more pleasant the job. The least skilled work, which seems most unpleasant, is also the worst paid. But it should be added that this feature is not confined to the capitalist societies; it is found in all known systems, the Soviet societies included.

Leaving aside the simple fact of inequality, the idea of exploitation rests upon the theory of surplus value, which reduced to essentials is as follows: the worker produces by his labor a certain value, and receives less than the value he has produced. The argument may be complicated by introducing the labor theory of value and the Marxist theory of wages, but I shall omit these, as they would take us too far afield – the crux of the matter is that the worker receives less in wages than he has produced by his labor, and the remainder goes to the capitalist as profit.

We must recognize that there is some truth in this argument. The worker receives in wages, and the mass of workers receives as a whole, a smaller value than it has produced. But it could not be otherwise in the type of modern economy which we have defined as progressive, where it is assumed that the society does not consume the total value it has produced in a year. In a totally planned economy there would also be surplus value; that is to say, a part of the value produced by the workers which would not be returned to them in the form of wages, but which would go to the society as a whole. In the Soviet economy the surplus value created by the worker over and above his wages goes to the whole society, which shares it out in accordance with the decision of the planning authority. In a capitalist economy where there is private ownership of the instruments of production, this surplus value passes through the intermediary individual incomes of the entrepreneurs. Thus, I am considering a capitalist economy in the pure state and assuming that the funds necessary for investment come from private saving, from the surplus of the individual incomes not consumed by their owners. In both cases there are invested surpluses. In a planned Soviet system the reinvestment of this surplus value and the sectors to which it should go are decided by the planning authority; in a capitalist system the surplus has to be reinvested partly at least as a result of the actions of individuals.

What are the possible disadvantages of a system in which surplus value is allocated through individual incomes? The surplus value meant for investment, in order to extend the apparatus of production, may be consumed by the owners of these incomes. If capitalists receive large profits and use them to buy luxuries, the capitalist system becomes detestable. But if most of the income going to capitalists is reinvested, it does not matter that the incomes are received by individuals and only later return to the various sectors of production. The first problem, therefore, is to discover the proportion of the surplus value which is consumed by the privileged class. The second is to determine the relative efficiency of the system of private production and the collective system. The third problem is to decide whether the planned distribution of investment is better or worse than the distribution of investment by the capital market.

In a modern capitalist economy such as the USA, how much of the surplus value goes to the capitalists? In 1955, for all private corporations in the USA, the total of profit was 48.6 billions of dollars out of which taxes took 21.6. From the remaining 27.0 only 10.5 were distributed as dividends, the rest remaining in the corporations as source of self-financing. In the year 1965, the total of profits was 73.1, of tax liability 29.5, of distributed dividends 18.0. The profit after taxes per dollar of sales was 4.2 cent in 1958, between 5 and 6 per cent in 1965 for private manufacturing corporations. Thus, in a developed capitalist society the proportion of profits distributed to shareholders is low compared with the total volume of wages, taxes and direct investment in the firm. Why is this percentage so low? Two factors limit the possibility of dividend distribution. First, competition. In a competitive economy capital must be reinvested in new equipment to avoid being outstripped in the battle between producers. The other factor is trade union pressure. Pessimists such as myself always tend to believe that the amount of exploitation is directly proportionate to men's ability to exploit their fellows. The more a social class is in a position to exploit other classes, the more it will do so. In the case of an underdeveloped capitalist society where there are only a few capitalists, inspired by the desire for luxurious living rather than by the capitalist spirit, the wage system is sometimes a detestable form of exploitation, both for those exploited and for society as a whole. Wages are below the level compatible with the collective resources, and large incomes are consumed, not reinvested. But in other societies governed by the wage system, there may be quite a different distribution of individual incomes and the surplus value created by the worker may return to society as a whole.

Nevertheless, the capitalist system, in the eyes of many critics, will always involve the disadvantage that surplus value is received as individual incomes. But in determining income levels the quality and efficiency of production and organisation count for infinitely more than the amount of profit. Look again at the figures I quoted for the USA, for non-financial, non-farm corporations. Not more than between 5 per cent and 6 per cent of the proceeds of sales go to the shareholders. The state normally takes more than twice as much as the amount distributed in profits and in periods of prosperity undistributed profits are higher than the total of dividends.

For moral reasons, dividends may be criticized because they make possible enormous individual incomes. But they do not determine directly the level of wages. One or two years of growth do not give to the wage-earner more than the theoretical and practically impossible redistribution of the profits of the corporations.

Part II

Laissez-Faire in Decline: from the Great Depression into the Post-war Era

5
The End of Laissez-faire (1926)*

John Maynard Keynes

I

The disposition towards public affairs, which we conveniently sum up as individualism and *laissez-faire*, drew its sustenance from many different rivulets of thought and springs of feeling. For more than a hundred years our philosophers ruled us because, by a miracle, they nearly all agreed or seemed to agree on this one thing. We do not dance even yet to a new tune. But a change is in the air. We hear but indistinctly what were once the clearest and most distinguishable voices which have ever instructed political mankind. The orchestra of diverse instruments, the chorus of articulate sound, is receding at last into the distance.

At the end of the seventeenth century the divine right of monarchs gave place to natural liberty and to the compact, and the divine right of the church to the principle of toleration, and to the view that a church is "a voluntary society of men," coming together, in a way which is "absolutely free and spontaneous."[1] Fifty years later the divine origin and absolute voice of duty gave place to the calculations of utility. In the hands of Locke and Hume these doctrines founded Individualism. The compact presumed rights in the individual; the new ethics, being no more than a scientific study of the consequences of rational self-love, placed the individual at the centre. "The sole trouble Virtue demands," said Hume, is that of just Calculation, and a

---

* From *Essays in Persuasion* (New York: London: Macmillan and W. W. Norton, 1963), pp. 358–73. This essay, which was published as a pamphlet by the Hogarth Press in July 1926, was based on the Sidney Ball Lecture given by Keynes at Oxford in November 1924 and a lecture given by him at the University of Berlin in June 1926. Chapters IV and V were used in *Essays in Persuasion*.

steady preference of the greater Happiness."[2] These ideas accorded with the practical notions of conservatives and of lawyers. They furnished a satisfactory intellectual foundation to the rights of property and to the liberty of the individual in possession to do what he liked with himself and with his own. This was one of the contributions of the eighteenth century to the air we still breathe.

The purpose of promoting the individual was to depose the monarch and the church; the effect – through the new ethical significance attributed to contract – was to buttress property and prescription. But it was not long before the claims of society raised themselves anew against the individual. Paley and Bentham accepted utilitarian hedonism[3] from the hands of Hume and his predecessors, but enlarged it into social utility. Rousseau took the Social Contract from Locke and drew out of it the General Will. In each case the transition was made by virtue of the new emphasis laid on equality. "Locke applies his Social Contract to modify the natural equality of mankind, so far as that phrase implies equality of property or even of privilege, in consideration of general security. In Rousseau's version equality is not only the starting-point but the goal."[4]

Paley and Bentham reached the same destination, but by different routes. Paley avoided an egoistic conclusion to his hedonism by a God from the machine. "Virtue," he says, "is the doing good to mankind, in obedience to the will of God, and for the sake of everlasting happiness" – in this way bringing back *I* and *others* to a parity. Bentham reached the same result by pure reason. There is no rational ground, he argued, for preferring the happiness of one individual, even oneself, to that of any other. Hence the greatest happiness of the greatest number is the sole rational object of conduct-taking utility from Hume, but forgetting that sage man's cynical corollary:

> 'Tis not contrary to reason to prefer the destruction of the whole world to the scratching of my finger. 'Tis not contrary to reason for me to choose my total ruin to prevent the least uneasiness of an Indian, or person totally unknown to me ... Reason is and ought only to be the slave of the passions, and can never pretend to any other office than to serve and obey them.

Rousseau derived equality from the state of nature, Paley from the will of God, Bentham from a mathematical law of indifference. Equality and altruism had thus entered political philosophy, and from Rousseau and Bentham in conjunction sprang both democracy and utilitarian socialism. This is the second current – sprang from long-dead controversies, and carried on its way by long-exploded sophistries – which still permeates our atmosphere of thought. But it did not drive out the former current. It mixed with it. The early nineteenth century performed the miraculous union. It harmonized the conservative individualism of Locke, Hume, Johnson, and Burke with the socialism and democratic egalitarianism of Rousseau, Paley, Bentham, and Godwin.[5]

Nevertheless, that age would have been hard put to it to achieve this harmony of opposites if it had not been for the *economists*, who sprang into prominence just at the right moment. The idea of a divine harmony between private advantage and the public good is already apparent in Paley. But it was the economists who gave the notion a good scientific basis. Suppose that by the working of natural laws individuals pursuing their own interests with enlightenment in conditions of freedom always tend to promote the general interest at the same time! Our philosophical difficulties are resolved – at least for the practical man, who can then concentrate his efforts on securing the necessary conditions of freedom. To the philosophical doctrine that government has no right to interfere, and the divine that it has no need to interfere, there is added a scientific proof that its interference is inexpedient. This is the third current of thought, just discoverable in Adam Smith, who was ready in the main to allow the public good to rest on "the natural effort of every individual to better his own condition," but not fully and self-consciously developed until the nineteenth century begins. The principle of *laissez-faire* had arrived to harmonize individualism and socialism, and to make at one Hume's egoism with the greatest good of the greatest number. The political philosopher could retire in favor of the business man – for the latter could attain the philosopher's *summum bonum* by just pursuing his own private profit.

Yet some other ingredients were needed to complete the pudding. First the corruption and incompetence of eighteenth century government, many legacies of which survived into the nineteenth. The individualism of the political philosophers pointed to *laissez-faire*. The divine or scientific harmony (as the case might be) between private interest and public advantage pointed to *laissez-faire*. But above all, the ineptitude of public administrators strongly prejudiced the practical man in favour of *laissez-faire* – a sentiment which has by no means disappeared. Almost everything which the State did in the eighteenth century in excess of its minimum functions was, or seemed, injurious or unsuccessful.

On the other hand, material progress between 1750 and 1850 came from individual initiative, and owed almost nothing to the directive influence of organised society as a whole. Thus practical experience reinforced *a priori* reasonings. The philosophers and the economists told us that for sundry deep reasons unfettered private enterprise would promote the greatest good of the whole. What could suit the business man better? And could a practical observer, looking about him, deny that the blessings of improvement which distinguished the age he lived in were traceable to the activities of individuals "on the make"? Thus the ground was fertile for a doctrine that, whether on divine, natural, or scientific grounds, state action should be narrowly confined and economic life left, unregulated so far as may be, to the skill and good sense of individual citizens actuated by the admirable motive of trying to get on in the world.

By the time that the influence of Paley and his like was waning, the innovations of Darwin were shaking the foundations of belief. Nothing could seem more opposed than the old doctrine and the new – the doctrine which looked on the world as the work of the divine watch-maker and the doctrine which seemed to draw all things out of Chance, Chaos, and Old Time. But at this one point the new ideas bolstered up the old. The economists were teaching that wealth, commerce, and machinery were the children of free competition – that free competition built London. But the Darwinians could go one better than that – free competition had built man. The human eye was no longer the demonstration of design, miraculously contriving all things for the best; it was the supreme achievement of chance, operating under conditions of free competition and *laissez-faire*. The principle of the survival of the fittest could be regarded as a vast generalization of the Ricardian economics. Socialistic interferences became, in the light of this grander synthesis, not merely inexpedient, but impious, as calculated to retard the onward movement of the mighty process by which we ourselves had risen like Aphrodite out of the primeval slime of ocean.

Therefore I trace the peculiar unity of the everyday political philosophy of the nineteenth century to the success with which it harmonised diversified and warring schools and united all good things to a single end. Hume and Paley, Burke and Rousseau, Godwin and Malthus, Cobbett and Huskisson, Bentham and Coleridge, Darwin and the Bishop of Oxford, were all, it was discovered, preaching practically the same thing – individualism and *laissez-faire*. This was the Church of England and those her apostles, whilst the company of the economists were there to prove that the least deviation into impiety involved financial ruin.

These reasons and this atmosphere are the explanations, whether we know it or not – and most of us in these degenerate days are largely ignorant in the matter – why we feel such a strong bias in favour of *laissez-faire*, and why state action to regulate the value of money, or the course of investment, or the population, provokes such passionate suspicions in many upright breasts. We have not read these authors; we should consider their arguments preposterous if they were to fall into our hands. Nevertheless we should not, I fancy, think as we do, if Hobbes, Locke, Hume, Rousseau, Paley, Adam Smith, Bentham, and Miss Martineau had not thought and written as they did. A study of the history of opinion is a necessary preliminary to the emancipation of the mind. I do not know which makes a man more conservative – to know nothing but the present, or nothing but the past.

II

I have said that it was the economists who furnished the scientific pretext by which the practical man could solve the contradiction between egoism and socialism which emerged out of the philosophizing of the eighteenth century and the decay of revealed religion. But having said this for shortness' sake, I hasten to qualify it. This is what the economists are *supposed* to have said. No such doctrine is really to be found in the writings of the greatest authorities. It is what the popularizers and the vulgarizers said. It is what the Utilitarians, who admitted Hume's egoism and Bentham's egalitarianism at the same time, were *driven* to believe in, if they were to effect a synthesis.[6] The language of the economists lent itself to the *laissez-faire* interpretation. But the popularity of the doctrine must be laid at the door of the political philosophers of the day, whom it happened to suit, rather than of the political economists.

The maxim *laissez-nous faire* is traditionally attributed to the merchant Legendre addressing Colbert some time towards the end of the seventeenth century.[7] But there is no doubt that the first writer to use the phrase, and to use it in clear association with the doctrine, is the Marquis d'Argenson about 1751.[8] The Marquis was the first man to wax passionate on the economic advantages of governments leaving trade alone. To govern better, he said, one must govern less.[9] The true cause of the decline of our manufactures, he declared, is the protection we have given to them.[10] "Laissez-faire, telle devrait être la devise de

toute puissance publique, depuis que le monde est civilisé."
"Detestable principe que celui de ne vouloir grandeur que par l'abaisse-
ment de nos voisins! Il n'y a que la méchanceté et la malignité du
coeur de satisfaites dans ce principe, et l'intérêt y est opposé. Laissez-
faire, morbleu! Laissez faire!!"*

Here we have the economic doctrine of *laissez-faire*, with its most
fervent expression in free trade, fully clothed. The phrases and the idea
must have passed current in Paris from that time on. But they were
slow to establish themselves in literature; and the tradition associating
with them the physiocrats, and particularly de Gournay and Quesnay,
finds little support in the writings of this school, though they were, of
course, proponents of the essential harmony of social and individual
interests. The phrase *laissez-faire* is not to be found in the works of
Adam Smith, of Ricardo, or of Malthus. Even the idea is not present in
a dogmatic form in any of these authors. Adam Smith, of course, was a
Free Trader and an opponent of many eighteenth-century restrictions
on trade. But his attitude towards the Navigation Acts and the usury
laws shows that he was not dogmatic. Even his famous passage about
"the invisible hand" reflects the philosophy which we associate with
Paley rather than the economic dogma of *laissez-faire*. As Sidgwick and
Cliff Leslie have pointed out, Adam Smith's advocacy of the "obvious
and simple system of natural liberty" is derived from his theistic and
optimistic view of the order of the world, as set forth in his *Theory of
Moral Sentiments*, rather than from any proposition of political
economy proper.[11] The phrase *laissez-faire* was, I think, first brought
into popular usage in England by a well-known passage of Dr
Franklin's.[12] It is not, indeed, until we come to the later works
of Bentham – who was not an economist at all – that we discover the
rule of *laissez-faire*, in the shape in which our grandfathers knew it,
adopted into the service of the Utilitarian philosophy. For example, in
A Manual of Political Economy,[13] he writes:

> The general rule is that nothing ought to be done or attempted by
> government; the motto or watchword of government, on these
> occasions, ought to be – Be quiet ... The request which agriculture,

---

* Editor's translation: "Laissez-faire, that ought to be the motto of the whole
public power, since the world was civilized." "Detestable principle such that
greatness is not to be achieved without the lowering of our neighbors! Only
meanness and malice of heart are satisfied by this principle, and the interest
there is opposed. Laissez-faire, morbleu! Laissez-faire!"

manufacturers, and commerce present to governments is as modest and reasonable as that which Diogenes made to Alexander: Stand out of my sunshine.

From this time on it was the political campaign for free trade, the influence of the so-called Manchester School and of the Benthamite Utilitarians, the utterances of secondary economic authorities, and the education stories of Miss Martineau and Mrs Marcet, that fixed *laissez-faire* in the popular mind as the practical conclusion of orthodox political economy – with this great difference, that the Malthusian view of population having been accepted in the meantime by this same school of thought, the optimistic *laissez-faire* of the last half of the eighteenth century gives place to the pessimistic *laissez-faire* of the first half of the nineteenth century.[14]

In Mrs Marcet's *Conversations on Political Economy* (1817) Caroline stands out as long as she can in favour of controlling the expenditure of the rich. But by page 418 she has to admit defeat:

> CAROLINE.   The more I learn upon this subject, the more I feel convinced that the interests of nations, as well as those of individuals, so far from being opposed to each other, are in the most perfect unison.
> MRS B.   Liberal and enlarged views will always lead to similar conclusions, and teach us to cherish sentiments of universal benevolence towards each other; hence the superiority of science over mere practical knowledge.

By 1850 the *Easy Lessons for the Use of Young People*, by Archbishop Whately, which the Society for Promoting Christian Knowledge was distributing wholesale, do not admit even of those doubts which Mrs B. allowed Caroline occasionally to entertain. "More harm than good is likely to be done," the little book concludes, "by almost any interference of Government with men's money transactions, whether letting and leasing, or buying and selling of any kind." *True* liberty is "that every man should be left free to dispose of his own property, his own time, and strength, and skill, in whatever way he himself may think fit, provided he does no wrong to his neighbours."

In short, the dogma had got hold of the educational machine; it had become a copybook maxim. The political philosophy, which the seventeenth and eighteenth centuries had forged in order to throw down kings and prelates, had been made milk for babes, and had literally entered the nursery.

Finally, in the works of Bastiat we reach the most extravagant and rhapsodical expression of the political economist's religion. In his *Harmonies Économiques,*

> I undertake [he says] to demonstrate the Harmony of those laws of Providence which govern human society. What makes these laws harmonious and not discordant is, that all principles, all motives, all springs of action, all interests, co-operate towards a grand final result ... And that result is, the indefinite approximation of all classes towards a level, which is always rising; in other words, the equalisation of individuals in the general *amelioration.*

And when, like other priests, he drafts his Credo, it runs as follows:

> I believe that He who has arranged the material universe has not withheld His regard from the arrangements of the social world. I believe that He has combined and caused to move in harmony free agents as well as inert molecules ... I believe that the invincible social tendency is a constant approximation of men towards a common moral, intellectual, and physical level, with, at the same time, a progressive and indefinite elevation of that level. I believe that all that is necessary to the gradual and peaceful development of humanity is that its tendencies should not be disturbed, nor have the liberty of their movements destroyed.

From the time of John Stuart Mill, economists of authority have been in strong reaction against all such ideas. "Scarcely a single English economist of repute," as Professor Cannan has expressed it, "will join in a frontal attack upon Socialism in general," though, as he also adds, "nearly every economist, whether of repute or not, is always ready to pick holes in most socialistic proposals."[15] Economists no longer have any link with the theological or political philosophies out of which the dogma of social harmony was born, and their scientific analysis leads them to no such conclusions.

Cairnes, in the introductory lecture on "Political Economy and *Laissez-faire,*" which he delivered at University College, London, in 1870, was perhaps the first orthodox economist to deliver a frontal attack upon *laissez-faire* in general. "The maxim of *laissez-faire,*" he declared, "has no scientific basis whatever, but is at best a mere handy rule of practice."[16] This, for fifty years past, has been the view of all leading economists. Some of the most important work of Alfred

Marshall – to take one instance – was directed to the elucidation of the leading cases in which private interest and social interest are *not* harmonious. Nevertheless, the guarded and undogmatic attitude of the best economists has not prevailed against the general opinion that an individualistic *laissez-faire* is both what they ought to teach and what in fact they do teach.

III

Economists, like other scientists, have chosen the hypothesis from which they set out, and which they offer to beginners, because it is the simplest, and not because it is the nearest to the facts. Partly for this reason, but partly, I admit, because they have been biased by the traditions of the subject, they have begun by assuming a state of affairs where the ideal distribution of productive resources can be brought about through individuals acting independently by the method of trial and error in such a way that those individuals who move in the right direction will destroy by competition those who move in the wrong direction. This implies that there must be no mercy or protection for those who embark their capital or their labor in the wrong direction. It is a method of bringing the most successful profit-makers to the top by a ruthless struggle for survival, which selects the most efficient by the bankruptcy of the less efficient. It does not count the cost of the struggle, but looks only to the benefits of the final result which are assumed to be permanent. The object of life being to crop the leaves off the branches up to the greatest possible height, the likeliest way of achieving this end is to leave the giraffes with the longest necks to starve out those whose necks are shorter.

Corresponding to this method of attaining the ideal distribution of the instruments of production between different purposes, there is a similar assumption as to how to attain the ideal distribution of what is available for consumption. In the first place, each individual will discover what amongst the possible objects of consumption *he* wants most by the method of trial and error "at the margin," and in this way not only will each consumer come to distribute his consumption most advantageously, but each object of consumption will find its way into the mouth of the consumer whose relish for it is greatest compared with that of the others, because that consumer will outbid the rest. Thus, if only we leave the giraffes to themselves, (1) the maximum quantity of leaves will be cropped because the giraffes with the longest necks will, by dint of starving out the others, get nearest to the trees;

(2) each giraffe will make for the leaves which he finds most succulent amongst those in reach; and (3) the giraffes whose relish for a given leaf is greatest will crane most to reach it. In this way more and juicier leaves will be swallowed, and each individual leaf will reach the throat which thinks it deserves most effort.

This assumption, however, of conditions where unhindered natural selection leads to progress, is only one of the two provisional assumptions which, taken as literal truth, have become the twin buttresses of *laissez-faire*. The other one is the efficacy, and indeed the necessity, of the opportunity for unlimited private money-making as an incentive to maximum effort. Profit accrues, under *laissez-faire*, to the individual who, whether by skill or good fortune, is found with his productive resources in the right place at the right time. A system which allows the skilful or fortunate individual to reap the whole fruits of this conjuncture evidently offers an immense incentive to the practice of the art of being in the right place at the right time. Thus one of the most powerful of human motives, namely, the love of money, is harnessed to the task of distributing economic resources in the way best calculated to increase wealth.

The parallelism between economic *laissez-faire* and Darwinianism, already briefly noted, is now seen, as Herbert Spencer was foremost to recognise, to be very close indeed. Just as Darwin invoked sexual love, acting through sexual selection, as an adjutant to natural selection by competition, to direct evolution along lines which should be desirable as well as effective, so the individualist invokes the love of money, acting through the pursuit of profit, as an adjutant to natural selection, to bring about the production on the greatest possible scale of what is most strongly desired as measured by exchange value.

The beauty and the simplicity of such a theory are so great that it is easy to forget that it follows not from the actual facts, but from an incomplete hypothesis introduced for the sake of simplicity. Apart from other objections to be mentioned later, the conclusion that individuals acting independently for their own advantage will produce the greatest aggregate of wealth, depends on a variety of unreal assumptions to the effect that the processes of production and consumption are in no way organic, that there exists a sufficient foreknowledge of conditions and requirements, and that there are adequate opportunities of obtaining this foreknowledge. For economists generally reserve for a later stage of their argument the complications which arise – (1) when the efficient units of production are large relatively to the units of consumption, (2) when overhead costs or joint costs are

present, (3) when internal economics tend to the aggregation of production, (4) when the time required for adjustments is long, (5) when
ignorance prevails over knowledge, and (6) when monopolies and
combinations interfere with equality in bargaining – they reserve, that
is to say, for a later stage their analysis of the actual facts. Moreover,
many of those who recognise that the simplified hypothesis does not
accurately correspond to fact conclude nevertheless that it does represent what is "natural" and therefore ideal. They regard the simplified
hypothesis as health, and the further complications as disease.

Yet besides this question of fact there are other considerations, familiar enough, which rightly bring into the calculation the cost and character of the competitive struggle itself, and the tendency for wealth to
be distributed where it is not appreciated most. If we have the welfare
of the giraffes at heart, we must not overlook the sufferings of the
shorter necks who are starved out, or the sweet leaves which fall to the
ground and are trampled underfoot in the struggle, or the overfeeding
of the long-necked ones, or the evil look of anxiety or struggling greed-
iness which overcasts the mild faces of the herd.

But the principles of *laissez-faire* have had other allies besides economic textbooks. It must be admitted that they have been confirmed in
the minds of sound thinkers and the reasonable public by the poor
quality of the opponent proposals – protectionism on one hand, and
Marxian socialism on the other. Yet these doctrines are both characterised, not only or chiefly by their infringing the general presumption
in favour of *laissez-faire*, but by mere logical fallacy. Both are examples
of poor thinking, of inability to analyze a process and follow it out to
its conclusion. The arguments against them, though reinforced by the
principle of *laissez-faire*, do not strictly require it. Of the two, protectionism is at least plausible, and the forces making for its popularity are
nothing to wonder at. But Marxian socialism must always remain a
portent to the historians of opinion – how a doctrine so illogical and
so dull can have exercised so powerful and enduring an influence over
the minds of men and, through them, the events of history. At any
rate, the obvious scientific deficiencies of these two schools greatly
contributed to the prestige and authority of nineteenth-century *laissez-
faire*.

Nor has the most notable divergence into centralized social action
on a great scale – the conduct of the late war – encouraged reformers or
dispelled old-fashioned prejudices. There is much to be said, it is true,
on both sides. War experience in the organisation of socialized production has left some near observers optimistically anxious to repeat it in

peace conditions. War socialism unquestionably achieved a production of wealth on a scale far greater than we ever knew in peace, for though the goods and services delivered were destined for immediate and fruitless extinction, none the less they were wealth. Nevertheless, the dissipation of effort was also prodigious, and the atmosphere of waste and not counting the cost was disgusting to any thrifty or provident spirit.

Finally, individualism and *laissez-faire* could not, in spite of their deep roots in the political and moral philosophies of the late eighteenth and early nineteenth centuries, have secured their lasting hold over the conduct of public affairs, if it had not been for their conformity with the needs and wishes of the business world of the day. They gave full scope to our erstwhile heroes, the great business men. "At least one-half of the best ability in the Western world," Marshall used to say, "is engaged in business." A great part of "the higher imagination" of the age was thus employed. It was on the activities of these men that our hopes of progress were centered:

> Men of this class [Marshall wrote][17] live in constantly shifting visions, fashioned in their own brains, of various routes to their desired end; of the difficulties which Nature will oppose to them on each route, and of the contrivances by which they hope to get the better of her opposition. This imagination gains little credit with the people, because it is not allowed to run riot; its strength is disciplined by a stronger will; and its highest glory is to have attained great ends by means so simple that no one will know, and none but experts will even guess, how a dozen other expedients, each suggesting as much brilliancy to the hasty observer, were set aside in favour of it. The imagination of such a man is employed, like that of the master chess-player, in forecasting the obstacles which may be opposed to the successful issue of his far-reaching projects, and constantly rejecting brilliant suggestions because he has pictured to himself the counter-strokes to them. His strong nervous force is at the opposite extreme of human nature from that nervous irresponsibility which conceives hasty Utopian schemes, and which is rather to be compared to the bold facility a weak player, who will speedily solve the most difficult chess problem by taking on himself to move the black men as well as the white.

This is a fine picture of the great captain of industry, the master-individualist, who serves us in serving himself, just as any other artist does. Yet this one, in his turn, is becoming a tarnished idol. We grow more doubtful whether it is he who will lead us into paradise by the hand.

These many elements have contributed to the current intellectual bias, the mental make-up, the orthodoxy of the day. The compelling force of many of the original reasons has disappeared but, as usual, the vitality of the conclusions outlasts them. To suggest social action for the public good to the City of London is like discussing the Origin of Species with a bishop sixty years ago. The first reaction is not intellectual, but moral. An orthodoxy is in question, and the more persuasive the arguments the graver the offence. Nevertheless, venturing into the den of the lethargic monster, at any rate I have traced his claims and pedigree so as to show that he has ruled over us rather by hereditary right than by personal merit.

IV

Let us clear from the ground the metaphysical or general principles upon which, from time to time, *laissez-faire* has been founded. It is *not* true that individuals possess a prescriptive "natural liberty" in their economic activities. There is *no* "compact" conferring perpetual rights on those who Have or on those who Acquire. The world is *not* so governed from above that private and social interest always coincide. It is *not* so managed here below that in practice they coincide. It is *not* a correct deduction from the principles of economics that enlightened self-interest always operates in the public interest. Nor is it true that self-interest generally *is* enlightened; more often individuals acting separately to promote their own ends are too ignorant or too weak to attain even these. Experience does *not* show that individuals, when they make up a social unit, are always less clear-sighted than when they act separately.

We cannot therefore settle on abstract grounds, but must handle on its merits in detail what Burke termed "one of the finest problems in legislation, namely, to determine what the State ought to take upon itself to direct by the public wisdom, and what it ought to leave, with as little interference as possible, to individual exertion."[18] We have to discriminate between what Bentham, in his forgotten but useful nomenclature, used to term *Agenda* and *Non-Agenda*, and to do this without Bentham's prior presumption that interference is, at the same time, "generally needless" and "generally pernicious."[19] Perhaps the chief task of economists at this hour is to distinguish afresh the *Agenda* of government from the *Non-Agenda*; and the companion task of politics is to devise forms of government within a democracy which shall be capable of accomplishing the *Agenda*. I will illustrate what I have in mind by two examples.

(1) I believe that in many cases the ideal size for the unit of control and organisation lies somewhere between the individual and the modern State. I suggest, therefore, that progress lies in the growth and the recognition of semi-autonomous bodies within the State-bodies whose criterion of action within their own field is solely the public good as they understand it, and from whose deliberations motives of private advantage are excluded, though some place it may still be necessary to leave, until the ambit of men's altruism grows wider, to the separate advantage of particular groups, classes, or faculties – bodies which in the ordinary course of affairs are mainly autonomous within their prescribed limitations, but are subject in the last resort to the sovereignty of the democracy expressed through Parliament.

I propose a return, it may be said, towards medieval conceptions of separate autonomies. But, in England at any rate, corporations are a mode of government which has never ceased to be important and is sympathetic to our institutions. It is easy to give examples, from what already exists, of separate autonomies which have attained or are approaching the mode I designate – the universities, the Bank of England, the Port of London Authority, even perhaps the railway companies. In Germany there are doubtless analogous instances.

But more interesting than these is the trend of joint stock institutions, when they have reached a certain age and size, to approximate to the status of public corporations rather than that of individualistic private enterprise. One of the most interesting and unnoticed developments of recent decades has been the tendency of big enterprise to socialize itself. A point arrives in the growth of a big institution – particularly a big railway or big public utility enterprise, but also a big bank or a big insurance company – at which the owners of the capital, i.e. the shareholders, are almost entirely dissociated from the management, with the result that the direct personal interest of the latter in the making of great profit becomes quite secondary. When this stage is reached, the general stability and reputation of the institution are the more considered by the management than the maximum of profit for the shareholders. The shareholders must be satisfied by conventionally adequate dividends; but once this is secured, the direct interest of the management often consists in avoiding criticism from the public and from the customers of the concern. This is particularly the case if their great size or semi-monopolistic position renders them conspicuous in the public eye and vulnerable to public attack. The extreme instance, perhaps, of this tendency in the case of an institution, theoretically the unrestricted property of private persons, is the Bank of England. It is almost true to say that there is no class of persons in the kingdom of whom the Governor of the Bank of England thinks less when he decides on his policy than of his shareholders. Their rights, in excess of their conventional dividend, have already sunk to the neighborhood of zero. But the same thing is partly true of many other big institutions. They are, as time goes on, socializing themselves.

Not that this is unmixed gain. The same causes promote conservatism and a waning of enterprise. In fact, we already have in these cases many of the faults as well as the advantages of State Socialism. Nevertheless, we see here, I think, a natural line of evolution. The battle of Socialism against unlimited private profit is being won in detail hour by hour. In these particular fields – it remains acute elsewhere – this is no longer the pressing problem. There is, for instance, no so-called important political question so really unimportant, so irrelevant to the reorganization of the economic life of Great Britain, as the nationalization of the railways.

It is true that many big undertakings, particularly public utility enterprises and other business requiring a large fixed capital, still need to be semi-socialized. But we must keep our minds flexible regarding the forms of this semi-socialism. We must take full advantage of the natural tendencies of the day, and we must probably prefer semi-autonomous corporations to organs of the central government for which ministers of State are directly responsible.

I criticize doctrinaire State Socialism, not because it seeks to engage men's altruistic impulses in the service of society, or because it departs from *laissez-faire*, or because it takes away from man's natural liberty to make a million, or because it has courage for bold experiments. All these things I applaud. I criticize it because it misses the significance of what is actually happening; because it is, in fact, little better than a dusty survival of a plan to meet the problems of fifty years ago, based on a misunderstanding of what someone said a hundred years ago. Nineteenth-century State Socialism sprang from Bentham, free competition, etc., and is in some respects a clearer, in some respects a more muddled version of just the same philosophy as underlies nineteenth-century individualism. Both equally laid all their stress on freedom, the one negatively to avoid limitations on existing freedom, the other positively to destroy natural or acquired monopolies. They are different reactions to the same intellectual atmosphere.

(2) I come next to a criterion of *Agenda* which is particularly relevant to what it is urgent and desirable to do in the near future. We must aim at separating those services which are *technically social* from those which are *technically individual*. The most important *Agenda* of the State relate not to those activities which private individuals are already fulfilling, but to those functions which fall outside the sphere of the individual, to those decisions which are made by *no one* if the State does not make them. The important thing for government is not to do things which individuals are doing already, and to do them a little better or a little worse; but to do those things which at present are not done at all.

It is not within the scope of my purpose on this occasion to develop practical policies. I limit myself, therefore, to naming some instances of what I mean from amongst those problems about which I happen to have thought most.

Many of the greatest economic evils of our time are the fruits of risk, uncertainty, and ignorance. It is because particular individuals, fortunate in situation or in abilities, are able to take advantage of uncertainty and ignorance, and also because for the same reason big business is often a lottery, that great inequalities of wealth come about; and these same factors are also the cause of the unemployment of labor, or the disappointment of reasonable business expectations, and of the impairment of efficiency and production. Yet the cure lies outside the operations of individuals; it may even be to the interest of individuals to aggravate the disease. I believe that the cure for these things is partly to be sought in the deliberate control of the currency and of credit by a central institution, and partly in the collection and dissemination on a great scale of data relating to the business situation, including the full publicity, by law if necessary, of all business facts which it is useful to know. These measures would involve society in exercising directive intelligence through some appropriate organ of action over many of the inner intricacies of private business, yet it would leave private initiative and enterprise unhindered. Even if these measures prove insufficient, nevertheless, they will furnish us with better knowledge than we have now for taking the next step.

My second example relates to savings and investment. I believe that some coordinated act of intelligent judgement is required as to the scale on which it is desirable that the community as a whole should save, the scale on which these savings should go abroad in the form of foreign investments, and whether the present organisation of the investment market distributes savings along the most nationally productive channels. I do not think that these matters should be left entirely to the chances of private judgement and private profits, as they are at present.

My third example concerns population. The time has already come when each country needs a considered national policy about what size of population, whether larger or smaller than at present or the same, is most expedient. And having settled this policy, we must take steps to carry it into operation. The time may arrive a little later when the community as a whole must pay attention to the innate quality as well as to the mere numbers of its future members.

V

These reflections have been directed towards possible improvements in the technique of modern capitalism by the agency of collective action. There is nothing in them which is seriously incompatible with what seems to me to be the essential characteristic of capitalism, namely the dependence upon an intense appeal to the money-making and money-loving instincts of individuals as the main motive force of the economic machine. Nor must I, so near to my end, stray towards other fields. Nevertheless, I may do well to remind you, in conclusion, that the fiercest contests and the most deeply felt divisions of opinion are likely to be waged in the coming years not round technical questions, where the arguments on either side are mainly economic, but round those which, for want of better words, may be called psychological or, perhaps, moral.

In Europe, or at least in some parts of Europe – but not, I think, in the United States of America – there is a latent reaction, somewhat widespread, against basing society to the extent that we do upon fostering, encouraging, and protecting the money-motives of individuals. A preference for arranging our affairs in such a way as to appeal to the money-motive as little as possible, rather than as much as possible, need not be entirely *a priori*, but may be based on the comparison of experiences. Different persons, according to their choice of profession, find the money-motive playing a large or a small part in their daily lives, and historians can tell us about other phases of social organisation in which this motive has played a much smaller part than it does now. Most religions and most philosophies deprecate, to say the least of it, a way of life mainly influenced by considerations of personal money profit. On the other hand, most men today reject ascetic notions and do not doubt the real advantages of wealth. Moreover, it seems obvious to them that one cannot do without the money-motive, and that, apart from certain admitted abuses, it does its job well. In the result the average man averts his attention from the problem, and has no clear idea what he really thinks and feels about the whole confounded matter. Confusion of thought and feeling leads to confusion of speech. Many people, who are really objecting to capitalism as a way of life, argue as though they were objecting to it on the ground of its inefficiency in attaining its own objects. Contrariwise, devotees of capitalism are often unduly conservative, and reject reforms in its technique, which might really strengthen and preserve it, for fear that they may prove to be first steps away from capitalism itself. Nevertheless, a time may be coming when we shall get clearer than at present as to when we are talking about capitalism as an efficient or inefficient technique, and when we are talking about it as desirable or objectionable in itself. For my part I think that capitalism, wisely managed, can probably be made more efficient for attaining economic ends than any alternative system yet in sight, but that in itself it is in many ways extremely objectionable. Our problem is to work out a social organisation which shall be as efficient as possible without offending our notions of a satisfactory way-of-life.

The next step forward must come, not from political agitation or premature experiments, but from thought. We need by an effort of the mind to elucidate our own feelings. At present our sympathy and our judgement are liable to be on different sides, which is a painful and paralysing state of mind. In the field of action reformers will not be successful until they can steadily pursue a clear and definite object with their intellects and their feelings in tune. There is no party in the world at present which appears to me to be pursuing right aims by right methods. Material poverty provides the incentive to change precisely in situations where there is very little margin for experiments. Material prosperity removes the incentive just when it might be safe to take a chance. Europe lacks the means, America the will, to make a move. We need a new set of convictions which spring naturally from a candid examination of our own inner feelings in relation to the outside facts.

Notes

1. Locke, *A Letter Concerning Toleration.*
2. *An Enquiry Concerning the Principles of Morals*, section LX.
3. "I omit," says Archdeacon Paley, "much usual declamation upon the dignity and capacity of our nature, the superiority of the soul to the body,

of the rational to the animal part of our constitution; upon the worthiness, refinement, and delicacy of some satisfactions, and the meanness, gross-ness, and sensuality of others: because I hold that pleasures differ in nothing but in continuance and intensity" (*Principles of Moral and Political Philosophy*, Bk I, Chap. 6).

4. Leslie Stephen, *English Thought in the Eighteenth Century*, II, p. 192.
5. Godwin carried *laissez-faire* so far that he thought *all* government an evil, in which Bentham almost agreed with him. The doctrine of equality becomes with him one of extreme individualism, verging on anarchy. "The universal exercise of private judgement," he says, "is a doctrine so unspeakably beau-tiful that the true politician will certainly feel infinite reluctance in admit-ting the idea of interfering with it" (see Leslie Stephen, *op. cit.*, II, p. 277).
6. One can sympathize with the view of Coleridge, as summarized by Leslie Stephen, that "the Utilitarians destroyed every element of cohesion, made Society a struggle of selfish interests, and struck at the very roots of all order, patriotism, poetry, and religion."
7. "Que faut-il faire pour vous aider?" asked Colbert. "Nous laisser faire," answered Legendre.
8. For the history of the phrase, see Oncken, 'Die Maxime Laissez faire et laissez passer," from whom most of the following quotations are taken. The claims of the Marquis d'Argenson were overlooked until Oncken put them forward, partly because the relevant passages published during his lifetime were anonymous (*Journal Economique*, 1751), and partly because his works were not published in full (though probably passed privately from hand to hand during his lifetime) until 1858 (*Mémoires et Journal inédit du Marquis d'Argenson*).
9. "Pour gouverner mieux, il faudrait gouverner moins."
10. "On ne peut dire autant de nos fabriques: la vraie cause de leur declin, c'est la protection outrée qu'on leur accorde."
11. Sidgwick, *Principles of Political Economy*, p. 20.
12. Bentham uses the expression "*laissez-nous faire*" (*Works*, p. 440).
13. Written in 1793, a chapter published in the *Bibliothèque Britannique* in 1798, and the whole first printed in Bowring's edition of his *Works* (1843).
14. Cf. Sidgwick, *op. cit.*, p. 22:

Even those economists, who adhered in the main to Adam Smith's limi-tations of the sphere of government, enforced these limitations sadly rather than triumphantly; not as admirers of the social order at present resulting from "natural liberty," but as convinced that it is at least prefer-able to any artificial order that government might be able to substitute for it.

15. *Theories of Production and Distribution*, p. 494.
16. Cairnes well described the "prevailing notion" in the following passage from the same lecture:

The prevailing notion is that P. E. [Political Economy] undertakes to show that wealth may be most rapidly accumulated and most fairly dis-tributed; that is to say, that human well-being may be most effectually promoted, by the simple process of leaving people to themselves; leaving individuals, that is to say, to follow the promptings of self-interest, unrestrained either by State or by the public opinion, so long as they abstain from force and fraud. This is the doctrine commonly known as *laissez-faire*; and accordingly political economy is, I think, very generally regarded as a sort of scientific rendering of this maxim – a vindication of freedom of individual enterprise and of contract as the one and sufficient solution of all industrial problems.

17. "The Social Possibilities of Economic Chivalry," *Economic Journal*, XVII (1907), p. 9.
18. Quoted by McCulloch in his *Principles of Political Economy*.
19. Bentham's *Manual of Political Economy*, published posthumously, in Bowring's edition (1843).

6

An Explanation of the 1929 Depression (1973)*

Charles P. Kindleberger

What produced the world depression of 1929, why was it so wide-spread, so deep, so long? Was it caused by real or monetary factors? Did it originate in the United States, in Europe, in the primary-producing countries of the periphery, in the relations among them? Was the fatal weakness the nature of the international capitalist system, or the way it was operated, i.e. the policies pursued by governments? Were such policies, to the extent they were important, the consequence of ignorance, short-sightedness or ill-will? Were the depth and length of the depression a reflection of the strength of the shock to a relatively stable system, or a measure of the system's instability in the presence of a blow or series of blows of normal force (however measured)? Or ... was the 1929 depression the consequence of United States monetary policy or a series of historical accidents? Inevitably in drawing the threads together there will be a considerable amount of confirmation of preconceptions. We are open to the accusation of having selected statistics, facts and incidents from the history of the decade which support a position chosen *a priori*. But we would claim that we have not knowingly suppressed any facts that do not fit the explanation which follows, nor ignored other explanations such as United States monetary policy (Friedman); misuse of the gold standard (Robbins); mistaken deflation (Keynes); secular stagnation (Hansen); structural disequilibrium (Svennilson); and the like. The chapter is entitled "An Explanation" not "The Explanation."

The explanation of this book is that the 1929 depression was so wide, so deep and so long because the international economic system

---

* From *The World in Depression 1929–1939* (Berkeley: University of California Press, 1973), pp. 291–307.

was rendered unstable by British inability and United States unwilling-ness to assume responsibility for stabilizing it in three particulars: (a) maintaining a relatively open market for distress goods; (b) providing counter-cyclical long-term lending; and (c) discounting in crisis. The shocks to the system from the overproduction of certain primary prod-ucts such as wheat; from the 1927 reduction of interest rates in the United States (if it was one); from the halt of lending to Germany in 1928; or from the stock-market crash of 1929 were not so great. Shocks of similar magnitude had been handled in the stock-market break in the spring of 1920 and the 1927 recession in the United States. The world economic system was unstable unless some country stabilized it, as Britain had done in the nineteenth century and up to 1913. In 1929, the British couldn't and the United States wouldn't. When every country turned to protect its national private interest, the world public interest went down the drain, and with it the private interests of all.

Aymmetry

If the world economy behaved symmetrically, there could be no world depression. A decline in the price of wheat might produce losses for farmers; it would, however, lead to gains in real purchasing power for consumers (shifts in real income from groups with different marginal rates of saving are ignored). Gold losses for one country would be deflationary, but gains for the recipient country would yield offsetting expansion. Contractive exchange appreciation would be matched by stimulating depreciation. The stock market could not absorb funds, since for every buyer that gives up money, there is a seller that gains it.

But symmetry is not the way of the world in all times and places, and not for the reason of interference by men with, say, the rules of the gold-standard game, or that New York as an international financial center was inexperienced. It happened that in Britain, from 1873 to 1913, foreign lending and domestic investment were maintained in continuous counterpoint. Domestic recession stimulated foreign lending; boom at home cut it down. But the boom at home expanded imports which provided an export stimulus abroad in place of domes-tic investment with borrowed funds. Counter-cyclical lending stabil-ized the system.

In the 1920s, United States foreign lending was positively correlated with domestic investment, not counterpoised. The boom of the 1920s was accompanied by foreign lending; the depression of the 1930s saw the capital flow reversed. In his *The United States and the World*

Economy, written in 1943, Hal Lary recorded the fundamental fact that the United States cut down on imports and lending at the same time. The cut in lending actually preceded the stock-market crash as investors were diverted from the boom in foreign bonds which followed the Dawes loan to the boom in domestic stocks dating from the spring of 1928. The deflationary pressure on Germany may be debated;[1] the pressure on the less developed countries at the periphery is clear cut.[2] Moreover, Britain joined the United States in reducing its lending in 1929 over 1928.[3]

Maintaining a market for distress goods can be regarded as another form of financing. Free trade has two dimensions: (a) to adapt domestic resources to changes in productive capacities abroad, and (b) to maintain the import market open in periods of stress. The first is more readily done by a rapidly growing country which needs to transfer resources out of less productive occupations and is willing to embrace the competition of imports. By holding firm to free trade during depression at some short-run cost to resources in import-competing lines, the second provides a market for surpluses accumulated abroad. Britain clung to free trade from 1846 (or some years thereafter, such as 1860, when all tariffs but those for revenue had been dismantled) until 1916. After 1873, she was not growing rapidly, but continued to adhere to free trade since her declining industries were exporters rather than import-competers. Her tenacity in adhering to free trade in depression may have been born of cultural lag and the free-trade tradition of Adam Smith, rather than of conscious service to the world economy.

The contrast is with the Smoot–Hawley Tariff Act of 1930. At the first hint of trouble in agriculture, Hoover reached for the Republican household remedy, as Schumpeter characterized it, in the face of a recommendation of the World Economic Conference of 1927 that nations of the world should adopt a tariff truce. The action was important less for its impact on the United States balance of payments, or as conduct unbecoming a creditor nation, than for its irresponsibility. The congressional rabble enlarged protection from agriculture to primary products and manufactures of all kinds, and Hoover, despite more than thirty formal protests from other countries and the advice of 1,000 economists, signed the Bill into law. This gave rise to (or at least did nothing to stop) a headlong stampede to protection and restrictions on imports, each country trying to ward off deflationary pressure of imports, and all together ensuring such pressure through mutual restriction of exports. As with exchange depreciation to raise domestic prices, the gain from one country was a loss for all. With tariff retaliation and competitive depreciation, mutual losses were certain. The formula of tariff truce and exchange stabilization proposed for the World Economic Conference of 1933 offered no positive means of raising prices or expanding employment. It would none the less have been significant as a means of slowing further decline. With no major country providing a market for distress goods, or willing to tolerate appreciation, much less furnish long-term capital or discounting facilities to countries suffering from payments difficulties, the fallacy of composition with the whole less than the sum of its parts ensured that deflation would roll on.

Initial conditions

The lack of leadership in providing discount facilities, anti-cyclical lending or in [an] open market for goods rendered the system unstable. So did the heritage of war, and especially the combination of reparations, war debts, overvaluation of the pound and undervaluation of the French franc. One should perhaps add the German inflation of 1923, which made that country paranoid in its subsequent attachment to deflation. The structural dislocations of war in excess production of wheat, sugar and wool, plus ships, cotton textiles and coal, were of less consequence and could have been cared for fairly readily by the price system if macroeconomic stability could have been preserved. The financial distortions made such stability difficult if not impossible to sustain. A far-seeing leadership on the part of the United States might have been willing to waive war debts, but it would have been difficult to persuade the American voter of the merit of the course, especially when Britain and France were receiving reparations. Britain was willing to forego reparations, to the extent that war debts were written off – an attitude of limited self-denial – but the suggestion that the French could write off reparations, after having paid them in 1871 and 1819, and after four years of cruel war, is to ask too much from history.

The failure to achieve a system of equilibrium exchange rates must be set down, like budget-balancing in government accounts, at the door of economic ignorance. In the British case, the urge was to restore the *status quo ante*; it was aided by destabilizing speculation. The selection of an exchange rate for the French franc was addressed much more clinically – as it could be, since restoration of the old par was out of the question – but too little account was taken of the earlier export of capital and the need for an import surplus to transfer it inward as it returned to France. This can be regarded as economic ignorance of a second order. In combination with war debts and reparations, the disequilibrium rates made the underlying position weak. It is interesting, though perhaps idle, to contemplate whether the depression could still have been avoided, or mitigated by some substantial fraction such as two thirds, if the United States had managed to keep open its market, maintain long-term capital flowing and provide lending of last resort through discounting in crisis. One great difficulty was that while the market for goods might be kept open by vetoing congressional tariff proposals, and discounting undertaken through government or central-bank action, there was no way in which governments of the day could sustain international lending. Foreign loans were made by the market, or largely not at all. Lending could be stopped by government fiat, as the Capital Issues Committee did from time to time in London; it was impossible for government to get the private market to start after it had stopped. And to substitute government loans for the market on anything but an emergency-discounting basis called for machinery which was virtually non-existent. The Bank of France would direct President Luther of the [German] Reichsbank to talk loans with private bankers. The Department of State could suggest that foreign governments talk to J. P. Morgan & Company. They could not produce loans. Leverage was weak.

British leadership

Not until 1931 was it clear that Britain could not provide the leadership. In the early 1920s, there were League of Nations programs for the stabilization of the currencies of Austria and Hungary. These were to a considerable extent British in spirit, with help of experts from Scandinavia, the Low Countries and the Dominions, such as staffed the League or Nations Economic and Financial Section. Later the Dawes and Young Plans to settle German reparations were dominated by British experts, with Americans serving as front men to foster the British hope of tying reparations to war debts. By 1931, British capacity for leadership had gone. In small part it had been dissipated in puerile central-bank quarrels between Norman and Moreau, although much of the competition for domination over the smaller central banks of Europe was the product of Moreau's imagination. (Benjamin Strong tried hard to arbitrate these quarrels, and his death in 1928 was a loss for the stability of the system.) More significant was the burden of French sterling balances, which inhibited Britain as a lender of last resort. In the June 1931 crises, the climax of weakness was reached on the second Austrian loan for the *Kreditanstalt* when Norman offered 50 million schillings or $7 million as a loan for one week. At the World Economic Conference in 1933, it was clear that Britain had turned away from a leading world role, cultivating the Commonwealth and freedom to manage sterling, and largely leaving it to the United States to devise a world program.

Lack of United States leadership

Revisionist historians, such as William A. Williams, insist that the United States undertook a leading world role under Charles E. Hughes as early as the Disarmament Conference of 1922.[4] It is difficult or impossible to find support for this position in the field of international economics, which supports the conventional wisdom of such historians as E. H. Carr, that "in 1918, world leadership was offered, by almost universal consent, to the United States … [and] was declined."[5] There was interest in the affairs of Europe in New York, in the Federal Reserve Bank of New York under Strong and Harrison, in the financial community represented by such people as Dwight Morrow, Thomas Lamont and Norman Davis. A few non-New Yorkers, such as Charles G. Dawes and Andrew Mellon, were brought into international finance and diplomacy. On the whole, however, the isolationism expressed by Henry Cabot Lodge in leading the rejection of the Versailles Treaty and United States adherence to the League of Nations typified the dominant sentiment. The United States was uncertain in its international role. It felt that the British were shrewder, more sophisticated, more devious in their negotiating tactics, so that the United States came out of international conferences losers. Stimson would have been willing to undertake a major discounting operation to rescue the Reichsmark in July 1931. Hoover, Mellon and (though from New York) Mills were opposed to sending good money after bad, as discounting calls for. In 1933, James Warburg, Moley, and, presumably, Woodin and Roosevelt still resisted sending good money after bad. Proposals for embryonic international monetary funds were legion; and even Britain presented one officially. They were uniformly turned down with a lecture on how much the United States had already lost in unpaid war debts and the Standstill Agreement.[6] It was not until 1942 that Harry D. White began preparing a world plan for discussion at Bretton Woods – together with the plan of Lord Keynes – a world plan for limited discounting.

Cooperation

Clarke conclu[ded] that central-bank cooperation was maintained up to mid 1928 but failed thereafter [in his work, *Central Bank Cooperation: 1924–31* (New York, 1967)]. In summary, such cooperation on matters such as hegemony over small central banks or the choice of an equilibrium exchange rate was inadequate before 1926, and the Bank of France supported the pound loyally (and expensively) in the late summer of 1931. A deeper question is whether cooperation as such would have been sufficient. In *America's Role in the World Economy*,[7] Alvin Hansen prescribed for the United States policies of maintenance of full employment at home and cooperation with international efforts at freer trade, restoring capital movements, improvement or the world monetary system and so on. With the advantage of hindsight, it appears that more than cooperation was provided, viz. leadership, and that mere cooperation would not have built the institutions and policies of the Organization for Economic Cooperation and Development, Group of Ten, Bank for International Settlements, International Monetary Fund, International Bank, General Agreement on Oil Tariffs and Trade, etc. As an acquaintance of the International Monetary Fund staff put it (admittedly to an American), if the United States does not take the leadership, nothing happens. Leadership may lack followership, and foolish or even sensible proposals may be defeated through lack of support. But the most sensible proposals emanating from small countries are valueless if they lack the capacity to carry them out and fail to enlist the countries that do. The World Economic Conference of 1933 did not lack ideas, as that of 1927 seems to have done. The one country capable of leadership was bemused by domestic concerns and stood aside.

One special form of cooperation would have been joint Anglo–American leadership in the economic affairs of the world. Economists usually agree that such arrangements, whether duopoly or bilateral monopoly, are unstable, and so do political scientists. Carr states explicitly that the hope for Pax Anglo-Saxonica was romantic and that Pax Americana "would be an easier contingency."[8] Vansittart, referring to the Standstill agreements and the German occupation of the Rhineland, wrote *à propos* of the World Economic Conference: "When action was required two years earlier, the two governments [British and American] sheltered behind each other like the British and French governments three years later."[9] With a duumvirate, a troika, or slightly wider forms of collective responsibility, the buck has no place to stop.

Changing leaders

Friedman and Schwartz make a great deal of the role in the great depression of the shift of monetary leadership in the United States from New York to Washington.[10] They suggest that this sounds far-fetched, since it is a "sound general principle that great events have great origins," but note that small events at times have large consequences through chain reactions and cumulative force. The universality of the asserted principle seems dubious to this observer;[11] the observation that shifts of the locus of leadership give rise to instability does not. Had they not focused so exclusively on monetary conditions in the United States, Friedman and Schwartz might have noted the accentuation of the depression which came with the transfer of the presidency from Hoover to Roosevelt (occurring after the money supply had been greatly enlarged); and the still more significant (in my judgment) transfer of leadership in the world economy from Whitehall to the White House.

This notion of the instability of a financial system with two centers, or of one where leadership is in process of being dropped by one and picked up by another, is cited by Edward Nevin as crucial to the collapse of the gold standard in 1931. He quotes Sir Ernest Harvey's testimony before the Macmillan Committee: "such leadership as we possess has been affected by the position which America has gained"; making a change in the ancient system as set out in the Macmillan Report, under which bank rate regulated the reserve position of the United Kingdom, and other countries adjusted their positions to that of Britain. He then went on to say, "Better that a motor car should be in charge of a poor driver than of two quite excellent drivers who are perpetually fighting to gain control of the vehicle."[12] The analogy of two excellent drivers fighting for control of the wheel may be more graphic than apposite. The instability seems rather to have come from the growing weakness of one driver, and the lack of sufficient interest in the other. William Adams Brown, Jr., describes the gold standard of the period as "without a focal point," meaning that it had two, but the conclusions of his monumental work do not dwell on this critical aspect of the world economy.[13]

Role of the small countries and France

One passenger in the vehicle which did not lack interest was France. And one group which lacked responsibility – to discontinue the metaphor, or perhaps they should be regarded as passengers in the back seat – consisted of the smaller countries: Belgium, the Netherlands, Switzerland, and Scandinavia. The smaller countries can be disposed of first. They are sometimes blamed, as in Born's analysis, for having acted irresponsibly in, say, converting sterling into gold in the summer of 1931, or raising tariffs with alacrity after 1930. There is, however, no universally accepted standard of behavior for small countries. On one showing, they lack power to affect the outcome of great events and are therefore privileged to look after the private national interest rather than concern themselves with the public good of stability in the world economy as a whole. On a somewhat higher ethical level, the small countries may be held [to the] Kantian Categorical Imperative, which enjoins them to act only in ways which can be generalized. In such circumstances, of course, they would not have withdrawn credits from Austria in the spring of 1931, nor from Germany and Britain in the summer, nor from the United States in the autumn. The economist chooses between these standards perhaps on the basis of comparative cost. If the Netherlands had known the cost of leaving its sterling unconverted into gold, it seems unlikely that it would have done so, even at the risk of accelerating the collapse of the pound and deepening of the world depression. It may be that such countries as Sweden, Canada and New Zealand that set high standards of international conduct – in foreign aid, contributions to United Nations peacekeeping missions, etc. – do so solely from ethical reasons; or they may choose among occasions to take largely the opportunities which are relatively cheap. One may thus note that the small countries contributed substantially to the deflation by the speed with which they cut imports, depreciated, or converted sterling and dollars into gold, but find it hard to blame them for it.[14]

There is another aspect to the role of small countries: they could offer programs for recovery because they knew that the major cost of programs adopted would fall on other countries. Proposals for an embryonic international monetary fund in the Washington discussions preceding the World Economic Conference of 1933 were put forward by Poland, Turkey, Belgium, the ILO., and one was made by Britain, though this latter was quickly withdrawn when the United States frowned upon it. Lacking resources to make these schemes effective, small countries were reduced to advisory roles without conviction, even when the proposals were sound. An essential ingredient of followership is to convince the leader that he is the author of the ideas which require the use of his resources.

The case of France is different. France sought power in its national interest, without adequately taking into account the repercussions of its positions on world economic or political stability. Its intransigence in the matter of reparations or the attempt to attach political conditions to the second Austrian credit of June 1931 or the contemplated German loan of July of that year illustrate the position. Hurt in the depreciation of sterling in September, the Bank of France, under strong political pressure at home, converted its dollars into gold in the private national interest during 1931-2, all the while protesting its cooperation and concern for the interest of the United States. The rivalry between the Bank of France and the Bank of England over which should take over the leadership in restoring independence to central banks and stabilization of currencies in Eastern Europe would be pathetic, had it not run risks of instability for the system as a whole when the French threatened to withdraw balances from London.

Not quite big enough to have responsibility forced on it, nor small enough to afford the luxury of irresponsibility, the French position in the inter-war period was unenviable. It had the power to act as a destabilizer, but was insufficiently powerful to stabilize. "Great Britain and the United States together were the active nucleus that replaced the single center of pre-war days, but the position and policy of France actively directed their mutual as well as their joint relations to the outlying countries."[15] In these circumstances France could be (and was) blamed for upsetting the system when she had no capacity to take it over and run it in the presence of two larger powers, one feeble, the other irresponsible.

Public v. private interest

Cynicism suggests that leadership is fully rewarded for its pains in prestige, and that no matter how much it protests its commitment to the public welfare, its fundamental concern is private. Bismarck insisted that free trade was the weapon of the dominant economy anxious to prevent others from following in its path. "The white man's burden" is an expression used today only in mockery. A country like France deliberately setting out to achieve prestige suggests that those with a concern for problem-solving, are either perfidious or self-deceiving. None the less there is a difference between accepting and declining responsibility for the way the system is run. The British accepted responsibility, although, as the 50 million schilling loan emphasizes, they were unable to discharge it. The French and the United States were unwilling to underwrite stability. Under Coolidge and Hoover, the United States refused to commit itself to any program of foreign reconstruction or currency stabilization, leaving these questions to the Federal Reserve System.[16] There was hardly any improvement in Roosevelt's commitment to the world economy until timidly in 1936, at the time of the Tripartite Monetary Pact, and ultimately during the Second World War. Inside France, as between France and the other leading powers, "all groups thought their opponents more united and dedicated than they were, and a concern for the general interest was virtually absent."[17]

Unable to cope with the public good, the British more and more turned their energy to the private. Keynes' advocacy of a tariff and the refusal to contemplate stabilization after 1931 are examples. One may find a hint or two in the documents that the initiative came from the Dominions rather than Britain.[18] For a time, until well after the war, the British economics profession and public almost drew the lesson that each country should take care of itself without regard to external effects.

The point is illustrated in the memorandum written by Hubert Henderson at the British Treasury in 1943, entitled "International Economic History of the Interwar Period."[19] This summarizes the crude view of the depression as resulting from nationalism and tariffs, the collapse of world trade, bilateralism and preferences and disregard of the advice of the League of Nations, leading to the conclusion that after the war there is need for the world to be more resolute in avoiding economic nationalism, and attempting to construct a freely working economic system with international credits, the reduction of trade barriers and the outlawry of qualitative regulation.[20] Henderson states that the history of the inter-war period provides no support for this view. He opposes exchange depreciation:

> there can be little doubt that the depreciation of the pound was in part responsible for the sharper fall in gold prices, and disillusionment is general in the United Kingdom and still more in the United States on the power of exchange depreciation to promote national recovery.[21]
>
> But the conventional view is false in all essential respects. The old international order has broken down for good. Nothing but futility and frustration can come from the attempt to set it up again. Individual countries must be free to regulate their external economies effectively, using control of capital movements, quantitative regulation, preferences, autonomous credit policies, etc.[22]

This foot-dragging, which Keynes shared during the 1930s and until late in the war, is understandable. It misses the main lesson of the inter-war years, however: that for the world economy to be stabilized, there has to be a stabilizer, one stabilizer.

Countercyclical capital movements

Assume that the United States had not led the way to destroying the trade mechanism through the Smoot–Hawley Tariff of 1930, and that a discounting mechanism had been available to cope with 1931. There would still have been a serious depression, if perhaps not so prolonged, owing to the failure of countercyclical lending, and the absence of machinery such as the World Bank or foreign aid coordinated through the Development Assistance Committee (DAC) of the Organization of Economic Cooperation and Development (OECD), to replace the private market with public funds. It remains puzzling that the foreign capital market in New York (and to a much lesser degree in London) started to come back in the spring of 1930, after the stock-market crash, and then relapsed. There was no panic, and no alarm, but "people felt the ground giving way under their feet."[23] Arthur Lewis's explanation of the relapse in terms of the decline of prices is perhaps not wholly satisfactory, nor is the "inexperience" of the New York capital market in international lending. They are all that is available. Even with anti-cyclical capital movements, there would have been a depression. With a flow of international capital positively correlated with business conditions in the lending country, the depression was inevitably severe. Add to this position, which was perhaps beyond the power of policy to correct in the existing state of knowledge, beggar-thy-neighbor tactics in trade and exchange depreciation, plus the unwillingness of the United States to serve as a lender of last resort in 1931, and the length and depth of the depression are explained.

There is one respect in which United States "inexperience" in lending might be said to be relevant to the pattern of lending. A new lender is likely to behave differently from an old lender because of the wider array of investment opportunities available to it. Consider a country which has been long engaged in international investment. Its foreign loans are likely to follow what may be called a "demand model," in which a given flow of savings is allocated between domestic and foreign uses depending upon the relative demands from them. A domestic boom diverts foreign loans to the home market. Depression at home and expansion abroad stimulates foreign lending. The result is a countercyclical pattern.

When a country begins lending abroad for the first time, however, there are likely to be a host of unfilled opportunities for foreign loans. As savings become available, they are invested at home and abroad, simultaneously. The more profits at home in boom, the more foreign investment. This is a "supply model," in which foreign lending depends on the availability of savings. Alteration between demand and supply models is evident in direct foreign investment. That it may apply to lending through foreign bonds is only a hypothesis. It would, however, explain why United States lending at the beginning of its career as a creditor was positively correlated with the domestic business cycle, whereas in Britain, the experienced lender, the pattern had been otherwise.

Relevance to the 1970s

Leadership is a word with negative connotations in the 1970s when participation in decision-making is regarded as more aesthetic. Much of the overtones of *der Führer* and *il Duce* remain. But if leadership is thought of as the provision of the public good of responsibility, rather than exploitation of followers or the private good of prestige, it remains a positive idea. It may one day be possible to pool sovereignties to limit the capacity of separate countries to work against the general interest; such pooling is virtually attained today in some of the functions needed to stabilize the world economic system, such as the Basle arrangements for swaps and short-term credits which, pending a world central bank, serve as a world rediscounting mechanism in crisis. In this area, and in the world agencies for maintaining freer trade and a liberal flow of capital and aid, however, leadership is necessary in the absence of delegated authority. That of the United States is beginning to slip. It is not yet clear that the rising strength of Europe in an enlarged European Economic Community [EEC] will be accompanied by an assertion of leadership in providing a market for distress or aggressive goods, in stabilizing the international flow of capital or in providing a discount mechanism for crisis. Presumably the Basle arrangements for the last will endure. There are indications that the European market for goods will remain ample, except in agriculture, which is an important exception from a world viewpoint. There is still some distance to go to stabilize the flow of capital countercyclically.

As the United States economic leadership in the world economy falters, and Europe gathers strength, three outcomes are politically stable; three unstable. Among the stable outcomes are continued or revived United States leadership, after the exchange controls of 1963 to 1969 and the 1970–71 wave of protectionism have been reversed; an assertion of leadership and assumption of responsibility for the stability of the world system by Europe; or an effective cession of economic sovereignty to international institutions: a world central bank, a world capital market, and an effective General Agreement on Tariffs and Trade. The last is the most attractive, but perhaps, because difficult, the least likely. As between the first two alternatives, the responsible citizen should be content with either, flipping a coin to decide, if the third alternative proves unavailable, simply to avoid the undesirable alternatives.

The three outcomes to be avoided because of their instability are: (a) the United States and the EEC vying for leadership of the world economy; (b) one unable to lead and the other unwilling, as in 1929 to 1933; and (c) each retaining a veto over programs of stability or strengthening of the system without seeking to secure positive programs of its own. The articles of agreement of the International Monetary Fund (IMF) were set up to provide the United States with a veto over action which it opposed. In the 1969 reform which legislated the addition of Special Drawing Rights (SDRs) to the monetary system, quotas of [the] IMF were adjusted to provide a veto to the EEC as well. This leaves open the possibility of stalemate, as in the United Nations Security Council, when two major powers are unable to agree. In the circumstances of the Security Council there is a danger of regressive spiral into war; the analog in the economic field is stalemate, and depression.

In these circumstances, the third positive alternative of international institutions with real authority and sovereignty is pressing.

Notes

1. See Heywood W. Fleisig, "Long-Term Capital Flows and the Great Depression: The Role of the United States, 1927–1933," unpublished dissertation, Yale University, 1968, *passim*, and Peter Temin, "The Beginning of the Depression in Germany," *Economic History Review*, 24(2) (May 1971), pp. 240–8. Fleisig and Temin argue over the size of the shock to the system. If the system is basically unstable, this issue is downgraded in importance.
2. Heywood Fleisig, "The United States and the World Periphery during the Early Years of the Great Depression," … in Herman van der Wee (ed.), *The Great Depression Revisited* (The Hague: Nijhoff, 1972).

3. *Editor's Note*: See Kindleberger, *The World in Depression*, Table 1, p. 56.
4. See, for example, William Applenian Williams, *The Tragedy of American Diplomacy* (Cleveland, OH: World Publishing Co. 1959), *passim*, but esp. Chapter IV, "The Legend of Isolationism." Mr Williams, a Marxist revisionist historian, states (p. 123): "Hoover did not grasp the fact that the depression was a sign of stagnation in a corporate economy which was born during the civil war and came to maturity in the decade from 1895 to 1905"; and (p. 128): "from the fall of 1932 Roosevelt and Hull stressed the importance of foreign trade for domestic revival and expansion and for world wide relief of conditions which caused war and revolution." It is difficult to see how a historian could ignore such evidence as the First Inaugural Address, cited earlier, to be able to make such a statement about Roosevelt.
5. Edward Hallett Carr, *The Twenty Years' Crisis, 1919–1939: An Introduction to the Study of International Relations* (London: Macmillan, 1939), 2nd edn (1946), p. 234.
6. Jorgen Pedersen blames the liquidity crisis of 1931 on the United States for its failure to support the German mark, and, when that had been forced to suspend gold payments, for its failure to underwrite sterling. See "Some Notes on the Economic Policy of the United States during the Period 1919–1932," in Hugo Hegeland (ed), *Money, Growth and Methodology*, in Honor of Johan Akerman, *Lund Social Science Studies* (Lund, 1961), pp. 490–1. This would be agreed today, and Professor Pedersen put it forward himself, as noted earlier, in 1933. As he himself points out, however (p. 494), the United States was acting with "the normal prejudices of the period."
7. Alvin Hansen, *America's Role in the World Economy* (New York: W. W. Norton, New York and London: Allen & Unwin, 1945).
8. Carr, *The Twenty Years' Crisis, 1919–39*, pp. 233–4.
9. Lord Vansittart, *The Mist Procession, the Autobiography of Lord Vansillart* (London: Hutchinson, 1958), p. 466.
10. Milton Friedman and Anna Jacobson Schwartz, *A Monetary History of the United States, 1867–1960* (Princeton: Princeton University Press, 1963), p. 419.
11. Cf. Benjamin Franklin, *Maxims Prefixed to Poor Richard's Almanac* (Philadelphia, 1757), "Little strokes fell great oaks," and "A little neglect may breed mischief: for want of a nail the shoe was lost; for want of a shoe the horse was lost; for want of a horse the rider was lost." The exception for cumulative feedback embraces the second quotation, but not the first.
12. Edward Nevin, *The Mechanism of Cheap Money: A Study of British Monetary Policy, 1931–1939* (Cardiff: University of Wales Press, 1955), pp. 9n., 12, 14.
13. William Adams Brown, Jr., *The International Gold Standard Reinterpreted, 1914–34* (New York: National Bureau of Economic Research, 1940), ii, p. 781: "The essential difference between the international gold standard of 1928–29 and that of 1914 was that when the world returned to gold after the war it built its international financial system around a nucleus of London and New York, and not a single center." The title of his Chapter 20 is "The Experiment of a Gold Exchange Standard without a Focal Point."

14. For an interesting political model of countries which are free-riders behind the leadership of others, see Norman Froelich and Joe A. Oppenheimer, "I Get Along with a Little Help from My Friends," *World Politics*, 23(1) (October 1970), pp. 104–20. But note, p. 119, that leadership is rewarded in this model rather than made to pay for the privilege, as implied where the responsibilities of leadership are maintaining an open market for goods, a countercyclical export of capital and a mechanism for rediscounting in crisis.
15. Brown, *The International Gold Standard Reinterpreted, 1914–1934*, p. 785.
16. Lester V. Chandler, *Benjamin Strong, Central Banker* (Washington, DC: The Brookings Institution, 1958), p. 255.
17. Alfred Sauvy, *Histoire économique de la France entre les deux guerres, 1: 1918–1931* (Paris: Fayard, 1965), p. 73.
18. See *Documents diplomatiques français, 1932–39*, 1ᵉʳ série (1932–1935), Tome (Paris: Imprimerie Nationale, 1967), 470, Bonnet to Paul-Boncour (9 July 1933), p. 871:

    One fact is evident: it is that Britain is not free. Its dominions and in particular Canada whose Prime Minister Bennett is a man of extraordinary violence have a predominant influence on her, to the point of modifying totally her opinion in the space of a few seconds.

    This is doubtless hyperbole.
19. See Hubert D. Henderson, *The Inter-war Years and Other Papers* (Oxford: Clarendon Press, 1955), pp. 236–95.
20. Ibid., pp. 236, 290.
21. Ibid., pp. 260, 262; see also p. 291:

    Of the various expedients which different governments employed in the 1930s, none produced more unfortunate results than deliberate exchange depreciation. It was the least helpful to the countries which tried it, and the most harmful to other countries.

22. Ibid., p. 293.
23. Joseph A. Schumpeter, *Business Cycles, A Theoretical, Historical and Statistical Analysis of the Capitalistic Process*, ii (New York and London: McGraw-Hill, 1939), p. 911.

7
Our Obsolete Market Mentality (1947)*

Karl Polanyi

The first century of the Machine Age is drawing to a close amid fear and trepidation. Its fabulous material success was due to the willing, indeed the enthusiastic, subordination of man to the needs of the machine. Liberal capitalism was in effect man's initial response to the challenge of the Industrial Revolution. In order to allow scope to the use of elaborate, powerful machinery, we transformed human economy into a self-adjusting system of markets, and cast our thoughts and values in the mold of this unique innovation.

Today, we begin to doubt the truth of some of these thoughts and the validity of some of these values. Outside the United States, liberal capitalism can hardly be said to exist any more. How to organize human life in a machine society is a question that confronts us anew. Behind the fading fabric of competitive capitalism there looms the portent of an industrial civilization, with its paralyzing division of labor, standardization of life, supremacy of mechanism over organism, and organization over spontaneity. Science itself is haunted by insanity. This is the abiding concern.

No mere reversion to the ideals of a past century can show us the way. We must brave the future, though this may involve us in an attempt to shift the place of industry in society so that the extraneous fact of the machine can be absorbed. The search for industrial democracy is not merely the search for a solution to the problems of capitalism, as most people imagine. It is a search for an answer to industry itself. Here lies the concrete problem of our civilization. Such a new dispensation requires an inner freedom for which we are but ill

*   From *Commentary*, (February 1947), pp. 109–17. Reprinted by permission of *Commentary*. © 1947 by the American Jewish Committee.

equipped. We find ourselves stultified by the legacy of a market-economy which bequeathed us oversimplified views of the function and role of the economic system in society. If the crisis is to be overcome, we must recapture a more realistic vision of the human world and shape our common purpose in the light of that recognition. Industrialism is a precariously grafted scion upon man's age-long existence. The outcome of the experiment is still hanging in the balance. But man is not a simple being and can die in more than one way. The question of individual freedom, so passionately raised in our generation, is only one aspect of this anxious problem. In truth, it forms part of a much wider and deeper need – the need for a new response to the total challenge of the machine.

Our condition can be described in these terms: Industrial civilization may yet undo man. But since the venture of a progressively artificial environment cannot, will not, and indeed, should not, be voluntarily discarded, the task of adapting life *in such a surrounding* to the requirements of human existence must be resolved if man is to continue on earth. No one can foretell whether such an adjustment is possible, or whether man must perish in the attempt. Hence the dark undertone of concern.

Meanwhile, the first phase of the Machine Age has run its course. It involved an organization of society that derived its name from its central institution, the market. This system is on the downgrade. Yet our practical philosophy was overwhelmingly shaped by this spectacular episode. Novel notions about man and society became current and gained the status of axioms. Here they are: As regards *man*, we were made to accept the heresy that his motives can be described as "material" and "ideal," and that the incentives on which everyday life is organized spring from the "material" motives. Both utilitarian liberalism and popular Marxism favored such views. As regards *society*, the kindred doctrine was propounded that its institutions were "determined" by the economic system. This opinion was even more popular with Marxists than with liberals.

Under a market-economy both assertions were, of course, true. *But only under such an economy.* In regard to the past, such a view was no more than an anachronism. In regard to the future, it was a mere prejudice. Yet under the influence of current schools of thought, reinforced by the authority of science and religion, politics and business, these strictly time-bound phenomena came to be regarded as timeless, as transcending the age of the market. To overcome such doctrines, which constrict our minds and souls and greatly enhance the difficulty of the life-saving adjustment, may require no less than a reform of our consciousness.

Market society

The birth of laissez-faire administered a shock to civilized man's views of himself, from the effects of which he never quite recovered. Only very gradually are we realizing what happened to us as recently as a century ago.

Liberal economy, this primary reaction of man to the machine, was a violent break with the conditions that preceded it. A chain-reaction was started – what before was merely isolated markets was transmuted into a self-regulating *system* of markets. And with the new economy, a new society sprang into being. The crucial step was this: labor and land were made into commodities, that is, they were treated *as if* produced for sale. Of course, they were not actually commodities, since they were either not produced at all (as land) or, if so, not for sale (as labor). Yet no more thoroughly effective fiction was ever devised. By buying and selling labor and land freely, the mechanism of the market was made to apply to them. There was now supply of labor, and demand for it; there was supply of land, and demand for it. Accordingly, there was a market price for the use of labor power, called wages, and a market price for the use of land, called rent. Labor and land were provided with markets of their own, similar to the commodities proper that were produced with their help. The true scope of such a step can be gauged if we remember that labor is only another name for man, and land for nature. The commodity fiction handed over the fate of man and nature to the play of an automaton running in its own grooves and governed by its own laws.

Nothing similar had ever been witnessed before. Under the mercantile regime, though it deliberately pressed for the creation of markets, the converse principle still operated. Labor and land were not entrusted to the market; they formed part of the organic structure of society. Where land was marketable, only the determination of price was, as a rule, left to the parties; where labor was subject to contract, wages themselves were usually assessed by public authority. Land stood under the custom of manor, monastery, and township, under common-law limitations concerning rights of real property; labor was regulated by laws against beggary and vagrancy, statutes of laborers and artificers, poor laws, guild and municipal ordinances. In effect, all societies known to anthropologists and historians restricted markets to commodities in the proper sense of the term.

Market-economy thus created a new type of society. The economic or productive system was here entrusted to a self-acting device. An institutional mechanism controlled human beings in their everyday activities as well as the resources of nature. This instrument of material welfare was under the sole control of the incentives of hunger and gain – or, more precisely, fear of going without the necessities of life, and expectation of profit. So long as no propertyless person could satisfy his craving for food without first selling his labor in the market, and so long as no propertied person was prevented from buying in the cheapest market and selling in the dearest, the blind mill would turn out ever-increasing amounts of commodities for the benefit of the human race. Fear of starvation with the worker, lure of profit with the employer, would keep the vast establishment running.

In this way an "economic sphere" came into existence that was sharply delimited from other institutions in society. Since no human aggregation can survive without a functioning productive apparatus, its embodiment in a distinct and separate sphere had the effect of making the "rest" of society dependent upon that sphere. This autonomous zone, again, was regulated by a mechanism that controlled its functioning. As a result, the market mechanism became determinative for the life of the body social. No wonder that the emergent human aggregation was an "economic" society to a degree previously never even approximated. "Economic motives" reigned supreme in a world of their own, and the individual was made to act on them under pain of being trodden under foot by the juggernaut market. Such a forced conversion to a utilitarian outlook fatefully warped Western man's understanding of himself.

This new world of "economic motives" was based on a fallacy. Intrinsically, hunger and gain are no more "economic" than love or hate, pride or prejudice. No human motive is per se economic. There is no such thing as a *sui generis* economic experience in the sense in which man may have a religious, aesthetic, or sexual experience. These latter give rise to motives that broadly aim at evoking similar experiences. In regard to material production these terms lack self-evident meaning.

The economic factor, which underlies all social life, no more gives rise to definite incentives than the equally universal law of gravitation. Assuredly, if we do not eat, we must perish, as much as if we were crushed under the weight of a falling rock. But the pangs of hunger are not automatically translated into an incentive to produce. Production is not an individual, but a collective affair. If an individual is hungry, there is nothing definite for him to do. Made desperate, he might rob or steal, but such an action can hardly be called productive. With man, the political animal, everything is given not by natural, but by social circumstance. What made the nineteenth century think of hunger and gain as "economic" was simply the organization of production under a market economy.

Hunger and gain are here linked with production through the need of "earning an income." For under such a system, man, if he is to keep alive, is compelled to buy goods on the market with the help of an income derived from selling other goods on the market. The name of these incomes – wages, rent, interest – varies accordingly to what is offered for sale: use of labor power, of land, or of money; the income called profit – the remuneration of the entrepreneur – derives from the sale of goods that fetch a higher price than the goods that go into the producing of them. Thus all incomes derive from sales, and all sales – directly or indirectly – contribute to production. The latter is, in effect, *incidental to the earning of an income*. So long as an individual is "earning an income," he is, automatically, contributing to production. Obviously, the system works only so long as individuals have a reason to indulge in the activity of "earning an income." The motives of hunger and gain – separately and conjointly – provide them with such a reason. These two motives are thus geared to production and, accordingly, are termed "economic." The semblance is compelling that hunger and gain are *the* incentives on which any economic system must rest. This assumption is baseless. Ranging over human societies, we find hunger and gain not appealed to as incentives to production, and where so appealed to, they are fused with other powerful motives.

Aristotle was right: man is not an economic, but a social being. He does not aim at safeguarding his individual interest in the acquisition of material possessions, but rather at ensuring social good will, social status, social assets. He values possessions primarily as a means to that end. His incentives are of that "mixed" character which we associate with the endeavor to gain social approval – productive efforts are no more than incidental to this. *Man's economy is, as a ride, submerged in his social relations*. The change from this to a society which was, on the contrary, submerged in the economic system was an entirely novel development.

The evidence of facts, I feel, should at this point be adduced. *First,* there are the discoveries of primitive economics. Two names are outstanding: Bronislaw Malinowski and Richard Thurnwald. They and some other research workers revolutionized our conceptions in this field and, by so doing, founded a new discipline. The myth of the individualistic savage had been exploded long ago. Neither the crude egotism, nor the apocryphal propensity to barter, truck, and exchange, nor even the tendency to cater to one's sell was in evidence. But equally discredited was the legend of the communistic psychology of the savage, his supposed lack of appreciation for his own personal interests. (Roughly, it appeared that man was very much the same all through the ages. Taking his institutions not in isolation, but in their interrelation, he was mostly found to be behaving in a manner broadly comprehensible to us.) What appeared as "communism" was the fact that the productive or economic system was usually arranged in such a fashion as not to threaten any individual with starvation. His place at the campfire, his share in the common resources, was secure to him, whatever part he happened to have played in hunt, pasture, tillage, or gardening. Here are a few instances: Under the *kraalland* system of the Kaffirs, "destitution is impossible; whosoever needs assistance receives it unquestioningly."[1] No Kwakiutl "ever ran the least risk of going hungry."[2] "There is no starvation in societies living on the subsistence margin."[3] In effect, the individual is not in danger of starving unless the community as a whole is in a like predicament. It is this absence of the menace of individual destitution that makes primitive society, in a sense, more humane than nineteenth-century society, and at the same time less "economic."

The same applies to the stimulus of individual gain. Again, a few quotations: "The characteristic feature of primitive economics is the absence of any desire to make profits from production and exchange."[4] "Gain, which is often the stimulus for work in more civilized communities, never acts as an impulse to work under the original native conditions."[5] If so-called economic motives were natural to man, we would have to judge all early and primitive societies as thoroughly unnatural.

Secondly, there is no difference between primitive and civilized society in this regard. Whether we turn to ancient city-state, despotic empire, feudalism, thirteenth-century urban life, sixteenth-century mercantile regime, or eighteenth-century regulationism – invariably the economic system is found to be merged in the social. Incentives spring from a large variety of sources, such as custom and tradition, public duty and private commitment, religious observance and political allegiance, judicial obligation and administrative regulation as established by prince, municipality, or guild. Rank and status, compulsion of law and threat of punishment, public praise and private reputation, insure that the individual contributes his share to production. Fear of privation or love of profit need not be altogether absent. Markets occur in all kinds of societies, and the figure of the merchant is familiar to many types of civilization. But isolated markets do not link up into an economy. The motive of gain was specific to merchants, as was valor to the knight, piety to the priest, and pride to the craftsman. The notion of making the motive of gain universal never entered the heads of our ancestors. At no time prior to the second quarter of the nineteenth century were markets more than a subordinate feature in society.

Thirdly, there was the startling abruptness of the change. Predominance of markets emerged not as a matter of degree, but of kind. Markets through which otherwise self-sufficient householders get rid of their surplus neither direct production nor provide the producer with his income.[6] This is only the case in a market-economy where all incomes derive from sales, and commodities are obtainable exclusively by purchase. A free market for labor was born in England only about a century ago. The ill-famed Poor Law Reform (1834) abolished the rough-and-ready provisions made for the paupers by patriarchal governments. The poorhouse was transformed from a refuge of the destitute into an abode of shame and mental torture to which even hunger and misery were preferable. Starvation or work was the alternative left to the poor. Thus was a competitive national market for labor created. Within a decade, the Bank Act (1844) established the principle of the gold standard; the making of money was removed from the hands of the government regardless of the effect upon the level of employment. Simultaneously, reform of land laws mobilized the land, and repeal of the Corn Laws (1846) created a world pool of grain, thereby making the unprotected Continental peasant-farmer subject to the whims of the market. Thus were established the three tenets of economic liberalism, the principle on which market economy was organized: that labor should find its price on the market; that money should be supplied by a self-adjusting mechanism; that commodities should be free to flow from country to country irrespective of the consequences – in brief, a labor market, the gold standard, and free trade. A self-inflammatory process was induced, as a result of which the formerly harmless market pattern expanded into a sociological enormity.

These facts roughly outline the genealogy of an "economic" society. Under such conditions the human world must appear as determined by "economic" motives. It is easy to see why. Single out whatever motive you please, and organize production in such a manner as to make that motive the individual's incentive to produce, and you will have induced a picture of man as altogether absorbed by that particular motive. Let that motive be religious, political, or aesthetic; let it be pride, prejudice, love, or envy; and man will appear as essentially religious, political, aesthetic, proud, prejudiced, engrossed in love or envy. Other motives, in contrast, will appear distant and shadowy since they cannot be relied upon to operate in the vital business of production. The particular motive selected will represent "real" man.

As a matter of fact, human beings will labor for a large variety of reasons as long as things are arranged accordingly. Monks traded for religious reasons, and monasteries became the largest trading establishments in Europe. The Kula trade of the Trobriand Islanders, one of the most intricate barter arrangements known to man, is mainly an aesthetic pursuit. Feudal economy was run on customary lines. With the Kwakiutl, the chief aim of industry seems to be to satisfy a point of honor. Under mercantile despotism, industry was often planned so as to serve power and glory. Accordingly, we tend to think of monks or villeins, Western Melanesians, the Kwakiutl, or seventeenth-century statesmen, as ruled by religion, aesthetics, custom, honor, or politics, respectively.

Under capitalism, every individual has to earn an income. If he is a worker, he has to sell his labor at current prices; if he is an owner, he has to make as high a profit as he can, for his standing with his fellows will depend upon the level of his income. Hunger and gain – even if vicariously – make them plow and sow, spin and weave, mine coal, and pilot planes. Consequently, members of such a society will think of themselves as governed by these twin motives. In actual fact, man was never as selfish as the theory demanded. Though the market mechanism brought his dependence upon material goods to the fore, "economic" motives never formed with him the sole incentive to work. In vain was he exhorted by economists and utilitarian moralists alike to discount in business all other motives than "material" ones. On closer investigation, he was still found to be acting on remarkably "mixed" motives, not excluding those of duty toward himself and others – and maybe, secretly, even enjoying work for its own sake.

However, we are not here concerned with actual, but with assumed motives, not with the psychology, but with the ideology of business.

Not on the former, but on the latter are views of man's nature based. For once society expects a definite behavior on the part of its members, and prevailing institutions become roughly capable of enforcing that behavior, opinions on human nature will tend to mirror the ideal whether it resembles actuality or not. Accordingly, hunger and gain were defined as economic motives, and man was supposed to be acting on them in everyday life, while his other motives appeared more ethereal and removed from humdrum existence. Honor and pride, civic obligation and moral duty, even self-respect and common decency, were now deemed irrelevant to production, and were significantly summed up in the word "ideal." Hence man was believed to consist of two components, one more akin to hunger and gain, the other to honor and power. The one was "material," the other "ideal"; the one "economic," the other "non-economic"; the one "rational," the other "non-rational." The Utilitarians went so far as to identify the two sets of terms, thus endowing the economic side of man's character with the aura of rationality. He who would have refused to imagine that he was acting for gain alone was thus considered not only immoral, but also mad.

Economic determinism

The market mechanism, moreover, created the delusion of economic determinism as a general law for all human society. Under a market-economy, of course, this law holds good. Indeed, the working of the economic system here not only "influences" the rest of society, but determines it – as in a triangle the sides not merely influence, but determine, the angles. Take the stratification of classes. Supply and demand in the labor market were identical with the classes of workers and employers, respectively. The social classes of capitalists, landowners, tenants, brokers, merchants, professionals, and so on, were delimited by the respective markets for land, money, and capital and their uses, or for various services. The income of these social classes was fixed by the market, their rank and position by their income. This was a complete reversal of the secular practice. In Maine's famous phrase, "contractus" replaced "status"; or, as Tönnies preferred to put it, "society" superseded "community"; or, in terms of the present article, instead of *the economic system being embedded in social relationships, these relationships were now embedded in the economic system.*

While social classes were directly, other institutions were indirectly determined by the market mechanism. State and government, marriage and the rearing of children, the organization of science and education, of religion and the arts, the choice of profession, the forms of habitation, the shape of settlements, the very aesthetics of private life – everything had to comply with the utilitarian pattern, or at least not interfere with the working of the market mechanism. But since very few human activities can be carried on in the void; even a saint needing his pillar, the indirect effect of the market system came very near to determining the whole of society. It was almost impossible to avoid the erroneous conclusion that as "economic" man was "real" man, so the economic system was "really" society.

Yet it would be truer to say that the basic human institutions abhor unmixed motives. Just as the provisioning of the individual and his family does not commonly rely on the motive of hunger, so the institution of the family is not based on the sexual motive. Sex, like hunger, is one of the most powerful of incentives when released from the control of other incentives. That is probably why the family in all its variety of forms is never allowed to center on the sexual instinct, with its intermittences and vagaries, but on the combination of a number of effective motives that prevent sex from destroying an institution on which so much of man's happiness depends. Sex in itself will never produce anything better than a brothel, and even then it might have to draw on some incentives of the market mechanism. An economic system actually relying for its mainspring on hunger would be almost as perverse as a family system based on the bare urge of sex.

To attempt to apply economic determinism to all human societies is little short of fantastic. Nothing is more obvious to the student of social anthropology than the variety of institutions found to be compatible with practically identical instruments of production. Only since the market was permitted to grind the human fabric into the featureless uniformity of selenic erosion has man's institutional creativeness been in abeyance. No wonder that his social imagination shows signs of fatigue. It may come to a point where he will no longer be able to recover the elasticity, the imaginative wealth and power, of his savage endowment.

No protest of mine, I realize, will save me from being taken for an "idealist." For he who decries the importance of "material" motives must, it seems, be relying on the strength of "ideal" ones. Yet no worse misunderstanding is possible. Hunger and gain have nothing specifically "material" about them. Pride, honor, and power, on the other hand, are not necessarily "higher" motives than hunger and gain.

The dichotomy itself, we assert, is arbitrary. Let us once more adduce the analogy of sex. Assuredly, a significant distinction between "higher" and "lower" motives can here be drawn. Yet, whether hunger or sex, it is pernicious to institutionalize the separation of the "material" and "ideal" components of man's being. As regards sex, this truth, so vital to man's essential wholeness, has been recognized all along; it is at the basis of the institution of marriage. But in the equally strategic field of economy, it has been neglected. This latter field has been "separated out" of society as the realm of hunger and gain. Our animal dependence upon food has been bared and the naked fear of starvation permitted to run loose. Our humiliating enslavement to the material, which all human culture is designed to mitigate, was deliberately made more rigorous. This is at the root of the "sickness of an acquisitive society" that Tawney warned of. And Robert Owen's genius was at its best when, a century before, he described the profit motive as "a principle entirely unfavorable to individual and public happiness."

The reality of society

I plead for the restoration of that unity of motives which should inform man in his everyday activity as a producer, for the reabsorption of the economic system in society, for the creative adaptation of our ways of life to an industrial environment.

On all these counts, laissez-faire philosophy, with its corollary of a marketing society, falls to the ground. It is responsible for the splitting up of man's vital unity into "real" man, bent on material values, and his "ideal" better self. It is paralyzing our social imagination by more or less unconsciously fostering the prejudice of economic determinism. It has done its service in that phase of industrial civilization which is behind us. At the price of impoverishing the individual, it enriched society. Today, we are faced with the vital task of restoring the fullness of life to the person, even though this may mean a technologically less efficient society. In different countries in different ways, classical liberalism is being discarded. On Right and Left and Middle, new avenues are being explored. British Social-Democrats, American New Dealers, and also European fascists and American anti-New Dealers of the various "managerialist" brands, reject the liberal utopia. Nor should the present political mood of rejection of everything Russian blind us to the achievement of the Russians in creative adjustment to some of the fundamental aspects of an industrial environment.

On general grounds, the Communist's expectation of the "withering away of the state" seems to me to combine elements of liberal utopianism with practical indifference to institutional freedoms. As regards the withering state, it is impossible to deny that industrial society is complex society, and no complex society can exist without organized power at the center. Yet, again, this fact is no excuse for the Communist's slurring over the question of concrete institutional freedoms. It is on this level of realism that the problem of individual freedom should be met. No human society is possible in which power and compulsion are absent, nor is a world in which force has no function. Liberal philosophy gave a false direction to our ideals in seeming to promise the fulfillment of such intrinsically utopian expectations.

But under the market system, society as a whole remained invisible. Anybody could imagine himself free from responsibility for those acts of compulsion on the part of the state which he, personally, repudiated, or for unemployment and destitution from which he, personally, did not benefit. Personally, he remained unentangled in the evils of power and economic value. In good conscience, he could deny their reality in the name of his imaginary freedom. Power and economic value are, indeed, a paradigm of social reality. Neither power nor economic value spring from human volition; non-co-operation is impossible in regard to them. The function of power is to insure that measure of conformity which is needed for the survival of the group: as David Hume showed, its ultimate source is opinion – and who could help holding opinions of some sort or other? Economic value, in any society, insures the usefulness of the goods produced; it is a seal set on the division of labor. Its source is human wants – and how could we be expected not to prefer one thing to another? Any opinion or desire, no matter what society we live in, will make us participants in the creation of power and the constituting of value. No freedom to do otherwise is conceivable. An ideal that would ban power and compulsion from society is intrinsically invalid. By ignoring this limitation on man's meaningful wishes, the marketing view of society reveals its essential immaturity.

Freedom in industrial society

The breakdown of market-economy imperils two kinds of freedoms: some good, some bad.

That the freedom to exploit one's fellows, or the freedom to make inordinate gains without commensurable service to the community, the freedom to keep technological inventions from being used for the public benefit, or the freedom to profit from public calamities secretly engineered for private advantage, may disappear, together with the free market, is all to the good. But the market economy under which these freedoms throve also produced freedoms that we prize highly. Freedom of conscience, freedom of speech, freedom of meeting, freedom of association, freedom to choose one's job – we cherish them for their own sake. Yet to a large extent they were by-products of the same economy that was also responsible for the evil freedoms.

The existence of a separate economic sphere in society created, as it were, a gap between politics and economics, between government and industry, that was in the nature of a no man's land. As division of sovereignty between pope and emperor left medieval princes in a condition of freedom sometimes bordering on anarchy, so division of sovereignty between government and industry in the nineteenth century allowed even the poor man to enjoy freedoms that partly compensated for his wretched status. Current skepticism in regard to the future of freedom largely rests on this. There are those who argue, like Hayek, that since free institutions were a product of market-economy, they must give place to serfdom once that economy disappears. There are others, like Burnham, who assert the inevitability of some new form of serfdom called "managerialism."

Arguments like these merely prove to what extent economistic prejudice is still rampant. For such determinism, as we have seen, is only another name for the market mechanism. It is hardly logical to argue the effects of its absence on the strength of an economic necessity that derives from its presence. And it is certainly contrary to Anglo-Saxon experience. Neither the freezing of labor nor selective service abrogated the essential freedoms of the American people, as anybody can witness who spent the crucial years 1940–43 in these States. Great Britain during the war introduced an all-round planned economy and did away with that separation of government and industry from which nineteenth-century freedom sprang, yet never were public liberties more securely entrenched than at the height of the emergency. In truth, we will have just as much freedom as we will desire to create and to safeguard. There is no one determinant in human society. Institutional guarantees of personal freedom are compatible with any economic system. In market society alone did the economic mechanism lay down the law.

What appears to our generation as the problem of capitalism is, in reality, the far greater problem of an industrial civilization. The economic liberal is blind to this fact. In defending capitalism as an economic system, he ignores the challenge of the Machine Age. Yet the dangers that make the bravest quake today transcend economy. The idyllic concerns of trust-busting and Taylorization have been superseded by Hiroshima. Scientific barbarism is dogging our footsteps. The Germans were planning a contrivance to make the sun emanate death rays. We, in fact, produced a burst of death rays that blotted out the sun. Yet the Germans had an evil philosophy, and we had a humane philosophy. In this we should learn to see the symbol of our peril.

Among those in America who are aware of the dimensions of the problem, two tendencies are discernible: some believe in elites and aristocracies, in managerialism and the corporation. They feel that the whole of society should be more intimately adjusted to the economic system, which they would wish to maintain unchanged. This is the ideal of the Brave New World, where the individual is conditioned to support an order that has been designed for him by such as are wiser than he. Others, on the contrary, believe that in a truly democratic society, the problem of industry would resolve itself through the planned intervention of the producers and consumers themselves. Such conscious and responsible action is, indeed, one of the embodiments of freedom in a complex society. But, as the contents of this article suggest, such an endeavor cannot be successful unless it is disciplined by a total view of man and society very different from that which we inherited from market economy.

Notes

1. L. P. Mair, *An African People in the Twentieth Century* (1934).
2. E. M. Loeb, *The Distribution and Function of Money in Early Society* (1936).
3. M. J. Herskovits, *The Economic Life of Primitive Peoples* (1940).
4. R. Thurnwald, *Economics in Primitive Communities* (1932).
5. B. Malinowski, *Argonauts of the Western Pacific* (1922).
6. *Editor's Note*: George Dalton, the editor of the collection where Polanyi's essay reappeared, added the following reference: "On such peripheral or petty markets as they function in Africa, see Paul Bohannan and George Dalton, 'Introduction,' to *Markets in Africa* (New York: Natural History Press, 1965)."

8

Capitalism in the Postwar World (1943)*

Joseph A. Schumpeter

I

For the purposes of this essay capitalism will be defined by three features of industrial society: private ownership of the physical means of production; private profits and private responsibility for losses; and the creation of means of payments – banknotes or deposits – by private banks. The first two features suffice to define private enterprise. But no concept of capitalism can be satisfactory without including the set of typically capitalistic phenomena covered by the third. Where it is absent we might speak of commercial society. By socialism we shall mean an institutional arrangement that vests the management of the productive process with some public authority.[1]

In trying to forecast the role, if any, that capitalism in the sense defined may be expected to play in the postwar world it is well to remember that its fate is not a question of the merits or demerits we may individually see in it. Our judgment about these is a matter of personal or groupwise preference that depends on interests and ideals largely determined by our personal or groupwise location in the social organism. What we mean when we say that we are for or against capitalism is that we like or dislike a certain civilization or scheme of life which is historically associated with the three economic features mentioned. But civilizations are incommensurable. Even if we agreed to neglect those cultural aspects which are what really matters to us, and to make the "desirability" of retaining or eliminating capitalism turn on some purely economic criterion – such as comparative productive

---

* From Seymour E. Harris (ed.), *Postwar Economic Problems* (New York: McGraw-Hill, 1943), pp. 113–26.

efficiency – we should never agree about the result. For even if those extraeconomic and largely extrarational preferences did not prevent us from admitting that any criterion could ever tell against the alternative we have chosen to espouse which they no doubt would in most cases – we should immediately challenge a criterion that did. No amount of honest intention to place oneself on the standpoint of the public welfare or of the nation's interest avails against that. For the point is precisely that these words carry different meanings for different minds. The only thing we can do in something like a scientific frame of mind is therefore to try to visualize, irrespective of our wishes, the actual situations which may be expected to emerge and the relative power of the groups which will be in a position to assert their interests and ideals in handling those situations.

Another point should be borne in mind. No social system is ever pure either in its economic or in its political aspects. As regards the former, structural principles, such as, in the case of commercial society, private management of the process of production and free contracting, are never fully carried to their logical consequences. People were at no time allowed to do with their own quite as they pleased, and society at all times limited the range within which they might freely contract. In the epoch of intact capitalism, law, custom, public opinion, and public administration enforced a certain amount of public planning, while in a society that had adopted the structural principles of socialism there was such a thing as Lenin's New Economic Policy that left room for a certain amount of *laissez faire*. It follows that, public management or planning being never either absent or complete, our question concerning the immediate future should not be couched in terms of "capitalism or socialism": there is a great variety of intermediate possibilities.

Still more important for social diagnosis and prognosis is, as we shall presently see, the fact that no society is ever homogeneous. By this I do not merely mean that the political sector of every society grows out of, and hence reflects, all the different interests and attitudes of the various groups and classes that the prevailing social system produces. I mean something much more fundamental: every society contains, at any given time, elements that are the products of different social systems. Thus, feudal society harbored, besides the lords and peasants and artisans that constituted the essential elements of its system, also other elements – traders, for instance, and certain classes of producers – that did not belong to the feudal organism and dwelt in towns which that organism failed to subjugate or to assimilate. In the capitalist epoch, the classes that are the products of the capitalist process are hardly ever found alone. Practically always they exist in symbiosis with an aristocracy and a peasantry of noncapitalist origin. And this fact is not only, as one might think, responsible for frictions and other secondary phenomena. It is of the essence of the social process. A purely capitalist society – consisting of nothing but entrepreneurs, capitalists, and proletarian workmen – would work in ways completely different from those we observe historically, if indeed it could exist at all.[2]

II

Both in its international and in its domestic aspects, capitalist economy is adapted to the requirements and habits of a normally pacific world. "Total war" under modern conditions calls for a concentration of effort much more stringent than the mechanism of capitalist markets can achieve. Wartime planning by government in fact suspends the normal operation of capitalist processes. In doing so it develops, on the one hand, economic structures and situations and, on the other hand, new social organs and positions of power which do not automatically disappear with the emergency that brought them into existence. They have to be liquidated, if at all, by a series of distinct measures which naturally meet resistance. We have seen that the outcome of the ensuing struggle will not depend on any abstract desirability of a return to prewar ways but on the political forces marshaled for and against it.

The strength of these forces in turn will depend, first, on the duration of the war in question and, second, on the vitality of the capitalist system independently of the war. Thus, in 1919, the United States emerged from a spell of wartime planning that had been both mild and short. The various war boards and their bureaucracies had not had time to get into full working order, let alone to settle into positions which they would have looked upon as permanent. The business world and the public in general had not had the time to get accustomed to their rule and to accept them as parts of the normal scheme of things. Moreover, all the groups that counted politically were fully determined to stand for private enterprise and in fact did not clearly perceive an alternative – which fact indicates precisely that the vitality of American capitalist society then was not yet substantially impaired.

This historical instance should not blind us to the possibility that events such as total war may influence social evolution more profoundly than words like "catastrophe" and "conflagration" imply. They may create situations so compelling as to impose permanent depar-

tures from the lines previously followed, and attitudes greatly at variance with any observed before. They may change the distribution of
political power in unpredictable ways. The bolshevist regime is obviously of more than passing importance; yet it could never have established itself without the First World War and the largely accidental
ways in which that war affected Russia. We may indeed succeed in
interpreting the break as the result of existing tendencies that were
merely accelerated by the war, and thus formally salvage historical
determinism as a philosophy. But this does not increase its value as a
working hypothesis.

There cannot be any doubt but that, in all countries concerned, the
present war effort will put existing social structures under severe strain
which may result in breakdown or fundamental transformation. The
chances for this to happen are presumably greater in vanquished countries, but the victor countries are by no means exempt from this possibility. All the more important is it to raise the question of what we
may term the tensile strength of the social systems that are being
exposed to that strain.

It is a commonplace that capitalist society is, and for some time has
been, in a state of decay. But there is no agreement about the precise
nature of that decay. Differences of opinion on this point can be conveniently described in terms of two theories.

There is, first, the familiar theory of Vanishing Investment
Opportunity.[3] It starts from an undeniable truth, more or less explicit
recognition of which constitutes its chief merit. Unlike other economic
systems, the capitalist system is geared to incessant economic change.
Its very nature implies recurrent industrial revolutions which are the
main sources of the profit and interest incomes of entrepreneurs and
capitalists and supply the main opportunities for new investments –
such as railroad building or the construction of electric-power plants –
and the main outlets for new savings. Whereas a stationary feudal
economy would still be a feudal economy, and a stationary socialist
economy would still be a socialist economy, stationary capitalism is a
contradiction in terms. This becomes evident when we survey its most
characteristic types, processes, and institutions, all of which would
become atrophic in a stationary world.

Now the theory in question holds that this is happening in our day.
That process of economic conquest is exhausting its possibilities. No
very great innovations are in prospect, and those minor ones that may
be said to be in the offing fail to stimulate entrepreneurship and investment either because they are capital-saving rather than capital-

consuming or else because they are more suited to public than to private management. Moreover the great impetus given to investment in the nineteenth century by the opportunity of opening up new countries and sources of raw materials has spent itself. Finally the falling birth rate and the consequent slackening of the rate of increase in population tend to dry up a source of particularly calculable investments. For all these reasons the saving–investment process, which is of obviously vital importance to capitalist society, works with increasing friction. Thrift, instead of being the means of expanding the industrial equipment becomes a cause of falling prices and of unemployment. Hence the necessity of injecting into an anemic system new purchasing power: the first and foremost application of this theory was in fact to provide a rationale for the [Keynesian] fiscal policies of the past decade. Hence also – so we may continue for our purpose – progressive paralysis of the political organs of capitalist society and reduced ability to withstand shocks or to defend itself against attack.

This theory cannot be adequately discussed here.[4] It must suffice to state that there does not seem to be any good reason for believing that, except as a temporary effect of the world crisis, the opportunity for great innovations in the economic process has been exhausted; that the tendency of innovations to become capital-saving to the required extent has been illustrated by examples but has not been established convincingly; that the opening up of new countries, even if we assume it to be completed, was but one of many opportunities and might be replaced by others – in fact has been replaced by others during the 1920s; that the falling birth rate, both through its direct effects on demand and through its indirect effects on motivation, may become economically significant in the future but that it could hardly be used in an explanation of the course of events in the 1930s, even if the relation between the rate of increase in population and economic progress were less complex than it actually is.

The theory of vanishing investment opportunity obviously invokes the factors mentioned in order to deduce from them a state of perennial inadequacy of profit expectations or, to use Lord Keynes's term, of the marginal efficiency of capital. It is only by this effect on profit expectations that those factors can be held to account for insufficient investment and, in turn, for underemployment. But, surely, if profit expectations are the operative link in the deduction, it is natural to stress another element the reality of which cannot be called into question and which acted on profit expectations much more obviously, *viz.*, the anti-capitalist policies adopted, in most European countries, ever since the First World War and, in the United States, since 1933. The fact that both in Europe and in the United States the capitalist process displayed unmistakable symptoms of strain exactly since the break in the legislative and administrative attitudes of public authority occurred may be significant. This element constitutes the pivot of the other theory.[5] It also starts from the proposition that capitalism is essentially a process of economic change and then goes on, as follows.

One of the most familiar phenomena of that process of change, the full importance of which was first recognized by Karl Marx, is the emergence of large-scale business, which to some extent tends to compete out of existence – or, to use the Marxian phrase, to "expropriate" – small or medium-sized firms. It stands to reason that, especially under conditions of democratic politics, this process weakens the political position of the industrial bourgeoisie, for a numerous stratum of businessmen owning and managing small or medium-sized firms is obviously much less exposed to political attack and in a much better position to withstand it than is a small number of salaried executives and large shareholders,[6] *quite irrespective of comparative economic performance or "service."* Moreover, within the big concern the pungent sense of property and the will to fight for it tooth and nail withers away: the big concern thus not only "expropriates" some of its competitors but also its own capitalist interest. Those executives and shareholders are not only in a less favorable position to defend their ground than were the owner-managers of old but they meet attack in a much weaker spirit. Big business is in fact but a midway house on the road toward socialism.

The capitalist process undermines the structure of capitalist society in many other ways. I shall mention two only. First, it tends to destroy, economically or socially, the position of what may be termed the protective strata. The rise of the bourgeoisie ousted from political leadership the old aristocracies who knew so much better how to rule than does the businessman. The factory destroyed the old crafts and the department or chain store destroys the small traders who counted at the polls. It also reduced, relatively at least, the number of farmers and peasants. And so on. Second, capitalist civilization is a rationalist civilization. It tends to eliminate extra- or hyperrational sanctions and habits of mind without which no society can exist.

Though the argument cannot be adequately developed, it should be clear that we have now before us the elements of a more realistic substitute for, or of a more realistic version of, the theory of vanishing investment opportunity and of the decay of capitalist society. The capitalist process itself produces, as effectively as it produces motorcars or refrigerators, a distribution of political power, an attitude of the public mind, and an orientation of the political sector that are at variance with its own law of life. It produces anti-capitalist policies, i.e., policies that, regardless of individual intentions, prevent it from functioning according to its logic, the implications of which increasingly meet moral disapproval. Modern principles of taxation, although only one among many manifestations, of the disintegration of capitalist society, afford perhaps the most telling illustration.

It is a nice question, on which it is much easier to differ than to agree, how far this decay has gone in any given case. Some symptoms showed in Europe before the First World War, but without it the majority of observers might have taken a long time in becoming aware of them. In the United States, the first unmistakable symptom of decay was perhaps the lack of spirit displayed by the bourgeoisie toward the end of the world crisis when the modal business-man proved that he was no longer up to the tests imposed by his own order of things. That the decay of capitalist society is very far advanced by now – everywhere – is not open to doubt. However much we may approve of some or all of the policies of the New Deal, we cannot fail to be struck by the absence of any serious resistance to them. A bourgeois society that meekly accepts the vast transfer of wealth accomplished in the United States during the 1930s – I am not speaking of war taxation – thereby testifies to its readiness to surrender, though it may not be ready to surrender to every type of conqueror. It is in such conditions that events like world wars may acquire an importance in shaping the history of institutional patterns which they could never acquire if they impinged on an intact social system.

III

We are now in a position to form an idea about the various possibilities concerning the capitalist order's survival in the postwar world. It is first necessary to visualize the economic and political situation that will confront the dominant political groups at the end of the war. In what follows we shall confine ourselves to the United States and consider no other case but that of complete victory.

Everybody is afraid of a postwar slump, threatening from a drastic reduction of military expenditure financed by inflationary methods as well as from mere reorientation of production. The all but general opinion seems to be that capitalist methods will be unequal to the task of reconstruction. This opinion in itself will be a political factor of first-rate importance. All the more essential is it to understand its rationale.

Viewed as a purely economic problem, that task might well turn out to be much easier than most people believe. It may happen that peace will be preceded by a period of decreasing military expenditure and of gradually increasing production for civilian consumption and also that the former will continue, though at a reduced rate, on a level much beyond that of prewar times. Either or both of these possibilities would greatly facilitate transition. But in any case, the wants of impoverished households will be so urgent and so calculable that any postwar slump that may be unavoidable would speedily give way to a reconstruction boom. Capitalist methods have proved equal to much more difficult tasks.

Nevertheless the opinion that the capitalist solution of the problem will prove unworkable or, at all events, unsatisfactory, may well be true. For, like any other system, capitalism cannot be expected to function efficiently except on its own terms, that is to say, in a social atmosphere that accepts its responsibilities and incentives and allows it sufficient freedom of action. As we have seen, however, such an atmosphere and the corresponding attitude of public authority have not existed for some time, do not exist now, and are obviously unlikely to exist in future. Capitalist management would hence have to solve the problems of reconstruction at home and abroad in the face of public antagonism, under burdens which eliminate capitalist motivation and make it impossible to accumulate venture capital, with risks of borrowing greatly increased,[7] without authority in the plant, and under the close control of a hostile bureaucracy. Deadlock so complete as to practically impose socialism as the only alternative is not inconceivable, but even conditions far removed from deadlock may preclude performance comparable to that of the past.

To be sure, a temporary revulsion of public sentiment in favor of *laissez faire* is not unthinkable. I need hardly stay however in order to show how very improbable it is. The public mind has renounced allegiance to the capitalist scheme of values. Private wealth is under a moral ban. All those bars to the effective functioning of capitalism embody what to most of us are cherished achievements. In particular, reduction of the fiscal burdens imposed upon the high income brackets and upon large-scale business and removal of administrative fetters would be highly unpopular and could hardly be carried to the requisite extent in a situation in which high rates of taxes on all incomes will continue to be necessary. Intellectuals and organized labor will emerge from the war in a radical frame of mind. Nobody will dare and, what is more, nobody will care to advocate what would have to be a return not only to prewar conditions but – substantially – to the conditions of 1929.

Nor will there be a motive for any of the political groups of significant importance to influence the public mind in a procapitalist direction. Any regime that may be established will have to court the farm group and to present attractive schemes of agricultural "planning." Farmers therefore might not be actively hostile to partial reversal of anti-capitalist policies – especially if their views about railroads were taken account of – but they will see little reason why they should go out of their way for the sake of it. Organized labor will find it impossible to abandon any of the positions it has conquered even if some labor leaders should entertain doubts as to their economic value. The strata of small and medium-sized business still constitute a factor which no regime can afford to neglect. But they can be satisfied without making any concessions to big business which embodies the achievements and the vital energies of the American economy.

Thus there is a reasonable chance that the bureaucratic apparatus of the Federal administration will hold its own. At the end of the war it will first of all be in possession. It will have outgrown initial difficulties and be in something like working order. It will have consolidated its position and have acquired enormous power. It will be a factor in its own right and stand ready to deal with the postwar emergency as it dealt with the war emergency. Political forces strong enough to liquidate the organs of the war economy as they were liquidated in 1919 are not in sight. There seems to be no reason why these organs should not succeed in establishing themselves as permanent institutions, especially as they will be in a position to serve the immediate interests of agriculture and of labor and hence derive support from these quarters. In this case a sort of *classe dirigente* may develop.

The nature, structure, and ideology of this managing class is not determined as yet. Many mutually exclusive possibilities exist both as to what it will eventually turn out to be and as to what it will eventually do. Disregarding all other aspects and placing ourselves on a purely economic standpoint, we may, however, out of a mash in full process of fermentation, select a few typical possibilities each of which corresponds to the views and interests of some existing subgroup.

1. The most obvious possibility is that the economic principles of the period immediately preceding the war will be applied to postwar problems – being consolidated and developed, revised and extended,

according to circumstances. In this case the policy of income-generating public expenditure would be continued, first in order to prevent or mitigate the postwar slump and after that as a permanent device for regulating the pulse of the nation's economic life. As the reader knows, this policy commands widespread support. The fear of the postwar slump may well silence such opposition as may be said to exist. And groups with completely different ultimate aims may agree on it because it is the easiest way toward all of them and carries the further advantage that none of them need be mentioned in advocating it.

Theorists are in the habit of dealing with this policy in the abstract. But its nature and consequences depend upon the complementary policies with which it is linked. In the case under discussion, these are taxation high enough and progressive enough to prevent private accumulation and in consequence the possibility that large-scale business should ever again, financially speaking, stand on its own feet and become independent of government; labor legislation that shifts questions of wages, hours, and factory discipline to the political sphere; and strict regulation, enforced by the threat of prompt prosecution, of the behavior of big business in every respect. Under these conditions, public income generation will automatically become permanent, quite irrespective of the factors stressed by the theories framed to prove its necessity from causes inherent in the saving–investment process of capitalist society.

Such a system will no doubt still be called capitalism. But it is capitalism in the oxygen tent–kept alive by artificial devices and paralyzed in all those functions that produced the successes of the past. The question why it should be kept alive at all is therefore bound to be put before long. Such concessions about relief from war rates of taxation and so on as are within practical politics, may temporarily change details of the picture and postpone the putting of that question, but cannot be expected to change essentials.

2. It will therefore be perfectly natural – in fact it may be a practical necessity – to take further steps toward state management.

To begin with, it is difficult to see what role will be left for non-public banking and finance in an economic world thoroughly dependent on government financing that is itself entirely independent of private voluntary saving. Government, to be sure, still goes through the motions of "borrowing" and "lending," pays and receives interest and so on. But the life has gone out of these forms and an administrative rationalization of what is actually being done could easily eliminate them. If we assume that capitalist methods will disappear gradually there will be a narrowing sphere of activity for banks as we know them also in the future. They may continue to keep accounts and to fill administrative functions for an indefinite time. But though this may facilitate transitions it does not alter the fact that, if we must stick to old words, government will develop into the sole banker.

Again, government spending as a permanent policy cannot fail to develop into governmental planning of investment. In fact, its failure to do so would be quite uneconomical. If government expenditure is to be the pivot of the economic process it stands to reason that the productive efforts propelled by that expenditure will in the end have to be directed by public authority. The government will from time to time have to proclaim a national goal which its expenditure is to serve – such as housing for the masses, completion of the electrification of the household, reorganization of the transport system and of urban life to make them fit the conditions created by the airplane – and to define the ways in which and the extent to which each particular goal is to be approached.

There is still another reason for this. Whatever the outcome of the war, the postwar world will hardly be a place for privately controlled trade and industrial venture. As to the first, it is not easy to see how private enterprise could cope with the conditions created by the immense differences as between countries in monetary and real cost of production that have developed of late.[8] From a purely commercial standpoint, and taking account of all the "rigidities" that will prevent adaptation, the United States might well be unable to export at all.[9] Quite apart from the political considerations that are bound to complicate the problem still further, international trade in commodities and services will have to be cut off from its old background of commercial calculation and have to be managed by political treaties, bilateral and multilateral. But this implies domestic public management just as the latter implies the public management of international economic relations.

As to the second, international industrial venture[s] involving long-term investment, the need for government leadership, perhaps on lend-lease lines, in an expansion that will inevitably carry imperialist features, is still more obvious. The spacious possibilities that open up under these heads should be noted not less than the sources such a system harbors of waste surpassing anything ever charged to the account of capitalism. It should also be noted that such a system leaves the managing bureaucracy free to allocate to private business as much or as little room as may be desired. Just as the TVA, a national venture, let contracts to private firms, so a similar national venture on the Yangtze, though initiated by government and controlled by it, may parcel out individual jobs to capitalist firms. Therefore, on the understanding that the essence of the bourgeois economy will be absent from the picture, we may call this system Guided Capitalism.

3. Some measures of nationalization will almost inevitably suggest themselves in a system of the type just discussed. Moreover, other measures – perhaps the nationalization or municipalization of utilities, of insurance, of mines – will be rendered easy by public support. It is difficult to foretell how far this tendency will go. The term "nationalization" does not sound well to every ear and it may be that other means of establishing no less complete public control, even if less rational and fraught with more friction, will be preferred by the political groups in power. But if the Federal government should follow this line to a significant extent, and if it should try to run the nationalized industries according to the principles of business rationality, Guided Capitalism would shade off into State Capitalism, a system that may be characterized by the following features: government ownership and management of selected industrial positions; complete control of government in the labor and capital market; government initiative in domestic and foreign enterprise.

4. It will always be a matter of taste whether a given way of running the economic engine be called socialist or not. On the one hand, disgruntled bourgeois spoke of socialism when the first municipal gas works and the first progressive income taxes put in appearance; on the other hand, socialist groups that are not "in on it" will never admit that anything not sanctified by Marxian doctrine can possibly be genuine socialism. Moreover, people care so much more for words than they do for things, that acceptance or avoidance of the term socialism may be dictated by tactical considerations. In this country, these considerations seem to tell against rather than for it so long as no violent break is on the cards.

If, however, we agree that advance on any of the lines we have briefly surveyed comes within the definition of gradual socialization, the problem narrows down considerably. Any approach to socialism other than by continued extension of government control and expropriation of the upper strata by taxation would no doubt meet resistance from the farm interest and from small and medium-sized business. Neither would put up a life-and-death fight in order to prevent the nationalization of big business – say, the corporations owning assets amounting to $50 million or more. But they presumably would fight against anything much more radical than this, particularly against anything which they recognize as a "revolution." Barring such a revolution which, while never impossible, cannot be expected to be successful, an amphibial state for the calculable future is certainly the most probable one. From a purely economic standpoint this may be regrettable. Such a state will suffer from a lot of frictions and inefficiencies that a return to the capitalist alternative or a resolute adoption of the socialist one would save, and it will not command the full motive power of either. On the other hand, amphibial states conserve many human values that would perish in others. Thus there may be as little reason for the fears of some as there is for the hopes of others.

Notes

1. It should be noted that this definition of socialism is not only purely economic but also purely formal. It says nothing about the structure and character of a socialist society, e.g., whether it is equalitarian or not, warlike or pacific, democratic or authoritarian. Friends and foes of socialism are in the habit of endowing their concept of it with additional traits and hence in general mean by it something much more specific.
2. Many readers will feel that while this might apply to European and Asiatic countries, it could not possibly apply to the United States. But it would be easy to enumerate the very particular conditions now rapidly passing – which explain why a purely bourgeois regime was in this case able to hold its own for so considerable a time.
3. The outstanding exponent of this theory is Prof. Alvin H. Hansen; see, e.g., his *Fiscal Policy and Business Cycles* (New York, 1941), Ch. 1, and his essay in S. E. Harris (ed.), *Postwar Economic Problems* (New York: McGraw-Hill, 1943).
4. I refer the reader to the discussion in my *Business Cycles* (New York, 1939), Vol. 11, Ch. XV.
5. I have developed it at length in my *Capitalism, Socialism, and Democracy* (1942), Part II.
6. Here, any adequate exposition of that theory would have to digress into political sociology in order to show that the behavior of a society toward a particular interest is primarily determined by the inducement and the opportunity for attacking it and only to a minor degree by what the observer according to his own standards may consider justifiable reasons for approving or disapproving of it. These reasons, so far as produced by political or intellectual agents, are simply rationalizations in the psychological sense.
7. High or highly progressive taxation of profits increases the risks of borrowing for purposes of long-run investment, because it absorbs profits the accumulation of which might be counted on to take care of subsequent losses.
8. This position in not inconsistent, however, with the theory of comparative costs.
9. The roots of this difficulty are in the prewar situation. One of the most curious contradictions in New Deal policy was its attempt to "liberalize" foreign trade while erecting a rigid economic structure at home.

Part III

The Golden Age of Capitalism: Large Corporations and the Regulatory State

9

The Technostructure, the Industrial System, and the State (1967)[*]

John Kenneth Galbraith

In the past, leadership in business organization was identified with the entrepreneur – the individual who united ownership or control of capital with capacity for organizing the other factors of production and, in most contexts, with a further capacity for innovation.[1] With the rise of the modern corporation, the emergence of the organization required by modern technology and planning and the divorce of the owner of the capital from control of the enterprise, the entrepreneur no longer exists as an individual person in the mature industrial enterprise.[2] Everyday discourse, except in the economics textbooks, recognizes this change. It replaces the entrepreneur, as the directing force of the enterprise, with management. This is a collective and imperfectly defined entity; in the large corporation it embraces chairman, president, those vice presidents with important staff or departmental responsibility, occupants of other major staff positions and, perhaps, division or department heads not included above. It includes, however, only a small proportion of those who, as participants, contribute information to group decisions. This latter group is very large; it extends from the most senior officials of the corporation to where it meets, at the outer perimeter, the white and blue collar workers whose function is to conform more or less mechanically to instruction or routine. It embraces all who bring specialized knowledge, talent or experience to group decision-making. This, not the management, is the guiding intelligence – the brain – of the enterprise. There is no name for all

---

[*] From *The New Industrial State* (Boston: Houghton Mifflin, 1967), pp. 70–1, 296–306, 308–17.

who participate in group decision-making or the organization which they form. I propose to call this organization the Technostructure.

I

Qualified manpower is decisive for the success of the industrial system. The education on which it depends is provided mostly in the public sector of the economy. By contrast, capital, which was once decisive, comes mostly from the private economy. The market for the most advanced technology and that which best allows of planning is also in the public sector. Much scientific and technical innovation comes from, or is sponsored by, the state or by publicly supported universities and research institutions. The state regulates the aggregate demand for the products of the industrial system. This is indispensable for its planning. And, still discreetly and with infirmity of intent, somewhat in the manner of a conservative cleric viewing an erotic statue, the state provides the wage and price regulation without which prices in the industrial system are unstable. Clearly the modern organized economy was designed with a perverse hand. For how, otherwise, could so many needs seeming so inescapable conspire to make a system which still rejoices in the name of free enterprise in truth be so dependent on government?

The industrial system, in fact, is inextricably associated with the state. In notable respects the mature corporation is an arm of the state. And the state, in important matters, is an instrument of the industrial system. This runs strongly counter to the accepted doctrine. That assumes and affirms a clear line between government and private business enterprise. The position of this line – what is given to the state and what is accorded to private enterprise – tells whether the society is socialist or non-socialist. Nothing is so important. Any union between public and private organization is held, by liberal and conservative alike, to be deviant sin. To the liberal it means that public power has been captured for private advantage and profit. To the conservative it means that high private prerogative has been lost to the state. In fact, the line between public and private authority in the industrial system is indistinct and in large measure imaginary, and the abhorrent association of public and private organizations is normal. When this is perceived, the central trends in American economic and political life become clear. On few matters is an effort to free the mind more rewarding.

The relationship between the technostructure and the state is very different from that between the state and the entrepreneurial enterprise. This difference is our point of departure.

II

The relationship between the state and the entrepreneurial corporation was, like all of the other relationships of this entity, principally pecuniary. It was also unstable with a tendency to be a zero sum game. The corporation might be strong. Then it would be independent of public restraint. It might even use public power to enhance its own revenues. Or the state might be strong in which case it curbed the private power, and therewith the profits, of the entrepreneur. If extremely powerful, the state would move to socialize such enterprise. Weakness on one side would be exploited by the other. Constant and reciprocal vigilance would be necessary to prevent domination of the state by business or of business by the state.

Such was the common view of the relationship between the entrepreneurial corporation and the state. The balance in this relationship is assumed to have altered over time. Seventy-five years ago, in the United States, it was believed that the corporation was naturally the paramount power. Business control of the state was the thing to fear. Men of subtle mind agreed with Marx that the state would come to be the executive committee of capitalist enterprise. With the passage of time, however, fear of business domination receded while fear of state domination increased. The corporation was once the octopus. This became the image of government. Where entrepreneurs had once gathered in the Senate to consider the needs of their class, they now gathered in convention to deplore the intentions of Washington. Golf, once an opportunity for consolidating power over some aspect of the life of the community, became an occasion for collective complaint about bureaucrats. Both the earlier and later fears reflect the circumstances of the entrepreneurial corporation. Though both continue to influence contemporary attitudes, neither reflects the modern reality.

As noted, the relationship of the entrepreneurial corporation to the state, in accordance with the principle of consistency, was primarily a pecuniary one. The state had much to offer that was of pecuniary advantage and, through taxation and regulation, it could do much to deny revenues to the corporation. The entrepreneurial corporation, in turn, had much with which to pay for what it wanted. And it had few legal or other barriers to doing so.

Thus the state, through the tariff, could accord the entrepreneur protection from foreign competition; it also had railroad, power or other public utility franchises to grant; it possessed land, mineral rights, forests and other natural resources for private exploitation; it could offer exemption or mitigation of taxes; and it could provide moral or armed support in managing refractory workers. As a further and important point, these and other benefits could all be given or withheld in response to relatively simple decision.

The entrepreneurial enterprise had, in turn, the ability to deploy financial resources for political ends that reflected its advantage. The entrepreneur unites in his own person the right to receive and dispose of the revenues of the enterprise. So revenues are at his command for purchase of votes, legislators or legislative action. If he is subject to some legal constraint in the expenditure of corporate funds for political purposes, he can transfer them, as dividends, to himself and his associates and spend from a privy purse. The public benefits so purchased accrue to the entrepreneur. This, along with the commitment to pecuniary motivation, meant that the entrepreneurial corporation had every incentive to spend for political advantage. The financial resources of the corporation could be fully deployed for political purposes and that by the men who derived personal advantage from doing so.

In a society where economic activity is subject strongly to pecuniary motivation, such motivation will seem normal in the relations between business firms and the state. It will be assumed that public officials will be responsive to opportunity for pecuniary gain. Nor will this seem totally iniquitous. Where the society approves and applauds moneymaking as the highest social purpose, public servants will often think it appropriate that they sell themselves or their decisions for what they are worth to the buyers.

In the heyday of the entrepreneurial corporation this occurred. The company town and the company-dominated state – California of the Southern Pacific, Montana of Anaconda, Pennsylvania of the steel and coal companies, Michigan of the automobile companies – were familiar features of the industrial landscape. It was assumed that Congressmen and Senators would be the spokesmen, paid or otherwise, of the industrial firms of their states or districts. From those so financed or controlled, the entrepreneurial corporation got much of what it wanted. The control was not absolute but it was sufficiently extensive to justify belief in corporate domination as a normal fact of life.

To this day, the independent entrepreneur – the highway contractor, insurance firm, real estate operator, loan shark – is the most important source of political funds and the principal remaining exponent of purchased influence. Those who have won major distinction in this general area in modern times have all been independent entrepreneurs. Texas oil operators, almost alone among modern businessmen, are able to obtain implicit obedience from their state's Congressional delegation.

While the entrepreneurial corporation had resources with which to purchase pecuniary opportunity from the state, it was also independent of the state. Its revenues were made in the market. Thence came its instructions. Had it need to fight the state, the battle might cost it money but it would not be mortal.

III

In time, as noted, the fear that the corporation would dominate the state was matched and replaced by the fear that the state would dominate business. This change occurred especially in the 1930s. There were two causes: the rise of the trade union and the response of the state to the new needs of the industrial system.

The Great Depression gave a strong impetus to the trade union movement. By destroying his alternatives and thus increasing the element of compulsion in his attachment to his job, the depression arrested any tendency for the worker to identify himself with the goals of his employer. And it made the union more important to the worker. He needed its support against pressures for wage reduction. As his alternatives dwindled the union compensated for his weakness and countered his sense of compulsion. As they grew in membership in this favorable environment, the unions became a factor in politics; as their role was adversary within the corporation so it was adversary in their influence on the state. What the unions lacked in financial resources they compensated for in voting power. They found an ally in the emerging educational and scientific[3] estate with its long-standing alienation from the entrepreneurial corporation. This, with some support from the farmers, was the heart of the Roosevelt coalition. It was easy for business enterprise to imagine that it was about to pass under the political authority of a state permanently dominated by the unions and the "intellectuals."

At the same time the entrepreneurial corporation was giving way steadily to the mature corporation and to control by the technostructure. In their study of the 200 largest nonfinancial corporations in 1930, Berle and Means found that, by then, 44 per cent of the firms by numbers and 58 per cent by wealth were effectively controlled by their management.[4]

For direct political action the technostructure is far more circumscribed than the entrepreneur. This is a matter of prime importance.

The members of the technostructure do not themselves receive the revenues of the corporation. An early gesture, designed to limit the political advantage of the business enterprise resulting from its wealth, prohibited the use of corporate funds for political purposes. This did not greatly hurt the entrepreneur; he could, as noted, transfer the funds to his own account as dividends and spend with impunity. But this the technostructure cannot do; it does not get the dividends.

Nor does it have the same incentive to do so. Bribery of public officials, purchase of the electorate or promiscuous use of financial power to influence public decision (e.g. the threat to discharge workers or close a plant) are not especially prestigious activities. They often result in unpleasant publicity; there is risk in all bribery that the practitioner's hand will slip and that he will be publicly pilloried by all who have not received his subvention and by the more adaptable of those who have. These risks were often worthwhile for the entrepreneur; the mantle of the sanguinary industrial pirate can be worn with some comfort if the wearer receives the loot. But it is not something one does on a salary.

The technostructure is also handicapped in its political activity by its collegial character. Political leadership, persuasion and action are activities of individuals; they are not readily undertaken by men who are accustomed to operating as a group. The mature corporation is run by committees. But the suborning of a legislature or even the persuasion of an electorate is accomplished, on the whole, by men working as individuals.

This point cannot be carried too far. The technostructure has ready access to communications media – press, television, radio – and thus to political influence. In mature corporations which have particular need for favorable political action – the alcoholic beverage industry has in the past been an example – executives pay themselves salaries which provide a margin for political purposes. Much minor bribery is still used by mature corporations to buy needed action or inaction from state legislatures. And ample funds are available for persuasive lobbying, as distinct from the older forms of direct purchase of legislators or votes. Nevertheless the conclusion stands. The technostructure of the mature corporation is far less able to deploy financial resources for political purposes than was the entrepreneurial corporation, has less incentive to do so and, in consequence of its group character, is far less effective in direct political action.

The opposition to the rising power of the state in the 1930s, like opposition to the rising power of the unions, was led not by the mature corporations but by the surviving entrepreneurs. The names of Ernest Weir, Thomas Girdler, Henry Ford, the du Ponts and Sewell Avery are associated with this resistance. General Motors, General Electric, US Steel and other mature corporations were much more inclined to accept such innovations as NRA [National Recovery Administration], to be somewhat more philosophical about Roosevelt and otherwise to accommodate themselves to the New Deal.

IV

Nor is this all. We have seen that much government activity has a very different effect on the entrepreneurial corporation as compared with the mature corporation. What is damaging to the first is benign for the second. This began to be evident in the 1930s and became increasingly so thereafter. The striking case was the regulation of aggregate demand. Such regulation, we have sufficiently seen, is essential for the effective planning of the industrial system and, accordingly, for the security and success of the technostructure. A large public sector, supported by a progressive tax structure and with such added offsets to declining-income as unemployment insurance, is not welcome in itself. But it is the fulcrum of the regulatory apparatus. Members of the technostructure do not themselves have to pay the corporation income tax which is a central part of this machinery. It falls on the stockholders or, given the control of prices, can be passed along to customers. Social security taxes and associated record-keeping are, for the technostructure, merely administrative problems to be solved.

The entrepreneurial corporation, by contrast, had less need for the regulation of aggregate demand, and its owners stood much more of the cost. Being in an earlier stage of development, it did less planning. So it was less troubled by fluctuations in demand. The entrepreneur was answerable to himself for a failure in earnings; however disagreeable, it did not necessarily threaten his survival. He had less organization to protect. Meanwhile since he sought, in principle, to maximize earnings, higher corporation taxes came out of that maximum and with incidence on himself. Similarly with his share of social security taxes. And similarly with administrative costs and annoyances.

Other accommodation by the state to the needs of the industrial system also had a contrasting effect. The entrepreneurial corporation, again as a result of its lower level of development, had less need for the trained personnel that the state provided. Its technology being more primitive, it had less to gain from public underwriting of research and markets. Unions, the subject of state encouragement and support, perform, we have just seen, a ministerial and communications role for the mature corporation;[5] for the entrepreneurial corporation their purpose remained the winning of a larger share of the profits. Restraints on prices which for the mature corporation helped insure wage and price stability could be a way of reducing returns for the entrepreneur.

It would be a mistake to paint this contrast in unduly sharp tones. The tendency nonetheless is unmistakable. What seemed, at first glance, to be a damaging accession of power by the state was damaging principally to the entrepreneurial corporation. For the mature corporation it was not. Rather, it reflected the accommodation of the state to its needs.

From the 1930s on, the fear of government by business seemed to be a uniform and permanent feature of the American political landscape:

> Opposition to government is more than disaffection from the policies of a particular party or administration. The [American business] creed contains a generalized distrust and scorn of politicians and bureaucrats, whatever the party and whatever the politics they advocate and execute.[6]

But appearances are deceiving. Until comparatively recent times the tone and attitude of business in these matters were set by the entrepreneurs. Being without the political inhibition of organization, they were most outspoken. Unlike members of the technostructure they also had grievances. The members of the technostructure said nothing or they echoed the complaints of the entrepreneurs about government for this was the conventional wisdom of the businessman. Or they reacted only to their need for autonomy on internal decisions. The staffs of the business organizations continued, under inertial guidance, to recite the liturgy of entrepreneurial complaint. Entrepreneurs did not see that the accommodation of the state to the needs of the mature corporation was a substantial source of their discomfort. They did not see that they were, in effect, the victims of a passive conspiracy between other businessmen and the state.

V

The threads may now be drawn together. Business in its relations with the state is anything but homogeneous. Once, in the day of the entrepreneur and the entrepreneurial corporation, it was so. And it was also transcendent in its direct political power – its power over votes and legislators. The mature corporation does not exercise similar power. But it has won an accommodation by the state to its needs that is highly favorable. And this accommodation has not been nearly so favorable to the surviving entrepreneurs. Their position in relation to the state has been substantially weakened. While they seemed to have the general support of all business they, in fact, did not.[7] The mature corporations were all the time seeking many of the things the entrepreneurs most opposed.

It will be evident that at this stage there is a certain puzzle in the political position of the mature corporation. As we have seen, its capacity for, and incentive to, direct political action – management of the electorate, control of legislatures, procurement of legislation – is much less than that of its entrepreneurial antecedents. But, at the same time, the trend of public policy has been highly favorable to its needs. If this is accidental it reflects from the point of view of the mature corporation one of the happiest conjunctions of circumstance in history. But to explain anything of this importance in the closely interlocked system we are here examining as an accident would be odd. And it is nothing of the kind. As the industrial system in general, and the mature corporation in particular, have lost direct political power, they have acquired other methods of influencing social action of far, far greater significance. These explain the benign tendencies, from their viewpoint, of the state.

VI

We have seen that the technostructure of the mature corporation neither deploys the resources nor has the incentive for purchase of political power. At the same time it has become much more dependent on the state. The entrepreneurial corporation, from public resources to favorable tariffs to tax concessions, had much to get from the state. And from adverse regulation and higher taxation it had considerable to lose. But, apart from the provision of law and order which on occasion it supplied to itself, it was not deeply dependent on the government. The mature corporation by contrast depends on the state for trained manpower, the regulation of aggregate demand, for stability in wages and prices. All are essential to the planning with which it replaces the market. The state, through military and other technical procurement, underwrites the corporation's largest capital commitments in its area of

most advanced technology. The mature corporation cannot buy political power. Yet, obviously, it would seem to require it.

Its influence on the state is, in fact, much greater than that of the
entrepreneurial corporation. Those who look for it usually look in the
wrong place. Given the past pre-eminence of pecuniary relationships,
they naturally look for these. They look for legislators who are in the
pay of corporations and for public officials who are responsive to
financial blandishment. They delve for five-per-centers and lobbyists
who dispense alcohol, mink, vicuña, freezers, hospitality in Nassau and
New York hotel suites and the attention of far more vivid and adaptable young women than the public servant encounters of an evening
in Falls Church. The best discovery of all is of a traditionalist who
carries money in a black bag. These last are rare but every year one or
more exponents of one or another of the techniques of bribery is discovered and drummed out of the company of respectable men, often
with the help of those who, until recently, had thought well of such
resourcefulness. These victims are the archaic survivors of an earlier era
and methodology. Their public destruction for minor peculation – it
rarely amounts to the price of the most insignificant modern weapon –
is a purification rite. Minor sin is washed away in an orgiastic burst of
indignation. Iniquitous influence is thus extirpated from government.
It may well be to the advantage of the industrial system that simple
men should continue to suppose that influence is exerted on the state
principally by such means.

Members of the technostructure, we have seen, identify themselves
with its goals because they find these goals superior to their own and
because there is a chance of adapting them to their own. The relationship of the technostructure of the mature corporation to the state is
the same. The state is strongly concerned with the stability of the
economy. And with its expansion or growth. And with education. And
with technical and scientific advance. And, most notably, with the
national defense. These are the national goals; they are sufficiently trite
so that one has a reassuring sense of the obvious in articulating them.
All have their counterpart in the needs and goals of the technostructure. It requires stability in demand for its planning. Growth brings
promotion and prestige. It requires trained manpower. It needs government underwriting of research and development. Military and other
technical procurement support its most developed form of planning.
At each point the government has goals with which the technostructure can identify itself. Or, plausibly, these goals reflect adaptation of
public goals to the goals of the technostructure. As the individual

serves the technostructure in response to a complex system of motivation in which identification and adaptation are extremely important,
so the same motivation is reflected in the relations of the mature corporation to the state. Again we find the principle of consistency rendering faithful service. Therein lies the influence of the mature
corporation – an influence which makes purely pecuniary relationships
pallid by comparison.

Let us now give these abstractions specific form – and put them to
test.

VII

The practical manifestation of this process is to be seen most clearly in
defense procurement. With the $60 billion it spends for this purpose
each year (as this is written) the Department of Defense supports, as
noted, the most highly developed planning in the industrial system. It
provides contracts of long duration, calling for large investment of
capital in areas of advanced technology. There is no risk of price fluctuations. There is full protection against any change in requirements, i.e.,
any change in demand. Should a contract be canceled the firm is protected on the investment it has made. For no other products can the
technostructure plan with such certainty and assurance. Given the
inevitability of planning, there is much attraction in circumstances
where it can be done so well.

This leads the technostructure to identify itself closely with the goals
of the armed services and, not infrequently, with the specific goals of
the particular service, Army, Navy or Air Force, which it most intimately serves. Simple association, as in the case of individual and
organization, supports this tendency. In consequence the technostructure comes to see the same urgency in weapons development, the same
security in technical pre-eminence, the same requirement for a particular weapons system, the same advantage in an enlarged mission for
(say) the Air Force or Navy, as does the particular service itself. Its
members develop the same commitment to these goals as do officers of
the services.

This relationship accords parallel opportunity for adaptation. The
need to combine the work of diverse specialists and technicians means
that the development of (say) a new weapons system requires organization. This the technostructure, and frequently it alone, can provide. So
the armed services are deeply dependent on their supplying corporations for technical development. And, in practice, numerous other

tasks requiring the resources of organization – the planning of logistics systems, planning and development of base facilities, even on occasion the definitions of the missions of a particular service or one of its branches – are contracted out to supplying corporations.

> In its rapid climb during the fifties, the Air Force fostered a growing band of private companies which took over a substantial part of regular military operations, including maintaining aircraft, firing rockets, building and maintaining launching sites, organizing and directing other contractors, and making major public decisions ... The Air Force's success over her sister services ... established the magic formula that all federal agencies soon imitated.[8]

A firm that is developing a new generation of fighter aircraft is in an admirable position to influence the design and equipment of the plane. It can have something to say on the mission for which it is adapted, the number of planes required, their deployment, and, by implication, on the choice of the enemy toward which it is directed. This will reflect the firm's own views, and, *pari passu*, its own needs. If the firm has been accorded a more explicit planning function, it helps to establish assumptions as to probable enemies, points of probable attack, the nature of the resulting hostilities and the other factors on which defense procurement depends. In conjunction with other such planning, including, of course, that of public agencies, it helps to establish the official view of defense requirements and therewith of some part of the foreign policy. These will be a broad reflection of the firm's own goals; it would be eccentric to expect otherwise.

This influence is not absolute. In the autumn of 1962, the Department of Defense canceled plans for further development of the Skybolt, a missile of disturbingly erratic behavior designed for launching in flight from a manned bomber. If successful, it would have insured, in turn, a further demand for manned bombers, a weapon which otherwise would be obsolescent. In advertising and other forms of persuasion, the putative manufacturer made a strong case for the eventual technical proficiency of Skybolt and its importance in the defensive strategy of the United States. It failed. But the failure was not in this last rather desperate effort but in the earlier inability to have it incorporated, without particular public discussion, in the general catalog of military needs. This would have been the normal manifestation of influence.

VIII

Not only are identification and adaptation important for influencing decisions by the technostructure on weapons procurement, they are very nearly the only source of such influence.

We have seen that the head of the modern corporation cannot order up a new civilian product in response to a major exercise of imagination. The toaster will be recalled. It must emerge from the teams of scientists, engineers, designers, production experts, market researchers and sales executives. That is why power has shifted to, and into, the technostructure. For the same reason the modern business firm cannot buy defense decisions favorable to itself. There is, to speak loosely, no decision available for purchase. There is, instead, a process of decision-making in which many people participate over a long period of time. Some are members of the technostructure, some of the public agency. From this process come decisions on the feasibility, need for and design of an anti-missile system, a new transport aircraft or a new warhead of unparalleled destructive power. By then familiarity with the design and other requirements, including possession of the requisite technical knowledge and experience, will have gone far to decide who gets the contract. A new contender, entering at this point, would have little chance. There is influence only if there has been this prior and intimate and long-continued participation.

This was not always so. When the Army contracted for mules, blankets, shoes or muskets, an open-handed lobbyist or a determined legislator could have influence on the award. Only a simple, single decision was required; to control the decision, or the man who made it, was to control the outcome. To this day the Congress retains a certain voice on whether army bases, arsenals, ships' repair facilities and other relatively uncomplicated installations of an earlier period are to be used or abandoned. It has at best limited and more often no voice at all in the decision to proceed with or abandon a weapons system, a nuclear propulsion system or a space vehicle or as to who the manufacturer will be. These decisions are taken by teams and committees and then passed for review through a hierarchy of teams and committees. Participation in this process is again the key to power. Even a superior Secretary of Defense is deeply subordinate to this group decision-making, and the usual one is utterly so.

IX

In the nature of the market, one organization or enterprise sells to another and the boundaries between the two are sharp. This same delineation characterizes the private firm selling (say) powdered milk to the Department of Agriculture. But when planning replaces the market, and identification and adaptation supplement pecuniary compensation, matters are very different. No sharp line separates government from the private firm; the line becomes very indistinct and even imaginary. Each organization is important to the other; members are intermingled in daily work; each organization comes to accept the other's goals; each adapts the goals of the other to its own. Each organization, accordingly, is an extension of the other. The large aerospace contractor is related to the Air Force by ties that, however different superficially, are in their substance the same as those that relate the Air Force to the United States government. Shared goals are the decisive link in each case.

This notion is rather fiercely resisted. Tradition, derived from the antecedent separation of government and its suppliers by the market, defends a sharp separation of public from private activity. Socialism is not an evocative word in the United States. The myth of separation helps to suppress any suggestion that the mature corporation in its public business is, in principle, a part of a larger public bureaucracy. It also helps the technostructure defend its autonomy – and protect itself from a good deal of awkward supervision. Government interference on rates of pay, expense accounts, plant location, executive nepotism and patronage and numerous other matters of public or political interest can be minimized (though not wholly resisted) on the grounds that this is a private operation. Expenditure of public funds by a public agency is governed by a stern ethic. Attitudes toward nominally private firms, even when spending public funds, are considerably more relaxed. Only those who wish to be fooled will, however, ignore the reality which is that the modern motivational system blurs the line into irrelevance.

Although the firm is related to the procurement agencies by shared goals, the result of identification and adaptation, these do not, of course, exclude pecuniary compensation and motivation. A motivational system that combines identification and adaptation with pecuniary reward is internally consistent and self-reinforcing.[9] But as pay fails to explain the relationship of a general or a Pentagon official to his job, so pecuniary motivation fails equally to explain the relationship of the mature corporation to the procurement agencies. To suppose that the modern weapons-maker offers his wares to the government only for pay and profit, as did the vintage maker of muskets, has an overtone of hardy, muscular intelligence which appeals to the social radical including the Marxist. But so to believe is to see almost nothing of the modern reality of industrial power.

Nor, of course, is this power exercised only in relation to the Department of Defense. The National Space Agency, the Atomic Energy Commission, the Federal Aviation Agency and other public bodies all underwrite industrial planning with long-term contracts involving large capital outlays and advanced technology. There are few mature corporations which do not have this relationship with the modern state.

X

Identification and adaptation cannot ordinarily be reconciled with political hostility to the state or any particular party or administration. As noted, the entrepreneurial corporation did not have an intimate and continuing dependence on the state; its fortunes in respect of the state were affected by individual and discreet actions – the award of a contract, sale of public lands, imposition of a tax or tariff, passage of a regulation which it could influence as such without worrying excessively about the general political environment. But the mature corporation has a continuing and intimate relationship for which doors must always be open and access to public officials always be easy and without tension. Adverse political action or even hostile oratory lessens this ease of access. Men arriving with their briefcases for the day's meetings in Washington or at Wright Field cannot have the added burden of explaining the testimony of a company president who has just attacked the government and all its minions hip and thigh.

But this is not a mere matter of expediency. Identification is a psychological phenomenon. If it is operative, there can be no mental or moral barriers to accepting the goals of the state. Such will be the consequence of political polemics and conflict. To denounce Democrats as destroyers of business and liberal Republicans as conscious agents of Communism is to proclaim one's alienation from their goals. For the technostructure it means rejecting the identification and therewith the adaptation which are the source of its power. This, obviously, makes no sense.

We have here a guide to the political tendencies of the modern large corporation. Increasingly it will be passive rather than active in politics. It will eschew any strong identification with a political party – as the entrepreneur is identified with the Republican Party. It will not speak out on partisan issues. To some extent, perhaps, it will take on the political coloration of whatever party is in office.

All of this is by way of protecting a much stronger and more vital position of influence as an extension of the arm of the bureaucracy. In this role the corporation can participate in the decisions that count. It can help shape the highly technical choices which, in turn, govern the demand for its own military and other products. It will have access to the decisions on military strategy which establish the need for such products. And it will help to shape the current beliefs or assumptions on foreign policy. These, obviously, are a far more important power. It is the difference between the formal grandeur of the legislative hearing and the shirt-sleeved rooms with blackboards and tables heavy with data, drawings and tapes where the important decisions, bit by bit, are actually made. The technostructure selects its theater of influence with discrimination and intelligence.

XI

Industrial planning, we have seen, requires the control of prices and the management of the consumer. As a result, instruction passes not alone from the sovereign consumer to the producer; it proceeds also from the producer to the consumer in accordance with the needs of the technostructure. This is the revised sequence. The revised sequence operates also in the field of public procurement.

Those who, for purposes of rebuttal, would wish to find that I had argued that all public spending is an accommodation to the needs of the modern corporation will be disappointed. The influence of the industrial firm on military procurement is singularly a matter where those who reach inconvenient conclusions are impelled to make themselves vulnerable by overstatement. They are then destroyed by those who say that, since they do not value exact truth, they do not value truth. I seek to be less obliging. I argue only for a complex two-way flow of influence. That, however, has deep consequences for public action ...

Notes

1. "To act with confidence beyond the range of familiar beacons and to overcome that resistance requires aptitudes that are present in only a small fraction of the population and [they] define the entrepreneurial type as well as

the entrepreneurial function." Joseph A. Schumpeter, *Capitalism, Socialism and Democracy*, 2nd edn (New York: Harper, 1947), p. 132.

2. He is still, of course, to be found in smaller firms and in larger ones that have yet to reach full maturity of organization. I deal with this evolution in the next chapters. [*Editor's Note*: In particular, Galbraith refers to Chapters VII and VIII of *The New Industrial State*, on "The Corporation" and "The Entrepreneur and the Technostructure," respectively.]

3. Still rather more educational in this period than scientific.

4. That is to say, the Board of Directors was selected by the management rather than by the stockholders and, in turn, selected the management. Adolf A. Berle, Jr. and Gardiner Means, *The Modern Corporation and Private Property* (New York: Macmillan, 1934), p. 94. In effective control of important decisions, as discussed in Chapter VIII [of *the New Industrial State*, "The Entrepreneur and the Technostructure", pp. 86–97], the erosion of the power of the owners had, unquestionably, gone much farther.

5. *Editor's Note*: See esp. Chapter XXIV, "The Industrial System and the Union II: The Ministerial Union," pp. 274–281, in *The New Industrial State, op. cit.*

6. Francis X. Sutton, Seymour E. Harris, Carl Kaysen and James Tobin, *The American Business Creed* (Cambridge: Harvard University Press, 1956).

7. In 1964, the independent entrepreneurs, large and small, were mostly for Senator Goldwater. His domestic program – shrinkage of the Federal government, less reliance on progressive taxes, aversion to social security – was consistent with their interest. It was not consistent with the interest of the technostructure and it is noteworthy that this group shifted in large numbers to the Democratic Party. On the changing political alignments of businessmen in this election as indicated by campaign contributions, see Herbert E. Alexander and Harold B. Meyers, "The Switch in Campaign Giving," *Fortune* (November 1965).

8. H. L. Nieburg, *In the Name of Science* (Chicago: Quadrangle Books, 1966), pp. 188, 189. This study, which appeared after this book had been substantially completed, provides admirably detailed documentation on the relation of government and technostructure as here outlined. Cf. particularly Chapters X and XI.

9. *Editor's Note*: See Chapter XI, "The General Theory of Motivation," in *The New Industrial State, op. cit.*, pp. 128–39.

10
The Military–industrial Complex and the New Industrial State (1968)*

Walter Adams

In *The New Industrial State*,[1] Galbraith finds that the giant corporation has achieved such dominance of American industry that it can control its environment and immunize itself from the discipline of all exogenous control mechanisms – especially the competitive market. Through separation of ownership from management, it has emancipated itself from the control of stockholders. By reinvestment of profits, it has eliminated the influence of the financier and the capital market. By brainwashing its clientele, it has insulated itself from consumer sovereignty. By possession of market power, it has come to dominate both suppliers and customers. By judicious identification with, and manipulation of, the state, it has achieved autonomy from government control. Whatever it cannot do for itself to assure survival and growth, a compliant government does on its behalf – assuring the maintenance of full employment; eliminating the risk of and subsidizing the investment in research and development; and assuring the supply of scientific and technical skills required by the modern technostructure. In return for this privileged autonomy, the industrial giant performs society's planning function. And this, according to Galbraith, is inevitable because technological imperatives dictate it. The market is dead, we are told; and there is no good reason to regret its passing.

This blueprint for technocracy, private socialism, and the corporate state suffers from three fundamental defects. First, it rests on the unproved premise that corporate giantism is an inevitable product of

---

* From *American Economic Review* (*Papers and Proceedings*), 58(2) (19680, pp. 652–65.

technological determinism. Second, it rests on the increasingly more dubious assumption that industrial and political power are confined to separate, distinct, and hermetically scaled compartments. Finally, it offers no policy guidance, and ignores the crucial questions of responsibility and accountability. If industrial giants, freed from all traditional checks and balances, are to perform society's planning function, what standards shall they use and what assurance is there of an automatic convergence between private and public advantage? What are the safeguards – other than the intellectual in politics – against arbitrary abuse of power, capricious, or defective decision making? Must society legitimize a self-sustaining, self-serving, self-justifying, and self-perpetuating industrial oligarchy as the price for efficiency and progress?

In this paper, I shall eschew a dreary and repetitive recital of the voluminous evidence that negates the Galbraith version of a crude technological determinism.[2] I shall also spare the reader any comments on the virtues of private planning – the proposition that what is good for General Motors is good for the country. Instead, I shall offer an alternative (and, hopefully, more realistic) explanation of the current levels of industrial concentration, in general, and the military–industrial complex, in particular.

I

My hypothesis – the obverse of Galbraith's – holds that industrial concentration is not the inevitable outgrowth of economic and technical forces, nor the product of spontaneous generation or natural selection. In this era of big government, concentration is often the result of unwise, man-made, discriminatory, privilege-creating governmental action. Defense contracts, R and D support, patent policy, tax privileges, stockpiling arrangements, tariffs and quotas, subsidies, etc., have far from a neutral effect on our industrial structure. In all these institutional arrangements, government plays a crucial, if not decisive, role.[3] Government, working through and in alliance with "private enterprise," becomes the keystone in an edifice of neomercantilism and industrial feudalism. In the process, the institutional fabric of society is transformed from economic capitalism to political capitalism.

My hypothesis is best explained in Schumpeterian power terms. According to Schumpeter, the capitalist process was rooted, not in classical price competition, but rather "the competition from the new commodity, the new technology, the new source of supply, the new type of organization – competition which commands a decisive cost or quality advantage and which strikes not at the margin of the profits and outputs of existing firms but at their very foundations and their very lives."[4] The very essence of capitalism, according to Schumpeter, was the "perennial gale of creative destruction" in which existing power positions and entrenched advantage were constantly displaced by new organizations and new power complexes. This gale of creative destruction was to be not only the harbinger of progress but also the built-in safeguard against the vices of monopoly and privilege.

What was obvious to Schumpeter and other analysts of economic power was also apparent to those who might suffer from the gales of change. They quickly and instinctively understood that storm shelters had to be built to protect themselves against this destructive force. The mechanism which was of undoubted public benefit carried with it exorbitant private costs. And, since private storm shelters in the form of cartels and monopolies were either unlawful, unfeasible, or inadequate, they turned increasingly to government for succor and support. By manipulation of the state for private ends, the possessors of entrenched power found the most felicitous instrument for insulating themselves against, and immunizing themselves from, the Schumpeterian gale.

It requires no exaggeration to argue that modern technology and the inherent dynamism of Schumpeterian competition are such that, in the absence of governmental interference and protection, some of the bulwarks of concentrated power could be successfully eroded. Government policy toward the petroleum industry is a case in point. Under the antitrust laws, it is a offense *per se* for private firms to fix prices or allocate markets, yet in the name of conservation the government does for the oil companies what they could not legally do for themselves. The process is familiar. The Bureau of Mines in the Department of Interior publishes monthly estimates of the market demand for petroleum (at current prices, of course). Under the Interstate Oil Compact, approved by Congress, these estimates are broken down into quotas for each of the oil producing states which, in turn, through various prorationing devices, allocate "allowable production" to individual wells. Oil produced in violation of these prorationing regulations is branded as "hot oil," and the federal government prohibits its shipment in interstate commerce. Also, to buttress this government sanctioned cartel against potential competition, oil imports by sea are limited to slightly more than one million barrels a day. Finally, to top off these indirect subsidies with more visible favors and to provide the proper incentives for an industry crucial to the national defense, the government authorizes oil companies to charge off a $27^1/_2$ per cent depletion allowance against their gross income. In all, the industry has been estimated to receive special favors of $3.5 billion (according to Milton Friedman[5]) and $4.0 billion (according to Morris Adelman[6]) – in addition to having a government sanctioned cartel provide the underpinning for its control of markets and prices.

Another case in point is the military–industrial complex, where the morganatic alliance between government and business is even clearer, bolder, and more positive. Here government not only permits and facilitates the entrenchment of private power but serves as its fountain-head. It creates and institutionalizes power concentrations which tend to breed on themselves and to defy public control. The scenario of events should be familiar. The "mad momentum" of an international weapons race militates toward large defense expenditures (currently at an annual rate of $75 billion). This generates a demand, not only for traditional, commercial, shelf items like food, clothing, fuel, and ammunition, but also for the development and production of sophisti-cated weaponry. Lacking a network of government-owned arsenals, such as produced the shot and cannon in the days of American inno-cence, or having dismantled the arsenals it did have, the government is forced to buy what it no longer can make. It becomes a monopsonistic buyer of products which are not yet designed or for which production experience is lacking. It buys at prices for which there is little prece-dent and hardly any yardsticks. It deals with contractors, a large per centage of whose business is locked into supplying defense, space, or atomic energy needs. It confronts powerful oligopolists in a market where technical capability rather than price is the controlling variable – in an atmosphere shrouded by multilateral uncertainty and constant warnings about imminent aggression. In the process, government becomes almost totally dependent on the chosen instruments, i.e., creatures of its own making, for effectuating public policy.[7] Lacking any viable in-house capabilities, competitive yardsticks, or the poten-tial for institutional competition, the government becomes – in the extreme – subservient to the private and special interests whose entrenched power bears the governmental seal.

This unique buyer–seller relationship, which defies analysis by con-ventional economic tools, lies at the root of the military–industrial complex and the new power configurations generated by it. The complex is not a conspiracy between the "merchants of death" and a band of lusty generals, but a natural coalition of interest groups with an economic, political, or professional stake in defense and space. It includes the armed services, the industrial contractors who produce for them, the labor unions that represent their workers, the lobbyists who tout their wares in the name of "free enterprise" and "national security," and the legislators who, for reasons of pork or patriotism, vote the sizable funds to underwrite the show. Every time the Congress authorizes a military appropriation, it creates a new constituency (i.e., propaganda machine) with a vested interest in its perpetuation and aggrandizement. Thus, the current proposal for an anti-ballistic-missile system, the "thin" variety of which would cost $5 billion and the "thick" variety $40 billion, and which would probably be obsolete by the time it was completed, has been estimated to involve 28 private contractors, with plants located in 42 states (i.e., 84 senators), and 172 congressional districts. Given the political reality of such situations and the economic power of the constituencies involved, there is little hope that an interaction of special interest groups will somehow cancel each other out and that there will emerge some compromise which serves the public interest. There is little assurance that the corporal's guard of auditors in the General Accounting Office or Galbraith's scientific professional elite or a handful of disinterested university analysts will constitute a dependable and adequate force of countervailing power. The danger remains that the "conjunction of an immense military establishment and a large arms industry," against which President Eisenhower warned, will become a Frankenstein threatening to control the contract state which brought it into being. The danger persists that power will be coalescing, not countervailing – that the political cloakroom will displace the economic market place.

It would be facile to conclude that the military–industrial complex and the new industrial state represent a price which society must pay – and inevitably so – because of national defense considerations or because of technological inexorability. But this would be to miss the point – to ignore the crucial political component in the institutional arrangements at issue. The military–industrial complex is only a special case illustrating the power problems inherent in the new industrial state. Both are created, protected, privileged, and subsidized by the state. Both represent a form of private socialism – a type of social planning through fragmented, special-interest chosen instruments operating in the "private" sector. Both represent a blending of private economic power and public political power. Both are reminiscent of the Elizabethan monopoly system and its abuse, corruption, favoritism, waste, and inefficiency – an *imperium in imperio*, without demonstrable public benefits, and without any built-in safeguards for the public interest. In sum, to the extent that they are creatures of political power and not the product of natural evolution, there is nothing inevitable about their survival and nothing inevitable about the public policies which spawn and preserve them.

II

Let us examine these public policies which lie at the base of the new industrial state, and particularly the military-industrial complex.

Defense and space contracts

These contracts, typically awarded on a negotiated rather than a competitive bid basis and as much the result of political as economic bargaining, convert the private contractor into a quasi-governmental, mercantilist corporation, maintained in a privileged position by "royal" franchise. The attendant abuses, especially the creation of entrenched power positions, are not inconsiderable.

In 1965, the US Comptroller General, an Eisenhower appointee, highlighted the following characteristics of the contract system before a congressional committee:

(1) excessive prices in relation to available pricing information,
(2) acceptance and payment by the government for defective equipment,
(3) charges to the government for costs applicable to contractors' commercial work,
(4) contractors' use of government-owned facilities for commercial work for extended periods without payment of rent to the government,
(5) duplicate billings to the government,
(6) unreasonable or excessive costs, and
(7) excessive progress payments held by contractors without payment of interest thereon.[8]

To this list could be added the procurement of items that were not needed, or in adequate supply elsewhere in the armed services, or were in fact being sold as surplus by the buying agency; indirect procurement through the prime contractor rather than direct purchase from the actual manufacturer – at far lower prices and without the pyramiding of overhead and profits; awarding of sole-source contracts for which the contractor had no special competency; the refusal by firms with overall systems responsibility to break out components for competitive bidding, or to furnish specifications for such bidding;[9] and finally, according to the Comptroller General, "excessive prices resulting from the failure of the agencies to request, or the contractors to furnish, current, accurate, and complete pricing data or from the failure to adequately evaluate such data when negotiating prices."[10] In quantitative terms, according to a summary of GAO studies covering the period from May 1963, to May 1964, there was ascertainable waste of $500 million in a 5 per cent sample of procurements.[11]

Perhaps it is unavoidable that in the procurement of complicated weapons systems, where uncertainty is pervasive and precedents are unavailable, cost estimates will be unduly inflated. As Peck and Scherer found in their study of twelve major weapon system development programs, actual costs exceeded predicted costs by 3.2 times on the average, with a range of actual versus predicted costs of from 70 to 700 per cent.[12] Recent prediction errors in the F-111 and Apollo programs, Scherer reports, are of the same order of magnitude.

One can sympathize with the contracting officers negotiating for complex and sophisticated weapons technology and still agree with the McClellan Committee's conclusion that the government should not abdicate its responsibilities for program management, nor delegate these responsibilities to private contractors, if it wants to avoid avoidable abuses and flagrant overcharges: "Even the most reputable and ethical contractor is placed in the conflicting position of managing a program where the feasibility, technical, and economic decisions which should be made by the customer – Government – are made by the producer-contractor," the Committee observed with charitable understatement. "The absence of competition, coupled with the urgency to get the program underway, removes normal safeguards against large profits and weakens the Government's negotiating position."[13]

On the other hand, one must understand the reluctance to endanger the national security because of excessive delays caused by punctilious bookkeeping. As Charles G. Dawes told a congressional committee investigating World War I procurement scandals:

> Sure we paid. We didn't dicker. Why, man alive, we had to win the war. We would have paid horse prices for sheep if sheep could have pulled artillery to the front. Oh, it's all right now to say we bought too much vinegar and too many cold chisels, but we saved the civil-

ization of the world. Damn it all, the business of an army is to win the war, not to quibble around with a lot of cheap buying. Hell and Maria, we weren't trying to keep a set of books, we were trying to win the war.[14]

Government R and D and patent

The awarding of government R and D contracts – and the disposition of patent rights thereunder – is another technique of creating, privileging, subsidizing, and entrenching private power. Again, this is a matter of man-made policy, not institutional inevitability. The importance of federal policy in this area derives from a number of characteristics of federally financed research. Since the Second World War, the government has generally paid for roughly 65 per cent of the nation's research and development, but performed only 15 per cent of the work. Two agencies, the Department of Defense and NASA, account for about 80 per cent of the government's R and D outlays. The lion's share of these outlays is concentrated in a few industries, notably aerospace, electronics, and communications. The concentration of R and D contracts is even greater than that of production contracts. There is high correlation between companies receiving R and D contracts and those receiving production contracts. Finally, the benefits of military R and D tend to spill over into civilian markets.[15]

The typical R and D contract, it should be noted, is a riskless cost-plus-fixed-fee venture. It usually protects the contractor against increases in labor and materials costs; it provides him with working capital in the form of periodic progress payments; it allows him to use government plant and equipment; in addition, it guarantees him a fee up to 15 per cent of the estimated cost. Nevertheless, some contractors demand additional incentives. With the arrogance characteristic of all privilege recipients, they want to extend and compound such privilege. "We recognize," says the vice-president of the Electronics Industries Association, a prime beneficiary of government-financed R and D, "that the ownership of a patent is a valuable property right entitled to protection against seizure by the Government without just compensation."[16] In this view, the patent is a right, not a privilege voluntarily bestowed by the government to effectuate a public purpose. By a curious perversion of logic, it becomes a vested privilege to which the private contractor is entitled and of which he is not supposed to be deprived without "just" compensation.

Characteristically, both the Department of Defense and NASA have accepted this argument for privilege creation and made it the cornerstone of their patent policies. The principle at issue requires little adumbration. Allowing a contractor to retain patents on research financed by and performed for the government, as Wassily Leontief points out, "is no more reasonable or economically sound than to bestow on contractors, who build a road financed by public funds, the right to collect tolls from the cars that will eventually use it"[17] – or the right to close the road altogether. It is tantamount to socializing the financial support for research while permitting private monopolization of its benefits. Moreover, as Admiral Rickver observed, firms receiving R and D contracts "are relatively few huge corporate entities already possessing great concentrated economic power. They are not ailing segments of the economy in need of public aid or subsidy. Nor are there any real reasons to offer patent give-aways in order to induce them to accept Defense Department research grants or contracts ... To claim that agencies cannot get firms to sign such contracts unless patent rights are given away strikes me as fanciful nonsense."[18]

Stockpiling of strategic and critical materials

This is an "ever normal granary" program, ostensibly designed to enable the United States to fight a war of specified duration, determined by the strategic assumptions of the Joint Chiefs of Staff. In reality, it is a price support program, the details of which are buried in secret government files and the "primary purpose" of which is to subsidize selected mining interests in the name of national security.[19] That, at least, was the conclusion of the exhaustive hearings conducted by the Symington Subcommittee of the Senate Armed Services Committee which examined the origin and growth of the national stockpile, the Defense Production Act inventory, and supplemental stockpile, which by 1961 had involved the expenditure $8.9 billion.[20]

These were the specific findings of the Symington Subcommittee:

1. Stockpile objectives were constantly manipulated to increase purchases regardless of national security needs. Thus, starting in 1954,

> to justify further purchases of lead and zinc, when use of the old formula or requirements versus supplies did not permit additional buying, basic strategic assumptions were changed, and objectives for each material were established. Under this new concept, the basic objective was determined under the usual method, but a new objective – the maximum objective – was arrived at by disallowing all supplies of a material from overseas. This had the effect, in many instances, of doubling the amount of a material that had to be

stockpiled. It was then discovered, however, that even this new system would not permit additional purchases of lead and zinc in the amounts needed to maintain higher prices for lead and zinc. Resort was then had to the arbitrary one-year rule. Under this rule objectives were set at one year's consumption of the total national economy during a normal year without regard to what our requirements and supplies were.[21]

In the case of some ores and minerals, an arbitrary six-month rule was adopted.

2. The buying programs to develop a domestic supply of certain ores, said the Committee,

can only be described as a failure ... Much of the material purchased was not needed. A substantial part of these ores did not meet the specifications of the stockpile. Nor was any domestic mobilization base established by these purchases as is indicated by the fact that when the purchases stopped production stopped as well.[22]

Moreover, contrary to expectations, most of the expenditures did not go to small business but to well-established mining companies; 86.7 per cent of the tungsten purchases, for example, were made from the ten largest producers.

3. The price support level of some materials, like tungsten, e.g., were set two or three times above world prices, thus allowing the contractors windfall profits by buying at low world prices and supplying the stockpile at artificially exorbitant prices.[23]

4. Premium prices were often paid to contractors on the assumption that it would be necessary for the contractor to incur substantial capital expenditures to perform under the contract. Yet the government was denied the right under these contracts to check whether the capital expenditures had in fact been made, or to inspect the contractor's book to ascertain his production costs, or to renegotiate the price if the anticipated high costs were not realized.[24]

5. When market prices for some materials, like copper, e.g., rose above the contractual stockpile price, producers were permitted to divert deliveries from the stockpile to private industry – without sharing this windfall with the government.[25]

6. When the Joint Chiefs of Staff changed their strategic assumptions from a five-year war to a three-year war, the stockpile administrators waited for two years before implementing the change. Felix Wormser,

Assistant Secretary of the Interior for Minerals Resources, who before and after his government service was vice-president of the nation's largest lead producer (St. Joseph Lead Co.), protested that such a change would constitute "a breach of faith with the mining industry."[26]

7. Disposals of excess supplies were resisted strenuously, and only in tin and rubber were any large-scale sales made. "It is significant," the Symington Committee noted wryly, "that there are no producers of natural rubber and tin in the United States and this could well account for the fact that the only two large disposals have been in these materials."[27]

The point need not be belabored. The rules for operating the national stockpiles as articulated by the industries concerned and their protagonists in government are fairly simple: The government must accumulate reserves against the most unthinkable eventualities. It must buy these materials at prices industry considers remunerative, regardless of world market conditions. This subsidy must be adequate to enable industry to operate profitably until such time as its services are required for mobilization in time of war. Finally, regardless of the available stocks, no disposal must ever be made from the stockpile. Such sales would not only endanger national security but also disturb market conditions and hence constitute unwarranted government interference with free enterprise.

Alienation of the public domain

To achieve or solidify their control over prices and markets, the giants of American industry cannot rely on the imperatives of modern technology. On the contrary, they must live in constant fear of the "creative destruction" wrought by new technology; and they must always be alert to the potential competition of substitute products and processes. Even more important, they must fight to contain, neutralize, and sterilize the "institutional" competition of the public domain which threatens to impose an intolerable regulatory yardstick on their operations. TVA is an embarrassment to the electric power monopoly, the communication satellite to AT&T dominance, navy shipyards to the shipbuilding cartel, and the Army's Redstone Arsenal and Jet Propulsion Laboratory to the condottieri of aerospace. Pressure must be exerted, therefore, to dismantle such operations, or to circumscribe their competitive viability, or to sell their facilities to private enterprise – in a manner which does not disturb the existing power structure and indeed might even entrench it more solidly. Here, again, governmental cooperation is required for implementation of this grand strategy, and this is a matter of political decision, not technological or economic inevitability.

The disposal of government-owned plants at the end of World War II underscores the nature of the power struggle and the availability of public policy alternatives.[28] In aluminum, the disposal program was a qualified success; Alcoa's prewar monopoly was broken, Kaiser and Reynolds sprang like Minerva from Jupiter's brow, and the aluminium industry was converted into a triopoly. Synthetic nitrogen production was also deconcentrated by the infusion of additional sellers. In steel, by contrast, the disposal program served to entrench and extend oligopoly dominance; the Geneva Steel plant, built at a cost of $202.4 million, was sold to the United States Steel Corporation for $47.5 million, and enabled US Steel to increase its regional control over the Pacific Coast and Mountain States market from 17.3 to a commanding 39 per cent. In synthetic rubber, the wartime operation of the government plants gave a handful of large firms enormous patent and know-how advantages for the postwar period, and the subsequent disposal program resulted in the sale of twenty-five plants to three firms controlling 47 per cent of the industry's capacity.

More recent is the controversy over the disposition of the government's oil shale lands, located in the Rocky Mountain States, and estimated to contain two trillion barrels of oil (i.e., six times the known oil reserves of the entire world).[29] It illustrates the public policy options which are available to influence the structure of markets and to cope with existing power concentrations. At issue are the ground rules to be established for the control and development of a resource valued at $2.5 to $3.5 trillion.[30]

The petroleum industry's plan, according to one of its spokesmen, is to create "an economic climate equivalent to that provided [for] crude oil." Under its plan, the oil companies would be allowed to carve out homestead-like leases from the public lands and would be eligible for the customary subsidy of 27 1/2 per cent depletion allowance in return for their development efforts. Shell Oil has already proposed to lease a "homestead" that would cover its refining requirements (at present rates) for the next 660 years; Sinclair has entered its more modest request for a tract that would fill its needs for 226 years; Humble's request would provide for the next 54 years; and Continental's for the next 27 years.[31] The desire to gain control of a potentially competitive resource is not coupled with any guarantee to produce from it; and if production should take place, it would be subject to the oligopolistic rationality of the oil majors, restrained from undue competitiveness by government proration regulations.

Opponents of this plan, notably John K. Galbraith, argue that this would be a free ride to monopoly for the big companies.

> Unless safeguards ... are carefully spelled out what would happen is that few of the majors would get these reserves as their reward. An eventual position in the basins would be their payoff. This would be in addition to the lands that they already own in most cases. Were there development, the processes for recovering the shale would then presumably be patented by them and reserved to them.[32]

Obviously there are policy alternatives, including *inter alia* TVA- and COMSAT-like arrangements. "Certainly," as Senator Hart, chairman of the Senate Antitrust Subcommittee put it, "the development of oil shale reserves should offer a unique opportunity for new sources of competition to penetrate the petroleum industry. And that opportunity depends substantially on Government policy."[33]

International trade barriers

No system based on protection, privilege, and subsidy is safe without barriers to foreign competition. Its beneficiaries recognize the rough validity of the Mancunian assumption that "free international trade is the best antimonopoly policy and the best guarantee for the maintenance of a healthy degree of free competition." Action is, therefore, necessary to protect domestic restrictionism against erosion and subversion from abroad. And governmental action is the most reliable technique available.

The steel industry, in its current clamor for tariffs and/or quotas, illustrates the rationale of (what *Barron's* calls) the "protection racket" (October 18, 1967). Roger Blough, congenitally unable to resist the ludicrous, observes that

> obviously there are many things in life that should and must be protected. For example, millions of our people – and a number of government agencies – are laudably striving to protect certain vanishing forms of Wildlife that are threatened with extinction; and one may reasonably wonder, I suppose, how far down the road to oblivion some of our major industries must go before they are deemed to merit similar concern.[34]

To this, the president of the American Iron & Steel Institutes adds the ominous warning that "a first-class power with global responsibilities cannot afford to rely for any important part of its needs on overseas sources of steel thousands of miles away. There is the constant danger that these sources may be cut off at a critical moment."[35] Finally, the United Steel Workers of America, upon whom Galbraith once relied as a source of countervailing power, and not to be outdone in their concern for the public interest and national security, lend their voice and not inconsiderable political influence to the fight for a quota law to limit steel imports.[36]

What is at stake, of course, is the steel industry's right to preserve its administered price structure, to remain the catalyst of seller's inflation, to impose periodic price squeezes on independent fabricators, to price itself out of world export markets, to encourage the growth of substitute materials, and to persist in its technological lethargy.[37] Specifically, the industry needs government help to validate its investment in "40 million tons of the wrong capacity – the open hearth furnace" which it built in the 1950s. This capacity, as *Fortune* points out, was "obsolete when it was built" and the industry by installing it "prepared itself for dying."[38] This is the $300 million blunder, the cost of which the industry would like to shift to the public by obtaining government protection from foreign competition.

The point need not be stressed. Tariffs, quotas, "anti-dumping" statutes, "Buy American" regulations, and similar devices are not only a tax on domestic consumers and a subsidy to sheltered industries, but the capstone of any policy to protect entrenched economic power. They are a crucial facet of the *Realpolitik* designed to preserve the discipline of a nation's *Ordnungswirtschaft*.

III

In conclusion, we may note that the problem at hand is not one of technological determinism which would militate toward fatalistic acceptance of the status quo. Nor is it rooted in the ineffectiveness of what Galbraith calls the charade of antitrust. Instead, it is largely a political problem of governmental creation, protection, and subsidization of private privilege. If this diagnosis is indeed correct, then public policy alternatives are available and a reasonably competitive market is more than a utopian policy objective.

Let me offer two general policy recommendations:

1. Most important is government noninterference in markets which in the absence of such interference would be workably competitive. In the words of Adam Smith, it may be difficult to "prevent people of the

same trade from sometimes assembling together," but government "ought to do nothing to facilitate such assemblies; much less to render them necessary." While assuring effective enforcement of the antitrust laws, government should abjure the role of the mercantilist state in sanctioning and legitimizing private privilege. One can only speculate on the quantitative benefits of such measures as the abolition of tariffs in concentrated industries, the deregulation of surface transportation from ICC control, or the elimination of the honeycomb of governmental supports for the petroleum price and power structure.

2. In those areas where competition cannot be allowed full sway or where government cannot avoid active participation in the economic game, the basic guidelines point to preserving the maximum amount of power decentralization feasible. This may require positive encouragement of institutional competition from whatever source available and, at the very least, the preservation of effective yardsticks by which to measure and control monopoly performance. In the national defense sector, for example, government must rebuild and preserve its in-house competence for R and D, systems engineering and management, and contract evaluation. As the Bell Report of 1962 concluded, "there are certain [management] functions which should under no circumstances be contracted out."[39] Basic policy and program decisions respecting the research and development effort – relating to "the types of work to be undertaken, when, by whom, and at what cost – must be made by full-time Government officials. Such officials must also be able to supervise the execution of work undertaken, and to evaluate the results."[40] In short, the government cannot surrender the yardsticks essential for the discharge of its responsibilities to the public.[41] And the public must recognize that the servants of the military–industrial state cannot be allowed to become its masters – either in the name of "free enterprise" or under the guise of promoting the "national security."

What I have said here is not likely to please those who rationalize the status quo by invoking some deterministic inevitability. I do not claim that what I have said is particularly new or startling. I do believe, however, that it is true and that, as Dr. Johnson said, men need not so much to be informed as reminded.

Notes

1. John K. Galbraith, *The New Industrial State* (Boston, 1967).
2. US Senate Select Committee on Small Business, *Planning, Regulation, and Competition, Hearings*, 90th Congress, 1st Session (1967), pp. 11–27, 53–66;

US Senate Subcommittee on Antitrust and Monopoly, *Economic Concentration, Hearings,* Parts 3 and 6 (Washington, DC, 1965 and 1967).

3. Walter Adams and Horace M. Gray, *Monopoly in America: The Government as Promoter* (New York, 1955).

4. Joseph A. Schumpeter, *Capitalism, Socialism, and Democracy* (New York, 1942), p. 84.

5. Milton Friedman, "Oil and the Middle East," *Newsweek* (June 26, 1967).

6. Morris A. Adelman, "Efficiency of Resource Use in Crude Petroleum: Abstract," *American Economic Review* (May, 1964).

7. David E. Bell, "Report to the President on Government R&D Contracting" (April 1962), printed in House Committee on Government Operations, *Systems Development and Management, Hearings,* Part 1, Appendix I, 87th Congress, 2nd Session (1962), pp. 191–337; Clark R. Mollenhoff, *The Pentagon* (New York, 1967); H. L. Nieburg, *In the Name of Science* (Chicago, 1966).

8. US House Committee on Government Operations, *Comptroller General Reports to Congress on Audits of Defense Contracts, Hearings,* 89th Congress, 1st Session (1965), p. 46.

9. US House Committee on Government Operations, *Comptroller General Reports to Congress on Audits of Defense Contracts, Hearings,* 89th Congress, 1st Session (1965); US Joint Economic Committee, *Background Materials on Economic Impact of Federal Procurement,* Washington, DC (various years, 1964–7); appendices contain lists and digests of General Accounting Office reports on defense activities to Congress.

10. US House Committee on Government Operations, *Comptroller General Reports to Congress on Audits of Defense Contracts, Hearings,* 89th Congress, 1st Session (1965), p. 46.

11. H. L. Nieburg, *In the Name of Science* (Chicago, 1966), p. 269.

12. Merton J. Peck and Frederic M. Scherer, *The Weapons Acquisition Process: An Economic Analysis* (Harvard Business School Division of Research, 1962), pp. 19–25.

13. US Senate Committee on Government Operations, *Pyramiding of Profits and Costs in the Missile Procurement Programs, Report No. 970,* 88th Congress, 2nd Session (1964), p. 141.

14. Mollenhoff, *The Pentagon,* pp. 53–54.

15. Richard J. Barber, *The Politics of Research* (Washington, DC, 1966), pp. 71–90.

16. US Senate Select Committee on Small Business, *Economic Aspects of Government Patent Policies, Hearings,* 88th Congress, 1st Session (1963), p. 132.

17. Ibid., p. 234.

18. Nieburg, *In the Name of Science,* p. 294.

19. US Senate Committee on Armed Services, Draft Report of the National Stockpile and Naval Petroleum Reserves Subcommittee, *Inquiry into the Strategic and Critical Material Stockpile of the United States,* 88th Congress, 1st Session (1963), pp. 36–45 .

20. Ibid., p. 4.

21. Ibid., pp. 4–5.

22. Ibid, pp. 8–9, 66.

23. Ibid., pp. 69–71.
24. Ibid., pp. 68–9.
25. Ibid., pp. 49–54.
26. Ibid., p. 251.
27. Ibid., p. 28.
28. Walter Adams and Horace M. Gray, *Monopoly in America: The Government as Promoter* (New York, 1955), pp. 117–41.
29. US Senate Subcommittee on Antitrust and Monopoly, *Competitive Aspects of Oil Shale Development, Hearings*, Part 1, 90th Congress, 1st Session (1967), pp. 106–7.
30. Ibid., pp. 403, 407.
31. Ibid., p. 455.
32. Ibid., p. 22.
33. Ibid., p. 3.
34. Roger M. Blough, "Progress Is Not Our Most Imported Product," Address at the Annual Meeting of the Indiana Manufactures Association, Indianapolis (November 16, 1967).
35. US Senate Committee on Finance, *Import Quota Legislation, Hearings*, Part 2, 90th Congress, 1st Session (1967), p. 830.
36. Ibid., pp. 888–96.
37. Ibid., pp. 846–88.
38. Ibid., p. 855.
39. Bell, "Report to the President on Government R&D Contracting," p. 213.
40. Ibid., pp. 214–15.
41. Nieburg, *In the Name of Science*, pp. 334–50.

11
Planning, Corporatism, and the Capitalist State (1985)*

Bill Jordan

Since the Second World War, an outstanding feature of advanced capitalist states has been the development of institutions and processes for organizing and coordinating their national economies. These emerged in the 1950s, waxed strongest in the 1960s and early 1970s, and have become the subjects of dispute and criticism since then. In this chapter I shall try to account for theories and practices which gave a key organizing role to the state under capitalism, and which suggested that market distributions were necessarily part of a political process. I shall look at the successes and failures of economic planning, and – using mainly examples from British experiences – outline structural and political shortcomings of this approach to the problems of the advanced industrialized economies of the 1980s.

The state in advanced capitalist countries is committed to maximizing national income. In an economy dominated by a few large national industrial firms, producing and selling the bulk of their output within national boundaries, a happy coincidence of interests occurs. Where their authority systems are somewhat similar in structure, and where top elites are drawn from similar social and educational backgrounds[1] it would be surprising if close organizational links between these major companies and the state did not develop. Where trade unions are also organized nationally, with centralized authority systems, it would be surprising if they were not to some extent drawn into the same process of consultation and coordination. To a considerable extent, such conditions prevailed in several of the advanced capitalist countries in the 1960s, and a range of institutions and processes

---

* From *The State: Authority and Autonomy* (Oxford: Blackwell, 1985), pp. 219–37.

for consultation and coordination developed according to the political and commercial traditions of each of these states.

However, with the increasing internationalization of production, this situation no longer prevails. The largest corporations in the advanced capitalist countries are increasingly international in their perspectives on production and profits, and their interests do not necessarily coincide with those of the national state in which they happen to be based. Economic dominance is shared between these multinational corporations, so that governments must deal both with home-based companies with many overseas interests, and with foreign companies with interests in their territories. Home-based industrial production, though still the primary generator of national income, has become a much less important determinant of employment levels. Whereas countries like Britain and Belgium had almost half of their workforces engaged in industrial production in the 1950s, by 1981 they had only 35.5 and 33.4 per cent, respectively in such jobs, while other advanced capitalist countries had even lower proportions. New patterns of labor utilization and income distribution raise quite different issues on employment and incomes policies, which cannot be resolved by coordination between the leaders of a few large firms, large unions and state officials.

Nonetheless, many theorists and politicians still argue that issues such as these should continue to be treated primarily as political issues, requiring planning and – if necessary – compulsory regulation. According to this school of thought, levels of prices, wages and employment are not, and never can be, determined primarily by market forces in advanced economies where large companies predominate. Accordingly, the internationalization of production, leading to even larger corporations, with still greater monopoly powers over the market, requires even stronger efforts by governments to ensure that the interests of all their citizens are protected and upheld. Against this, those who insist that market forces alone can be relied upon to distribute resources efficiently and fairly, and that this process can only occur internationally, have insisted that attempts at national economic planning merely cause distortions which are damaging to prosperity. These planned distortions require constant reinforcement, leading ultimately towards closed, centrally planned, backward and repressive national economies.

Capitalist economic planning also rekindled interest in Marxist theories of the state. The evidence of institutional coordination between government and large-scale industry was a *prima facie* case for arguing either that the state served capital's needs for accumulation, or that it served the class needs of the bourgeoisie. In this chapter I shall also try to give brief attention to the light shed by Marxist analyses on planning, corporatism and social democracy, and to the problems of the Marxist approach.

Justifications of planning

Economic planning was pioneered in Western European states with political and intellectual traditions of corporatism. But postwar or "liberal" corporatism was different from both pre-capitalist and authoritarian (fascist) corporatism.[2] It was not set up as a challenge to parliamentari[ani]sm, or a denial of individual civil or political rights; the role of the state was not so much leadership as orchestrating a bargain and compromise between representatives of major interest groups; and these interests (especially industrial capital and the trade unions) were treated as being interdependent, and capable of benefiting from cooperation to maximize national output. The spur to this cooperation was postwar reconstruction and the opportunities of using new Keynesian insights and methods in overcoming obstacles to growth. Its objectives included economic targets and aggregates, social policy formulation and a consensus on values – a whole design for a regulated and integrated social and economic system. Its forms varied between the formal and structured and the informal and *ad hoc*. In these countries, with their traditions of corporatist institutions, and given the dominance of the major national corporations, state coordination through economic planning needed little new justification.

In Britain and the United States, planning had been used to coordinate the wartime economy, but state direction was perceived as inconsistent with market principles. After the war, planning institutions and controls were rapidly dismantled, and it was only in response to the success of the Western European systems that the advantages of corporatist methods began to be discussed. Hence there was a far greater need for theoretical justifications for the use of planning, and for a political debate about its principles.

In the 1950s, a kind of political and theoretical consensus developed in the capitalist world around the grafting of Keynes's insights in macroeconomics onto neoclassical microeconomic analysis. Keynesian theory was taken to apply in the short run, when market imperfections prevented the national system from reaching equilibrium; if the state countered these with fiscal and monetary policy, neoclassical mechanisms could then be relied upon. This theory accommodated practices as diverse as those of the French and the Japanese; it was as if most successful politicians and business leaders had been brought up on a diet of Paul Samuelson's economic writings.[3]

However, in the late 1950s and early 1960s a number of economists were developing theories which challenged this orthodoxy. Building on the work of Roy Harrod before the war, Joan Robinson and Nicolas Kaldor challenged neoclassical theories in the fields of capital accumulation and income distribution;[4] their ideas were further developed by Piero Sraffa and Michal Kalecki, whose work cast doubt on all the elements of neoclassical production theory.[5] A small but insistent group of post-Keynesians therefore increasingly rejected every aspect of neoclassical analysis. They saw the rate of investment as crucial for economic growth, but problematic because it depended on levels of aggregate demand – so government had to be concerned with maintaining both consumption and investment, and the balance between them. In the process of development and change, in which new industries, firms, technologies and products played a key role, high levels of investment were required. But funds for investment were drawn mainly from firms' savings out of profits. Large, oligopolistic corporations set prices according to their long-term plans and prospects, and required a "mark-up" over costs which could support their long-term targets, to give high and growing rates of investment. This could only be achieved through control over workers' claims on national income, and a planned share for profits.[6]

The post-Keynesians questioned the whole marginalist analysis of production theory and income distribution. In neoclassical theory, the distribution of income is determined by the price at which each individual can sell the services of the factor of production he possesses in the competitive market, and the price of the factor service should be equal to the value of its marginal product. But Keynes argued that money wages and real wages did not necessarily move in the same direction, so that workers' sacrifices in money wages would not necessarily lead to falls in real wages and hence to increased employment; and Sraffa denied that the quantity of capital could be measured, and hence whether it was possible to calculate a relationship between this quantity and its price. He also showed that a system of equilibrium prices for factors could be derived independently of any marginal changes and without direct recognition of the role played by demand for factor services. Hence the notion of a mechanism by which factors were substituted for each other in production was undermined, and the notion of a structural link between production and the market came under question.[7]

If, as this analysis suggested, neither the demand for labor nor its supply depended on the real wage, then the labor market was not a true market, because the wage-rate could not clear the market, and variations in the wage-rate could not eliminate unemployment. Post-Keynesians drew attention to the segmentation of the labor market, and the very different rates of wages, employment conditions and productivity rates (even in the same industries) in different sectors of the same economy.[8] They emphasized the differences between the structure of the "core" oligopolistic sector, with high wages, high productivity, and relatively stable employment, and the more backward sector, with lower wages, less advanced methods, lower productivity and unstable employment conditions. Hence total employment levels have little to do with marginal productivity. The supply of labor depends on demographic factors; when aggregate demand in the economy falls, the oligopolistic sector raises its demand for qualifications for long-term employees: the peripheral sector follows suit, and the most vulnerable groups – the unskilled, women, blacks, etc. – become vulnerable to long-term unemployment. Adjustments to wages cannot eliminate this unemployment, which responds only to changes in aggregate demand, not to wage-levels, real or monetary.

However, this apparently damaging critique of neoclassical social market theorists' "solutions" to national economic problems in the advanced industrialized economies itself raises formidable difficulties. If investment is the key to growth, and a high and rising share of investment is the crucial factor, how is this to be achieved? If neither profits nor wages are determined by marginal products, or by supply and demand, but merely by social and political conventions, what conventions should apply, and how should they be enforced? If final income distribution for consumption need bear no relation to original wages and profits, and neoclassical incentives are irrelevant to production decisions, then what distribution is appropriate, and how is it to be agreed? But if the control of the share of wages in national income is essential in order to guarantee required levels of investment, how will workers accept a wages policy in the absence of the prices policy that post-Keynesians see as potentially damaging to profits and investment? Finally, if the economy is seen as divided between a (hitherto expanding) oligopolistic, price-setting, high-technology, high-wage sector and a (hitherto contracting) competitive, low-technology, low-wage sector, how can economic planning affect an apparent reversal in the relationship between these two sectors, with the "core" sector contracting both output and employment and the "peripheral" sector slowly expanding, in most of the advanced capitalist countries? Appelbaum puts the problem succinctly when she writes that implicit in the post-Keynesian model is "the need for social and economic planning to determine the secular growth rate, to eliminate poverty, to improve the standard of living of workers and others, and to enable investment to take place at the appropriate socially determined rate". This in turn implies that such planning requires political institutions and political controls which do not exist, and would have to be brought into existence:

> Furthermore, such planning would result in socially imposed limits on the megacorp's ability to determine its own margin above costs and to make investment decisions. But such policies are necessary if economic growth, full employment, and a rising standard of living are not to be sacrificed in the attempt to end inflation by conventional means.[9]

In all the advanced capitalist countries, attempts were made to establish state institutions and processes to achieve these goals, containing some elements of fiscal and monetary manipulation, economic planning and corporatist methods. In all they seemed to achieve a degree of acceptance and success in the 1960s; but in most they have been increasingly questioned, criticized, modified or discarded since the postwar boom ended in the early 1970s.

Criticisms of planning

Some smaller countries (such as Austria and Sweden) have maintained the political continuity and consensus which were necessary conditions for corporatist methods, once economic growth began to falter; in the rest, serious difficulties have occurred. Even before the slower growth of the 1970s, planning and corporatism were criticized by market theorists and politicians, and by Marxists – by the former for inefficiency, and by the latter for bogus claims of class neutrality.

According to the market theorists, attempts to plan the national economy's growth are pointless because development occurs internationally. The determinants of national growth rates are on the supply side, and lie in the rate of growth of the labor force and the rate of technological change. Demand plays a passive role; if the supply factors allow growth, then it will fall into line, and equilibrium will be reached at full employment in conditions of perfect competition. Attempts at state coordination divert attention away from crucial market indicators and towards misleading aggregates.[10] Whereas the price mechanism can function as an overall coordinator of all the subtly interconnected elements in the economic system, is highly sensitive to change, and provides links between not obviously related variables, governments' attempts to influence aggregates are necessarily clumsy and crude. Efforts by the state to modify the *general* level of prices, *aggregate* demand, or *total* employment levels had weakened the price mechanism and caused chronic distortion in the allocation of resources. Efficient allocation can only occur if *relative* wages and prices are determined by market forces.[11]

What no system of coordination can do (neither state planning nor the price mechanism) is eliminate uncertainty or the need for change. Market theorists accuse post-Keynesians and planners of mistaking the consequences of inevitable miscalculations for failures of the market. The price system is the best way of signalling known data to millions of separate decision-makers, all making separate plans. It can bring them into some degree of coordination, but it cannot bring them into perfect harmony – indeed, it is precisely because information cannot be perfect or complete that a market economy is the best form of coordination, because the market is its own information system. As von Mises argues:

> If all people were to anticipate correctly the future state of the market, the entrepreneurs would neither earn any profits nor suffer any losses ... Profit and loss are ever-present features only on account of the fact that ceaseless change in the economic data makes again and again new discrepancies, and constantly the need for new adjustments originate.[12]

Attempts to provide greater certainty or eliminate losses through state coordination merely distort, and create inefficient allocation. Planners cannot hope to distinguish between which new enterprises are to succeed and which to fail. Hence they are reduced to supporting and rescuing ailing old enterprises, either directly (e.g. nationalization) or indirectly, through regional or monetary policy – a process derided by market theorists as "picking losers".[13]

Other critics of planning have argued that there are severe political consequences that arise from the attempt at state coordination,

because the government is subjected to demands from so many interest groups, and on behalf of so many social needs. Because the state
has allowed itself to be seen as controlling key decisions over investment, employment levels, incomes and so on, it is besieged with pressures to solve problems by spending money, or allocating other
resources. The result is that it is "overloaded" with demands, spends
too much and intervenes too frequently, leading to inflation and mis-
allocation. Furthermore, governments have used their powers to dispense resources through state agencies to buy off key sectors of the
electorate near election times, or to increase general spending power to
attract votes. Some authors have claimed to identify a political trade
cycle associated with this use of economic management for election-
eering purposes. With slower growth since the mid-1960s, the state has
found increasing difficulties in meeting the demands to which its
activities and election promises have given rise. Some authors have
argued that key economic decisions should be insulated from the
democratic process; others simply suggest that expectations must be
lowered, through resistance to pressures.[14]

In practice, the differences between governments heavily influenced
by post-Keynesian theories and those which have adopted monetarist
and market frameworks have not been as great as these theoretical dis-
agreements suggest. If we take the British experience as an example,
despite a commitment to "democratic" (as opposed to "totalitarian")
planning, the Attlee government quickly abandoned its attempt to plan
economic aggregates in 1947–8.[15] The National Plan of 1965 – an ambitious attempt to boost exports, reduce imports, increase industrial investment, control spending on social services, improve productivity and
curb wage increases – was abandoned in 1966. Large-scale and long-term
plans for coordination and target setting were dropped in favour of *ad
hoc* interventions, often in crises, an approach which continued in
1974–9. Similarly, Conservative pledges to reduce state activity, cut
spending, simplify administration and strengthen market systems have
been modified by events – spectacularly in the case of the Heath government in 1972–3, and considerably in the case of the Thatcher government after 1979. Whether in rescuing ailing industries or in providing
employment through state schemes, market-orientated governments
have been drawn into the field they would rather leave alone, while
Labour planners have been defeated in their more grandiose intentions
by market forces and the hostility of both business and trade unions.

The Marxist critique sees capitalist state planning as serving the
needs of capital, and mainly as a method of curbing the demands of

labor. Some authors regard the state's interventions as necessary to guarantee capital accumulation, or to ensure that the general interests of capital are served, as against particular interests or fractions of capital. Others see the state's role as the expression of capital's ability to represent its class interests as those of the nation as a whole, and hence economic planning as part of the process of political hegemony. Many see the failures of planning in terms similar to those of the "overload" theory – that the state experienced a fiscal crisis as a result of excessive or conflicting demands upon it, either because of the requirements of accelerated accumulation, or as a result of conflicts between these needs and its legitimating functions (such as the increased provision of social services). Marxist theories describe and explain planning activities and institutions in terms of a bewildering variety of "needs" and "resolutions", the main themes of which concern parallel concentrations of economic and political power in monopolistic corporations and the state's executive, and the need for class-conscious coordination between the economy and a range of expanding government agencies.[16]

Such accounts suffer from the same difficulties as earlier Marxist theories of the development of the state in explaining exactly how it is related to class interests.[17] Furthermore, they do not explain the persistent suspicion of the state among capitalists in many countries, especially those with liberal democratic traditions. As Crouch has commented:

> The *central* reason why capitalist interests mistrust the state is not the fear that it will be other fractions of capital which gain its favour (though this may sometimes be the case) but that it will be responsive to class interests other than those of capital. The attempts of Marxist analysis to get round this problem are not convincing.[18]

According to Marxist theories, planning and corporatism are alternative strategies for the subordination of labor when control through markets is problematic. Some theorists suggest that labor might have opportunities to bargain itself advantages under this system, or even possibly some common interests with capital which could be furthered through it; but all agree that it is a class concept which belongs to the analysis of the state in a capitalist society.[19] This means that the rise and decline of planning have both to be accounted for in terms of changes in class interests, or contradictions in capitalist development. But such analyses are distressingly circular, since the possibility of a change in the state superstructure without a corresponding shift in the economic base cannot arise.

My own analysis would suggest that postwar economic planning in the advanced capitalist countries developed from a number of historical factors, theoretical proposals and organizational changes. Both fascism and wartime mobilization had provided experiences of corporatism and planning. Keynesian ideas suggested that governments and industrialists could both benefit, in their shared concerns for maximization, from consultation and cooperation over long-term goal setting, particularly over major projects, involving lengthy and expensive research and development. The growth of government departments and the concentration of firms into larger corporations allowed institutions for such cooperation and joint planning to develop easily and naturally, especially in countries like Japan, with no democratic political institutions or liberal traditions to resist them, and West Germany and Italy with their interwar experiences of corporatism. In the United States, by contrast, planning was never developed systematically or institutionalized, except in the field of military projects, while in Britain, with its strong traditions of liberalism and its independent labor movement, attempts to use planning for purposes of wage restraint met with only temporary success.

Why then has planning waned in most of these countries? The major factor seems to me to have been the internationalization of industrial production, and particularly the relocation of much heavy industry in the newly industrializing countries. This has meant that multinational corporations in the advanced countries have been reluctant to plan with their national governments, or at least reluctant to commit themselves to attempts to increase output and employment in their home countries. While as investors they have been keen to exploit privileges and benefits both at home and overseas, their maximization of profits and growth as international enterprises has been at odds with national governments' attempts to maximize national output and income. This change has been reflected in the theory about planning developed in the 1970s.

Planning and multinational corporations

European countries which adopted economic planning and achieved rapid growth of national incomes in the 1960s were unable to sustain the same rates of growth in the 1970s. Above all, industrial production, which had provided the expansionary thrust during the postwar boom, grew only slowly during that decade; in Britain it grew hardly at all, so that (following the deflationary policies of the Conservative government after 1979) industrial output (excluding North Sea oil and natural gas) was at the same level in 1983 as it had been in 1967. Meanwhile, some newly industrializing countries were achieving far higher rates of growth of industrial output, based mainly on the heavy industries that were declining in the advanced economies, and using substantial investment from multinational companies based in the advanced industrialized countries. An alternative explanation was required by those who rejected market theories both of the declining growth rates of the previously successful economies, and of the chronic failure of the British economy, in spite of attempts at imitating European methods.

The experience of British governments since the Second World War seemed to suggest:

1 That output and investment in productive industry were crucial to the success of any planning about the distribution of resources in the economy. The instruments of "democratic planning" were inadequate to influence these magnitudes while productive industry was in almost exclusively private hands. Output targets consistently fell below planned levels, and even where proportions of investment were as planned, this was used to save costs (and especially labor costs) rather than to increase output.

2 That in the absence of any control over these factors, both state planning for the growth of national income, and the redistribution of resources (either between import and exports, or between the incomes of one group of consumers and another), were largely futile.

3 That increasing aggregate demand in the economy was insufficient to achieve increased output and investment in productive industry. This had been the tactic of the Conservative governments, in 1963–4 (when Reginald Maudling was Chancellor of the Exchequer) and 1972–4 (when Anthony Barber was Chancellor). The results in both cases seemed to be consumer spending booms, rapid rises in imports, and increased property speculation, but insufficient improvements in industrial output or investment.

In the mid-1970s, the British Labour Party reassessed its approach to planning, in the light of these problems, using concepts from post-Keynesian theory, and fusing them with some elements of the Marxist analysis. In this its thinking closely resembled that of some of the European socialist parties, and especially the French, with the result that there were marked similarities between the Labour Party's "alternative economic strategy" of the early 1980s, and the programme of the Mitterrand socialists in France. The new approach was perhaps most cogently expressed in Stuart Holland's book *The Socialist Challenge*, published in 1975. Holland is a Labour MP, and his book was a conscious attempt to supplant Anthony Crosland's *The Future of Socialism*, with its optimistic conclusions about the taming of capitalism through Keynesian economic management and the welfare state.

According to Holland, the crisis in the British economy and the failure of Keynesian methods could both be traced to "a new mode of production which has divorced macro policy from microstructure".[20] This was the advent of "the new *meso*economic sector which controls the commanding heights of big business in the national and international economy", consisting of monopoly multinational capital, which had interposed itself between the macroeconomic and microeconomic spheres.[21] The power of this sector frustrated national planning, which was in principle capable of harnessing any mixture of *national* enterprises to required levels of growth of output, investment, exports, jobs and incomes, but which required new mechanisms to harness the power of the largely international mesoeconomic sector to national purposes.

Holland referred to the new strategy as a restoration of national economic sovereignty, correcting the erosion of state power which had occurred through the growth of multinational enterprises. His solution was to nationalize some of these corporations – enough to shift the balance of power from the private to the public sector. He argued that in this way the state could set the pace in the active, manufacturing sector of industry, rather than controlling only the passive infrastructure. Capitalism and the market were consistent with socialism once the state controlled these key firms, and could force genuine competition on the large corporations, in place of oligopoly; the new approach to planning aimed at restoring the competitive mixed economy, in which output, investment and employment levels could be pulled upward by state initiatives.[22]

This theory still drew heavily on optimistic precedents from planning in Western European economies before the oil price crisis; but by the early 1980s it was clear that the European countries were locked into much the same cycle of stagnant industrial output, rising unemployment and decaying regions as Britain had been for over a decade. While the French economy under the Mitterrand regime did not suffer quite as disastrous a decline in industrial production and employment as the British economy did under Margaret Thatcher, it hardly sustained the claims made for these methods, either in terms of growth or in terms of "socialist transformation".

The implausible elements in the new strategy might be summarized as follows:

1 Multinational corporations make their plans according to international opportunities for profit. During the period when European industrial output has grown only slowly they have continued to increase their international output, investment and employment levels quite rapidly; they have simply concentrated a certain type of production in the advanced industrialized countries, and developed other types elsewhere. Only a real change in the international balance of opportunities could persuade them to make rational choices in favour of a different pattern.

2 Faster growth in the advanced industrialized economies might require lower levels of industrial employment, not higher. Higher productivity and profits might only be achievable through further reductions in the workforce. Choices might have to be made between growth and full employment.

3 If growth was to be the first priority, and industrial employment levels continued to fall (as had been the case for over a decade in Britain, and more recently in other European countries), then the state would be forced to redistribute a larger and larger proportion of income away from workers and towards the newly redundant population. This would require it to devise ways of doing so which could be perceived as just by both groups.

4 The same would be true of regional policy, where rapid growth might require the concentration of industry in already prosperous regions, and some system of support for decaying regions based on the profits or the wages generated there.

5 The socialist alternative still saw high levels of industrial employment and output as the basis for a healthy economy; but this was the approach which required the most comprehensive state controls. The essential point of the post-Keynesian model was that there could be no overall planning without political controls over decisions about output, investment and the incomes of both workers and claimants. The incomes policy elements were largely obscured

by socialist programmes, because the trade unions found controls politically unacceptable.

All this amounts to saying that the planning methods which were so successful in Western Europe during the postwar boom years required special conditions for their success. Rapid growth allowed simultaneous increases in investment, wage-levels and social provision, which avoided serious conflicts; when slow growth made choices between these priorities necessary, conflicts could not be contained within corporatist frameworks. In those countries at that time there was a preponderance of large national industrial companies, exerting a dominant influence on the economy, and willing to cooperate and consult with governments. Where countries had major overseas interests and where their currencies had an international role (as in the USA and Britain), finance capital was powerful and had interests which were not necessarily in line with those of national industrial firms. These interests were more concerned with preserving "sound money" than with promoting industrial production or national economic growth. In Britain, for instance, the City's longstanding links with the Treasury through the Bank of England proved more effective than the new institutions for linking the loosely knit industrial corporations with the state through the National Economic Development Corporation, the Department of Trade and Industry, and so on.[23] This traditional strength of British finance capital, and weakness of industrial capital, helps explain why Britain is the most obvious and extreme example of the trends I have identified; but these are recognizable in less extreme forms in other advanced capitalist countries.

Furthermore, once a significant number of major firms cease to be national and become international in scope, their interests become much more similar to those of finance capital. Whereas the large national firm can only increase profits and accumulate by increasing output or saving costs at home, the international corporation has the flexibility to diversify its productive methods and relocate parts of its operations in other countries. When Adam Smith and the later neoclassical theorists wrote about the mobility of capital they did not anticipate the speed and case with which international corporations would be able to switch between production bases in different countries; nor did Keynes take account of the possibility that a major industrial sector of the "national" economy might in fact be more concerned with profits earned abroad than with maximizing home production. Thus the growth of multinational corporations introduces entirely new elements into the process of managing a national economy, as international trade is replaced by international production.

This process of internationalization of production was initially slow, and largely obscured by the continuation of the earlier process of concentration and centralization in larger national firms, with more complex financial and managerial structures.[24] But theorists have drawn attention to the qualitative differences inherent in the recent move towards international corporations, in which the firm moves from being "the process that gives rise to the product" to becoming "the network of elements required to be juxtaposed and rearranged in relation to one another to fill functional-system objectives".[25] Characteristically, the headquarters of such corporations are right away from any productive centres, and are concerned exclusively with strategic planning of operations, leaving tactical decisions about output, use of factors, etc., to a management tier at a level equivalent to the national firm.[26] Kindleberger has described this change as an adaptation to the challenges and opportunities of the internationalization of production, and he has drawn attention to the problems of the nation state in meeting these same challenges.[27]

Above all, this flexible structure and strategic international planning allows the multinational corporation to make use of opportunities for new combinations which take account of such particular national differences as tax regulations, environmental controls, investment incentives and subsidies, as well as the prices of the factors of production. In this way, multinational corporations become more like international banks, and their decisions over production more like decisions over international monetary flows.[28]

Even more fundamentally, the internationalization of production creates for the first time the possibility of productive processes which are not tied to any particular form of property rights or productive relations. ... [The] evolution of modern nation states and commercial enterprises [are] inextricably linked, and ... the link was through the definition and guaranteeing of property rights, and for specific productive relations derive[d] from them. With the evolution of multinational corporations this link is broken. The corporation can diversify its production between nation states, each with very different property rights and productive relations. Just as capitalist banks have given credit to communist governments, so multinational corporations have relocated production in communist countries, benefiting from low labor costs and strict industrial discipline.

The real issue of modern economic management is not the close integration between national capital and state agencies, but the fact that international capital has transcended the nation state. It has burst out of the fetters of particular property rights and productive relations, which between the seventeenth century and the Second World War seemed to be the necessary protection offered by the state to capital. The issue therefore is how the state is to respond to its apparent redundancy – to the fact that multinational corporations now seem able to use its protection and assistance without depending upon them. It is that the state's priorities for national maximization of income and employment no longer accord with the multinational corporation's priorities for maximization through quick adaptability and flexibility in a fluid international situation.

An important attempt at a new type of adaptation to these new relationships has been made in Britain, the country most crucially affected, because of its long tradition of overseas investments, the importance of its international financial role, and the weakness of its national industrial base.

The rejection of planning, along with the whole concept of corporate economic management, by the Thatcher government in Britain seems to signify a recognition that the oligopolistic sector of British industry cannot readily be harnessed to targets of national output and investment programmes. Previous governments (both Conservative and Labour) appeared to believe that they could reconcile the international scope of the plans of these major corporations with their national growth objectives, and bargain with them and the trade unions to achieve a degree of control over economic development through political negotiation. The Thatcher government has accepted that the scope for such negotiations is limited so long as the major determinants of the corporations' decisions are outside the national framework, and so long as the state has no ability or mandate to override their decisions. The relative ease with which the Thatcher government has excluded the trade unions from any part in decision-making indicates that corporatist theories overestimated both the significance of the unions' corporate power (at least in a situation of rising unemployment and falling working-class expectations) and capital's "need", through the state, to control this through corporate planning.

The Thatcher government's approach to economic policy ostensibly returns to a model based on the competitive market. In reality, its major break with the post-Keynesian model is in recognizing the international development of production and the impossibility of containing this within the framework of the kinds of institutions that emerged in the 1960s. This means that its strength is not derived from "harnessing" corporate power to national purposes, or from a "fusion" between the political power executive and the economic power of big corporations. It stems from a recognition of a role for the state in determining the social order which is *not* derived directly from productive relations.

During the era when economic management and planning dominated governments' perceptions of the role of the state's institutions, it appeared that this post-Keynesian model of the "superstructure" was the logical counterpart of the economic "base". It corresponded neatly with the emergence of the oligopolistic sector of industry in the form of large national firms, and the increasingly important role of the major trade unions. Since the relationship between these producer groups appeared to be the crucial factor shaping the economic order, and hence the social order derived from it, it was logical for the state to be a forum for coordination of political and economic decision-making, involving these major corporate powers. The experience of the 1970s suggests that this model was misleading. In economic terms, British development was far more influenced by external factors – the pattern of overseas investment, the terms of the IMF loan of 1976, the terms of membership of the EEC [European Economic Community] – than by negotiated settlements between the representatives of the producer interest groups.

In the model of the state developed by the Conservatives under Margaret Thatcher, no concerted effort is made to plan *national* targets on such aggregates as investment and output, or even national income. The government emphasizes the need for international trade and competition, and for British firms to improve their efficiency in order to compete more successfully. There is more emphasis on encouraging small firms and entrepreneurial initiative. The organizational structure of economic planning and corporate consultation remains largely intact, but much less faith is placed in it as an instrument of the state.

This approach by no means resolves the many conflicts and tensions in the British economy. For instance there are clear and occasionally visible rifts between those sections of the CBI [Confederation of British Industries] which represent predominantly British capital (including the chairman himself and the former managing director of British Leyland, who believe that they would benefit from policies which allowed lower interest rates and increased demand), and the international companies and financial interests, which largely endorse the Thatcher government's policies. However, since even these mild dissenters strongly approve the government's policies in relation to many other aspects of the economy (for instance, trade union "reform"), their criticisms are very muted. Above all, even though the Thatcher government initially had disastrous effects on the profits of British industry, it has proved more successful in holding down wages and curbing trade union intransigence than any of its postwar predecessors.

Conclusions

The example of British economic policy illustrates the difficulties of attempts to apply post-Keynesian theory in the context of a modern advanced economy. It is one thing to argue that relative income shares are largely conventionally or politically determined; it is quite another to achieve the political consensus required to control or alter these shares. It is one thing to suggest that aggregates such as investment levels are of crucial importance; it is quite another to achieve effective power over the size and direction of total investment. In the British mixed economy, governments could command neither consensus nor control.

This was partly connected with the internationalization of industrial production. What British governments were apparently trying to achieve was quite contrary to the direction of this development. Increased output by British industry would have required a volume and type of investment, an increase in productivity, a control of wages and above all a guarantee of profits that reversed the whole trend in the advanced industrialized countries, as well as its own record of the previous decade. If the aim of planning was simultaneously to modernize and expand British productive industry, this was doomed by forces outside Britain, so long as these forces were allowed to influence the British economy.

By the end of the 1970s, the Conservatives were able credibly to argue that the choice lay between a closed, protectionist economy with increasing political controls, or an open, free-market one, which took its chance in international competition. Effective protection of Britain's industrial base would have required not merely exchange controls, tariff barriers and import quotas, but also a rigid incomes policy; and these trends would have been cumulative. In their taunts that Labour's policies led towards an Eastern European model, the Conservatives were merely taking the logic of post-Keynesian economic theory to its own unpalatable conclusions. Their subsequent electoral victories demonstrated the lack of support for such measures, and particularly for the incomes policies that had been such a disastrous part of previous Labour governments' strategies.

By contrast, the free-market approach made little attempt to defend Britain's industrial base. It relied on the increased self-sufficiency in food that had occurred in the 1970s to compensate for the adverse balance of manufactures trade which eventually occurred in 1983. It allowed international forces to transform the British economy into one that relied more and more on the export of raw materials (oil especially) and services, and less the export of industrial products.

In political terms, the success of these policies seems to lie in their ability to combine a strongly internationalist approach to economic policies with the rhetoric of the shopkeeper or small businessman. This of course is true to the tradition of Adam Smith: that however destructive the giant forces of international development may seem, they are ultimately beneficial and liberating, and operate according to exactly the same principles as the local trade and industry of the village community. It does not really matter whether the mechanisms of price and income determination work precisely according to marginalist theory so long as this rhetoric conforms so closely to the established perceptions and thought processes of a large proportion of the electorate. By swimming with the tide of economic development, the Thatcher government is able to exonerate itself from responsibility for the least pleasant aspects of change, and claim credit for its more acceptable features.

It could be argued that the mistake of British economic planning lay not so much in its theoretical basis as in its attempts to bring about the impossible. By swimming so very much *against* the tide of international development, it was forced either to fail, or to use instruments which were politically unacceptable. If it had been able to identify more achievable aims, it might well have earned itself a better reputation. This presumably was the secret behind the more successful attempts at planning in France and Italy, up to the mid-1970s.

However, since the mid-1970s, planning in Britain and France has come to be associated exclusively with an attempt to promote growth through a rebuilding of the "industrial base", and particularly with reducing unemployment through the creation of new jobs in productive industry. It has also been associated with the attempt to resist international capitalist forces through the use of the power of the state – and hence with an emphasis on national economic and political sovereignty.[29] This notion of a return to past industrial glories, and to a "right to work" for all, as a means of defending the living standards of the working class, represents a narrow and backwardlooking interpretation of the socialist tradition and of economic planning. Planning becomes concerned with one particular variable or one particular outcome. It leads to a rigid approach, such as that of the USSR where ... it is inextricably linked with certain "goals of production", which always require a particular type of result.[30] Socialist planning is supposed to be concerned with designing a society in which social needs are met, and the benefits of cooperation are maximized. The task of discovering such a design cannot be a once-for-all exercise, nor can it be left in the hands of a group of experts; it requires adaptation to changing economic circumstances, and a dialogue between planners and people.[31]

Notes

1. Ralph Miliband, *The State in Capitalist Society* (London: Weidenfeld & Nicolson, 1969), Chapters 2 and 3.
2. P. C. Schmitter and G. Lembruch (eds), *Trends Towards Corporatist Intermediation* (London: Sage, 1979).
3. See for instance, Paul Samuelson, *Economics* (New York: McGraw-Hill, [1948] 1976).
4. Joan Robinson, *The Accumulation of Capital* (London: Macmillan, 1956); Nicolas Kaldor, *Essays on Value and Distribution* (London: Duckworth and Glencoe: Free Press, 1960).
5. Piero Sraffa, *The Production of Commodities by Means of Commodities* (Cambridge: Cambridge University Press, 1960); Michal Kalecki, *Studies in the Theory of the Business Cycle* (New York: Kelly, 1966).
6. See for instance, J. Cornwall, "Macrodynamics", in A. S. Eichner (ed.), *A Guide to Post-Keynesian Economics* (London: Macmillan, 1979), p. 29.
7. Richard X. Chase, "Production Theory", in Eichner (ed.), *Post-Keynesian Economics*, p. 79.
8. See Chapter 10, "The Development of the World Economy," pp. 188–218, in Jordan, *The State. Authority and Autonomy* (Oxford: Basil Blackwell, 1985).
9. Eileen Appelbaum, "The Labour Market", in Eichner (ed.), *Post-Keynesian Economics*, p. 100.
10. See for instance, F. A. Hayek, *A Tiger by the Tail* (London: Institute of Economic Affairs, 1972).
11. F. A. Hayek, *Full Development at Any Price?* (London: Institute of Economic Affairs, 1975), Occasional Paper, 45.
12. L. von Mises, *Planning for Freedom* (South Holland, Ill.: Libertarian Press, 1974), pp. 108–9.
13. John Burton, *Picking Losers ... ? The Political Economy of Industrial Policy* (London: Institute of Economic Affairs, 1983), Hobart Paper, 99.
14. See for instance, S. Brittan, "Inflation and Democracy", in F. Hirsch and J. H. Goldthorpe (eds), *The Political Economy of Inflation* (London: Robertson, 1978); R. Rose and G. Peters, *The Political Consequences of Economic Overload* (Strathclyde: University of Strathclyde, Centre for the Study of Public Policy, 1977).

15. These contrasting terms were used in the government's Economic Survey (1947), quoted in Joan Mitchell, *Groundwork to Economic Planning* (London: Secker & Warburg, 1966).
16. See for instance J. Holloway and S. Piciotto (eds), *State and Capital* (Arnold, 1978); N. Poulantzas (ed.), *La Crise de L'Etat* (Paris: PUF, 1976); J. O'Connor, *The Fiscal Crisis of the State* (New York: St. Martin's Press, 1973); I. Gough, *The Political Economy of the Welfare State* (London: Macmillan, 1979). I shall not review these or other Marxist theories here because this has been comprehensively done by Jessop [see e.g. n. 17 below] and they suffer from the common weakness of reducing state power to the power exercised by capitalists.
17. See Bob Jessop, *The Capitalist State. Marxist Theories and Methods* (London: Robertson, 1982).
18. Colin Crouch, "The State, Capital and Liberal Democracy", in C. Crouch (ed.), *State and Economy in Contemporary Capitalism* (New York: St Martin's Press, 1979), p. 27.
19. Ibid., p. 19.
20. Stuart Holland, *The Socialist Challenge* (London: Quartet, 1975), pp. 14–15.
21. Ibid.
22. Ibid., pp. 185–8.
23. Frank Longstreth, "The City, Industry and the State," in Crouch (ed.), *State and Economy*.
24. See Alfred Chandler, *Strategy and Structure* (Garden City: Doubleday, 1966).
25. D. Schon, "The Future of American Industry", *The Listener* (July 2, 1970).
26. Alfred Chandler and Fritz Redlich, "Recent Developments in American Business Administrations and their Conceptualisation", *Business History Review*, Spring (1961).
27. Charles Kindleberger, *American Business Abroad* (New Haven: Yale University Press, 1969), Lecture 6.
28. Gilles Paquet, "The Multinational Firm and the Nation State as Institutional Forms", in G. Paquet (ed.), *The Multinational Firm and the Nation State* (Don Mills, Out.: Collier-Macmillan, 1972).
29. See for instance, F. Cripps, J. Griffith, F. Morrell, J. Reid, P. Townsend and S. Weir, *Manifesto: A Radical Strategy for Britain's Future* (Pan, 1981).
30. See B. Jordan, "The Centrally Planned Economies", in *The State: Authority and Autonomy*, pp. 238–9.
31. See ibid., Part III: "Alternative Designs," pp. 281–356.

12
Some Contradictions of the Modern Welfare State (1981)*

Claus Offe

The welfare state has served as the major peace formula of advanced capitalist democracies for the period following the Second World War. This peace formula basically consists, first, in the explicit obligation of the state apparatus to provide assistance and support (either in money or in kind) to those citizens who suffer from specific needs and risks which are characteristic of the market society; such assistance is provided as a matter of legal claims granted to the citizens. Second, the welfare state is based on the recognition of the formal role of labor unions both in collective bargaining and the formation of public policy. Both of these structural components of the welfare state are considered to limit and mitigate class conflict, to balance the asymmetrical power relation of labor and capital, and thus to overcome the condition of disruptive struggle and contradictions that was the most prominent feature of pre-welfare state, or liberal, capitalism. In sum, the welfare state has been celebrated throughout the post-war period as the political solution to societal contradictions.

Until quite recently, this seemed to be the converging view of political elites both in countries in which the welfare state is fully developed (for example, Great Britain, Sweden), and in those where it is still an incompletely realized model. Political conflict in these latter societies, such as the USA, was not centred on the basic desirability and

* From *Contradictions of the Welfare State*, trans. John Keane (Cambridge, Mass: MIT Press, 1984), pp. 147–61. This essay was first presented as a paper to the Facoltà de Scienze Politiche, Università di Perugia, Italy (February 1980). It is here reprinted, with minor alterations, from the version published in *Praxis International*, I (3) (October 1981), pp. 219–29.

functional indispensability, but on the pace and modalities of the implementation of the welfare state model.

This was true, with very minor exceptions, until the mid 1970s. From that point on we see that in many capitalist societies this established peace formula itself becomes the object of doubts, fundamental critique, and political conflict. It appears that the most widely accepted device of political problem-solving has itself become problematic, and that, at any rate, the unquestioning confidence in the welfare state and its future expansion has rapidly vanished. It is to these doubts and criticisms that I will direct our attention. The point to start with is the observation that the almost universally accepted model of creating a measure of social peace and harmony in European post-war societies has itself become the source of new contradictions and political divisions in the 1970s.

Historically, the welfare state has been the combined outcome of a variety of factors which change in composition from country to country. Social democratic reformism, Christian socialism, enlightened conservative political and economic elites, and large industrial unions were the most important forces which fought for and conceded more and more comprehensive compulsory insurance schemes, labor protection legislation, minimum wages, the expansion of health and education facilities and state-subsidized housing, as well as the recognition of unions as legitimate economic and political representatives of labor. These continuous developments in Western societies were often dramatically accelerated in a context of intense social conflict and crisis, particularly under war and post-war conditions. The accomplishments which were won under conditions of war and in post-war periods were regularly maintained, and added to them were the innovations that could be introduced in periods of prosperity and growth. In the light of the Keynesian doctrine of economic policy, the welfare state came to be seen not so much as a burden imposed upon the economy, but as a built-in economic and political stabilizer which could help to regenerate the forces of economic growth and prevent the economy from spiralling downward into deep recessions. Thus, a variety of quite heterogeneous ends (ranging from reactionary pre-emptive strikes against the working-class movement in the case of Bismarck to socialist reformism in the case of the Weimar social democrats [in Germany: Ed.]; from the social–political consolidation of war and defence economies to the stabilization of the business cycle, etc.) converged on the adoption of identical institutional means which today make up the welfare state. It is exactly its multi-functional character, its ability to serve many conflicting ends and strategies simultaneously, which made the political arrangement of the welfare state so attractive to a broad alliance of heterogeneous forces. But it is equally true that the very diversity of the forces that inaugurated and supported the welfare state could not be accommodated forever within the institutional framework which today appears to come increasingly under attack. The machinery of class compromise has itself become the object of class conflict.

The attack from the right

The sharp economic recession of the mid 1970s has given rise to an intellectually and politically powerful renaissance of neo-*laissez-faire* and monetarist economic doctrines. These doctrines amount to a fundamental critique of the welfare state that is seen to be the illness of what it pretends to be the cure: rather than effectively harmonizing the conflicts of a market society, it exacerbates them and prevents the forces of social peace and progress (namely, the forces of the marketplace) from functioning properly and beneficially. This is said to be so for two major reasons. First, the welfare state apparatus imposes a burden of taxation and regulation upon capital which amounts to a *disincentive to investment*. Second, at the same time, the welfare state grants claims, entitlements and collective power positions to workers and unions which amount to a *disincentive to work*, or at least to work as hard and productively as they would be forced to under the reign of unfettered market forces. Taken together, these two effects lead into a dynamic of declining growth and increased expectations, of economic "demand overload" (known as inflation) as well as political demand overload ("ungovernability"), which can be satisfied less and less by the available output.

As obvious as the reactionary political uses are that this analysis is usually meant to support or suggest, it may well be that the truth of the analysis itself is greater than the desirability of its practical conclusions. Although the democratic Left has often measured the former by the latter, the two deserve at least a separate evaluation. In my view the above analysis is not so much false in what it says but in what it remains silent about.

For instance, to take up the first point of the conservative analysis: is it not true that, under conditions of declining growth rates and vehement competition on domestic and international markets, individual capitalists, at least those firms which do not enjoy the privileges of the monopolistic sector, have many good reasons to consider the prospects for investment and profits bleak, and to blame the welfare state, which imposes social security taxes and a great variety of regulations on them, for reducing profitability even further? Is it not true that the power position of unions, which, in turn, is based on rights they have won through industrial relations, collective bargaining, and other laws, is great enough to make an increasing number of industrial producers unprofitable or to force them to seek investment opportunities abroad? And is it not also true that capitalist firms will make investment (and hence employment) decisions according to criteria of expected profitability, and that they consequently will fail to invest as soon as long-term profitability is considered unattractive by them, thus causing an aggregate relative decline in the production output of the economy?

To be sure, no one would deny that there are causes of declining growth rates and capitalists' failure to invest which have nothing to do with the impact of the welfare state upon business, but which are rather to be looked for in inherent crisis tendencies of the capitalist economy such as overaccumulation, the business cycle, or uncontrolled technical change. But even if so, it still might make sense to alleviate the hardship imposed upon capital – and therefore, by definition, upon the rest of society, within the confines of a capitalist society – by dropping some of the burdens and constraints of the welfare state. This, of course, is exactly what most proponents of this argument are suggesting as a practical consequence. But after all, so the fairly compelling logic of the argument continues, who benefits from the operation of a welfare state that undermines and eventually destroys the production system upon which it has to rely in order to make its own promises become true? Does not a kind of "welfare" become merely nominal and worthless anyway that punishes capital by a high burden of costs and hence everyone else by inflation, unemployment, or both? In my view, the valuable insight to be gained from the type of analysis I have just described is this: the welfare state, rather than being a separate and autonomous source of well-being which provides incomes and services as a citizen right, is itself highly dependent upon the prosperity and continued profitability of the economy. While being designed to be a cure to some ills of capitalist accumulation, the nature of the illness is such that it may force the patient to refrain from using the cure.

A conceivable objection to the above argument would be that capitalists and conservative political elites "exaggerate" the harm imposed upon them by welfare state arrangements. To be sure, in the political game they have good tactical reasons to make the welfare state burden appear more intolerable than it "really" is. The question boils down then to what we mean by – and how we measure – "reality" in this context. In answering this question, we will have to keep in mind that the power position of private investors includes the power to *define* reality. That is to say, whatever they *consider* an intolerable burden in fact is an intolerable burden which will *in fact* lead to a declining propensity to invest, at least as long as they can expect to effectively reduce welfare-state-related costs by applying such economic sanctions. The debate about whether or not the welfare state is "really" squeezing profits is thus purely academic because investors are in a position to *create the reality – and the effects – of "profit squeeze."*

The second major argument of the conservative analysis postulates that the effect of the welfare state is a disincentive to work. "Labour does not work!" was one of the slogans in the campaign that brought Margaret Thatcher into the office of the British Prime Minister. But, again, the analytical content of the argument must be carefully separated from the political uses to which it is put. And, again, this analytical argument can, often contrary to the intentions of its proponents, be read in a way that does make a lot of empirical sense. For instance, there is little doubt that elaborate labor protection legislation puts workers in a position to resist practices of exploitation that would be applied, as a rule, in the absence of such regulations. Powerful and recognized unions can in fact obtain wage increases in excess of productivity increases. And extensive social security provisions make it easier – at least for some workers, for some of the time – to avoid undesirable jobs. Large-scale unemployment insurance covering most of the working population makes unemployment less undesirable for many workers and thus partially obstructs the reserve army mechanism. Thus, the welfare state has made the exploitation of labor more complicated and less predictable. On the other side, as the welfare state imposes regulations and rights upon the labor-capital exchange that goes on in production, while leaving the authority structure and the property relations of production itself untouched, it is hardly surprising to see that the workers are not, as a rule, so intrinsically motivated to work that they would work as productively as they possibly could. In other words, the welfare state maintains the control of capital over production, and thus the basic source of industrial and class conflict between labor and capital; by no means does it establish anything resembling "workers' control". At the same time, it strengthens workers' potential for resistance against capital's control – the net effect being that an unchanged conflict is fought out with means that have changed in favor of labor. Exploitative production relations coexist with expanded possibilities to resist, escape and mitigate exploitation. While the *reason* for struggle remained unchanged, the *means* of struggle increased for the workers. It is not surprising to see that this condition undermines the "work ethic", or at least requires more costly and less reliable strategies to enforce such an ethic.[1]

My point, so far, is that the two key arguments of the liberal-conservative analysis are valid to a large extent, contrary to what critics from the Left have often argued. The basic fault I see in this analysis has less to do with what it explicitly states than with what it leaves out of its consideration. Every political theory worth its name has to answer two questions. First, what is the desirable form of the organization of society and state and how can we demonstrate that it is at all "workable", i.e., consistent with our basic normative and factual assumptions about social life? This is the problem of defining a consistent *model* or goal of transformation. Second, how do we get there? This is the problem of identifying the dynamic forces and *strategies* that could bring about the transformation.

The conservative analysis of the welfare state fails on both counts. To start with the latter problem, it is extremely hard today in Western Europe to conceive of a promising political strategy that would aim at even partially eliminating the established institutional components of the welfare state, to say nothing about its wholesale abolition. That is to say, the welfare state has, in a certain sense, become an irreversible structure, the abolition of which would require nothing less than the abolition of political democracy and the unions, as well as fundamental changes in the party system. A political force that could bring about such dramatic changes is nowhere visible as a significant factor, Right-wing middle-class populist movements that occasionally spring up in some countries notwithstanding. Moreover, it is a well-known fact from political opinion research that the fiercest advocates of *laissez-faire* capitalism and economic individualism show marked differences between their *general* ideological outlook and their willingness to have *special* transfers, subsidies, and social security schemes abandoned from which they *personally* derive benefits. Thus, in the absence of a powerful ideological and organizational undercurrent in Western politics (such as a neo-fascist or authoritarian one), the vision of overcoming the welfare state and resurrecting a "healthy" market economy is not much more than the politically impotent day-dream of some ideologues of the old middle class. This class is nowhere strong enough to effect, as the examples of Margaret Thatcher and – hypothetically – Ronald Reagan demonstrate, more than marginal alterations of an institutional scheme that such figures, too, have to accept as given when taking office.

Even more significant, however, is the second failure of the conservative analysis; its failure to demonstrate that "advanced-capitalism-*minus*-the-welfare-state" would actually be a workable model. The reasons why it is not, and consequently why the neo-*laissez-faire* ideology would be a very dangerous cure even *if* it could be administered, are fairly obvious. In the absence of large-scale state-subsidized housing, public education and health services, as well as extensive compulsory social security schemes, the working of an industrial economy would be simply inconceivable. Given the conditions and requirements of urbanization, large-scale concentration of labor power in industrial production plants, rapid technical, economic and regional change, the reduced ability of the family to cope with the difficulties of life in industrial society, the secularization of the moral order, the quantitative reduction and growing dependence of the propertied middle classes – all of which are well-known characteristics of capitalist social structures – the sudden disappearance of the welfare state would leave the system in a state of exploding conflict and anarchy. The embarrassing secret of the welfare state is that, while its impact upon capitalist accumulation may well become destructive (as the conservative analysis so emphatically demonstrates), its abolition would be plainly disruptive (a fact that is systematically ignored by the conservative critics). The contradiction is that while capitalism cannot coexist *with*, neither can it exist *without*, the welfare state. This is exactly the condition to which we refer when using the concept "contradiction". The flaw in the conservative analysis is in the one-sided emphasis it puts on the first side of this contradiction, and its silence about the second one. This basic contradiction of the capitalist welfare state could, of course, be thought to be a mere "dilemma" which then would be "solved" or "managed" by a circumspect balancing of the two components. This, however, would presuppose two things, both of which are at least highly uncertain: first, that there is something like an "optimum point" at which the order-maintaining functions of the welfare state are preserved while its disruptive effects are avoided; and, second, if so, that political procedures and administrative practices will be sufficiently "rational" to accomplish this precarious balance. Before I consider the prospects for this solution, let me first summarize some elements of the contending socialist critique of the welfare state.

The critique from the socialist left

Although it would be nonsensical to deny the fact that the struggle for labor protection legislation, expanded social services, social security and the recognition of unions led by the working-class movement for over a century now has brought substantial improvements of the living conditions of most wage earners, the socialist critique of the welfare state is, nevertheless, a fundamental one. It can be summarized in three points which we will consider in turn. The welfare state is said to be:

1 ineffective and inefficient;
2 repressive;
3 conditioning a false ("ideological") understanding of social and political reality within the working class.

In sum, it is a device to stabilize, rather than a step in the transformation of, capitalist society.

In spite of the undeniable gains in the living conditions of wage earners, the institutional structure of the welfare state has done little or nothing to alter the income distribution between the two principal classes of labor and capital. The huge machinery of redistribution does not work in the vertical, but in the horizontal direction, namely, *within* the class of wage earners. A further aspect of its ineffectiveness is that the welfare state does not *eliminate the causes* of individual contingencies and needs (such as work-related diseases, the disorganization of cities by the capitalist real estate market, the obsolescence of skills, unemployment, etc.), but *compensates for* (parts of) *the consequences* of such events (by the provision of health services and health insurance, housing subsidies, training and re-training facilities, unemployment benefits and the like). Generally speaking, the kind of social intervention most typical of the welfare state is always "too late," and hence its *ex post facto* measures are more costly and less effective than a more "causal" type of intervention would allow them to be. This is a generally recognized dilemma of social policy-making, the standard answer to which is the recommendation to adopt more "preventive" strategies. Equally generally, however, it is also recognized that effective prevention would almost everywhere mean interfering with the prerogatives of investors and management, i.e., the sphere of the market and private property which the welfare state has only very limited legal and *de facto* powers to regulate.

A further argument pointing at the ineffectiveness of the welfare state emphasizes the constant threat to which social policies and social services are exposed due to the fiscal crisis of the state, which, in turn, is a reflection of both cyclical and structural discontinuities of the process of accumulation. All West European countries experienced a sharp economic recession in the mid 1970s, and we know of many examples of cutting social policy expenditures in response to the fiscal consequences of this recession. But even if and when the absolute and relative rise of social policy expenditures as a percentage of GNP continues uninterrupted, it is by no means certain, as Ian Gough and others before him have argued, that increases in the expenditures are paralleled by increases in real "welfare". The dual fallacy, known in the technical literature as the "spending-serving-cliché", is this: first, a marginal increase in expenditures must not necessarily correspond to a marginal increment in the "outputs" of the welfare state apparatus; it may well be used up in feeding the bureaucratic machinery itself. But, second, even if the output (say of health services) is increased, a still larger increase in the level of risks and needs (or a qualitative change of these) may occur on the part of the clients or recipients of such services, so as to make the net effect negative.

The bureaucratic and professional form through which the welfare state dispenses its services is increasingly seen to be a source of its own inefficiency. Bureaucracies absorb more resources and provide less services than other democratic and decentralized structures of social policy could. The reason why the bureaucratic form of administering social services is maintained in spite of its inefficiency and ineffectiveness, which becomes increasingly obvious to more and more observers, must, therefore, be connected with the social control function exercised by centralized welfare bureaucracies. This analysis leads to the critique of the *repressiveness* of the welfare state, its social control aspect. Such repressiveness is, in the view of the critics, indicated by the fact that, in order to qualify for the benefits and services of the welfare state, the client must not only prove his or her "need," but must also be a *deserving* client – a client, that is, who complies with the dominant economic, political, and cultural standards and norms of the society. The heavier the needs, the stricter these requirements tend to be defined. Only if, for instance, the unemployed are willing to keep themselves available for any alternative employment (often considerably inferior to the job they have lost) that eventually may be made available to them by employment agencies are they entitled to unemployment benefits; and the claim for welfare payments to the poor is everywhere made conditional upon their conformity to standards of behaviour which the better-to-do strata of the population are perfectly free to violate. In these and many other cases, the welfare state can be looked upon as an exchange transaction in which material benefits for the needy are traded for their submissive recognition of the "moral order" of the society which generates such need. One important pre-condition for obtaining the services of the welfare state is the ability of the individual to comply with the routines and requirements of welfare bureaucracies and service organizations, an ability which, needless to say, often is inversely correlated to need itself.

A third major aspect of the socialist critique of the welfare state is to demonstrate its *political-ideological* control function. The welfare state is seen not only as the source of benefits and services, but, at the same time, as the source of false conceptions about historical reality which have damaging effects for working-class consciousness, organization and struggle. First of all, the welfare state creates the false image of two separated spheres of working-class life. On the one side, the sphere of work, the economy, production and "primary" income distribution; on the other, the sphere of citizenship, the state, reproduction and "secondary" distribution. This division of the socio–political world obscures the causal and functional links and ties that exist between the two, and thus prevents the formation of a political understanding which views society as a coherent totality-to-be-changed. That is to say, the structural arrangements of the welfare state tend to make people ignore or forget that the needs and contingencies which the welfare state responds to are themselves constituted, directly or indirectly, in the sphere of work and production, that the welfare state itself is materially and institutionally constrained by the dynamics of the sphere of production, and that a reliable conception of social security does, therefore, presuppose not only the expansion of "citizen rights", but of "workers rights" in the process of production. Contrary to such insights, which are part of the analytical starting points of any conceivable socialist strategy of societal transformation, the inherent symbolic indoctrination of the welfare state suggests the ideas of class co-operation, the disjunction of economic and political struggles, and the evidently more and more ill-based confidence in an ever-continuing cycle of economic growth and social security.

The welfare state and political change

What emerges from our sketchy comparative discussion of the "Right" and the "Left" analyses of the welfare state are three points on which the liberal–conservative and the socialist critics exhibit somewhat surprising parallels.

First, contrary to the ideological consensus that flourished in some of the most advanced welfare states throughout the 1950s and 1960s, nowhere is the welfare state believed any longer to be the promising and permanently valid answer to the problems of the socio–political order of advanced capitalist economies. Critics in both camps have become more vociferous and fundamental in their negative appraisal of welfare state arrangements.

Second, neither of the two approaches to the welfare state could and would be prepared, in the best interest of its respective clientele, to abandon the welfare state, as it performs essential and indispensable functions both for the accumulation process as well as for the social and economic well-being of the working class.

Third, while there is, on the conservative side, neither a consistent theory nor a realistic strategy about the social order of a non-welfare state (as I have argued before), it is not perfectly evident that the situation is much better on the Left where one could possibly speak of a consistent theory of socialism, but certainly not of an agreed-upon and realistic strategy for its construction. In the absence of the latter, the welfare state remains a theoretically contested, though in reality firmly entrenched, fact of the social order of advanced capitalist societies. In short, it appears that the welfare state, while being contested both from the Right and the Left, will not be easily replaced by a conservative or progressive alternative.

To be sure, there are a number of normative models of the social and economic order which are, however, advocated by intellectuals and other minorities rather than being supported by any broad political current. One is the neo-*laissez-faire* model according to which the welfare state can and should be abolished so that the resurrection of the free and harmonious market society can take place. This solution is typically supported by political forces from the old middle class, such as farmers and shopkeepers, who also often favor tax-resistance movements. The political problem with this solution is that the further and more evenly capitalist modernization has taken place within one country, the smaller the social base of this backward-looking alternative will be. Its polar opposite is a model favored by elements of the new middle class, combining "post-material" values with certain ideas inherited from the anarchist and syndicalist tradition of political thought. This model would imply that the functions of the welfare state could be taken over by libertarian, egalitarian and largely self-reliant communities working within a highly decentralized and debureaucratized setting.

Typically, both of these alternative models have no more than a very marginal role to play as long as they fail to form alliances with one of the principal classes, respectively, and the political forces representing them. But such alliances, either between the old middle class and the centres of capital or the new middle class and the established working-class organizations, are immensely difficult to form and sustain. Nevertheless, it would probably not be too speculative an assumption to expect such struggles for new alliances to occupy the stage of social policy and welfare state reform in the years to come. In my view, three potential alternative outcomes of these political efforts can be envisaged.

First, under conditions of heightened economic crisis and international tension, a relative success of the neo-*laissez-faire* coalition, based on an alliance of big capital and the old middle class, is not entirely to be excluded as a possibility. Second, in countries with a strong social democratic (and possibly also in those with a strong Euro-communist) element, it is more likely that new forms of interest intermediation and relatively peaceful accommodation will emerge which are designed to determine the "right dose" of welfare state expansion, i.e., one that is compatible both with the requirements of accumulation as well as with the key demands of working-class organizations. This model would involve the extensive reliance on "neo-corporatist" or "tripartite" modes of decision-making, carried out by representatives of highly centralized employers' organizations and unions under the supervision of specialized agencies of the state. This second conceivable configuration, however, will operate, especially under economic crisis conditions, at the expense not only of the old middle class, but also of those sectors of the working class which are less well organized and represented within such highly exclusive frameworks of inter-group negotiation and decision-making. Not entirely inconceivable is, third, a type of alliance that combines working-class organizations and elements from the new middle class on the basis of a non-bureaucratic, decentralized, and egalitarian model of a self-reliant "welfare society". Proponents of this solution are to be found within the new social movements who find some resonance in the theoretical ideas of authors like Illich, Gorz, Touraine, Cooley and others.

Rather than speculating about the likely outcome of this configuration of forces and ideas, which would require a much more detailed analysis than is possible within the confines of this essay, I want to turn in my concluding remarks to the nature of the political process which will eventually decide one or the other of these outcomes. This process can best be conceived of as consisting of three tiers, or three cumulative arenas of conflict. The first and most obvious is the arena of political *decision-making within the state apparatus*. Its actors are political elites competing with each other for electoral victories and scarce resources. They decide on social policy programmes, legislations and budgets. This is the most superficial and most visible level of politics, the one publicized by the media and involved whenever the citizen is called upon to act in his or her political role, for example, as voter.

But this is by no means the only level at which political power is generated, distributed and utilized. For the space of possible decisions of political elites is determined by societal forces that, on a far less visible level, shape and change the politicians' view and perception of reality, i.e., of the alternatives open to decision-making and the consequences to be expected from each of the alternatives. This is the level at which the agenda of politics and the relative priority of issues and solutions is determined, and the durability of alliances and compromises is conditioned. On this level, it is more difficult to identify specific actors; the forces operating here are most often the aggregate outcome of a multitude of anonymous actors and actions which nevertheless shape the politicians' view of reality and space of action. Examples of such conditioning forces are events in the international environment (such as wars or revolutions), macro-economic indicators (terms of trade, growth rates, changes in the level of unemployment and inflation, etc.), and changes in the cultural parameters of social life (ranging from the rates of secondary school attendance to divorce rates). The experience of these indicators shapes the elites' image of reality, their view of what they can and must do, what they have to expect as consequences of their actions, and what they must refrain from doing. The important point here is this: although the power to structure the politicians' reality, agenda and attention cannot be as easily traced back to personal actors as is the case on the first level of political conflict, there is, nevertheless, a *matrix of social power* according to which social classes, collective actors and other social categories have a greater chance of shaping and reshaping political reality, opening or closing the political agenda, than others. Access to and control over the means of production, the means of organization and the means of communication are highly unevenly distributed within the social structure, and each of them can be utilized, to a different degree of effectiveness, to shape and to challenge what politicians perceive as their *environment of decision-making*. The relative weight of these different resources which, partly, may balance each other, but which also can be concentrated in the hands of one and the same class or group, depends also on cyclical and conjunctural variations which may allow a group to exploit its specific social power to a larger or smaller extent at different points in time.

Underlying this second level of politics (the social power matrix), however, is a third level at which changes within the matrix itself occur, i.e., changes in the relative "weight" collective actors enjoy in shaping the agenda of politics. If, as we have argued before, the second level consists in the process of shaping the space of political action by the exercise of veto power, blackmail, threat, mobilization and social discourse about political issues, or merely the silent force of "antici- pated reaction", this does not mean that the amount and effectiveness of political resources that each social class and social category controls must remain fixed. That is to say, social power is never great enough to reproduce itself eternally. Power positions are, almost by definition, contested and hence subject to change and redistribution. The struggle for the *redistribution of social power* is what takes place on the third, and most fundamental, level of politics. For instance, the market power, or political legitimacy, or the organizational strength that one group or class has enjoyed so far may be restricted (with the effect of making the political agenda less vulnerable vis-à-vis this group), or another group may open up new channels of influence, may form new alliances, or win a hegemonic position through the appeal to new values, ideals and visions. Both relative losses of power and relative gains in power can be promoted, facilitated or triggered off (if only through the unequivocal demonstration of failures) on the level of formal politics. The veto power attached to certain groups can be limited and constrained, and the institutional underpinnings of social power can be abolished. It therefore appears that the three levels are interrelated, not in a strictly hierarchical but in a cyclical manner: although the action space of level one ("formal politics") is largely determined by the matrix of social power ("level two"), it may itself facilitate and promote a revi- sion of the distribution of social power ("level three"). And the state of democratic politics would thus have to be looked upon as both deter- mined by, and a potential determinant of, social power.

I trust that I can leave it to the reader to apply this analytical model of the political process to the contemporary controversy about the welfare state that I have reviewed and discussed, and, thereby, to explore the extent of its usefulness. The question with which I wish to conclude is as much of academic as it is of political significance: will the agenda of the welfare state, its space of action and future development, be shaped and limited by the matrix of social power of advanced capitalist social structures? Or will it, conversely, itself open up possibilities of reshaping this matrix, either through its own accomplishments or failures?

Note

1. A corollary argument often used in the conservative analysis is this: not only does the welfare state undermine the *quality* of working behavior by inducing workers to be more "demanding" and, at the same time, less willing to spend strong efforts on their work, etc., but also it cuts the *quantity* of available productive labor. This is said to be so because the welfare state ideology puts strong emphasis on public sector services, bureaucratic careers, and especially education and training, all of which drain the labor market of "productive" labor in a variety of ways.

Part IV

Restructuring Business, Labor, and Government: Deindustrialization, Entrepreneurialism, and the Decline of Labor

13

Closed Plants, Lost Jobs: Consequences of Deindustrialization (1982)*

Barry Bluestone and Bennett Harrison

Just after the Second World War, in one fell swoop the Chance–Vought Division of United Aircraft moved an entire industrial complex from Bridgeport, Connecticut, to Dallas, Texas. This particular relocation, which had financial assistance from the federal government, has been described as one of the most spectacular migrations in industrial history – fifteen hundred people, two thousand machines, and fifty million pounds of equipment were involved.[1]

The relocation of Chance–Vought was an especially dramatic example of the "runaway shop." Even today, when companies literally pick up and move, the wholesale disruption of people's lives garners newspaper and TV headlines. Especially when the move is from the "Frostbelt" – the states of the old industrial Northeast and upper Midwest – to the "Sunbelt" or overseas, it reinforces the popular impression that "capital flight" is a matter of manufacturing firms literally relocating their plant and equipment into areas where wages are lower, unions are weaker, and local government provides the good business climate that corporate managers dream about. And there is no question that such dramatic relocations *do* occur; during the decade of the 1970s, we estimate that between 450,000 and 650,000 jobs in the private sector, in both manufacturing and non-manufacturing, were wiped out somewhere in the United States by

---

* From *The Deindustrialization of America* (New York: Basic Books, 1982), pp. 25–9, 31–6, 37–8, 39–43, 44–8; subsequently cited as *DoA*. The original chapter also contains several lengthy endnotes that are not reproduced here (notably notes 5, 7, 14, 16, 27–29) – along with two tables.

the movement of both large and small runaway shops. But it turns out that such physical relocations are only the tip of a huge iceberg. When the employment lost as a direct result of plant, store, and office *shutdowns* during the 1970s is added to the job loss associated with runaway shops, it appears that more than 32 million jobs were destroyed. Together, runaways, shutdowns, and permanent physical cutbacks short of complete closure may have cost the country as many as 38 million jobs.

The process of capital disinvestment in older plants, industries, or regions, and reinvestment in other activities or places, can take many forms. For example, when General Electric builds a new steam iron factory in Singapore and subsequently sells an older one outside of Los Angeles, thus eliminating nearly a thousand jobs in the process, that is capital shift. Or when Pratt & Whitney Aircraft or the Ford Motor Company transfers subcontracts for machine-tooled parts from local suppliers to shops located in other countries, causing widespread layoffs in Connecticut and outright plant shutdowns in Michigan, that, too, is capital flight. Private disinvestment in a particular locale occurs when a conglomerate buys a business that was operating profitably in one place and moves it to another, as Norton Simon has done with the Max Factor cosmetics firm, shifting production from California to Tennessee. The loss in social productivity is even greater – going beyond the mere shifting of existing facilities around the map – when a conglomerate acquires a profitable company, milks it of its cash, runs it into the ground, and then closes it down altogether. By all accounts this is what happened to the Youngstown Sheet and Tube Company, a steel mill in Ohio's Mahoning Valley, after it was acquired by the Lykes Corporation (now itself part of the giant Ling–Temco–Vought (LTV) conglomerate).

Remarkable as it may seem, in a country whose national census bureau regularly pokes into the minutest details of people's private lives, measuring how many children they have or why their mothers did not go to work last week, the government makes only the most minimal demands on private companies to report their investment transactions. Data on the investment decisions by managers in the service sector are almost completely nonexistent, even though hospitals, supermarkets, and television stations obviously buy and sell buildings and machinery, too. Because companies are virtually allowed to select depreciation schedules from a menu offered by the Internal Revenue Service to fit their cash flow requirements, official published statistics on the extent to which an industry's capital stock is being run down by its managers have become artifacts of the political process, almost useless for measuring actual disinvestment.

Few people have the necessary time, access, or money to pierce the veil of secrecy that firms have thrown up around their investment transactions. With the federal government unwilling to require companies to disclose the details of their investment activities, direct measurement of all of the many different forms of capital movement is virtually impossible. What we can measure now – thanks not to any government program, but to the availability of information generated by the private sector itself, for its own internal use – are plant (as well as office, store, shop, and warehouse) relocations and shutdowns.[2]

Over the decade of the 1970s, in twelve states, plant closings shut down more jobs than were added through new start-ups. Elsewhere, jobs created by the opening of new business establishments barely offset the losses connected with the closings of older ones (except in those states containing the mining and energy industries, where the net growth was considerable). But even where more new plants were opened than shut down, millions of workers, their families, and their communities experienced severe economic and emotional dislocation. Typically, the businesses that started up were located in different places and in different industries (usually services rather than manufacturing); they required different skills, paid lower wages, provided less job security, or simply would not hire the people who had been laid off.

Private business investment and disinvestment in the US, 1969–76

Dun and Bradstreet Incorporated (D & B) [a private business credit-rating service] keeps detailed records on various aspects of the economic activity of American businesses. The 1969–76 Dun's Identifiers File covers nearly 5.6 million business establishments. About 88 per cent of these are independently owned and operated; the rest are the branches, subsidiaries, and headquarters of corporations. The data are especially valuable in that they refer to the activity of each of a company's workplaces or *establishments*, rather than reporting only on the aggregate behavior of the company or *firm* as a whole.

Yet even this detailed data source does not permit the measurement of investment and disinvestment per se. Rather, the D & B file breaks down net job change over time in a given industry in a particular location into the sum of:

- employment created as a result of new plant, store, or office openings in the original location, *plus*
- employment generated through the relocation of an existing plant, store, or office into this location, *plus*
- jobs created through the expansion of establishments that were already operating in this location at the beginning of the period of analysis

minus those elements of employment change that make tip job loss:

- employment destroyed through establishment closures
- jobs lost as the result of the physical "outmigration" of establishments that used to do business in this location
- jobs destroyed through the contraction of existing plants, stores, and shops.

Employment gains and losses associated with the opening, closing, and relocation of a business establishment are unambiguously the result of private investment and disinvestment activity. This is not so with the expansion and contraction data. Employment change associated with expansion over some period of time usually includes some jobs that have been added to an existing plant or store, with little or no new physical investment having taken place – economists call this "increased utilization of existing productive capacity. The remaining job growth *is* the result of the addition of new physical capacity, for example, a new wing on a building, three new machines, or the rehabilitation of an existing conveyer belt. But there is no way to separate these two sources of job change out of the D & B data labeled "expansions." The same holds for the information on "contractions." (Later in this chapter we will show how one researcher has made some headway in connection with this by conducting his own extensive interviews with a sample of the companies monitored by D & B.)

Thus, when a company opens, closes, or physically relocates one of its individual establishments, private investment or disinvestment occurs and can be measured in terms of the number of jobs that are created or destroyed at that location. When employment expands in a particular industry in a particular place, there may be some new investment, but that is not certain. Conversely, when employment contracts within existing establishments, it can only be inferred that some disinvestment *might* have occurred. Like so many other researchers who have worked with these data, we have relied on the help of David Birch.[3]

...

In the United States, between 1969 and 1976, private investment in new plants created about 25 million jobs. This amounts to an average of 3.6 million jobs created each year as the direct result of plant openings. On the other hand, by 1976 shutdowns had wiped out 39 per cent of the jobs that had existed in 1969 – a total of 2.2 million jobs over seven years, or on average, about 3.2 million jobs destroyed each year. Therefore, about 110 jobs were created by new plant openings for every 100 jobs destroyed by plants shutting down.

This relationship between the openings and closings of plants varied substantially among the various regions of the country (and even within regions...). Jobs created through new business start-ups generally exceeded job losses resulting from shutdowns in the Midwest and the Sunbelt, although more jobs were terminated than created even in some of the Sunbelt states, such as Delaware, Idaho, and Utah.[4] On the other hand, in every state in the Northeast, private industry destroyed more jobs through plant closings than it created through new openings. Whether 22 million jobs destroyed through shutdowns represents socially unacceptable or (as Thurow would have it) insufficiently rapid capital shift is the subject of [Chapters 3 & 4 of *DoA*]. But one thing ought to be immediately clear: plant closings are not confined to the old industrial "Frostbelt"; they occur in large numbers in every region of the country and as such they are a national phenomenon.

Indeed the greatest surprise is in the South. We know that the overall pace of economic growth has been greater in the sixteen states making up this region than anywhere else. But even in spite of its legendary "good business climate," between 1969 and 1976 industry apparently saw fit to withdraw enough of its capital there to destroy almost 7 million jobs as a direct result of shutdowns, with another 3.8 million lost through cutbacks in existing operations.

Up to this point, the behavior of establishments of all sizes has been taken into account. But considering the political furor over shutdowns and their impacts on people and communities, it is surely the large manufacturing plants that have caused the greatest concern. What can be said about this category of private industry? Birch has begun to address this question by estimating what the chances are that an establishment that is in business on a particular date will still be there at some future time, or will have closed during the period.[5] Not surprisingly, the larger the facility, the less likely it is to be shut down, even during recessions. Of all "small" establishments (those with between one and twenty employees) existing in 1969, between one half and three fifths were out of business by 1976, depending upon industry and region. The chances of survival were a little better for small manufacturing plants than for non-manufacturing establishments, and generally worse in the Midwest than elsewhere.

Knowing the fragile economic markets within which small companies operate, none of this should be particularly surprising. But the rate for large enterprises certainly is. The proportion of establishments with 500 or more employees that closed their doors sometime between 1969 and 1976 ranged from 15 per cent to more than 35 per cent, again depending on region and industrial sector. This is a tale of shutdown – a key element in the overall rate of capital disinvestment – far beyond anything that anyone ever expected to find. It should be emphasized once again that these data refer to individual establishments, that is, stores, plants, and shops, and not to whole companies. The failure rate of companies has, of course, been much lower.

...

By far the largest absolute number of closings of large, established (pre-1970) manufacturing plants occurred in the Northeast. With only 24 per cent of the nation's population in 1970, the Northeast suffered 39 per cent of the shutdowns of this type of establishment.

Still, what is perhaps even more dramatic is the large absolute number of closings of this scale that took place in the South. During this seven-year period, one out of every three existing plants shut down operations. In fact, the proportion of pre-1970 large manufacturing plants that closed by the end of 1976 was actually higher in the South than in any other part of the country!

There is a widespread tendency to view an entire region as though it were homogeneous. This is reflected in the media's (and Congress's) obsession with the "Sunbelt–Frostbelt" imagery. However, evidence has been uncovered of extraordinarily uneven development within regions, including the Sunbelt. During the late 1960s and early 1970s, Massachusetts was considered a terminal case. Yet just over its border, the southern towns of New Hampshire were experiencing an unprecedented boom. The same holds true in the South. While Houston, Dallas, and Oklahoma City were brimming with new migrants who were lured to these areas by oil, chemicals, and new manufacturing opportunities, older areas of the South were crumbling. Some of this loss was no doubt due to rural to urban relocation. But a new wave of US reinvestment abroad – in textiles, apparel, electronics assembly, and other labor-intensive industries – was probably an even larger factor. These were the industrial sectors on which the (especially the rural) "New South" of post-World War II America was established, and which were being seriously eroded by shutdowns in the years during and after the Vietnam War. For example, during the 1970s, almost 60 per cent of all the textile mill closings in the United States occurred in the South.[6]

So far, these results pool the corner grocer, the multinational corporation's branch plant, and the successful family business that is acquired by a diversified conglomerate. For several reasons, the data should be broken down according to who owns the business. Small, independently owned, and often family-run, firms might be expected to have high failure rates because they are generally more vulnerable to the business cycle, suffer more restricted access to debt finance (and/or must pay more for it), and have no "parent" or home office to bail them out of trouble. Corporate branch plants presumably have all of these advantages – along with access to the corporation's own internally retained earnings – as, in theory, do the subsidiaries of conglomerates.

Unquestionably, most plant shutdowns are the unplanned outcome of intensified domestic and international corporate rivalry. But ... there are often real profits to be made when a cash-conscious corporate management deliberately writes off a still viable plant, or when the central managers of a diversified conglomerate deliberately milk a subsidiary of its cash flow and then shut it down (if they cannot find another buyer). In these cases, plant shutdowns are likely to be the result of a planned strategy to increase company-wide profits. On the other hand, the closing of an independently owned business is more likely to be the result of a truly involuntary failure.

Our estimates of start-ups and closings by type of ownership are unfortunately limited at the moment to New England. Similar counts could indeed be constructed for other states and regions, but Birch has not done so, and the extract used here from the D & B file is limited to this area.

Between 1969 and 1976 plant closings in Massachusetts cost the state about 730,000 jobs (about 40 per cent of the stock of jobs at the beginning of the period). For New England as a whole, the closings eliminated slightly more than 1.4 million jobs. Corporations and conglomerates together were responsible for a disproportionate amount of job destruction – about 15 per cent of the establishment "deaths," but half of all the jobs lost. Moreover, our own fieldwork on subcontracting and procurement networks in this region convinces us that a great many of those closings of independently owned businesses were the indirect result of losses of orders and other spillovers generated by the corporate shutdowns.[7]

The ways in which ownership affects the likelihood of an establishment shutdown (and indeed whether new openings exceed closings) vary among industries. Take two industries that are highly important to, and quite typical of the old and new economic bases of, the region: metalworking machinery and department stores. For every new job created in these industries in New England by an independently owned business, 1.6 jobs were destroyed in metalworking and 1.0 in department stores. But in establishments controlled by conglomerates, for every job created, 4.6 jobs were destroyed in metalworking, while 4.0 were eliminated in department stores. The same pattern of disproportionate closing activity by conglomerates took place in women's apparel, shoes, computers, aircraft engines, supermarkets, hotels, and motels.[8]

The deindustrialization wave of the late 1970s

The D & B data with which to update a systematic, region-by-region analysis of shutdowns and contractions beyond the end of 1976 have not been made available. But even if just a projection were made from the previous finding of about 3.2 million jobs lost per year in the country as a result of plant closures alone (not counting redundancies created by private disinvestment short of total shutdown), it would be concluded that, over the whole decade of the 1970s, a minimum of 32 million jobs were probably eliminated in the United States as a direct result of private disinvestment in plant and equipment. Making the (very conservative) assumption that one third of the job loss associated with establishment contractions was attributable to disinvestment short of complete shutdown (with another two thirds connected to personnel layoffs not accompanied by reductions in physical productive capacity), then … it may be inferred that, all together, over 38 million jobs were lost through private disinvestment during the 1970s. That would seem to be deindustrialization with a vengeance. It certainly creates skepticism about the claim that not enough "creative destruction" is taking place in America.

In fact, there is good reason to believe that these estimates may actually *undercount* the total job loss for the decade. The reason is that a truly major wave of closings and retrenchments in some of the country's most basic industries – autos, steel, and tires – struck American workers during the last several years of the period. Corporate managers in these and many other industries found themselves confronting an unprecedented profit squeeze associated with intensified international competition and chronic stagflation. Especially in their older product lines, these managers were forced to become more cost conscious than at probably any time since the Second World War. To cut costs, firms focussed their attention on cutting jobs.

Faced with the challenge of old plant and equipment that had been inadequately maintained or upgraded, and confronted by workers whose costs of living (and therefore wage requirements) were also being driven up by inflation, American industrial managers in the closing years of the 1970s resorted to truly draconian measures. Wholesale rationalization and industrial restructuring were undertaken. Sometimes, capital was removed from domestic facilities and reinvested outside the country. There was a growing tendency for managers to use profits that had been made, for example, in steel and oil to diversify into totally unrelated activities – that is, to follow the conglomerate model. Some companies moved plants from highly unionized areas in the North and the Far West into the South. And most dramatically of all, there was an unprecedented wave of total plant shutdowns in some of the most well known companies in the United States. As had been true even before 1976, these shutdowns occurred throughout the country, even in the Sunbelt.

Between January 1979 and December 1980, domestic automobile manufacturers closed or announced the imminent shutdown of twenty facilities employing over 50,000 workers. As a consequence of these closings and of the output reductions in other auto plants, suppliers of materials, parts, and components to the automotive industry closed nearly 100 plants, eliminating the jobs of about 80,000 additional workers. Altogether, the downturn in the industry in just these two years may have boosted unemployment in the supplier network by anywhere from 350,000 to 650,000 jobs – depending on whether the Congressional Budget Office or the AFL–CIO is making the estimate.[9]

Among the major permanent closings in the last years of the decade were thirteen Chrysler plants employing nearly 31,000 workers, five Ford plants including the huge facility at Mahwah, New Jersey, and seven plants in the General Motors system.[10] Of these twenty-five shutdowns, eleven were located in Michigan and six more were in other midwestern states. But even the Sunbelt lost some of its automobile capacity. Ford shut down its large Los Angeles assembly plant in 1980, while Chrysler closed a small facility in Florida. In 1981–82, the wave became a flood, affecting every region of the country.

...

As we now know, the invasion of the domestic auto market by Japanese manufacturers and the spurt in oil prices after 1973 combined to force huge cutbacks in domestic car production. It was inevitable that American tire manufacturers would feel the brunt as well. Moreover, while these companies had held out as long as they could from replacing the old bias-ply technology with the far longer-lasting radial tires, competition from foreign radial manufacturers such as France's Michelin and Japan's Bridgestone finally forced the Americans into their own major restructuring program. According to the Research Department of the United Rubber Workers of America, between mid-1975 and early 1981, there were twenty-four domestic plant shutdowns, eleven of them in Sunbelt cities, accompanied by nearly 20,000 permanent layoffs. (The *New York Times* reported on April 19, 1980, that some of these shutdowns involved radial tire plants, as well as the "obsolete" bias-ply factories.)

Eleven of the closed facilities had been part of the Firestone Tire and Rubber Company. Others had been operated by Goodyear, B. F. Goodrich, Uniroyal, and several smaller firms. Even while they were shutting down their older plants, rather than upgrading them or building new facilities in the same cities, Goodyear and Uniroyal were simultaneously expanding into other parts of the Sunbelt as well as overseas. Uniroyal now produces tires in Brazil, Turkey, Spain, and Australia. The company with the fewest actual closings during this period, General Tire, had already completed its own restructuring process earlier by successfully diverting profits from its tire business into television, radio, cable television, rocket-propulsion equipment, plastics, soft drink bottling, and a commercial airline.[11]

In one industry after another, the late 1970s was a time for unprecedented retrenchment. Combined with the continued trend toward the differential branching of operations based in older industrial areas into places with cheaper or less well organized labor, these restructuring schemes produced a spate of newspaper articles.

But if the most widely publicized shutdowns in the closing years of the 1970s were in the North, southern workers had their own deindustrialization with which to contend. Once thriving towns, Fayetteville, Tennessee; Tupelo, Mississippi; Guntersville and Muscle Shoals, Alabama; and Kennett, Missouri, which had experienced seemingly unlimited industrial growth in the years after World War II, were losing one plant after another by the late 1970s. While the typical closure was the small family business unable to survive in the face of chronic inflation and rising labor costs, the branches of major corporations such as Scoville Industries and Monsanto Chemical were also shut down. In fact, observed the chief economist of the Tennessee Valley Authority, "many of these towns had been in trouble for much of the decade." By 1980–81, unemployment rates in many of the more industrialized southern areas stood above 10 per cent. Of the 170 acres in Fayetteville's new industrial park on the east side of the city, 150 were vacant in early 1981. These are the kinds of conditions normally associated with the old mill towns of New England.[12]

Other Sunbelt states experienced unexpected waves of plant closings during the late 1970s and into the early 1980s. None was more unprepared for such a shock than the state of California.[13] ... From South Gate to Hayward to Sacramento, across the state as a whole, in the single year 1980, at least 150 major plants closed their doors permanently, displacing more than 37,000 workers. The problem has taken on epidemic proportions, affecting industries as varied as automobiles and trucks, rubber, steel, textiles, lumber, food processing, and housewares.

The diversion of corporate investment into the acquisition of existing businesses

While conglomerates controlled a small per centage of all businesses before 1976 (although they were responsible for a much larger proportion of all jobs), conglomerate behavior – the acquisition of existing facilities in diverse product and service lines bearing little or no relation to the acquirer's original industry – seems to have increased during the closing years of the decade. Thus, for example, during the three years following 1976, the US Steel Corporation reduced its capital expenditures in steel making by a fifth. Profits were redirected into the acquisition of chemical firms, shopping malls, and other activities; so much so that, by 1979, forty-six cents of every new dollar of US Steel capital investment was going into the corporation's non-steel ventures. Moreover, in 1979 while each dollar of depreciated non-steel plant and equipment was being replaced by $2.90 of new capital investment, in the steel operations the replacement rate was only $1.40.[14]

In other industries, General Electric makes everything from toaster ovens to jet engines. And Mobil Oil acquired the Montgomery Ward

department store chain and the Container Corporation of America. In 1979 alone, according to *Business Week*, US corporations made acquisitions totalling $40 billion – more than the total spent on research and development by all private firms in the nation.[15]
...

In the United States during the 1970s, two out of every three new *Fortune* 500 manufacturing plants were actually not "new" at all, but rather acquired from other owners. In every region, the majority of factories added to these corporations' holdings were acquired rather than built anew. This fraction was greater in the Frostbelt than in the Sunbelt, attaining its highest level in the mid-Atlantic states of New York, New Jersey, and Pennsylvania. There, more than three out of every four manufacturing plants that were added to the ownership rolls of the *Fortune* 500 during the last decade resulted from acquisitions of already existing facilities rather than from investment in new plant and equipment.

Moreover, during the 1970s these 410 corporations physically expanded only *one in seven* of the plants they owned at the start of the decade. Even in the West South Central region, where the oil industry is centered, only one out of every five manufacturing or processing plants was physically expanded.[16]

The "exporting" of jobs through foreign investment by american corporations

Even as they have been disinvesting in domestic industry, US corporations have continued to shift capital beyond the country's borders, into Canada, Western Europe, and the Third World. As a result, since the end of the Second World War, the growth of American corporate investment in other countries has been enormous. Between 1950 and 1980, direct foreign investment by US businesses increased sixteen times, from about $12 billion to $192 billion. Over the same period, gross private domestic investment grew less than half as rapidly, from $54 billion to about $400 billion.[17] The total overseas output of American multinational corporations is now larger than the gross domestic product of every country in the world except the United States and the Soviet Union.

During the decade of 1957–67 alone, a third of all US transportation equipment plants were located abroad. For chemicals, the ratio was 25 per cent; for machinery, it was 20 per cent.[18] By the end of the 1970s, overseas profits accounted for a third or more of the overall profits of the hundred largest multinational producers and banks in the United States. In some corporations, the fraction was much higher. In 1979, for example, 94 per cent of the profits of the Ford Motor Company came from overseas operations; for Coca Cola, it was 63 per cent. In 1977, Citicorp derived 83 per cent of its banking profits from its overseas operations.[19]

During the early 1970s, a great ideological struggle was waged around the question of whether and to what extent American workers were hurt or helped by the multinationals' overseas investment activities. The Research Department of the AFL-CIO insisted that domestic jobs were being destroyed. The multinationals' chief Washington lobbyist, the Emergency Committee for American Trade, with help from Harvard Business School and Commerce Department studies, tried to make the opposite case.[20]

The central question in what Richard Barnet and Ronald Müller call "the great statistical battle" is: What would or could the multinationals have done had they not been allowed to invest overseas? Assuming that they would have tried to export an equivalent volume of goods and services from their domestic home base, could they have succeeded? Or would foreign competitors have stolen their overseas markets? Might some of those markets never have been brought into existence without the presence of the multinationals "on the scene" to advertise, elicit, and otherwise "develop" customers? And if the multinationals had not been able to produce abroad for sale back into the United States, would they have tried to meet that domestic demand by expanding production and employment at home?

Believing that American firms would not have attempted an equivalent level of production inside the United States (for domestic sale and for export), or that, having tried, they would have failed to penetrate or hold onto their foreign markets, the conclusion can be reached that foreign investment does, on balance, create jobs at home. Conversely, the assumption that at least some of those foreign markets could be supplied by ordinary exports rather than through the creation of overseas branches or subsidiaries, and that American companies would expand production at home if they had no other way to meet the domestic demand for T-shirts, toys, and electronic components, leads to the conclusion that foreign investment does indeed on balance destroy domestic jobs.

On this question, the protagonists, each in his own way, have tended to make the most extremely favorable assumptions for their respective positions .... The corporate formulation is also incomplete to the extent that it ignores access to cheap foreign labor used in producing commodities overseas for *sale in the United States* as a motive for their foreign investment. Twenty-nine per cent of all US imports in 1976 came from the output of overseas plants and majority-owned subsidiaries of American multinational corporations. As Pogo once said: "We have met the enemy and he is us!"

Whether government-imposed restrictions on foreign investment would have forced US multinational corporations to make alternative investments at home instead, is really impossible to say. A slightly different (and answerable) question is this: Had they gone ahead and invested domestically, and had that additional capital gone into a mix of activities similar to what American industry was in fact already putting its capital into at home, how many new jobs might have been created, and for whom? Most important, would this have been a larger number than the jobs lost as a result of the enforced inability of American multinationals to invest abroad?

...

In 1970 US corporations undertook $10 billion in direct foreign investment. Frank and Freeman find that "even though sales in foreign markets would [have shrunk] by more than half in the event of a ban on foreign investment, such a ban would nevertheless be likely to produce [a net] increase in domestic employment demand."[21] Workers in the nonelectrical machinery sector were by far the most severely affected by this foreign investment. Among a series of calculations based on different assumptions about international competitiveness and relative production costs, the average domestic job loss resulting from that $10 billion of foreign investment was determined to be about 160,000 for 1970, with about 44,000 of these displaced jobs in nonmanufacturing (in 1970, direct US foreign investment in services, mining, and construction was $5.3 billion, over half of the $10 billion total). Using a 1970 input–output table, indirect manufacturing job loss – the elimination of work in (mostly domestic) companies supplying producers' goods to the multinationals – was estimated to average another 105,000. Moreover, had the $10 billion stayed at home, the duration of joblessness in American labor markets in 1970 would have decreased on the average from 6.4 to 5.3 weeks, with an attendant decrease in unemployment insurance and welfare payments.

Frank and Freeman conclude from their number crunching that "even allowing for considerable deficiencies in the data, the net impact of foreign investment by US multinationals is a substantial domestic employment demand reduction."[22] Specifically, every $1 billion of direct private US foreign investment seems to eliminate (on balance) about 26,500 domestic jobs.

Raymond Vernon of the Harvard Business School has argued that even if American multinationals' overseas activities do displace domestic production jobs, they nevertheless create new jobs in the home offices of these corporations – in finance, management, information systems, and clerical work.[23] To this position, Barnet and Müller have a strongly worded response. In the mind of the theorist, perhaps

> jobs may be interchangeable. In the real world, they are not. A total of 250,000 new jobs gained in corporate headquarters does not, in any political or human sense, offset 250,000 old jobs lost on the production line. When Lynn, Massachusetts becomes a ghost of its former self, its jobless citizens find little satisfaction in reading about the new headquarters building on Park Avenue and all the secretaries it will employ.[24]

This issue of who loses the most from the domestic employment impacts of overseas investment by American corporations is addressed in the second half of the Frank–Freeman study. When the job losses estimated earlier are translated into an occupational forecast for the United States, it is found that machinists, machine operators, craftspersons, and clerical workers suffer the greatest degree of economic dislocation from foreign investment. Note that office workers are not immune.

Finally, the authors report on the estimated impacts on US government revenues, wages, and labor's share of the national income. The foreign investment obviously drives domestic government revenues below what they would have been had the $10 billion been invested domestically. The simple reason for this is that the profits made on overseas investments generate an anemic tax return to the US Treasury, due to the way our Internal Revenue Code subsidizes foreign investment through special tax credits.[25]

As for the impacts of foreign investments on labor income, wages at home are estimated to be lower by between 3 per cent and 13 per cent, depending on one's assumption about the differential premium on profits demanded by American multinationals as a condition for investing overseas. The lower the premium, the more jobs created outside the United States, and the greater the consequent domestic wage loss. Finally, labor's share of national income is estimated to have been between 2 per cent and 6 per cent lower than it would have been had the foreign investment been redirected to the domestic economy.

Conclusion

What is to be made of all this? What people seem to be feeling (and what almost all analysts in universities and in the media seem to be studiously misunderstanding) is a deepening sense of *insecurity*, growing out of the collapse all around them of the traditional economic base of their communities. Their very jobs are being pulled out from under them. And instead of providing new employment opportunities, a higher standard of living, and enhanced security, the decisions of corporate managers are doing just the opposite.

Working people's feelings about this are not without foundation. Deindustrialization is occurring – on a surprisingly massive scale. It can be seen from North to South and East to West. It is happening as the largest, most powerful corporations in the nation shut down older plants in the industrial zones of the New South and overseas; as small businesses confront bankruptcy, close down themselves, or are bought up, milked dry, and then shut down later by larger firms; and as more and more corporations become multinational and conglomerate in nature, shifting finance capital (and even capital goods) all over the map (often at lightning speed) in an effort to maximize their own profits and increase their span of control over the global economic system.

It may well be, as David Birch has found, that only about 2 per cent of all private sector annual employment change in the United States now results from the actual physical relocations of businesses – the classic runaway shop.[26] But as has been seen, such a limited image of the nature and magnitude of capital shift hardly scratches the surface. Counting only those effects that are presently "countable" – plant closings, relocations, and estimated physical contractions – a sizeable fraction of all the private sector jobs that existed at the beeginning of the decade of the 1970s had been destroyed by the end of the decade through private disinvestment in the productive capacity of the American economy. How social disorganization of this magnitude can be considered "insufficient" for the achievement of some abstract notion of a "healthy economy" is, to be frank, beyond understanding.

Nevertheless, the question remains: How much economic dislocation is *too much* dislocation? Or, in Lester Thurow's words, has the pace of private disinvestment in (mainly) older industries been too *slow*? To deal with that question requires a look at what has been happening to the people and the communities that have experienced job loss as a result of the deindustrialization of America during the 1970s and early 1980s. To the extent that the economic, social, and psychological dislocation that they have experienced has largely been transitory, it would be difficult to conclude that the pace of deindustrialization has been too great. But if large numbers of workers, families, and communities are found to have been seriously injured by these economic processes, then there are stronger grounds for supporting the hunch that the pace of private capital mobility in the modern era has become unacceptably rapid; indeed, perhaps even out of control.

Notes

1. William Glenn Cunningham, "Postwar Developments and the Location of the Aircraft Industry in 1950," in G. R. Simonson (ed.), *The History of the American Aircraft Industry* (Cambridge, Mass.: MIT Press, 1968), p. 190; and R. C. Estall, *New England: A Study in Industrial Adjustment* (New York: Praeger, 1966), p. 163.
2. Most of this chapter is devoted to a presentation of our findings on closings, relocations, and the "export" of jobs through foreign investment in the 1970s. Toward the end, however, we will look briefly at new estimates of some indirect forms of industrial disinvestment: namely, the extent to which the largest manufacturing corporations have been putting their capital into buying up existing facilities rather than constructing new ones, and whether these corporations physically expanded the plants they already had on line at the beginning of the decade. Other measures of deindustrialization appear in Chapter 6 [of *DoA*], in the context of case studies of particular industries and companies.
3. David L. Birch, *The Job Generation Process* (Cambridge, Mass.: MIT Program on Neighborhood and Regional Change, 1979).
4. Of course, social problems can arise even where there is a net gain in employment. It is often difficult for those who are shut out of jobs in one sector to obtain jobs in the industries that are growing elsewhere in the region. It is also true that the jobs in the expanding industries often do not pay wages commensurate with what those who have been laid off used to earn. These questions [are] investigated in Chapters 3 and 4 of *DoA*.
5. *Editor's Note*: His detailed findings are reproduced in Table A.2 in the Appendix of *DoA*.
6. "Can Congress Control Runaways?," *Dollars and Sense*, 51 (November, 1979), p. 9.
7. *Editor's Note*: This important issue is discussed in Chapter 3 of *DoA*.
8. *Editor's Note*: See table A.3 in the Appendix of *DoA*.
9. Carol MacLennan and John O'Donnell, "The Effects of the Automotive Transition on Employment: A Plant and Community Study," Transportation Systems Center, US Department of Transportation (December 1980). As we know now, the epidemic of auto closures has become a tidal wave in the 1980s.
10. "America's Restructured Economy," *Business Week* (1 June, 1981), p. 87.

11. Ron Shinn, "Through the Wringer at Goodyear," *New York Times* (24 May, 1981), p. F1.
12. Reginald Stuart, "Boom in Sunbelt Bypasses Older Industrial Towns in the South," *New York Times* (4 June, 1981), p. 18.
13. California Association for Local Economic Development, *Economic Adjustment Report* 1(1) (August–September, 1981), pp. 1–2.
14. United States Steel Corporation, *Annual Corporate Reports* and *K-10 Reports to the Securities and Exchange Commission* for the years 1976–1979 ...
15. "The Reindustrialization of America," *Business Week* (30 June, 1980), p. 78.
16. *Editor's Note*: Table A.4 in the appendix of *DoA* presents some of Duke University Professor of Management Roger Schmenner's results in greater detail. See Roger Schmenner, "The Location Decisions of Large, Multiplant Companies" (Cambridge, Mass.: MIT–Harvard Joint Center for Urban Studies, 1980), manuscript.
17. Council of Economic Advisors, *Economic Report of the President 1981* (Washington, DC: US Government Printing Office, 1981), Tables B-1, B-103.
18. John M. Volpe, "The Effect of the Multinational Corporation on American Labor," PhD dissertation, (New York University, 1972), Tables 2-1, 2-4.
19. William M. Bulkeley, "As US Economy Falters, Multinationals Put Increased Stress on Overseas Business," *Wall Street Journal* (11 December, 1979), p. 48; Robert D. Hershey, Jr., "Banking's International Face," *New York Times* (5 February, 1978), pp. 38–9.
20. See Robert B. Stobaugh *et al.*, *US Multinational Enterprises and the American Economy*, in US Office of International Investment, Bureau of International Commerce, US Department of Commerce, *The Multinational Corporation: Studies on US Foreign Investment* (Washington, DC: US Government Printing Office, 1972), vol. 1.
21. Robert H. Frank and Richard T. Freeman, "The Distributional Consequences of Direct Foreign Investment," in William G. Dewald (ed.), *The Impact of International Trade and Investment on Employment. A Conference of the US Department of Labor* (Washington, DC: US Government Printing Office, 1978), p. 153.
22. Ibid., p. 156.
23. Raymond Vernon, *Sovereignty at Bay* (New York: Basic Books, 1971).
24. Richard Barnet and Ronald Müller, *Global Reach* (New York: Simon & Schuster, 1973), p. 302.
25. *Editor's Note:* See Frank and Freeman, "The Distributional Consequences," *op. cit.*, p. 164. See also Chapter 5 of *DoA*.
26. Birch, *the Job Generation Process*, *op. cit.*; and David L. Birch, "Who Creates Jobs?," *The Public Interest*, 65 (Fall 1981), p. 71.

14

Toward a Policy Agenda for Competitiveness (1987)*

Stephen S. Cohen and John Zysman

The current economic transition – the transformation of industrial society – sets an agenda of change and policy choice. Competitive adjustment … will be built on the ability to generate and apply product and process innovation. Competitive advantage will rest not just on product innovation, but on sustained manufacturing expertise. Those economies that diffuse and apply technologies widely will find advantage because they will both create markets for new and advanced technologies and transform traditional industries in the process. But there is nothing inevitable about the outcome. However, the policies we adopt will be an important element in determining the choice we make about the outcome we create.

Creating economic resources

How in an era of transition can government help create advantage? It can do so principally by substantially upgrading the quality of what goes into production, the factors of production – raw materials, capital, labor – and the networks and rules that affect how those factors are combined – the economic infrastructure. Government must act primarily at the second level of the policy hierarchy.[1] Even traditional theory suggests this. Comparative advantage rests on the relative factor proportions required in the production of different types of goods – that is, a nation will tend to specialize in those sectors that require factors of production that it has in abundance.

---

* From *Manufacturing Matters: The Myth of the Post-Industrial Economy* (New York: Basic Books, 1987), pp. 220–34, 242–3.

Classical trade theory does not worry about how a nation got its particular pattern of comparative advantage, just what it is. National factor endowments are not, however, simply given by nature; they are, to an extent that matters, created over time by policy. Moreover, policy powerfully affects the real price and quality of these inputs, and does so all the more when the crucial endowments involve technology, know-how, and skills. Let us look at the effect of policy on, respectively, land (raw materials), capital, and labor (which includes technological know-how) – the basic inputs to the economy.

Raw materials

The power of policy to create advantage by creating national factor endowments and affecting their quality and price is evident even in the case of raw materials. Geology is a natural given; economics isn't. Policy can play a role – a big role – in transforming geological factors into factors of production. In economics the question is not what raw materials a country can locate beneath its soil, but at what price they can be delivered to the point of use. And delivered price can be massively influenced by policy. One country may have abundant coal or iron or copper in the ground, but since the coal is deeply buried in isolated areas, the cost of getting it to the surface and shipped to the point of use may be very high. A second country may have no iron, coal, or copper, but may have decided to invest massively in port facilities and ships; it may be able to buy the raw materials at prices lower than that of its naturally endowed competitor. Japan, for example, has been blessed by a relatively solid absence of natural resources: no iron, no oil, no copper, though to their regret, the Japanese do have some coal. Japan consciously set out to turn its lack of raw materials to an advantage. It located steel mills on the coast, invested in modern port and off-loading facilities, and innovated in shipping design and production, while at the same time obtaining access to and control of raw materials around the world. The delivered price to Japanese producers of such raw materials as coal, iron ore, and copper has often been at prices lower than that paid by its competitors who have such resources in the ground. Indeed, Britain and France, as well as other naturally endowed nations, have been compelled by domestic political pressures to maintain high-cost domestic production of coal and other raw materials; their resource endowments have become comparative disadvantages.

Infrastructure development was the key policy choice involved in transforming a geological disadvantage in raw materials into an economic advantage. The provision of infrastructure can be considered a market-perfecting policy; infrastructure improvements make markets work better by eliminating "frictions," in this case – as with ancient Roman and modern American roads and harbors – the frictions of physical distance.

Capital

If policy, along with lots of effort, can decisively influence even the most "natural" of production factors – raw materials – it can play a bigger role in the other factors – such as capital – which are clearly not a matter of natural endowment. The level of savings, the allocation of access to that pool of savings, and the price of that money to different kinds of users are not simply matters of "natural" market forces. They are strongly affected, sometimes even set, by domestic and international policy decisions.

Sometimes the decisive character of policy is overlooked and people start to believe that capital costs or savings rates lie in our national character, so let us construct some illustrative examples of policies that have enormous impact. Let us make the market for savings competitive by eliminating traditional ceilings on interest paid to small savers; open the market to all borrowers, worldwide; allow interest payments on housing and consumer goods to be deducted from income for tax purposes; and create a social security system whose benefits are not based on actual past savings but on entitlements funded from current taxes. If we follow these policies, the cost of funds will rise. This is clearly the American case. Now let us choose a different set of policies. Let us fund pensions entirely from the earnings of past savings; administer the flow of funds to limit and to discourage consumer credit, which will not be granted tax advantages; keep a lid on interest paid to small savers; and moreover, limit foreign access to the pool of domestic savings thus generated. This is clearly the Japanese case (at least up through the mid-1980s). Other things being equal, as the economists say, savings will be higher in Japan, the pool of savings more readily available to national industrial investment, and crucially, the costs of capital will be lower in Japan than in the United States.

Our choice on capital costs – keeping America's higher than that of our most powerful competitor – has substantial consequences. Since Japanese capital costs are lower than ours, Japanese firms will have an advantage in capital-intensive businesses and an incentive to convert competition into a game of capital-intensive manufacturing, something they have done, with disproportionate benefit to themselves in industry after industry, most recently in semiconductors. In this way the nature of competition is itself shaped by policy, ours and that of other governments. A big difference, however, is that, for the most part, our policies are being set with little concern for competitiveness while those of our most successful competitors are being strategically determined.

Not only do the differences between American policies for capital and those of other countries matter, but it is no longer possible to just have a domestic policy for savings and investment. We must make the policy with attention to international markets and do so strategically, with an eye to foreign government policies. International markets and the strategic logic of policy now make even seemingly simple and direct solutions into complex conundrums. It may prove more difficult than expected to gain or close a cost-of-capital disadvantage. Take the deficit. Can it be assumed that slashing it would lower the competitive disadvantage of US firms in capital costs? The answer must be: only maybe. First, a reduction in US government borrowings should relieve demand pressure on capital markets. Interest rates should then decline. But there is no reason to assume that foreign governments would not take advantage of that reduction to lower their interest rates and thereby negate any catching up on the costs of capital. Also, and more important, if world capital markets were indeed open – and the US market is, for both borrowers and lenders – there is no reason to assume that US savings, even if lent at lower prices, would be chan-neled into onshore US productive investments; they could go, as they have in the past, to finance French nuclear power plants, or Korean semiconductor factories, or nonproductive spending in Latin America, or to finance American spending on housing and on imported goods. This is not to say, "Don't slash the deficit." It will have a big and posi-tive impact on US industry. But that impact might well come less through lowering the relative costs of capital to US industry than through lowering the exchange rate of the dollar. The point is that the impacts are strategically determined; the effects of our move will depend upon the responses of policy makers in other nations.

If international capital markets were truly open, it wouldn't necessar-ily matter where the savings took place. American, Swedish, and Dutch firms could draw on Japanese savings at those same low rates of inter-est Japanese firms enjoy. However, in the Japanese case, policy has pre-vented this. Foreigners who might have wanted to draw on the Japanese national pool of savings have, until now, had only limited access. That capital cost differentials have been an important element in international competition in recent years is largely the result of a Japanese policy choice. The policies were originally established to generate capital in postwar Japan, when investment funds were short. They have simply never been dismantled. In an international economist's dream world, perhaps the whole question for America and for others could be mooted by eliminating the possibility of substantial international capital cost differentials. In recent years there has been much movement in opening capital markets – though many of the capital markets in the advanced countries, especially Japan, the biggest after the United States, are far from open. In a world of open capital markets – that is, in a single world capital market – in which there were no successful national policies to favor certain sectors in the pricing and allocation of capital, competitive advantage in capital-intensive production – long a US strength and now a weakness – would be hard for anyone to achieve. Capital cost differentials – and policies designed to foster them – would cease to be a strategic concern of government and would drop out of the international competitiveness equation. It would be a solution to the policy problem in that it would simply eliminate it. In fact, international capital markets are already open enough, large enough, and efficient enough that the advanced countries will not be able to build capital barriers to entry against new producers.

If the prices and availabilities of raw materials, as well as the costs and availabilities of capital become smaller and smaller factors in differentiating production possibilities and costs across nations, the burden of competitiveness will fall on much softer factors of production: the ability to generate and use the most advanced technologies, the intelligence and dutifulness of the work force, and the relative ability of organizations to combine smart and flexible technology with smart and flexible people. The level of skill – perhaps education or productive smarts are better words – and the flexibility, robustness, and astuteness with which that intelligence is organized and mobilized will become the critical differentiating factor. This leads us to technology and education.

Technology

Technological development and diffusion, we have suggested, is where advanced countries may be able to gain an edge and establish themselves during the transition. Importantly, this is an area in which it is widely accepted that markets often fail, and because of that it is an area where government policy can make a major difference to competitiveness. The root of market failure is to be found in the fact that the social gains from technological investment and use often exceed even the enormous private gains. Since the socially optimal amount of effort will not occur spontaneously through markets, government support is considered appropriate to capture these externalities. There are an abundance of historic policies in America and in countries around the world aimed at making the markets for technologies work more effectively, or at least more effectively for them. In Japan the government adopted strategies in advanced electronics and manufacturing to encourage technological development in Japanese firms by funding what we call "generic" technology, thereby lowering the risk to firms entering new technological arenas. It has adopted ambitious policies to diffuse NC machine tools and robots among small producers who would otherwise be reluctant and slow to adopt these new apparatuses. In the United States the famed agricultural extension service and the land grant colleges were organized to develop and diffuse agricultural technology and upgrade skills in the agricultural sector. They were, as these things go, extraordinarily successful policies. In all these cases governments have acted, in the language of economics, to correct market failures. The improved use of labor and capital embedded in new technology gives advantages to firms that accumulate national comparative advantage in the high-value-added sectors.

For the development and, critically, the diffusion of today's production technologies, America currently has created two major disadvantages for itself. First, the American investment in civilian technologies now lags behind that of its partners. Civilian spin-offs from military R&D could, of course, offset some of that disadvantage. But studies at BRIE and elsewhere suggest that these commercial advantages are now much more restricted than they were in the 1950s and early 1960s.[2] While it is difficult to judge the effect of military development and procurement on civilian industry, on balance the impact is, in our view, to distort the capacity of firms to adjust to competitive international markets. To promote civilian R&D, government can do a number of things. It can subsidize, directly or through taxes, firms that undertake or increase levels of R&D. The R&D tax shelters and tax credits are instances of such policies. Government can also support the basic scientific research and the education required to transform basic science into products. Policy can promote more applied research. Here, often, there is a concern that government will either support the wrong firms or the wrong technologies. There are ways of avoiding that problem.

In critical areas such as semiconductors or new materials, support for generic technological development is a means of addressing international competitive problems. In current American policy there is a category called "basic science," which is heavily funded in the United States. Pour money into the science machine, the theory goes, and out will come product and economic growth. Of course the Japanese did fine without pouring much in at that point. They borrowed the results of that basic research from elsewhere, usually the US, at no or very low cost. There is a second category called "product development." In between basic science and product development is a third category known as "applied science" – the application of basic principles to something useful. In fact, policy makers need to examine these categories more carefully. At any moment a range of products will depend on resolving particular scientific problems or building up enough knowledge about particular materials or processes. Those problems are not basic science, but they precede product development. In the sweep of applied technologies and science, certain problems can be identified that are likely to have substantial economic consequences if solved. Here is where the Japanese have put their money.[3] It is the generic quality of these technologies, which are essential to many products but not specific to any, that permits joint research corporations among competing firms such as Microelectronics and Computer Technology Corporation to be established. In passing we should note that Bell Laboratories once played this role with extraordinary distinction. It was a national treasure and resource, a center of research that solved many generic problems and pumped the results into the national and, indeed, the international industrial community. The AT&T divestiture, the breakup of the Bell System, has changed the nature of Bell Laboratories' role in the economy. Generic research is a suitable and underdeveloped target of competitiveness policy.

Second, there is the task of diffusing the use of emerging technologies. In the nineteenth century American policy took the lead in this area when we established the Agricultural Extension Service both to do research for farmers, none of whom could individually conduct that research, and to diffuse this advanced agricultural know-how. That policy had a strong and positive impact on raising the competitiveness of American high-income agriculture. In the twentieth century the Japanese have created a virtual manufacturing and machine-tool extension service.[4] It does for a broad range of industry what the Agricultural Extension Service did for American farmers, introducing them to new ideas and equipment and providing technical expertise to help them choose and use that equipment productively. Japanese policy has gone even further. It has organized programs to help small and medium-sized firms lease and purchase the advanced equipment vital for increasing their competitiveness and, therefore, the competitiveness of other Japanese firms linked to them. These policies have helped Japan diffuse NC machine tools and robots among smaller producers, who would ordinarily be slow to adopt new techniques, much faster and more broadly than in the United States. A Manufacturing Extension Service, patterned after the Agricultural Extension Service, would be a good device for bringing new technologies into smaller US firms. It would help US competitiveness across a range of industries, not just those that make the technologies. With a similar objective of diffusing technology, but at a much higher technical level, the National Science Foundation is purchasing a number of supercomputers for major US universities to train the next generation of computer scientists on the newest, albeit very expensive, machines rather than on outdated technologies. Technological diffusion is critical because the current industrial transition is being driven by the application of emerging transformative technologies to traditional sectors. When microelectronics, new materials, and biotechnology touch established products, those established products, as well as the processes to make them, are altered. Moreover, the new technologies interconnect, creating an economywide wave of advance.

There are now extensive international markets in technology. Just as international capital markets have made investment funds more widely available, technology, which diffuses ever-more rapidly, is more quickly available to more potential producers. Consequently, the way technology is employed will prove decisive. That will turn, in our view, on the character of the US work force. Technology will be a complement not an alternative to a skilled work force.

Education and smarts

In the present transition, the nature of work force skills and the level of those skills will change. However, the distant and disembodied force of technological development driven by competitive pressures will not unilaterally determine the kinds and number of skills that a competitive US economy will require. Skill requirements – the market's demands for labor – will be significantly shaped by skill availabilities, and not only in the static and conventional sense of markets always clearing at some price. Work at BRIE suggests the hypothesis that the availability (or scarcity) of skills shapes competitive strategies as well as the development of particular technologies.[5] This has always been the case:

> We can see it as far back in the American past as in the origins of mass production of muskets, an organizational and technological response to perceived shortages of craft skills. Former Labor Secretary Ray Marshall has observed a similar phenomena in the period after World War II. He argues that the GI Bill played a key role in creating a supply of well educated workers that shaped a demand for their skills. A similar adjustment to skill availability also occurred during the 1960s when highly trained solid state electronics engineers – the result of government grants to graduate engineering education during the 1950s – began to enter the labor force in significant numbers. Educated labor is an economic resource that is strongly shaped by policy. In this transition it may prove decisive. We should admit that our close work with the Carnegie Forum on Education and the Economy during the last year simply confirmed our own biases. Nonetheless it does appear that "organized smarts" will massively determine a nation's competitive success in the current transition. An educated, skilled labor force broadens rather than forecloses choice in the competitive development and application of technologies. In the end it permits firms to get new technology into place more cheaply.
>
> Similarly our research and the work of others suggests that across the industrial spectrum, competitive mastery of the new technologies rests on successful employment of workers' skills. In continuous processing plants, for example, microprocessor based instrumentation generates a large integrated data base. To maximize the power of the technology, workers have to be able to monitor, analyze, and intervene in the continual flow of electronic data; they have to "both theoretically apprehend the data and convert their understanding into articulate processes in order to communicate it to others." Similarly metal workers using computer-controlled machine tools need to rely on a reservoir of craft skills to prevent disastrous breakdowns and bottlenecks in the production process. In white collar industries the introduction of office automation technologies makes it possible for clerical workers to assume functions formerly reserved for professionals, but only if they are sufficiently skilled to use the new technology and sufficiently educated to understand the new functions. Even the speed of change itself places new demands on the work force, requiring that it adapt continually to new products and new processes.[6]

Labor as a factor of production is not just people, but people with particular skills, attitudes, and habits. Production can be organized differently with literate workers than it can in an illiterate community, to take just one element of the labor package. The skill base of a nation and how it is employed is likely to be the decisive factor in determining national competitiveness – the country's ranking in the international hierarchy of wealth and power. America has a rather substantial range for choice in this matter. The pool of skills is a product of education policy. In the nineteenth century America benefited from a uniquely egalitarian system of public education that produced an unusually broadly skilled work force. At one time America could be confident that, in competition with Europe, its egalitarian, literate, and homogeneous community of skilled workers represented a distinctive asset. We cannot have such confidence now. We have lost that advantage. American literacy rates are low: functional illiteracy of US seventeen-year-olds is estimated to be somewhere between 8 and 20 per cent.[7] Some estimates are radically higher. Less than 1 per cent of the Japanese population[8] is functionally illiterate. On the basis of internationally administered achievement tests, American high school seniors do very poorly in international achievement comparisons – worse than the students of any other developed nation.[9] The number of engineers *per capita* in Japan is roughly double that of the United States.[10] Unless we avert this, the United States will find itself with one of the lowest skilled work forces among the advanced countries, and this will directly and powerfully shape our pattern of advantage, converting it to a pattern of disadvantage in industries that can employ high-wage labor.

Unless we have the skills to employ the new production possibilities, no amount of investment capital will make us competitive with countries that have invested in human as well as in physical capital. Economic development and productivity in Japan and the newly industrializing countries rests firmly on their development of a skilled work force. The unexpected and impressive success of Korea in advanced electronics is an excellent illustration of creating advantage through factor policies, especially skills policy. That nation entered electronics with none of the three necessary elements: it had no supply of skilled electronics engineers or technicians, little capital, and no homegrown technology. It sent its promising young people off to MIT and Berkeley, borrowed the money, licensed the technology, and built, over the years, an emerging and probably self-regenerating comparative advantage in electronics. An explicit policy about skills and an all-out effort to develop them was an indispensable element in Korea's success in electronics. It is not just that their labor was cheap, but that it was disciplined and – for the production tasks needed – educated and skilled. Now, as our competitors, both the newly industrializing countries and the advanced economies of Europe and Japan, move into higher and higher value-added production, the educational levels of their work forces and the investment in education at all levels of their societies are increasing more than proportionally. The United States will not again be the economy with the most skilled work force. The question is whether we will find ourselves at a substantial disadvantage.

Equally important, the skill pool of the population shapes how technology is used. Firms in different countries use different production technologies; cars are made differently in Britain, Japan, and the United States.[11] The origins of those differences do not lie ... simply in the cost of different factors of production. Rather they reflect different approaches to the problems of manufacturing – different solutions to be found under different social conditions and in which labor and capital costs are merely one element. Indeed, there are many instances in which factories in different countries use identical machines in radically different ways and achieve distinctly different results in terms of productivity.

Certainly, until five years ago the debate over how robots should be used was on different tracks in the United States and Japan, with the Japanese emphasizing production flexibility and the Americans emphasizing labor replacement.[12] There are clues emerging, not systematic evidence but clues, that the consequences of the new competition and technology for the labor force depends on how it is used. How the technology is used depends on the problems it is called on to solve. If there is a shortage of skilled labor, then the technologies will evolve in ways that require less skilled labor. Where skilled labor is abundant, technology can emerge to reinforce the abilities of the work force.

In the formulation we have chosen – seeing the economy through factors of production – skills appear as the most important element of policy affecting labor. Yet, if the optic is shifted slightly, it is the organization of labor relations and the character of labor–management conflict that will shape the technological strategies of firms. Where skilled labor is absent but technological development is easy to attain, technology will be used to substitute for the missing labor. However, where skilled labor is abundant but powerful and perceived by management as an obstacle to corporate operations, the technology will be used to displace the work force and eliminate the obstacle – the power a skilled work force can exert over operations in plant and shop floor.

The technology will be used to eliminate perceived obstacles to management strategies and autonomy. Consequently, labor relations are a vital counterpart to work force skills. This is not a technical matter of the best way to arrange "bargaining" and negotiations. Rather, it is a matter of resolving the conflicts between labor and management in a manner that assures flexibility and encourages participation and cooperation. In one form or another this involves security of employment. The politics of labor is the vital counterpart to the politics of education.

America has substantial choice here. We could try a strategy of stripping skills out of jobs. We can try to replace skilled labor – on the shop floor and in the office – with technology and offshore that which we can't replace or think we can't yet replace. ... [H]ow the technology is to be developed and how it will be used is not determined.[13] It is a question of choice or, more accurately, a question that will be resolved by a long series of iterative choices, each one being influenced by the previous one.

Shaping and using technologies to displace skilled labor runs deep and serious national risks. At any single moment it may be possible for a firm to pursue this tactic, but it will start us down a dangerous technological path, one that in the long run will make national competitiveness in world markets difficult. There are three dangers or risks. First, we suspect that technologies that displace skilled workers are more rigid and less flexible than those that complement and require skills. Such production systems are inherently more capital-intensive. They generally require far higher levels of capital investment and technological complexity to achieve comparable results. In part, as a consequence of the greater investment of capital and the elimination of skills, entire production systems must be reformed from the top down in larger discrete steps. They are more difficult to reform from within. This simply reinforces a weakness of American firms – their inability to adapt rapidly to changing technologies. Second, worker replacement technologies are harder to develop and more expensive to implement. Take, for instance, artificial intelligence control systems for production. If they are used to supplement worker skills, they can be much simpler than if they must embody vast levels of expertise and knowledge required to replace the workers. Look at the Bay Area Rapid Transit system (BART) in San Francisco. The technological dream was to replace drivers with an automated control system. To do so required enormous development costs and heavy capital investment. Yet, that system has never worked. In sum, simpler technologies that rest on worker skills will be implemented sooner and be more widely diffused, we hypothesize, because they are easier to develop and cheaper. But, we must not exaggerate. Fully automated factories will emerge and do provide remarkable efficiencies. Yet the question, we suspect, is how one closes on the design of such "lights out" operations. If the automated factory implements production systems initially developed progressively with skilled labor and less automated technologies, they are likely to move into operation smoothly and effectively. When the design is conceived whole cloth by engineers and cast into concrete and machines, serious difficulties may be expected. In other words, skilled labor may be a decisive element in the experimentation required to develop new production systems. Third, and centrally, can we as a nation – as opposed to an individual firm or even the sum of individual firms – really adopt fundamental strategies based on stripping labor skills from jobs and, therefore, accepting a relative decline in overall educational levels?

To pose the question as a national choice raises some unpleasant fundamentals about the different strategies that can be used to contend with our competitiveness problem. For the nation, the low-skill choice leads to dead ends. Competition on wage rates is one dead end. We cannot, we are learning, keep capital costs substantially lower in America than abroad, so that American unskilled labor could command much higher wages than foreign unskilled labor because it could be given much more powerful tools with which to work. It is also a fantasy to hope that an elite group of American engineers can keep production technology in this country so far ahead of technology in other advanced countries and developing nations that we can retain decisive production or product advantage. The realities of the past few years should by now have shattered that illusion.

That America will lose if it takes the low-skill route does not mean that America will close down or that all Americans will lose. It does, however, mean that most of us will lose a lot, and that this country will be transformed in ways that many of us find terribly unattractive. We would become more like a Latin American society. We could have a small minority of high-skilled research, development, production, and service jobs coexisting with a majority of low-skilled, low-wage jobs, and massive underemployment and unemployment. For the vast majority of Americans, living standards would deteriorate rapidly – probably along with social equality and political democracy – as, in order to compete, manufacturing and services move offshore and automation strips the remaining labor content from the remaining US goods and services. It is not an attractive scenario.

The new infrastructure: telecommunications and organized smarts

Infrastructure, as we have just seen, remains vital, even in its most traditional forms: ports, rails, and roads. But the critical form of infrastructure is now telecommunications. [Elsewhere, we] made this argument and showed how the development of new telecommunications-based technologies and their adaptation in a vast range of commercial settings are radically altering production strategies and recasting the competitive equation.[14]

[We] also showed how different nations are responding differently to the possibilities of the new telecommunications. Japan, in particular, is making an enormous effort, investing way ahead of market, to provide the most sophisticated possibilities to the broadest possible range of users – that is, to both small and large businesses (and even households). The United States, on the other hand, has devised policies that focus on providing, at very rapid speed, new and sophisticated technologies primarily to big users. It is, in the final analysis, a policy that conceives of telecommunications as an investment service purchased through the market by firms. And the United States has cleared away the obstacles to letting the market fit the technology to those clients who occupy the biggest places in the launch markets – the big users. The Japanese strategy is differently conceived. It sees telecom primarily as an infrastructure, and the Japanese government is setting the pace and the form of that infrastructural investment in order to orient and improve the working of the market. The improvements they have in mind are clear: get the benefits of the new technology to small- and middle-sized firms as well as big ones so that it will help them to compete in the ever-more difficult international competitive environment. That strategy aims at helping not only small Japanese firms but also, because many of them are subcontractors to big firms, at increasing the competitiveness of those large firms. At the same time, by investing ahead of market demand, Japanese infrastructural policy structures and launches what Japanese policy makers consider the most important high-tech sector for the future–enhanced telecommunications – in a way designed to enhance mightily the competitive advantage of Japanese firms.

Infrastructural policy cannot be divorced from competitiveness policy. But telecom, however enhanced, is more than a physical and software network that, once laid in, will quickly give a nation's producers a launch market lead down the learning curve and, when applied broadly, will offer vital production advantages to that nation's producers. Ultimately, productive use of that infrastructure depends upon the "quality" of the person on the other end of the line. That takes us back to the new economics of educated and organized "smarts," which treats national endowments of trained intelligence as productive infrastructure for the entire economy as well as just assets (actual or potential) for a particular firm.

Put more formally, as the division of labor becomes more and more complex – and that, after all, is what the colossal growth of producer services represents – the productivity of any worker, or any firm, depends on that of workers in other firms. The workers in other firms provide not simply a priced and purchasable input that can be warehoused and used as needed. Instead, they are integrated into the production, "on-line" as it were. The telecom revolution is all about enhancing the interactive approach to complex production. The productivity of a doctor, for example, is substantially a function of the ability of the patient to describe symptoms accurately and quickly and to understand complex instructions the first time through, as well as a function of the productivity of lab technicians, medical-imaging centers, and insurance claims processors, to name but a few. They are all external to the doctor's organization. In still more formal terms, when a firm's production function is written out in mathematical form, the factors that determine output are listed, rather like the ingredients in a cooking recipe: so much capital, so much raw materials, so much labor, and so on. But there is a whole set of factors that are not generally included in the written equation; they remain implicit. One such factor is public order: revolutions that will disrupt production are not listed; power outages that will short-circuit the works are also not factored in. The implicit part is growing bigger, or at least it is changing its composition. As the division of labor extends itself, the production function of any firm – be it a manufacturer or a service firm – is becoming increasingly dependent upon the production function of other firms. If this is not true, we have no explanation for the growth of services to producers ... It becomes harder and harder to shield or isolate the productivity of your firm from that of other firms – clients as well as providers – and from the organizations upon which your own productivity depends; for example, by buying up all the good people, because your good people have to interact with their less good people. Accountants, lawyers, travel agents, financial advisers, and consultants of all sorts confront similar "interdependent" production functions. So do software writers, venture capitalists, and air traffic controllers. Production more and more resembles an on-line network.

...

Conclusion

In many ways America is in a particularly fortunate position insofar as making policy to improve competitiveness is concerned. We have done so little that there is a huge layer of easy things we can do before we get to the hard ones. And those easy ones have by far the biggest impact. Most countries have already geared their basic economic policies toward international competition. We haven't. That gives us a kind of "advantage of backwardness" position in policy making. It is a little like energy conservation a few years back. The United States had done so little in that direction compared to Europe or Japan that, while other countries were at a stage where they had to take very difficult measures, we could do easier things – things they had done years before – and get huge returns. The same is true in competitiveness policy. Only let's hope that in competitiveness policy we take better advantage of our privileged position. Because we have done so little in the past to shape policy to the goal of competitiveness, we are, among all our competitors, uniquely privileged.

Notes

1. *Editor's Note*: See Stephen S. Cohen and John Zysman, *Manufacturing Matters*, Chapter 14, "Policy and Competitiveness in a Changing World Economy," pp. 211–19.
2. For a compelling argument as well as an excellent source of reference on the limited spinoff benefits of Pentagon R&D, see Jay Stowsky, "Beating Our Plowshares into Double-Edged Swords: The Impact of Pentagon Policies on the Commercialization of Advanced Technologies," *BRIE Working Paper*, 17 (1986).
3. See Kenichi Ohmae, "Japan's Industrial Policy for High-Technology Industries" (paper prepared for the Conference on Japanese Industrial Policy in Comparative Perspective, New York, 17–19 March 1984), pp. 31–6, 52–6.
4. The ... Houdaille scandal is a case in point. See the legal brief entitled: Houdaille Industries, Inc., Petitioner: 31 July 1982, "Petition to the President of the United States Through the Office of the United States Trade Representative for the Exercise of Presidential Discretion Authorized by Section 103 of the Revenue Act of 1971," 26 USC sect. 48(a)(7)(D).
5. See for instance Barbara Baran and Carol Parsons, "Technology and Skills: A Literature Review" (paper prepared for the Carnegie Forum on Education and the Economy, January 1986); see also Richard Gordon and Linda M.

Kimball, "High Technology, Employment, and the Challenges to Education," *Working Paper*, 1 (Silicon Valley Research Group, July 1985), pp. 84 ff.

6. See Baran and Parsons, "Technology and Skills."
7. Jonathan Kozol, *Illiterate America* (New York: New American Library, 1985), p. 4.
8. See Herbert J. Walberg, "Scientific Literacy and Economic Productivity in International Perspective," *Daedalus*, 112 (Spring 1983).
9. Ibid., p. 7.
10. Walberg, "Scientific Literacy and Economic Productivity."
11. See the description of different national automotive production systems in Alan Altschuler *et al.*, "The Competitive Balance," in Alan Altschuler *et al.*, *The Future of the Automobile* (Cambridge, Mass: MIT Press, 1984), pp. 145–75; see also Chapters 7 and 8 in National Research Council, *The Competitive Status of the US Auto Industry: A Study of the Influences of Technology in Determining International Industrial Competitive Advantage* (Washington, D.C.: National Academy Press, 1982), pp. 109–32.
12. Traditionally, American firms have been slow to recognize the need to retrain existing labor, preferring instead the time tested short-run palliative of massive layoffs. Recently, however, IBM has been making headway in retraining its workers to work with automated production technologies. See the *Wall Street Journal* (14 April, 1986), p, 1; for an account of similar developments in West Germany, see the *Wall Street Journal* (23 April, 1986), p. 1.
13. *Editor's Note*: Stephen S. Cohen and John Zysman, *Manufacturing Matters*, Part II, "Managing the Transition," Chapters 6–12, pp. 79–199.
14. *Editor's Note*: See Stephen S. Cohen and John Zysman, *Manufacturing Matters*, Chapter 11, "Dimensions of the Transition: The New Telecommunications Revolution," pp. 150–77.

15

Restructuring and the Working Class (1988)*

Joyce Kolko

...

[A] discussion of "restructuring" as it pertains to labor should begin with a definition of labor as a class. As in considerations of capital and the state, it is important to distinguish the systemic from the structural features in such a definition for, again, most of the generalizations about the "new" working class are based on transitional structural conditions.

Whether the nature of work is industrial or service, whether workers are employed as clerks or as miners, in transport or in construction, are skilled or unskilled, organized or not, well paid or earning subsistence wages, composed of minorities, natives, or migrants, or are unemployed are all important *structural* factors to examine. These structural features change and are restructured, but they are all subject to the *systemic* components, which determine the nature of the working class in the capitalist system at any time and place, whether in conditions of crisis or of "prosperity." These features include labor as a commodity in the production process; its vulnerability to immiseration; exploitation; and the class struggle (objective and/or subjective). One of the most important factors, other than the workers' role as producers, is their vulnerability as an expendable commodity.

...

I find it useful to delineate the constant features of the working class in formulating a definition, for as with the other categories, one can in this way avoid the tendency to generalize on and extrapolate the structural features. This delineation is less urgent today than in the recent

---

* From *Restructuring the World Economy* (New York: Pantheon, 1988), pp. 305–24, 327, 329–31, 343–345.

past, because social reality is starker under the condition of prolonged economic crisis, and there is now less inclination to dwell superficially on the appearance of prosperity and what it may mean for a changing working class.

The working class clearly extends beyond the occupational category of the industrial proletariat, which by the 1980s was less than half of the wage earners. Paul Mattick rightly pointed out,

> it is then not its *occupational character* that characterizes the prole-tariat but its *social position* as wage labor. The diminution of the industrial working class implies the growth of the working class irrespective of the type of employment (or unemployment) it is engaged in.[1]

Its essential trait is the sale of labor for wages, productive and non-productive.

...

[A] definition of class is based not on income but on the origin of income, be it wages or property, and is linked to the relations of production. In America part of the ideology has been to define nearly the whole of society as "middle class" and to use the terms *upper, middle* and *lower,* not to indicate income distribution but to exclude the terms *capitalist* and *working class* or *bourgeoisie* and *proletariat.* The ideologists thus made a part of the working class "middle class," on the basis of a family income of a certain level, usually with more than one earner. When a number of economists recently concluded that one result of the restructuring of the economy was a shrinking of the middle class, with higher income at the top and growing numbers at the bottom, there were widespread expressions of genuine consternation.

Income distribution is one critical aspect of class, of course, and the figures say much about a society's susceptibility to a crisis of underconsumption. Even when it was widely claimed that American capitalism had achieved a more equitable distribution, the empirical evidence revealed a contrary story, as Gabriel Kolko demonstrated in 1962, when the prevalence of this illusion among economists and others was at its height.[2] And the maintenance of a certain level of consumption during the periods of full employment and rising inflation increasingly depended on more than one earner in a household and the use of credit.

The conclusion of many writers that the working class becomes "bourgeoisified" by owning commodities or a house, or by having a high nominal income, or that elements of the bourgeoisie become "proletarianized" as their conditions of work change and they are vulnerable to unemployment, was highly superficial. Except over time and with generational change, there is far more to class than is measured by income. More income for workers does not change their relations of exploitation or their vulnerability as a commodity. Their enhanced bargaining position reached in the cyclical peak and near full employment as in France and Italy in the late 1960s, crumbles in times of crisis. The downward mobility of the bourgeois usually produces not solidarity with the working class but bitterness: such individuals retain the cultural and ideological baggage of their class. Working-class identity is determined by a whole matrix of associations in an individual's life, not merely by his or her income or occupation. It is crucial to emphasize the important systemic factor – the worker's vulnerability as an expendable commodity in the capitalist system. A worker's middle-class living standard has never been secure.

The conceptual myth that the working class would steadily become more affluent and an aristocracy of labor formed the basis of multiple generalizations, and it was rudely shattered in the recent condition of the world economy. It was also an example of the tendency to extrapolate current structural conditions rather than to focus on the systemic factors of capitalism. To be vulnerable, expendable, and increasingly superfluous has always been a reality for labor. And in this context the International Labor Organization (ILO) estimated that in the last twenty years of the twentieth century, one-third more people will enter the labor force each year, at a time of shrinking employment worldwide, than between 1950 and 1975, when employment was expanding.[3]

The OECD's 1979 report, *Interfutures*, declared,

> On the whole, Western civilization has, during the last 150 years, succeeded in integrating its internal proletariat [which it attributed to an expanding middle class] ... However, this civilization is now confronted by the problem of its external proletariat.[4]

Putting aside the fact that these nations in the OECD were in the process of dis-"integrating" their "internal proletariat," the structural conditions of the laboring classes in the less-developed capitalist countries have deteriorated rapidly as they are forced to bear the brunt of the restructuring of their society, seriously worsening the special "problem of its external proletariat."

Restructuring employment

The decade since the mid-1970s has seen fundamental changes in employment that are crucial to the restructuring of the economy and the nature of work. As has been widely noted, the most significant new characteristics for the entire industrial capitalist world, in addition to the export of jobs in search of cheap labor, have been the shift from relatively high-wage factory work in heavy industry to low-wage service occupations, the importance of part-time and temporary employment, and the predominance of lower-wage women workers in the occupations with expanding employment. These changes were largely the outcome of the objective operations of the system. But their advantages for capital and for the state were quickly apparent, and they were adopted as part of a conscious strategy to restructure the economy. The contradictions in these developments are all too evident as well.

In the United States, where 4.0 million jobs were added between 1958 and 1968, the Labor Department found in 1985 that 2.3 million manufacturing jobs had disappeared since 1980, some 90 per cent of them probably permanently, and most of these were in high-wage, organized heavy industry. Its studies argued that the economy was moving on two paths–service producing and goods producing. The workers in the fast-growing service industries were earning, on the average, $5,000 less than those in the industries with a shrinking work force. In the factories of the new industries, such as electronics, assembly jobs are few and low paying.

In the organized heavy-industry sector, business has demanded concessions and a rollback of previously won wage and benefit gains as part of its general offensive to cut costs and to take advantage of the economic crisis to change the relations with labor that had developed over the preceding thirty years. Union concessions on wages and benefits in settlements with US employers numbered 159 in 1982 and 430 in 1983. In 1982 some 38 per cent of the unionized workers took wage cuts, and 15 per cent had no increase. These concessions did not diminish layoffs. The most common form of wage concession accepted by the unions, usually under the threat of closure and relocation, was the dual wage and benefit system for new and old workers. The airline, auto, trucking, copper, and aerospace industries negotiated new-worker wage cuts of $4–$5 per hour in 1983. Frequently, the old workers were fired, so the two-tier system soon became the major grievance.

In addition to wage concessions, there were many other "givebacks" pertaining to work rules and working conditions in the labor contracts negotiated in the 1980s. Often the savings gained by union concessions intended to maintain employment and production were spent by management on more automation or financial speculation. Inevitable workers' resistance to these trends led in the mid-1980s to an increase in local strike action over company reductions in job security and benefits. Workers soon realized, especially in the steel industry, that when they made concessions the company often closed the plant anyway. Black male workers suffered most in the shift of employment away from manufacturing, for it was in the factory that they had been able to secure relatively high-wage jobs since the Second World War.

When industries close or restructure with automation, the change is dramatic. Workers habituated to high wages, benefits, and continued rises are confronted with falling wages and worsening conditions, if they are lucky enough still to have a job, or unemployment and the admonition to find a job in the low-paying services.

Service work

According to an OECD report, "since the beginning of the 1970s [the service sector] has been the only sector to create jobs in most member countries" in the OECD.[5] The US Bureau of Labor Statistics estimated in 1985 that the most rapidly growing sector in the American economy until 1995 would be janitors, fast-food workers, nurses' aides, and clerical workers. They expected a demand for only 120,000 computer programmers. By 1986 fully 81 per cent of the new jobs in the United States were in services, compared with 66 per cent in 1985 and 52 per cent in 1984, and the vast majority of them were near the bottom of the wage ladder. The trend accelerated in 1987 when 94 per cent of new employment was in the services. Three-fifths of the 8.1 million new jobs, service and nonservice, since 1979 have paid $7,000 a year or less.

The initial growth in service was linked to the expansion of the public sector. But the government sector, which accounted for one-third of the growth before 1975, accounted for only 15 per cent of the growth between 1976 and 1982 and has since contracted further because of ... fiscal constraints. Services in the private sector in the OECD countries, by contrast, are considered the only expanding employment sector in the economy. It was estimated in 1984 that up to 65–70 per cent of the jobs in Europe were in the services of all sorts and that three out of four American workers were.

But service work is a heterogeneous category. In the United States health services were by 1981 the largest component, with 29.5 per cent of all service workers, and 80 per cent of them were women. Next is the category of business services, with 16.9 per cent. Work in the business services increasingly consists of feeding data into computers, an extremely boring task, performed in nearly total isolation from other workers, usually on a piecework pay scale, and under constant electronic surveillance by supervisors. In "wholesale and retail trade," the number of workers rose front 8.7 million in 1950 to over 18.0 million in 1982. In the "recovery" beginning in 1983, all of the employment growth was in the private sector services, primarily in new small retail trade enterprises. Service workers' wages fell over the decade, and the new employment came in what were considered "dead-end" jobs. On the average, service sector pay was two-thirds that of manufacturing. In all the services there was a higher than average proportion of women, blacks, and part-time workers.

In manufacturing, as well, the per centage of service as opposed to production workers increased. In 1978 the figure was 23 per cent in the United States, 35 per cent in the FRG, 27 per cent in France, and 25 per cent in Sweden. In the 1980s such nonproduction workers made up 80 per cent of the new employment in US manufacturing.

When employment statistics in North America and Europe are compared, the gain of 18.0 million jobs in the United States and the loss of 1.5 million in Europe since 1973 has been attributed by government officials and businessmen to the "rigidities" of wages and other social benefits in the European economies that are absent in America. And in good part, among other factors discussed later, it does reflect the differing social attitudes in America and Europe. In the United States unemployment benefits are both shorter and lower; this forces workers to take any job and makes it mandatory for child-rearing women to seek work to supplement the family income. Their work is invariably in the service sector.

But service workers are now as vulnerable to automation as production workers. Employment in banking doubled between 1968 and 1983, but the new technology has helped halt or reverse that trend. By the 1980s even the computer programmer's work was being automated. Automation is increasingly evident in those industries where labor is the important component of cost, such as the insurance industry, where labor is 60 per cent of business expenses. And clerical and other white-collar workers in the manufacturing industries were also susceptible to unemployment in the great industrial cost cutting over this decade. White-collar work fell 4.0 per cent in the steel industry, and 15 per cent in the auto industry, totaling one million lost jobs since 1979. Other industries, such as oil, were also rapidly automating clerical jobs in the mid-1980s. While the cyclical pattern of service joblessness in manufacturing has matched overall unemployment, in the recession employment also increased, as women reentered the labor force for new forms of service work.

There is another factor behind these statistics of growth and decline of jobs in services and manufacturing. In the OECD nations business services have had the highest growth, and personal services as well as transport and communication have declined. This is because manufacturing companies, which once produced their own services, began to contract them to specialized companies and temporary manpower firms and because the same jobs are listed differently in the statistics. And it also explains why the service sector is smaller in the FRG, where manufacturers have not followed this trend and still produce their own services, giving a different employment picture. The classification of "personal services" has declined with machinery, whether it is a matter of household machines replacing laundries or of vending machines, or the workers are part of the "underground economy" and not listed statistically.

The nature of work

In addition to sectoral shifts in employment, work itself is being restructured. Part-time, homework, temporary, and other forms of "cost-free" labor are replacing traditional employment in both service and production. Such forms account for the expansion of employment in the United States because of the absence of the so-called rigidities in the labor market that existed in most of the European economies. The official celebration of the growth of employment in the United States in the 1980s, compared with that in other industrial countries, ignored the fact that it was part-time work that had increased while the number of hours worked and weekly earnings had declined. A worker is statistically employed in the United States if he or she works at least three hours a day for three days a week or if the work is temporary. What used to be a recession tactic has now become a structural feature of the economy. This fragmentation of the work force is a crucial dimension of the restructuring of the economy. "Personnel is not a fixed cost anymore," proclaimed the satisfied head of a temporary-employment agency, summing up this important trend in employment.[6]

Since 1980 the number of part-time workers in the United States has grown 58 per cent, to one-fourth of the total of those employed. While such work is preferred by many, 17 per cent of all American workers were part-time workers who desired full-time work, the number having doubled since 1980. One-third of the jobs in retail trade and the service sector are part-time, although most part-time work is in production. The workers in these realms are in circumstances scarcely better than those of the unemployed, and they naturally make up the bulk of the "working poor." Their advantages to the employer are obvious: there are no costs such as sick pay, health insurance, or vacations. Wages are usually nearly one-half those for a full-time worker, and a transient labor force is usually unorganized. This expansion of part-time work obviously depends on a large reserve army of unemployed.

Part-time work is especially prevalent in the new high-tech sector of the economy, in those very industries that are allegedly the great hopes for replacing the employment disappearing from heavy industry. In California's Silicon Valley, the labor force is unorganized and as flexible as the automation. The workers are hired for short periods adjusted to the frequent peaks and slumps in the industry, and the part-time employees are frequently 30 per cent of the total.

Part-time work is the trend in the rest of the OECD states as well. It has increased 50 per cent in the FRG since the early 1970s, to 12 per cent of the workers, and in Sweden it composes 25 per cent of all jobs. In Japan the use of part-time workers has been termed the "second secret weapon" of its competitive success.[7] (The first was workers' acceptance of long overtime hours.) And many in Japan work full-time hours for part-time wages and no benefits. Part-time jobs and temporary work increased over the 1970s, but it did so exponentially after 1980, when there was only one temporary-employment agency in Tokyo. By 1985 there were nearly 150. Some large companies had begun to hire out their own permanent workers to other companies needing temporary employees. It was a natural corollary to the system of lifetime full-time employees and shifting demand in manufacturing. So-called lifetime employment, in any case, has never affected more than 25 per cent of the Japanese workers. More and more companies have forced these workers into early retirement during the 1980s. And because there are minimal social services in Japan and the cost of living is exorbitant, the government developed a plan to export its elderly to low-cost countries. According to a Tokyo businessman, Japanese corporations concluded by 1983 that "the removal of people [permanent employees] is the only way to make money."[8] Japanese business prefers the part-time flexible work force for the same reason that capitalists elsewhere do – it lowers costs.

Temporary work is similar to part-time. The director of staffing at Citibank said, "Face it. Labor costs are a major item. You are not paying the same fringe benefits to temporaries, and this is one way for industry to keep costs within reason."[9]

Many industries have restructured to a much smaller "permanent" work force, and temporary or "contingent" workers have become an integral part of their adjustment to cyclical changes and of their efforts to lower costs. Over the 1980s the number of jobs defined as temporary grew at 20 per cent a year in the United States. Temporary workers are most prevalent in office work and are a major restraint on labor's organizing efforts. In Japan contract temporary workers used seasonally to expand manufacturing production are not listed statistically, but in steel, for instance, they constitute up to 4.0 per cent of the labor force. Temporary and part-time workers earn 30–50 per cent less than permanent workers. But this structural factor in Japanese capitalism is also emerging in US industry, where the unions and companies increasingly agree to permanent employment for a small group of core workers to be supplemented by part-time or temporary workers.

Also increasing over the past decade in the United States has been the old technique of homework and sweatshops, made possible by an increase in the number of illegal migrants. These are often linked with workers spending nine hours in the shop and taking the work home for additional hours of piecework. The home computer has also made it possible for much office work to be done in the home. The number who work at home rose fourfold since 1980, to nearly nine million.

All these factors mean that in Japan, and increasingly throughout Europe and North America, there is a trend toward a duality in the work force: a shrinking number of full-time permanent employees and a growing number of temporary or part-time workers for the giant industries, and the bulk of the workers in low-paying, insecure jobs with the thousands of small subcontractors to industry or in the services.[10]

Woman's work

Throughout the OECD countries low-wage jobs are performed by women, minorities, and immigrants. Both objectively and intentionally, this situation is lowering the general wage level of all these economies. And the growth of women in the work force has paralleled the growth of service work in the economy. Some 60–85 per cent of the employed women in the OECD states are in ... services.

As inflation increased and real wages began to fall, two earners maintained family income and the growth of credit sustained consumption beyond income by nearly one-fifth. In the United States the percentage of women in the labor force jumped from 36.5 per cent in 1960 to 54.0 per cent in 1985, the chief growth being among married women between twenty-five and thirty-four, whose participation rose from 28 per cent to 65 per cent. In over 50 per cent of the families with children, both parents work, including nearly half of all women with children under six years. The gap between the wages of men and women declined after 1978, but falling wages for male workers were the origin of the change. Yet, despite more than one income earner, household spending power fell in the 1980s, and in 1986 it was below that of 1979, and continued to fall in 1987.

The new factories in high-tech and service industries in Europe also moved toward the greater use of part-time, migrant, and women workers. This trend became their means to restructure the economy and increase employment. In Japan the part-time workers, increasingly crucial to the operations of the Japanese economy, have been predominantly women, whose participation has increased 7-8 per cent a year since 1980 and accounted for 90 per cent of those part-time workers who are statistically counted. In trade they already outnumber full-time workers.

In the LDCs, in every country with free-trade zones, over 80 per cent of the workers are young women between the ages of sixteen and twenty-four, who are particularly prevalent in the electronics and garment industries. Their wages are often half of those of men, and a dearth of options forces them to work the longest hours. Many studies have chronicled the marginally subsistence wages and dangerous working conditions that wear out the health of these workers in a few years. Either they are replaced from the local labor reserve or the company moves elsewhere, as many aspiring nations advertise the young women in their labor force at competitive terms.

In addition to the changes in the nature and type of work in the visible or legal economy, there has been an expansion of the "underground economy" in the OECD countries – that is, work outside of the state social security, minimum wage, and other legal labor standards. Mounting unemployment has only favored its growth. In Britain it is estimated to be 5–15 per cent of ... GNP. In the United States the comparable figure is reputed to be somewhere between 4.5 per cent and 6.0 per cent of ... GNP, rising, not surprisingly, since the mid-1970s. The estimate is largest for Italy, at 30 per cent. Such illegal labor parallels the LDC economies' vast "informal sector," where massive unemployment and extremes of exploitation are hidden. There one of the principal causes has been the displacement of the peasants, with the mechanization of agricultural production oriented toward the world market and with the increasing penetration of capitalist organization into the countryside, transforming many peasants into agrarian wage workers or into migrants to the urban areas in search of work.

Great diversity of activity characterizes the informal sector in the LDCs. That sector includes petty sales, services, such as shoeshines, pedicabs, and domestic work, as well as manufacturing and repair. Various bureaucrats in the international organizations have called the informal sector an example of enterprise and ingenuity and urged governments to provide credit to its various "entrepreneurs." In many large cities in Asia and Latin America, it is the activity of 50–70 per cent of the total "employment"; in Africa it absorbs 40–60 per cent of the urban labor force. For the most part, this large mass barely ekes out a subsistence at the bottom income layer of the urban society, living in squatter dwellings devoid of elementary services like water and sanitation in and around the vast urban sprawls that now make up the cities of the Third World.

However, as a number of analysts have demonstrated, a substantial part of this sector is really integrated into the industrializing, so-called formal sector and serves as "underground" labor for much of the work in that part of the economy, thereby allowing capitalists to avoid the extra cost, minimal as it is, and the labor relations problems of regular employment. This is especially true of the clothing, furniture, and handicrafts industries, where established companies supply materials on credit. Garbage pickers for recycling are in this way also part of the "formal" industrial economy. And the " informal" workers are important in the circulation of goods, as the ubiquitous street peddlers in Third World cities are often controlled by companies on an informal basis. They earn a bare subsistence margin in sales, out of which they also usually pay interest on credit from the supplier of whatever goods they sell. The informal-sector worker is vital for the profitability of many companies, large and small.

Evidence shows that this sector loses, whatever the condition of the economy. When there was high growth of the GNP, in countries like

Brazil, this segment of the population actually became poorer, although it was an important component of that growth. In periods of recession and austerity, their ranks are swollen by those who have lost regular jobs, the "visible" unemployed. And there is always a vast rural reserve enlarging this informal sector, as the process of displacing peasants continues. During the period from 1981 to 1984 agricultural employment rose in most Latin American countries – in Brazil by 4 per cent a year – with depression in the urban formal sector as would-be migrants clung to the land because of yet worse conditions in the cities.

Wages

The restructuring of employment in the industrialized countries achieved its principal aim of a generalized lowering of wages. As the OECD economists noted in 1985, a chief feature of the recovery was the "widespread fall in labor share of national income and the associated rise in the profit share and profits. Another related development has been the decline ... of real wages in many countries."[11]
...

In the United States there was growth in real income until the beginning of the economic crisis in 1974. Real wages then began to decline, fell significantly in 1980, remaining at the point attained in the early 1960s and more than 12 per cent below the 1972–73 peak, and were expected to fall in 1987 for the fifth year of the decade. Real income fell 5 per cent between 1978 and 1986 in manufacturing, as companies cut costs. Cutbacks or a freeze in even nominal wages took place in the recession in 1981 and continued for the following three years. According to *Business Week*, it was "the first major deceleration since the massive wage cuts in the largely nonunion economy of the early 1930s."[12] The first negotiated wage cut was the UAW [United Auto Workers] agreement with Chrysler in 1980 to trade a 12 per cent pay cut for job security. Unions, such as the IVE and UAW at GM factories, have bargained for a two-tier work and wage structure to protect the jobs of their existing members. The OECD, in noting all the concessions during the 1980s, commented, "What is novel is continuing union acquiescence ... despite a comparatively strong recovery in activity and profits."[13] Only in the FRG and in Japan did the unions demand to share in the rising profits. By 1986 American rank-and-file workers had begun to resist the union's readiness to make concessions.

By sector of the economy, the differential in wages is also outstanding. The average hourly wage of a service worker in the private sector is significantly less than that of a manufacturing worker. And in the competitive high-tech industry, as in the garment industry of old, wages are low.

The wage differential between blacks and whites and men and women in the same occupation widened in the United States in the 1980s. But US consumption continued to be higher than wages would indicate in the mid-1980s, since many workers turned to credit. In 1986, consumer debt amounted to a record 19 per cent of all take-home pay, a pattern that portended much greater problems for the future.

...

Prolonged unemployment at a high level was the major cause of the decline in wages. The OECD concluded that in the United States "wage moderation has been so pronounced as to suggest that there may have been an underlying change of behavior" in wage demands.[14] In fact, they found that the evidence was clear in the United States that wages follow rather than lead price inflation and that there was "little empirical support" for a prospective catch-up demand in wages, even where profits were high and rising. The statistics showed that, in the decade following 1973, average nonagricultural real wages in America fell 16 per cent and average household income by 11 per cent.

Since there was a sharp decline or stagnation in real wages in most countries, government officials could observe that this major goal in restructuring their economies had been successfully achieved either through the direct struggle between capital and labor or through state policies. Because bargaining positions depend on the condition of the general economy, real wages may rise at various times, but they are always vulnerable to a reversal and to the perpetual struggle to lower labor costs. The outcome of the gains of labor, in the context of other developments in the economy, was an acceleration of international investment in low-wage areas and investment in automation and other countermoves opposing labor in the late 1970s and 1980s, against a background of rising unemployment.

In the LDCs, of course, barely subsistence wages of a couple of dollars a day in many countries and less than three dollars an hour in the NIC's modern factories have been the major "comparative advantage" in the international division of labor for the labor intensive assembly tasks. These low wages have fallen drastically in real terms in the 1980s, for example, by 33 per cent in Brazil and over 28 per cent in Mexico in 1981–85, because of the restructuring policies in many nations, as the price subsidies for basic needs have been reduced or eliminated.

Productivity

Productivity revolves around the question of how much more can be produced with a given amount of labor or, in a capitalist economy that cannot sell what is produced, how labor cost can be reduced for a limited production. Productivity, then, is the rate of exploitation. Increases can be achieved by maintaining the same output with fewer workers, more labor per worker, or the introduction of new technology.

...

Because of the high rate of mechanization across the economy historically, the United States still has the highest absolute productivity, although the rate of growth is one of the lowest in the industrial countries. But even of the ten official causes of low productivity growth in the United States, only three relate to workers – the so-called declining work ethic, equal opportunity laws, and union "featherbedding." The rest are attributed to government fiscal policies and regulation that diverts investment funds that (supposedly) would go into automation. One politically motivated advocate of deregulation even did a semiofficial study (for the Brookings Institution) that sought to demonstrate that government regulation was the most important cause in the decline of US productivity in the period 1968–78. Many capitalists attributed the decline in productivity to a lack of investable capital, because of high taxes, wages, and falling profit. According to this viewpoint, as productivity depends on "incorporating new technology into new production facilities," business takeovers, rather than new investment, have become one of the greatest barriers to improved productivity.[15] The crude measure of productivity is output divided by hours worked; a more informative measure is output related to all factors of production. And some economists did conclude in 1980, "[T]he slow growth of investment has probably been the major cause of inadequate productivity growth."[16]

Much of American management now views the rigid Taylor organization of production as a barrier to increases in productivity with the new technology. Changes in work rules for many companies, even more than lower wages, are the most sought-after concessions from their workers. They need "flexible" workers and flexible work rules to accompany their flexible automation. Many companies have merged job classifications, eliminating "superfluous" workers and lowering costs. In many cases, it is now the unions that demand strict job assignments and work segmentation in order to protect jobs. This was especially true of skilled workers, who were increasingly being reclassified as "helpers." Change in work rules, rather than wages, was the most frequent cause of strikes in the early 1980s.

There has also been more experimentation in what is termed quality of work life or worker participation or productivity teams, in many cases modeled on Japanese factory organization, in an attempt to raise productivity and lower costs. "Teamwork" and a profitable manipulation of "job satisfaction" impulses are supposed to replace the old assembly line. These measures have usually been linked to a reduction of the work force around a core group, to be extended seasonally by part-time and temporary workers. But a 1981 review of such efforts between 1975 and 1980 found that 75 per cent did not last more than two years. For the workers, in a time of high unemployment, wages and job security are the critical factors. In more prosperous times the boredom and pace of the assembly line rise in importance.

...

Productivity questions in the capitalist industrial economies are merely a foil with which to extract greater concessions from the workers. The system's perennial problem is not inadequate productivity but overproduction.

The earlier US advantage in productivity over the LDCs had diminished by the 1970s. Labor productivity in the foreign subsidiaries in electronics assembly was 92 per cent of that in the United States; in some it was even higher by the early 1970s, because of the intensity (long hours) of work–ten or more hours a day and often seven days a week. And according to the OECD:

> the technologies transferred tend to be the most efficient ones and, in many cases, the most capital-intensive ... because in some developing countries with very disciplined manpower the capital equipment can be operated longer per day or per year, and therefore the original investment can be recovered more rapidly.[17]

The work week is generally 20–30 per cent longer than the OECD average. Needless to say, there is a little concern with health or safety standards. One of the most successful of the NICs, South Korea, has the world's longest average work week, varying over recent years from fifty-four to sixty hours, one of the worst health and safety records –

officially, there were 1,728 deaths and over 140,000 serious injuries in work-related accidents in 1985. The extreme regimentation of work in South Korea is usually compared to that in an army, and workers commonly stand at attention and salute their supervisors. High productivity is achieved in the process of superexploitation and absolute repression.

...

Unions

With the restructuring of employment have also come major changes in labor organizations in the industrialized countries. The OECD wrote in December 1985, "Labour power as measured by union membership and strike activity has fallen to post-war lows in most countries ..."[18] This situation clearly reflected the restructuring of employment in general, especially the highly organized heavy-industry sector, as well as the enormous increase in unemployment throughout the OECD countries, which especially affected the unionized industries. But it also was a response in many countries to two subjective factors – an all-out effort by capital to smash the unions and a growing recognition on the part of the workers that unions could not protect their interests.

During the twenty-five years of the precrisis "golden age," union strength grew and wages and benefits were secured regularly. Unions had rationalized the system of wages with industry-wide bargaining and provided regularity and order in labor management in prosperous times. This was particularly true for the unions in capital goods and other oligopolistic industries, such as automobiles, where increased labor costs were passed on to the buyer. Certain concentrated industries allowed a union strength not available in the less concentrated and more competitive industries, where the market conditions did not permit price administration. When demand for their product was high, the companies were loath to lose sales in prolonged labor disputes.

By 1980 the negotiating environment had been transformed. In a time of increased competitive pressures, falling profits, and the other conditions of the economic crisis, even the unions' narrow goals, and willingness to offer concessions, were not enough. By 1983 the corporate appetite had been whetted by the concessions, and an all-out struggle for more began. US corporations had resisted the initial organization of unions, but in times of high demand the oligopolistic industries tolerated and even found the unions useful, as long as they could pass on their costs. They also accepted them if they were able to secure wage cuts and other concessions. But their relationship was wholly dependent not only on the nature of the industry but also on the condition of the general economy. The very industries where unions had had their greatest strength were those with the highest unemployment in the 1980s.

In the restructuring of the 1980s industrywide wage bargaining in many industries where it had been the rule collapsed and reverted to the company or plant level. All the gains of previous decades began to crumble, as unions made concessions in order to prevent a threatened bankruptcy or to gain the promise of job security for a core of the existing work force. The unions remained useful to the industries as they negotiated these concessions. The companies secured two-tier wage scales, pay cuts, contingent workers, new work rules, and subcontracts, while the unions won pay raises of 1.2 per cent in 1986, a rate that had been falling steadily since 1980.

During the recession of the 1980s, many US unions agreed to freeze or cut wages and benefits and change work rules, enlarge jobs by adding duties, and restrict seniority in most of the basic industries. This form of bargaining continued into the so-called recovery, especially in industries like steel that remained depressed. But it became increasingly evident to the workers that concessions did not forestall what they were intended to and that concession bargaining had evolved into a pattern. However, in response to the call from the membership for renewed militancy, the AFL–CIO council declared, "Today's economic and political climate makes it imperative that unions follow realistic bargaining strategies ... not 'all-or-nothing' stances." It also advocated community pressure as an alternative to strikes, as well as experiments in labor–management cooperation.[19]

Unions began their own staff layoffs and raided other union territory to sustain their income. National unions' servicing of locals declined sharply. As safety conditions deteriorated, protests to the government regulatory agency diminished. The ILO complained in 1985 about cutbacks in safety regulations that were increasing the number of accidents throughout the OECD. The American union bureaucracy's leadership, calloused as always by its high salaries and affluent life-style to the needs of the rank and file, nevertheless feared a complete disintegration of its dues-paying base as workers began, out of necessity, to act independently on a local level.

There has been a marked shift in the American workers' attitude toward unions over the past three decades. In 1950, unions won 73 per cent of the elections to organize new locals. By 1970 the figure had dropped to 58 per cent, and in 1982 only 46 per cent agreed to unionize. In addition, the number of elections to decertify an existing union from representing the workers rose from 216 in 1959 to more than 900 in 1980. Between 1980 and 1984 union membership fell 2.7 million among employed workers, to just under one-fifth of the labor force, down from a peak of 35.5 per cent in 1945. A larger per centage of black workers are organized, but with the changing job structure the number of organized workers has fallen among all ethnic groups. The drop was largely due to the employment decline in basic industry. This rate of membership is relatively low compared with that in Europe and Japan. And the length of the US contracts – over half of them are for three years – is also exceptional by international standards and was especially damaging to workers' real income during the inflation of the 1970s. In each of the first three years of the "recovery" in the 1980s, union wages rose less than inflation and nonunion pay.

By 1986, American companies were demanding changes in all work rules – from washroom breaks to seniority. A number of firms, particularly in steel, threatened closures to gain rule changes. Most of the strikes in the mid-1980s were over changes in work rules and, increasingly, against union-negotiated contracts. The Japanese foreign investors in the United States, on the other hand, try to prevent organization of their plants, often by paying wages higher than the going rate and introducing other so-called nonadversary, consultative working conditions. But, as in Japan, the work pace is faster and soon creates conflict.

The attempt to organize clerical workers has been relatively unsuccessful. Only 14 per cent were organized in 1986, in large part because of the growing role of temporary and part-time workers. In Japan, as well, unions have been unable to organize service workers.

Socialists in power have had an important effect in reducing labor protest against the austerity policies. One union official in France exclaimed in 1984:

> Ten years ago, if we had seen the kind of layoffs we're seeing now or the cuts in purchasing power, we would have shut down the big companies and waged war on the capitalists – and tried to change the government to boot. Today there's an appreciation that a reaction like that doesn't fit the times.[20]

And an official of the Trade Union Institute in Brussels observed with resignation in 1985:

Somehow governments in Western Europe of whatever political coloration feel now that they ought to be tougher. Many of the problems would exist even if there were socialist governments in every capital, because the economic crisis cannot be escaped.[21]

...

As usual, during recessions and with high unemployment, the number of strikes diminished greatly in the OECD countries as a whole. The fear of unemployment led many workers to try to negotiate either individually or at a local level. And in the mid-1980s an OECD report noted with considerable satisfaction, "Labour power as measured by union membership and strike activity has fallen to post-war lows in most countries, with little prospect of immediate reversal."[22] While the observation did describe the situation in the first half of the 1980s, it was rash indeed to make predictions, for scarcely had the ink dried on their report than workers in Spain, Greece, France, and Holland, and in other places on a smaller scale, called major strikes and/or demonstrations independently of their trade unions.

...

Conclusion

A crucial consequence of the entire restructuring process in the OECD countries has been to reverse the position that labor had attained over the preceding decades. This restructuring – both objective, as the outcome of the operations of the capitalist system, and as a subjective offensive of capital and the state in the class struggle – created a basically new condition for labor in the 1980s.

The changes in the nature of work have tremendous implications for the future development of capitalism, as technology aggravates a trend toward unemployment and lower living standards in the context of all the other crisis features in the world economy. While offering the potential, in a different social system, of strengthening the forces of production and liberating workers from dangerous and monotonous work, the technological changes, now as in the past, are used as a weapon against labor. Technology has made possible the reduction of the cost of labor in production – in an increasing number of cases, by eliminating labor altogether. The introduction of new technology in industry's cost-cutting efforts in order to compete in the world market has sharply polarized incomes and jobs, shrinking middle-income employment. And if the costs of labor-substituting technology fall as fast as the cost of labor, it will continue to replace high-wage workers. The contradiction to this trend is that the technology must be used and amortized, whereas living labor can be hired and fired at will.

Unemployment at levels unprecedented since the Great Depression has persisted with little change during the so-called cyclical recoveries, and it has been accompanied by shrinking state support in terms of compensation. The option of migration has closed in the OECD countries and is closing in the OPEC states as well. Workers are the targets everywhere, as states struggle to renew investment incentives and compete for capital. The labor force is being "restructured" to a lower level of income and part-time and temporary work has become increasingly common.

The workers' conditions in the developing countries deteriorated on all levels, as the various factors of the crisis in the world economy increasingly bore in on them, from all sides. Unemployment, worsening wages and working conditions for the minority of full-time workers, increased cost of living for all, as subsidies of basic essentials are removed, increased harassment in the squatter settlements, and a greater influx from the countryside, as conditions there continue to fall, determined the life experience of the vast majority.

All these structural changes have made relevant once more Marx's prognosis of growing immiseration with growing concentration of wealth. This is developing disastrously in the LDCs and increasingly in the OECD nations as well. For a period during the 1970s the standard of living in many countries in the OECD was maintained by two income earners in a family, or through the use of credit that raised the income bracket and consumption level of many working-class families for a brief period, but those factors are no longer sufficient. New jobs for the working class are low-wage jobs, and two earners now may make less than one did a decade ago – and unemployment increasingly strikes both earners as well. At the other extreme, in the United States after the mid-1970s, there was a sharp acceleration of the concentration of wealth. One study for the US Congress concluded that the holdings of the top one-half of one per cent of the population rose from about 15 per cent of total wealth in 1976 to approximately 38 per cent in 1983.[23] Yet the contradictions for capitalism in all these developments are equally evident. This struggle with labor at the point of production costs shrinks the market that capitalists must have in order to realize profits.

Class conflict between capital and labor in the relations of production and for greater shares of national income, an essential aspect or

systemic feature of capitalism, exists even when a political consciousness regarding the direction of that struggle is absent or when it is suppressed. The class struggle is always waged more or less vigorously
against labor. In the late 1970s and 1980s it was a reaction against the
significant gains of labor during the period 1968–72, especially in
Europe, gains resulting in higher wages at a time when competition
was gathering momentum among most capitalists in the world
economy. The struggle is now being waged relentlessly by capital and
the state to reduce systematically the cost of labor and its share in the
national income, to weaken the working-class organization and movement, to restructure the work process globally, and to compensate for
the state's fiscal crisis by further reducing expenditures for health and
welfare.

But labor must resist or remain a victim. In many LDCs there has
been worker resistance to government austerity programs and worsening conditions. Inevitably, by 1987, after over a decade of absorbing
the systematic reduction of living standards and the threat of permanent unemployment, workers in France, Spain, and Greece, independently of the trade unions, had made it known through mass strikes
and/or demonstrations that it was no longer possible to proceed with
the restructuring policies without mounting opposition. In other parts
of the world, too, there is evidence of growing resistance. Workers
acted against an array of institutional forces committed to the preservation of the status quo or, in most cases now, to a reversal of even the
modest gains in social welfare won over the preceding decades. These
actions evoked surprise at the time and place, yet they should not
have, for labor militancy and class struggle are also systemic in capitalism. They can be expected in general even if they are usually unexpected in the specific; the potential is always there.

Of one thing we may be sure: there will be renewed periods of militancy and spontaneous active struggle on the part of the working class
in the industrial nations. When and where one cannot predict. But
there can be no illusion. The process of restructuring is well advanced,
and radical social change for the benefit of labor will not come about
without active resistance and mobilization.

Notes

1. Paul Mattick, *Marxism: Last Refuge of the Bourgeoisie*, ed. Paul Mattick, Jr.
   (Armonk, NY, 1983), pp. 117–18. This significant book is the last work by
   this important Marxist. It and his other works are of enduring value in
   studying the contemporary capitalist system.

2. Gabriel Kolko, *Wealth and Power in America: An Analysis of Social Class and Income Distribution* (New York: Praeger, 1962).
3. Cited in Richard Barnet, *The Lean Years* (New York: Simon & Schuster, 1980), p. 258. See also *OECD Observer* (April–May 1987), p. 14, which declared the annual increase in the LCDs alone was 60 million people.
4. OECD, *Interfutures: Facing the Future: Mastering the Probable and Managing the Unpredictable* (1st revision edn] (Paris, 1979), p. 8.
5. OECD, *Employment Outlook* (September 1984), p. 40.
6. *Business Week* (April 1, 1985), p. 63.
7. *Far Eastern Economic Review* (December 19, 1985), p. 57.
8. *Business Week* (September 5, 1983), p. 96.
9. *International Herald Tribune* (October 28, 1985).
10. See *Far Eastern Economic Review* (December 19, 1985), p. 57.
11. David Coe and Francisco Gagliardi, "Nominal Wage Determination in Ten OECD Countries," *OECD Working Papers*, 19 (Paris, 1985), p. 27.
12. *Business Week* (June, 14, 1982), p. 66.
13. OECD, *Economic Outlook* (December 1985), p. 39.
14. OECD, *Economic Outlook* (December 1985), p. 42.
15. *Wall Street Journal* (January, 29, 1979).
16. United Nations, *World Economic Survey* (1979–1980), p. 27.
17. OECD, *Interfutures, op. cit.*, p. 159.
18. Reported in *International Herald Tribune* (January 23, 1985).
19. *Ibid.* (May 5, 1986).
20. *Business Week* (November, 26, 1984), p. 84.
21. *International Herald Tribune* (January 23, 1985).
22. OECD, *Economic Outlook* (December 1985) p. 41.
23. US Congress, Joint Economic Committee, *The Concentration of Wealth in the United States: Trends in the Distribution of Wealth Among American Families* (Washington, DC, 1986), p. 44.

16
The Social Construction of Efficiency (1990)*

Neil Fligstein

Efficiency can be defined as the conception of control that produces the relatively higher likelihood of growth and profits for firms given the existing set of social, political, and economic circumstances. This definition takes into account the three most important factors necessary for the firm to prosper: a conception of control held by its top managers, the existence of a stable organizational field, and a political system that does not question the legality of the courses of action taken in the organizational field.

This view provides a model as to how and why different courses of action are established by large firms, how they are maintained, and what forces are likely to produce their transformation. Conceptions of control are world views that define one firm's relationship with others, what appropriate behavior is for firms of that type, and how those kinds of organizations ought to work. They imply certain strategies and structures. In essence, conceptions of control and the organizational fields they create define how markets are structured for firms. They are efficient in the sense that they provide firms with growth and profits relative to other conceptions of control. To the degree that firms in established fields continue to prosper, the fields remain stable. New conceptions of control which are legal and produce more growth and profits than the existing system will spread. They will do so because of their relative success, but also because they provide a threat to systems of existing power in other organizational fields.

The motive to find new conceptions of control with appropriate courses of action is always present. But there have been very few con-

---

* From *The Transformation of Corporate Control* (Cambridge, Mass.: Harvard University Press, 1990), pp. 295–314.

ceptions of control. The difficulty of establishing a new conception of control is that managers must construct it in the context of the existing social world. The problem is compounded by the fact that organizations already profit from a given conception of control and the power arrangement of the existing organizational field. Managers are also constrained by their organizations, which have selected them on the basis of their allegiance to a certain view of the firm, by their own world views, and by their organizational field.

The state maintains the institutional conditions for stable organizational fields and can provide the stimulus for change. Since it defines what the rules are for the existence of organizations and their relationships with other firms, it encourages and discourages different conceptions of control. The central theme of [*The Transformation of Corporate Control* is] that the conceptions of control and socially constructed organizational fields of large firms have emerged through interaction with the political and legal system in the United States. Managers and entrepreneurs have tried to impose their view of the sociologically efficient organization of markets on others. Then the government has decided which of these is legal given the popular political and economic ideologies. If the state disapproves of the conception of control, it is no longer efficient and the organizational field that defines the market must be reconstructed. The direct, manufacturing, sales and marketing, and finance conceptions of control were alternative ways to produce higher rates of growth and profits for large firms. The emergence and spread of these conceptions depended on their relative success and their eventual displacement depended on the institutional structure of state–firm relations.

From this perspective, the key problem of direct control was that it was illegal. Predatory trade practices, cartels, and monopolies preserved profits and kept organizations in existence. As ways to organize markets, they created the possibility of growth and profits. But because they were illegal in the United States forms of direct control could not guarantee profits or growth for large firms. The manufacturing conception of control proved acceptable to government agencies. It aided in the creation of organizational fields with leading firms that enforced prices by focusing on indirect forms of control: vertical integration of suppliers and customers, public pricing decisions, and the threat of ruinous competition. Hence managers in firms in these organizational fields were assured of profits and growth. The Depression brought limits to the manufacturing conception of control. In industries dominated by this conception, managers favored moving toward more

formal price arrangements and maintaining prices by cutting production. Instead of trying to expand and grow, firms tried to preserve what
they could and guarantee themselves at least short-term profits.

The sales and marketing conception shifted attention away from the
control over price and production toward market share as a measure of
how well the firm was doing. Sales and marketing managers realized
that to guarantee any profits at all, a firm needed growth. An efficient
firm was one that was growing in its main markets or diversifying into
new and more rapidly growing markets. These strategies were efficient
relative to the manufacturing ones because, given the existing political
situation and definition of markets, they made money. The realization
of managers after the Depression that concentration on production
alone would not guarantee survival meant that they had a much different sense of efficiency. The relative advantage of the sales and marketing view of efficiency was that even in bad economic times firms could
enhance their survival prospects by finding markets for their goods.

The organizational fields of the large corporation consequently were
redefined in terms of entire industries. More important, the relations
between firms became less directly competitive. Managers in firms
fought over market share, not the right to exist. Product lines were
diversified and managers concentrated on differentiating their products in order to avoid continued direct competition. Firms and organizational fields driven by sales and marketing executives were generally
not prosecuted by antitrust authorities because the antitrust laws were
intended to prevent the lessening of competition by direct control.
If managers in firms avoided direct confrontation, they were not
violating the law.

The finance conception of control took the sales and marketing conception one step further. If growth and profits were the essential goals
of the corporation, they could be best achieved by financially evaluat-
ing all firm activities. Because firms were already significantly
diversified and the antitrust authorities were renewing their efforts
against concentration and vertical and horizontal mergers, finance
managers were able to improve their growth and profits by using
financial tools to evaluate, buy, and sell assets in many industries. The
finance conception of control destroyed some organizational fields
defined in single industry terms because the leading firms in those
industries were bought and made part of a larger firm. Managers in
firms operating with finance strategies changed the rules no matter
what the managers in firms in a given organizational field wanted. The
finance view of efficiency dominates the corporate world today. It

proved its relative success by taking advantage of the antitrust climate and diversification to produce spectacular rates of growth.

Of course, the ability to measure financial performance is itself a social construction. The common belief is that the ultimate measure of a corporation's worth is its stock price or price/earnings ratio. When managers in both corporations and the financial community become more aware of those numbers, their importance increases. For instance, if CEOs spend most of their time attempting to manipulate stock prices, then they are less likely to worry about the underlying fundamentals of their firms. Such an orientation can produce an obsession with short-run profits and fluctuations of the stock price and a lack of attention to replacing capital stock and investing in future products. The finance conception of efficiency that focuses narrowly on financial data results in a socially constructed view of the firm as assets which are used to obtain short-run returns and keep the stock price high.

It is usual to contrast the view I propose here with the dominant historical view, which emphasizes the market as the key to understanding change in large-scale corporations. There are three kinds of economic efficiency to consider. First, efficiency implied the need to achieve economies of scale and lower costs to compete in markets. This was done by implementing the newest production technology and increasing the scale of production. Second, managers built integrated organizations as they took over the role of markets in making decisions regarding the allocation or resources, the production of inputs, and control over outputs. Managers who created hierarchies were able to show higher profits than those who used markets because they were less susceptible to the vagaries of markets that were unreliable and more costly in providing suppliers and customers. Finally, the multiproduct firm was efficient as it used the capital of the firm to spread risks across product lines thereby increasing the stability of the corporation. Together, these different efficiencies increased the scale of corporate enterprise.[1]

The cause of all three forms of efficiency was the market. The market generally refers to how the price of a given commodity is determined by the balance of the supply and demand. The social organization surrounding this price mechanism is the dependent variable that determines that efficient organizations – those that produce at low cost – survive and inefficient organizations die. All organizational innovations are reactions to the market.

This view of the market gives rise to the following story of the history of the large modern corporation. Around 1860 national markets for commodities came into existence. These markets were possible because of canals, railroads, and the telegraph system. Once they were built the transportation costs for commodities dropped significantly which allowed firms to increase their scale of operation. Firm size expanded and costs decreased as competition intensified. The largest producers became the most efficient producers. The term efficiency here refers to economies or scale.

But the large scale of production required enormous amounts of capital. If supply of inputs or sale of outputs was halted the firm could not take advantage of possible economies of scale. This uncertainty in the market caused the organization to expand. Firms began to control their suppliers and customers by absorbing more functions.[2] Hence the large modern firm was the model of efficiency in two senses: it maximized productive capacity by using the best and cheapest technology and by guaranteeing itself suppliers and customers.

The next stage in achieving more efficiency was the redeployment of capital to create the multidivisional, multiproduct firm. The market was influential in this transformation because it provided firms with the opportunity to produce multiple related products and thereby enter new markets. In order to control the new multiproduct firm, the multidivisional form was invented. The multidivisional, multiproduct form was efficient in a new sense: it insured the growth and profitability of the firm by spreading risk to many businesses.

At first glance the market-driven efficiency theory seems parallel to mine. But there are a number of major differences. The key problem is that these theoretical notions suggest that market processes are outside of social processes and therefore require no explanation. They do not involve the setting up of social institutions that reflect the interests of powerful groups. Instead, this view assumes that the price mechanism is constantly encouraging more and more efficient forms of social organization. The types of efficiency that get called into play from this perspective are a result of interactions between producers and consumers in the market. The efficiency demands of markets operate in a functionalist, seamless manner. Opportunities are recognized by rational managers and entrepreneurs whose actions are oriented toward the exploitation of profitable possibilities and organizational forms follow. Even in accounts that stress the failure of the market to provide resources and stability, the institutional response of managers and entrepreneurs is to create efficient social organization.[3]

From my perspective, once powerful interests legitimized capitalistic institutions in the United States they constructed markets to aid private gains. Sociological efficiencies resulted because of these institutional interactions between firms, organizational fields, and the state. The structuring of markets to produce growth and profits was limited by the existing conceptions of control, the strategies they implied, and their legality. Instead of markets calling forth efficient forms or social organization, political and social interactions produced the structuring of sociologically efficient markets.

A social organization that produced efficiency replaced another only when the former was illegal or in crisis. The social structure of markets and its relation to the state caused changes in their organization. In other words, the forms of social organization produced the market, not the reverse. The central mistake made in traditional accounts of the history or the large corporation is that by reading history backwards economic historians have known how things turned out and thereby were able to impute what kind of social institutions must have been called forth by efficient markets. By beginning with how managers, entrepreneurs, and politicians in each historical epoch constructed their worlds, one understands that the development was in the opposite direction. The institutions created markets that were dominated by a given conception of control that produced relatively more growth and profit and were legal.

Since the courses of action taken by managers and entrepreneurs were framed in worlds with quite different rules and understandings, it is difficult to see how economic arguments can account for what happened historically. The plausibility of economic efficiency stories rests more on their abstract character and ability to round out the edges of historical evidence and provide a pleasing and simple version of what occurred. Most of the evidence presented here is hard to rectify with such a view. One could account post hoc for this evidence, but that would not be scientific.

The basic economic argument about competitive markets is that the firms that produce the most cheaply will dominate. It is also asserted that such markets will reach a point at which production stops when the most efficient producer no longer makes money. Both of these claims are problematic. Historically, the problem has been that there are often a number of firms with similar technologies and hence similar levels of efficiency. Firms with similar technologies begin to lose money if they continue to allow prices to drop. But instead of discontinuing production of that line, they lose money until they go out of business.

This creates a paradox. If competitive markets are enforced, firms of similar efficient technologies will eventually drive one another out of business. If that occurs throughout the economy, the result is economic recession or depression. The so-called efficient market results in large-scale economic dislocation and the destruction of efficient producers.

The result of the cutthroat competition in the nineteenth century, however, was to create powerful organizations that sought direct control of competitive markets and to act efficiently from a sociological point of view. In order to account for the historical events of this period, the economic analyst has to ignore the overwhelming evidence that the conceptions of control of managers and entrepreneurs from 1880 to 1920 were oriented toward controlling competition. I have already shown that the best predictor of whether or not all industry engaged in the turn of the century merger movement was whether or not the industry had attempted to form cartels. In spite of abundant evidence that the owners and managers of large corporations were engaged in such efforts, the conventional wisdom asserts that such efforts were doomed to failure and that the search for economies of scale motivated managerial decisions.[4]

Because the economic model already assumes that market processes will dominate social interaction, the only possible outcome from that perspective is economic efficiency. Hence, economic accounts have to downplay the social and political search for stability and focus on arguments concerning economics of scale. They also have to ignore the role of the state in defining what behavior is acceptable from firms. The only reason that direct forms of control did not work was because they were illegal. In a different political system, for instance Western Europe and Japan before the Second World War, direct forms of control produced more stable outcomes.

The central ideas of the efficiency approach also require an unrealistic view of the motives and actions of managers and entrepreneurs. In the context of the competitive market, managers and entrepreneurs are actors who choose courses of action that conform to the rules of markets by acting only to improve their situations in those markets. The theory of action, one that stresses rationality or bounded rationality, requires actors to know and behave in ways that have little to do with how courses of action were constructed. The interpretation of the history of the corporation that stresses efficiency ignores the central fact that managers and entrepreneurs were constantly trying to escape or control competition, not engage in it. These actors were also well aware that markets were social constructions that revolved around systems or power, both private and public. As such, the rules or markets could be changed by powerful corporate actors and the government.

The central argument I propose here is that managers rarely know what is economically efficient. They have a sense of controlling a market or market share and to some degree can control costs. But the driving force for managers, just as it is for any kind of social actor, is to preserve their organizations and further their individual and collective interests. To do so they must define their situations, including what constitutes a market. In that process, they construct a conception of control that includes strategies and structures and helps to define their organizational fields.

Economists have tended toward two views of managers: omnipotent or irrelevant. These views account for the alleged efficiency and rationality or the firm. From the omnipotent perspective or the microeconomics of the firm, managers and entrepreneurs understand their markets and production processes quite well. They respond to markets by expanding and contracting production and utilize the best technology and the fewest labor inputs to achieve results. The firm is efficient because of the actions taken by managers and entrepreneurs. Inefficiency is caused by managers who do not act rationally, that is, they do not mix the factors of production to maximize outcomes.

The other perspective suggests that markets select successful firms, technologies, and products. The actions of managers and entrepreneurs are almost irrelevant. In an economy with few barriers to entry, no firm will be able to prevent others from entering a successful market nor prevent more efficient producers from emerging. In essence, no matter what managers do the market will encourage efficiency. The market is the final arbiter of efficiency and managers who are successful are efficient because the market is efficient.

The problem with these views is that they place either too much or too little weight on the two central constructs, managerial autonomy and the market. In my opinion managers must construct views about what constitutes efficient action that are historically determined. There have been very few conceptions of control yet each reflects the thinking of the period and the problems managers perceived. The goal of their actions has been to produce social conditions that stabilized their organizations. Managers' actions are highly constrained; they tend to go with what has worked in the immediate past or with the conventional wisdom guiding their organizational fields. When they innovate, it is to gain, preserve, or recover an advantage in some organizational field.

The problem with relying on the market to determine what is efficient is that all markets are comprised of a social structure of set of rules which preserve the power and interests of the largest organizations. When the rules no longer produce positive results for those in control, the rules are changed. In the case of competitive markets, the managers and entrepreneurs in the largest firms have tried to opt out of them because their existence implies competition that will end in the ruin of them all.

The point of view I provide here has a number of improvements over the traditional economic view of the various transformations of the large corporation. First, it does not assume the rationality of action or some absolute standard of efficiency. There is not one most efficient mode of organization, nor is there only one way in which organizational goals can be pursued. Instead, my view requires that one understand the rationale for an action. Second, it implies that the social construction of the world is as important as the "objective" character of the world. In this sense, managers are neither more nor less intelligent than any other social actors.

Additionally, it allows for the rules by which worlds are constructed to be negotiated and changed. Organizational conceptions, structures, fields, and performance are the outcome of the key interactions between managers, their organizations and fields, and the actors who control government agencies. The market as the driving force of economic history is replaced by the variety of constructions of institutional arrangements in the economic and political sphere and the dynamics of those arrangements. The market and the rules that govern it are the product of those interactions.

The most important feature of this point of view is that it does not rely upon the functionalism implied by the economic point of view expressed earlier. Since it is often difficult to tell who the winners and losers are, and hence what the winning and losing strategies are, there can be no one best way to achieve profitability. By dropping the notion that the most efficient economic solution is the predominant one and accepting that efficiency is a social construction, one can then see how the transformation of conceptions or control and their strategies rely on organizational dynamics and the interaction between organizations, their leaders, and the state.

A comparative consideration

To prove the difficulty of the functionalist position exemplified by the use of market logic, let's consider some other cases. If the economists are right, the most efficient form will emerge in every market society either because the market will select that form or because managers will adopt it. Factors such as the intervention of the state, conceptions of control, and organizational strategies and structures should not have an impact on the shape of the large modern firm. There should be convergence in form across societies of roughly equal levels of development in the conceptions of control and the strategies and structures of the largest firms. If economic theory is correct and the market selects the most efficient form, the large, multiproduct, multidivisional firm that grows through mergers should be the dominant social organization across nation states. Hence, the Japanese, German, British, and French large firms will mirror the large American firms.

In contrast, if the view that markets are constructed in the context of strategic interactions between firms and states is correct, such convergence should not be observed. This brief consideration of other countries is intended to illustrate and suggest that an organizational theory of the economy grounded in a view of how managers and entrepreneurs construct actions and how they spread to other organizations will bring us more understanding of large American firms than an approach that assumes that the most efficient form will emerge either through market processes or by managerial choice.

There are a number of problems in considering the evidence. The measurement of product mix and mergers in different countries is uneven and cannot always be compared. The role of the state in the postwar era was complex and differed by country. Before the war, the Japanese, German, French, and British governments encouraged cartels to varying degrees. After the war, the American occupation forces tried to break up the large Japanese trading companies and German cartels. The United States forced its antitrust laws on both of these countries. Generally, these laws did not change the cooperation between firms or between the government and the firms. But the philosophy of open international markets pushed on these countries by US policymakers encouraged the firms and governments to pursue policies that blended competition and cooperation. Another problem that makes comparison difficult is that the US firms were used as role models for some countries. The French and British governments thought that the large size of US firms was most responsible for their effectiveness so they encouraged mergers. Some of the convergence of these countries reflects this conscious policy rather than the workings of the market.

The British government supported cartel arrangements in the prewar era and suppressed them afterward. The Monopolies and Restrictive Practices Act of 1948 created a tribunal to consider possible anticompetitive practices. Between 1956 and 1973 four pieces of legislation were passed that made it increasingly difficult to restrain trade.[5] The British approach allowed some restrictive trade practices if positive competitive effects on international markets could be shown. This differed from the American antitrust laws which condemned all restrictive trade practices.[6]

The 1956 legislation made cartels illegal. Cartels were thought to prevent competition and reward inefficient producers. At the same time, the British government began to promote mergers and both Conservative and Labour parties embraced the policy. They argued that in order to compete effectively both domestically and internationally, economies of scale were needed. They thought mergers were the most effective mechanism to achieve those economies most rapidly.[7]

Not surprisingly, a large-scale merger movement began in the mid-1950s and continued until 1973. The aggregate concentration in the British economy increased greatly as the 100 largest British manufacturing firms increased their share of output from 2 per cent in 1949 to almost 41 per cent in 1970. Concentration within industries also increased substantially during that time.[8] Most of these increases in concentration were due to mergers. The 100 largest manufacturing firms in the United States increased their aggregate share from about 20 per cent in 1950 to roughly 32 per cent in 1970 and there was little increase in concentration within product lines. One can conclude that the British merger movement created more aggregate industrial concentration within product lines as well. It is interesting to note that at the same time the British economy suffered greatly.

As these increases in aggregate and product market concentration became evident, new legislation was passed. The Monopolies and Mergers Act of 1965 set up administrative machinery to evaluate the effects of mergers on competition and prevent anticompetitive mergers. Between 1965 and 1973, 83 per cent of the mergers investigated were horizontal in character.[9] In 1964, only 16.2 per cent of the mergers undertaken by the 159 largest British firms were product related or unrelated. By 1969, 63.6 per cent of these mergers were in these categories.[10] The British merger policy worked like the Celler–Kefauver Act: it encouraged firms to diversify and shy away from vertical and horizontal mergers that would attract the attention of antitrust authorities.

The overall result of the British policy toward mergers in the postwar era can be seen in the following figures. In 1950, 80 of the 100 largest British manufacturing enterprises were product dominant compared to

62 in the United States in 1948. By 1970, 38 of the 100 largest firms in Great Britain were primarily producing one product, 56 were producing related products, and only 6 were conglomerates.[11] In the United States in 1969, 24 were product dominant, 56 were product related, and 20 were product unrelated. British firms diversified substantially during the period, but they remained less diversified than their American counterparts. It could be argued that these differences reflect the differences in the antitrust laws. In this country horizontal and vertical mergers were consistently shunned after the war. In Britain such mergers were encouraged. Even when public policy turned somewhat against them, they remained a substantial component of overall mergers. The purest form of the finance conception, the acquisitive conglomerate, was not as important in the British context as in the American.

The German case shows more clearly the differences in national policies. In prewar Germany, cartels dominated the economy. The Allied forces instituted an ordinance prohibiting cartels and monopolies in 1947. This law became the 1957 Act against Restraint of Competition. The main target of the act was cartels, but substantial numbers of cartel situations were excluded from it including agreements related to rebates, standardization, specialization, rationalization of production, foreign trade, patents, and industrial secrets.[12] The 1973 amendments to the act brought abuse of market position under the law. Such abuses were left undefined and the laws were much weaker than the Sherman or Clayton acts in specifying what constituted restraints of trade. In 1974 an antimerger act went into effect that required clearance for mergers by an agency called B Kart A. The agency decides whether a merger helps or hurts competition in the relevant markets and prevents anticompetitive mergers.[13]

The German antitrust laws operated to encourage economic cooperation between firms. But that cooperation was directed toward export markets, economies of scale, and new technology. The cartel arrangements were used most effectively to promote these strategies. The German banks played a central role as German firms relied on banks for most of their financing. In 1965 German firms relied on internal funds for 32 per cent of financing, banks for 44 per cent of their financing, the bond market for 20 per cent, and the stock market for only 8 per cent.[14] The typical merger in Germany was vertical or horizontal and not oriented toward diversification. In the 1950s it was common for a producer to purchase stock in other firms, but not to merge the two firms. Managers in German firms have never engaged in merger for growth.

The 1950s and 1960s were periods of low merger activity in Germany. Mergers picked up in 1969 and peaked in 1977.[15] During the 1970s vertical and horizontal mergers comprised between 83 and 89 per cent of the largest mergers in the German economy. Vertical mergers increased from 7.9 per cent of the total in 1971 to 24 per cent in 1977 and outnumbered the 1976 and 1977 mergers for diversification. At the same time industrial concentration increased in Germany both in aggregate and product terms.[16]

These results suggest that the strategies of German firms were quite unlike those of their American and British counterparts. The German government and banking system worked with firms to increase their international competitiveness. The managers of German firms were not highly rewarded for increasing their stock prices or the size or their firm. Instead, their system promoted cooperation between firms to increase the scale of production and compete effectively in the world economy. The institutional system produced results markedly different from the American system.

The French case shows a different dynamic than the German one. Whereas the German government left the economy in the hands or the private sector and offered incentives to that sector, the French state has taken a more active role in promoting corporate transformation. Many of the largest French firms are publicly owned and many of the private firms are profoundly affected by the French government. It has been estimated that the French government owns half of the capital stock in France and controls firms in the tobacco, coal mining, railway, airlines, utilities, communications, automobile, oil, chemical, shipping, aircraft, banking, insurance, and advertising industries.[17] The French government exerts control over the economy through its control over investment and regulation of various industries.

The industrial policy of the French government in the 1960s greatly affected the number and types of mergers that occurred. The French government passed an anticartel law in 1956 and amended that law to include monopolistic practices in 1963.[18] Generally, the law was not enforced. Instead, the government decided that to compete with American firms, French firms needed to imitate their American counterparts. Since French firms were smaller than American firms, it was thought that they needed to be larger to generate economics of scale and increase innovation. The French government therefore began to encourage mergers by directly engineering various mergers and cartel arrangements in both the private and public sectors. In 1965 the government tried to promote mergers by reducing taxes on firms that engaged in them.[19]

The effects of these policies became evident throughout the 1960s and early 1970s. Mergers picked up in 1963 and remained high until 1973. The peak of the movement coincided with the tax incentives that existed from 1965 to 1969. Industrial concentration increased, particularly from 1965 to 1969. Between 1970 and 1972, 48 per cent of the mergers were classified as horizontal, 23 per cent as vertical, and 29 per cent as product related and unrelated. Using broad definitions of diversification, it has been estimated that 48 of the 100 largest French firms were product dominant, 42 product related, and 10 product unrelated in 1970. While there was some diversification in the French economy, the large French firm was less diversified than large firms in the other countries.

The Japanese case is perhaps the most interesting. The largest Japanese firms are diversified and rival American firms in size. In 1980, 37 of the 102 largest Japanese firms were classified as product dominant, 59 as product related, and 6 as product unrelated.[20] These levels of diversification are less than the United States, particularly in terms of product unrelated firms. However, the Japanese firms have one important quality that distinguishes them from the American firms. The expansion into new product lines is almost always done through internal growth, not mergers.

The emergence of the modern Japanese corporation is the subject of much speculation. Its development most parallels the German situation. Before the Second World War Japan's economy was dominated by a small group of large holding companies, each owned by extended families, that were called Zaibatsu.[21] The American Occupation Force tried to break up the power of the Zaibatsu and establish a competitive market system based on the US model. Four steps were undertaken to achieve this: the Zaibatsu organizations were dissolved and their component parts became independent firms; attempts were made to break up concentration in large-scale industry; senior executives of the Zaibatsu were removed; and an antimonopoly act was passed.[22] The only part of this program that was at all effective was the breaking up of the Zaibatsu and the replacement of their chief executives. By the early 1950s efforts at deconcentration bogged down and the Zaibatsu returned as loose coalitions of firms.

Cooperation within the Japanese economy was encouraged throughout the 1950s and 1960s. Three distinct forms of industrial groupings appeared. First, loose federations of firms that were former members of the Zaibatsu began to buy stock in one another's corporations. They created informal associations that promoted cooperation and competition. Members of the group relied on the banks within the group for financing as well as one another for joint ventures into new products. Second, coalitions of firms began to gravitate toward large banks for their capital needs. The banks played the major role in the postwar era in terms of financing firms and owning stock. Like German firms, Japanese firms relied on banks for the bulk of their outside funds to fuel expansion. The banks also became major shareholders and exerted great control over the firms. Banks often encouraged their corporate customers to cooperate on new ventures. Third, large firms organized their subsidiaries and suppliers into loose groups. These associations would sometimes involve ownership and sometimes just long-term supplier relations.[23]

The Japanese government also played a role in this development. The Ministry of International Trade and Industry (MITI) encouraged cooperative efforts among Japanese firms, particularly in developing and implementing technology for goods for foreign export. But MITI's efforts could not have worked without a structure of industry that promoted cooperation. The development of new products in Japan tended not to occur through mergers. Although some mergers were encouraged in order to create more efficient firms, especially in the 1960s, the general tendency has been to produce new products internally or through joint ventures.

The focus on the internal generation of ideas can be seen more clearly when one considers the backgrounds of Japanese executives. In 1978 it was found that about 50 per cent of Japanese top management came up through the production ranks while 26 per cent came up through marketing and only 5 per cent came up through finance or accounting.[24] Almost 76 per cent of the new products were developed from ideas that were internally generated as opposed to ideas brought in from the outside.[25] The focus of Japanese top managers, even in diversified firms, is on product development and production first, marketing second, and finance last.

Japanese firms are able to make long-term investments in new industries for a number of reasons. First, the financial community does not impose rigid standards on short-term rates of profit and growth. The Japanese bankers view their loans and investments on a more long-term basis. This means that managers are rewarded for long-term performance and have less need to opt for measures that increase only short-run profitability. Second, the Japanese government has encouraged firms to cooperate on the creation of new products, especially on those that could result in substantial export markets. It has also encouraged investment in new industries and aided in exiting from older industries. Finally, the Japanese firms compete strenuously with one another in domestic and foreign markets. While cooperation exists within groups, competition is the rule between them. The result is that the large Japanese firm is able to create new products, adopt the most modern manufacturing processes, take a number of years to enter a market, and achieve success.

The finance conception, which dominates the largest American firms, does not drive the largest Japanese firms. The interaction between Japanese firms and their government has produced a large diversified corporation that grows, not through acquisition, but through internal expansion. The institutional milieu that produced the Japanese firms may be one of the primary reasons that they have an advantage over American firms.

The most diversified large firms in the world are American, followed by the British, Japanese, German, and French firms. The American firms are substantially more diversified, particularly the production unrelated ones. Underlying these levels of diversification, however, are quite different conceptions or growth. The British firms have taken the American example of mergers for growth the most seriously and their largest firms most resemble the large American firms. The Japanese and German firms are in an institutional setting that encourages them to grow internally and cooperate with other firms, particularly in the development of products for export. Banks play important roles in these societies as providers of funds for expansion. Their stock markets have lesser roles. The French case is the most anomalous because the French government is the most intrusive in the organization of its economy. The large French firms are the least diversified, but more highly concentrated than their counterparts.

While this cursory review is partially speculative, there does not exist strong evidence for a convergence of the conceptions of control across societies. Indeed, the evidence suggests that unique interactions between the state and the largest firms in the economies of various advanced countries has resulted in different organizational forms driven by different sets of actors operating with different conceptions of control. There exists no abstract market that disciplines firms to one and only one efficient standard. Instead, industrial organization reflects the unique experiences of national economies.

312 The Social Construction of Efficiency

The future of the large American corporation

The problems of the American economy can be understood in the context I outline here. The finance conception that dominates the large American corporation is the product of a complex set of institutional structures. It maintains its advantage because it has been more successful than other tactics in guaranteeing the existence and growth of the largest firms in the unique context of the American economic and political system. Any change of the structure of American business will, thus, have to be a more successful tactic to preserve the power, size, and growth of the largest firms.

It is not just its relative success that holds the finance conception in place. The world of top managers is now more concerned with the firm's position in the stock market and with its accounting records. The finance conception evaluates the consequence of any course of action in purely financial terms. Any possible shift in that view will require an alternative world view that challenges the financial perspective by creating firm growth more predictably. A shift is also dependent on a crisis in the current point of view.

One could argue that such a crisis exists today. The 1970s were not good years for the largest firms and the 1980s have forced them to expand their view of organizational fields to encompass the international market. The large firm is in crisis because it cannot meet the competitive challenge of firms in other countries. The finance conception has been used throughout the 1980s as the solution to this problem. Mergers, acquisitions, and divestitures have been tried to encourage efficiency by eliminating unproductive product lines and ineffective managements. Their success remains to be seen. The short-run financial perspective of American managers is even more reinforced by the restructuring and increase of American business debt.

The effect on conceptions of control will depend on the ability of the managers of the largest firms to construct new solutions to this current crisis. Any new view must overtake the power of the stock market and finance executives to dictate a concern with short-run profits. Investment will need to be made for the long run. Such a structural change will probably require increased cooperation between firms to create and implement new technology. That cooperation will in turn require a radical shift in antitrust philosophy. Consequently the federal government's role in this transformation may be pivotal. One could speculate that an American industrial policy would allow more cooperation and joint ventures and discourage mergers that only create highly leveraged firms. In any case, these changes would have to produce spectacularly successful examples. The examples may be among the firms that are somewhat smaller than the largest firms because they are able to take advantage of changed conditions. These firms would also, at least initially, have to stay out of the stock market where the pressures to produce short-run profits would overwhelm long-run plans.

An alternative scenario would be the continuation of already existing tendencies. Smaller firms could continue to innovate and larger firms then purchase their assets. While this would continue to fuel the growth of the largest firms, its long-run effects on the economy might be continued decline. American firms have already exited from a number of important markets, leaving them to foreign competitors. Much depends on how the federal government changes the rules by which capital is depreciated, mergers are executed, and cooperation between firms is allowed. Any shift will require structural changes that produce advantages for a new conception of the corporation and disadvantages for the finance conception.

... [T]he modern corporation in its American form ... is driven by financial considerations, is highly diversified, and uses mergers and divestitures to expand and restrict product lines. Its future will be determined by further unique interaction between the large corporations and the state.

Notes

1. Alfred D. Chandler, Jr., *Strategy and Structure* (Cambridge, Mass.: MIT Press, 1962); Alfred D. Chandler, Jr., *The Visible Hand* (Cambridge, Mass.: Harvard University Press, 1977); Oliver E. Williamson, *Markets and Hierarchies: Analysis of Antitrust Implications* (New York: Free Press, 1975).
2. Chandler, *The Visible Hand*, Chapter 1.
3. Williamson, *Markets and Hierachies*.
4. Chandler, *The Visible Hand*, Chapter 1.
5. K. D. George and C. L. Joll, *Competition Policy in the UK and the EEC* (Cambridge: Cambridge University Press, 1975), pp. 10–14.
6. Ibid., p. 15.
7. Leslie Hannah, *The Rise of the Corporate Economy* (London: Methuen, 1976), pp. 150–81.
8. S. J. Prais, *The Evolution of Giant Firms in Britain* (Cambridge: Cambridge University Press, 1976), p. 5.
9. Michael A. Utton, "British Merger Policy," in K. D. George and C. L. Joll, *Competition Policy in the UK and the EEC* (Cambridge: Cambridge University Press, 1975), pp. 96–98.
10. Alexis P. Jacquemin and Henry W. de Jong, *European Industrial Organization* (London: Macmillan, 1977), pp. 106–8.

11. Derek F. Channon, *The Strategy and Structure of British Enterprise* (Boston: Harvard Business School, 1973), p. 67.
12. J. R. Cable, J. P. R. Palfrey and J. W. Runge, "Federal Republic of Germany, 1962–74," in Dennis C. Mueller (ed.), *The Determinants and Effects of Mergers* (Cambridge, Mass.: Oelschlaeger, Gunn & Hain, 1980), p. 114.
13. Ibid., p. 115.
14. Gareth P. Dyas and Heinz T. Thanheiser, *The Emerging European Enterprise* (London: Macmillan, 1976), p. 57.
15. Cable *et al.*, "Federal Republic of Germany," pp. 110–15.
16. Dyas and Thanheiser, *Emerging European Enterprise*, p. 50.
17. Ibid., p. 168.
18. F. Jenny and A. P. Weber, "France, 1962–1972," in Dennis C. Mueller (ed.), *The Determinants and Effects of Mergers* (Cambridge, Mass.: Oelschlaeger, Gunn & Hain, 1980), pp. 141–2.
19. Ibid., pp. 142–3.
20. Toyohiro Kono, *Strategy and Structure of Japanese Enterprises* (Londn: Macmillan, 1984), p. 80.
21. Michael Y. Yoshino, *Japan's Managerial System* (Cambridge, Mass.: MIT Press, 1968), pp. 118–19.
22. Ibid., p. 123.
23. Ibid., pp. 139–48.
24. Kono, *Strategy and Structure of Japanese Enterprises*, p. 33.
25. Ibid., p. 219.

Part V

Multinational Corporations Prepare the Global Economy: The Integration of Markets and the Erosion of the Nation-state

17

The International Monetary Order in Crisis (1977)*

Fred L. Block

The struggle of the United States to increase its freedom of action in international monetary affairs destroyed the old Bretton Woods system. Step by step, the United States either broke the rules of the old order or forced other countries to break them. The rule-breaking was deemed necessary at each step to save the international monetary system from an even greater crisis. The first major alteration of the rules was the creation of the gold pool in 1961, which relieved the US of part of the responsibility of maintaining the gold price at $35 an ounce. The next step was the unilateral renunciation by the United States in 1968 of the obligation to provide gold to private purchasers at the $35-an-ounce price. This was followed three years later by the decision to close the gold window to official purchasers as well. The United States also renounced its informal obligations as a reserve currency country by blocking access to its capital markets, and the imposition of the 10 per cent import surcharge in August 1971 was a blatant violation of rules governing international trade. Finally, the United States was largely responsible for the final significant rule violation, the end of the regime of fixed exchange rates. The continuation of the US deficit left foreign countries that did not want to accumulate additional dollars with only two options: instituting potentially dangerous controls over capital inflows or floating their currencies. Since the second alternative seemed less risky, it was the one for which Western Europe and Japan eventually opted.

---

* From *The Origins of International Economic Disorder. A Study of United States International Monetary Policy from the Second World War to the Present* (Berkeley: University of California Press, 1977), pp. 203–25.

It can be argued that each of these rule changes is part of a gradual evolution to a new monetary order, but there can be no doubt that the evolutionary process is still far from complete. The international monetary system, as it presently exists, lacks the institutional structure to deal smoothly either with special shocks such as the oil price rises or with the day-to-day problems of inflation and balance-of-payments adjustment. Even though the international monetary system survived the strain of financing the huge trade deficits of the oil-consuming nations during 1974, there were some periods when that survival seemed problematic. And it remains to be seen how the system will be able to cope with some of the shocks that certainly lie ahead. But the most telling critique of the present international monetary system is that the system has heightened the problem of global inflation. An analysis of the problem of inflation also provides a glimpse of the kinds of reforms that are necessary to create an international monetary order that minimizes, rather than maximizes, the strain between national economies and the world economy.

The problem of inflation

It hardly needs repeating that mounting inflationary pressure has been the characteristic problem of developed capitalist nations in the past fifteen years. While there are a multitude of explanations for this inflationary pressure, it is increasingly recognized that the inflationary dynamic is deeply rooted in the structure of contemporary capitalism.[1] It seems that the very success of advanced capitalism in using Keynesian techniques to moderate the severity of the business cycle has created the current problem with inflation. Since the Second World War, the developed economies have not experienced the "purification" of a major depression that lowers wages, prices, and interest rates. Instead, all of those have risen, if not steadily, relentlessly. In fact, it appears that in contemporary capitalism almost any strain generates new price rises and parallel wage gains. Even during periods of economic recession, significant price rises occur as capitalists attempt to make up for lagging profits by increasing their profit per unit sold. Such violations of the law of supply and demand, and parallel violations on the side of wages, are made possible by the market power exercised by giant corporations and the more powerful of the trade unions. This market power is a major factor in making contemporary capitalism so prone to inflationary pressure.

This means also that the capacity of governments to take effective action to control inflation is limited. The orthodox cure for inflation is a deliberate effort to slow the pace of economic activity through fiscal or monetary action. However, since market power makes it possible for firms and unions to increase prices and wages even in periods of recession, the economic slowdown might have to be quite severe before such wage and price rises are halted. The problem is that the lower the level of economic activity and the higher the rate of unemployment, the greater the social and economic risks. Not only is there a threat of social unrest or rebellion resulting from high rates of unemployment, but there is the clear danger of a general economic collapse if economic activity drops too far. A severe reduction in the level of economic activity threatens to produce widespread corporate, personal, and governmental bankruptcies that could easily spiral out of control. Finally, even if deflation is relatively successful in eliminating inflation, it might well mean that inflationary pressures, once economic expansion begins again, will be stronger than before. This can happen because low levels of investment during the period of deflation can lead to strains on capacity once expansion begins anew.[2]

The major alternative to deflation as an anti-inflationary strategy has been the development of an incomes policy, a government-imposed system of wage and price controls. The idea of such controls is to maintain a constant relationship between profits and wages through administrative measures rather than through market forces and inflation. While controls of this sort appear to have some initial success in halting inflation, they tend to break down over time. The continued existence of the controls places the state in the center of the struggle over the distribution of the social product. In this position it is difficult for the state to preserve its pretense of neutrality in the class struggle while simultaneously defending the existing distribution of income between wages and profits. To protect their electoral base, politicians usually opt for an end to controls in order to extricate themselves from a dangerous position. However, the pressure for elimination of controls is often exerted by capitalists as well as by labor. Capitalists attempt to raise profits by subverting the controls through the downgrading of product quality and the creation of artificial shortages. These efforts mean that the logic of long-term price controls points to increased government regulation of product quality, investment decisions, and profit levels. However, this is a logic that capitalist firms strenuously resist, because it threatens their decision-making autonomy. So instead of pursuing a logic of expanded controls, the state usually simply abandons the experiment with wage and price controls.

The inadequacy of the standard policy tools for controlling inflation in advanced capitalism would be a serious problem even if each of these economies existed in isolation. However, the openness of the world economy to flows of goods and capital across national boundaries makes the inadequacy of the anti-inflation tools even more dramatic. Illustrating the complexities that flow from the openness of the world economy, to take one example, are the potential, ironic consequences of domestic monetary policies. The normal use of monetary policy to prevent an overheating of the domestic economy involves pushing interest rates up. However, higher interest rates can attract capital from abroad, which will act as a stimulus to the domestic economy. A country that has been able to avoid inflation with a tight money policy can find itself overwhelmed by an inflow of capital attracted by high interest rates and a low rate of inflation. The inflow of capital can quickly destroy the government's work in holding inflation in check. Similarly, government efforts to slow the rate of economic activity by making credit scarce and expensive can be subverted by the ability of major corporations, particularly multinationals, to finance new expansion with capital borrowed at lower interest rates abroad. The national government's ability to control the domestic economy – already limited by the relative ineffectiveness of anti-inflationary tools – is further impaired by the openness of the international economy.[3]

Inflationary pressures in one national economy can also spill over into other economies through spreading shortages of commodities. Agricultural shortfalls, production bottlenecks, sharply increased speculative purchases, and even sudden growth in consumer demand can lead one country to increase its imports of certain products rapidly, resulting in parallel shortages in other countries. Inflation is exported by bidding up the price of certain commodities, and the increased price of those goods sets off price rises for related products. Again, a country that has kept to a relatively low level of inflation might find its price structure thrown into disarray by booming foreign demand.[4]

The problem of inflation has been further complicated in recent years by the relatively anarchic organization of international liquidity. At times, an excess of international liquidity has heightened the inflationary pressure on national economies. Excessive international liquidity more or less assures that there will be large capital inflows into low-inflation countries, and it also facilitates worldwide price increases in the same way that an excess of domestic liquidity contributes to inflation. The anarchic organization of international liquidity can be traced to American failure to perform adequately the tasks of an international financial center. The quantity of dollars pumped abroad through the US deficit often bore little relation to the quantity needed for gradual increments in official and private reserves. Furthermore, US policies encouraged the rise of the Eurodollar market that provides another important source of international liquidity. However, the expansion or contraction in the Eurodollar market's contribution to global liquidity is not subject to governmental regulation. In fact, there is some evidence that the supply of Eurodollars expands at precisely the time when the US authorities are attempting to slow the growth of the domestic money supply.[5]

There are, then, a variety of ways in which inflationary pressures can be transmitted from one country to another in the present system. If these various processes equalized the rate of inflation in all countries, the problem of balance-of-payments adjustment would be greatly reduced. However, that equalization does not occur. National rates of inflation vary according to specific national conditions, and the vulnerability of economies to imported inflations also differs dramatically. The consequence is that nations will have widely different rates of inflation depending on their own level of business activity, their vulnerability to imported inflation, the ability of their authorities to moderate wage demands, the rate of productivity advance, and other factors. Sharp differences in inflation levels most often lead to balance-of-payments problems for high-inflation countries. Not only do high rates of inflation tend to weaken the balance of trade, but inflationary pressure also results in capital outflows as investors switch to assets in more stable currencies.

Overcoming this kind of inflation-induced balance-of-payments deficit is the heart of the adjustment problem in contemporary capitalism. And it is the ineffectiveness and unreliability of the major anti-deflationary tools that makes this kind of adjustment so difficult. The process is further complicated by the reluctance of low-inflation countries with balance-of-payments surpluses to share the burden of adjustment. If low-inflation countries allowed their rates of inflation to rise by a portion of the difference between the low and high rates, the task of high-inflation countries would be more manageable. However, there is no institutional mechanism for forcing the low-inflation countries in this direction, and they are extremely reluctant to increase their rates of inflation through deliberate action. Low-inflation countries tend to see their success in holding inflation in check as an indicator of social health, and taking action to stimulate more inflation is seen as the equivalent of planning an epidemic of a dangerous disease. The fear is that a higher rate of inflation would destroy the existing delicate balance between labor and capital and begin a period of intense conflict over the distribution of the social product that could push the rate of inflation completely out of control.[6]

Exchange rate adjustments

The orthodox economic solution to balance-of-payments deficits caused by high rates of inflation is a downward shift in the deficit country's exchange rate. ... The problem is that this mechanism often fails to work in the way that economic theory indicates it should. Devaluations are designed to restore international equilibrium through a market device. Lower prices abroad for a country's exports are supposed to increase the volume of exports, while higher prices for imported goods will diminish total import volume. Increased exports and decreased imports mean a reduction in overall consumption. However, if a country's labor movement is anxious to preserve the existing level of real income, it will fight for wage increases to compensate for the losses due to devaluation.[7] If successful, this could set off a new inflationary spiral that would easily eliminate the potential trade gain from devaluation. Even when devaluations are combined with efforts to control inflation through monetary or fiscal restraint, the strength of unions in key sectors can still prevent the reduction in real incomes that devaluations are intended to produce.

Another problem with devaluations is their uncertain effects on the trade balance. A variety of products are not particularly responsive to price changes. Imports of crucial raw materials, many agricultural goods, petroleum, and other commodities might well continue at the same volume despite higher prices, since demand is not sensitive to price changes of 5 or 15 or 25 per cent. Similarly, exports of a similar range of products might not increase in volume despite lower unit prices, resulting in a drop in total export receipts for those goods. Another range of products are traded internationally under conditions of oligopolistic pricing, so that these goods are also relatively insensitive to price changes. Producers of certain goods, for example, might not even bother to reduce the foreign-currency cost of export goods that have been priced in another currency, increasing their profits per item regardless of volume. Depending on the specific composition of a country's exports and imports, it is possible that the impact of a devaluation on a country's trade balance might be the reverse of what was intended. The increased cost of necessary imports and decreased receipts on certain exports might outweigh the savings from discouraged imports and the gains from increased receipts for price-sensitive exports. But it is difficult to assess in advance whether the impact of a devaluation on the trade balance will be negative, neutral, or positive. The outcome depends significantly on the willingness or eagerness of a country's exporters to cut their foreign-currency prices and to pursue aggressively the new opportunities for expanded exports. It also depends on the nation's success in inducing the working class to accept a reduction in real earnings.

Since exchange rate changes do not automatically restore balance-of-payments equilibrium and sometimes even have adverse effects, floating exchange rates are not the universal panacea that they have been alleged to be.[8] An international monetary order in which exchange rates are free to find their "correct" level in the free market could work only if real-wage levels could be readily lowered. For real incomes to be successfully reduced without inflation in contemporary society seems to require, at the very least, a concerted and conscious policy by business and government. The advocates of floating exchange rates, however, generally assume that the market will accomplish this reduction by itself. In fact, it seems possible that, instead of facilitating adjustment, freely floating exchange rates would contribute to inflationary pressure because they would eliminate a traditional incentive for anti-inflationary actions – the defense of the existing exchange rate and the country's stock of currency reserves.

But whether exchange rates float freely or are more fixed, the problem remains that exchange rate changes, the major means of balance-of-payments adjustment, can serve to intensify inflationary pressures. The same is true of the other major techniques of balance-of-payments adjustment. Deflation, as already noted, can increase inflationary pressures over the short term or the long term. Attempts to adjust the balance of payments by raising domestic interest rates to attract capital flows can accelerate inflation when borrowers pass along the costs of higher interest rates to customers.[9] Even efforts to restrict imports, such as the import surcharges used temporarily by Britain and the United States, can have the effect of driving up certain critical prices. The consequence of all of these adjustment techniques is a classical vicious circle: rising domestic prices require balance-of-payments adjustment, but balance-of-payments adjustment leads to rising domestic prices. The severity of this cycle can be attenuated, since the rate of domestic inflation is affected by a wide variety of different factors. Yet the point remains that the adjustment mechanisms within the present international monetary system can work to intensify the tendency toward inflation, which is already the most critical economic problem of advanced capitalism.

The need for reform

The problem of inflation provides a dramatic illustration of the inadequacy of the present international monetary system, dramatic because accelerating inflation poses a fundamental threat to political and social order. To the extent to which present international monetary arrangements actually accelerate inflation or simply make it more difficult to control, it is clear that those arrangements are in need of repair. Still, there are those who take a sanguine view of today's international monetary system and argue that reform is not urgently needed because there is a gradual evolution toward a stronger, more stable order based on a high level of international cooperation. However, this optimistic view rests on the assumption that domestic solutions will work to curb inflationary pressures and that, with the problem of inflation reduced, the present system will work adequately. Such a view is unrealistic if, in fact, strong inflationary pressures are endemic to capitalism at its current stage of development. To be sure, the intensity of inflation will rise and fall over time, but I would argue that it is utopian to expect a sudden return to an era of stable prices or price rises limited to 2–3 per cent a year. Once high levels of inflation are seen as virtually inevitable, it follows that international monetary reform is necessary to create a monetary order better fitted to the task of neutralizing these inflationary pressures.

The problem of inflation and the related issues of exchange rate adjustment and international liquidity do not exhaust the reasons for international monetary reform being urgently needed. The crisis created by the increase in petroleum prices in 1973–74 revealed that the institutional apparatus for international crisis management is underdeveloped. For one thing, there is no adequate supervision of the Eurodollar banking system that had to bear much of the burden of recycling the petrodollars. For another, the IMF's resources are too limited for the kind of bailing-out operations that might have proved necessary. Of course, the world economy did survive the crisis, and a number of ad hoc measures succeeded in staving off disaster. But a sanguine view is justified only if one believes that the oil price crisis was simply a once-only phenomenon. If one sees other major international economic crises as likely,[10] it follows that the international monetary system needs an institutional structure powerful enough to cushion the impact of such crises. Such an institutional structure would minimize the need for last-ditch diplomacy to devise ad hoc means of crisis management. The strengthened institutional structure would decrease the danger that is always present in ad hoc arrangements – that one or two key nations might demand too high a price for cooperation in the ad hoc solution, thus creating a diplomatic deadlock that would make effective intervention impossible.

The shape of reform

The type of international monetary reform necessary to neutralize inflationary pressures and to facilitate global crisis management would involve both strengthening of supranational institutions and a higher level of economic coordination among the developed nations. Supranational institutions would be necessary to regulate smoothly the supply of international liquidity and to regulate international capital markets, such as the Eurodollar market. A strengthened supranational agency would also provide a first line of defense in crisis management, because it would control enough resources to perform bail-out operations without complex negotiations. Improved economic coordination among nations would ease the adjustment problem by dividing the burden among surplus and deficit nations. Coordination would also mean a much higher level of exchange of information about economic conditions and intended policies, so that deficit nations would be able to formulate a mix of policies for balance-of-payments adjustment based on the best possible information about the economic environment. Coordination would have to go far beyond the relatively low level of consultation that has already been achieved, and it would have to involve agreement on the acceptability of different types of economic intervention.[11] The supranational institutions would then be able to enforce those agreements.

While it is relatively easy to specify the types of reforms necessary for the successful management of an open world economy, it is extremely difficult to imagine the means by which those reforms would be implemented. Historically, the successful efforts at international monetary reform have been those organized by a single hegemonic power, but there exists today no single nation or group of confederated nations that has that kind of economic and political dominance. In the absence of a hegemonic power, there seem to be only two possible political foundations for effective international monetary reform. The first is the concerted exercise of political leverage by the multinational corporations. The second is the development of a joint partnership among the United States, Japan, and the major nations of Western Europe that would include a common program for international monetary reform. I will argue, however, that neither of these alternatives is likely to provide the necessary political base for reform.

The global corporations and international monetary reform

Those who celebrate the rise of the multinational corporation have often argued that the nation-state is no longer a viable economic unit. The nation-state, they assert, acts as a fetter on economic progress in the same way that principalities and duchies slowed the rise of capitalism before the creation of national markets. Multinationals must waste endless resources contending with dozens of different governments, each with a complex web of specific regulations that limit the ability of the multinational to organize its global activity in the most rational and efficient way.[12] While abolishing the nation-state seems unrealistic, the creation of a series of international institutions that would allow multinationals to operate as though the capitalist world economy were one nation has been advocated. This would involve an international system of corporate charters, patent arrangements, and antitrust and tax regulations. These arrangements would require mechanisms for adjudication and for enforcement on an international level. Along with the supranational structure required for these purposes, it would make sense to create an agency that would regulate international capital markets and an international central bank that would regulate the world's supply of liquidity. This would involve the creation of a formidable network of supranational economic agencies that would gradually relieve national governments of almost all authority over international economic matters.[13]

This is simply a modern version of the nineteenth-century utopian vision of a self-regulating international market. The only difference is that the contemporary view recognizes that the world market cannot adequately regulate itself, so that a supranational authority is required. Yet this authority would be fundamentally similar to the self-regulating market because it would be above politics; it would allow economic activity to proceed without interruption, except for the minimum necessary to assure order. Implicit here is the myth that there is basically one natural way of organizing the world economy, which would ultimately bring equal benefits to all classes and all nations. The whole thrust of the present study has been to argue that the specific way in which the world economy is organized has important consequences for the distribution of resources among nations and within nations, and this means that the specific organization of that world economy can never be "above politics." It is politics.

Just as the nineteenth-century effort to establish a self-regulating international market was based on Great Britain's international political and military hegemony, so the contemporary vision of supranational regulation of the world economy has flourished in the context of US international hegemony. American political, economic, and military power has been critical in making the world safe for multinational enterprises. But as the international position of the United States has begun to slip, it is increasingly argued that the same safety for multinational enterprises can be assured by a supranational authority divorced from the political and military power exercised by nations. Yet such an argument must be based on either extreme naiveté or self-interested cynicism. The men who run the multinationals are well aware that the exercise of political, economic, and military power is necessary to give them the freedom to continue their global operations.[14] Unless a supranational agency were invested with such powers, which seems quite unlikely, the agency would have to co-exist with the exercise of those powers by national governments. But under such conditions, it would be extremely improbable that the supranational agency would be able to disregard differences in national power in making its decisions. If several major nations were carrying the bulk of the military burden of keeping the world safe for multinational enterprises, could a supranational agency avoid favoring the corporations based in those nations? And if it did, why should those nations continue to bear the burden without gaining advantages?

The issue is starker if one looks at the idea of supranational regulation from the point of view of a particular multinational corporation. In the present order, that corporation gets a certain amount of support from the government of its base country. That support, whether it takes the form of preferential access to government contracts, diplomatic clout, or tax benefits, is useful in competing with foreign-based firms, especially those whose governments are able to provide less adequate support. If, however, a transition were made to supranational regulation, all of these forms of support would have to be eliminated to lessen the impact of national politics on the world economy. Each company would face the supranational agency on an equal footing. It seems obvious that American-based multinationals, in particular, would stand to lose a great deal by no longer having exclusive access to US diplomatic power.

In reality, the idea of supranational regulation of the world economy is simply an ideological smoke screen that the multinationals use in their campaign to lessen governmental regulation of their activities. It is certainly true that the multinationals want to minimize regulation by governments at home and abroad, but it does not follow from that that they have no interest in national governments. They want diplomatic and economic support from their home nation, but they want it with no strings attached. So they use an anti-nation-state ideology when they want to avoid regulation, but usually become quite patriotic when they need something from the government. No matter how hypocritical, the patriotism indicates their fundamental dependence on the power of their particular home government. That dependence makes it extremely unlikely that the multinationals will throw their weight behind efforts to replace national governmental regulation with supranational regulations.

This does not mean that any form of internationalization of economic regulation is impossible. International conventions and even effective international regulations can be developed in areas such as patents where the common interest among nations is strong and national practices are relatively similar. It is also possible that some limited form of supranational central banking could evolve, as long as it concentrated on creation of reserves and the management of international capital markets, leaving governments free to determine their own policies. The point is that the more ambitious vision of international economic management or of a highly interventionist international central bank will not be realized. And any progress toward effective international institutions would likely be interrupted or reversed when one nation feels that its international position is being undermined or unfairly limited by the international arrangements. In sum, the rise of multinational corporations does not increase the likelihood that international economic coordination will be handed over to a supranational agency, because conflict of interests among nation-states continues unabated. The only viable foundation for the further elaboration and development of supranational institutions would be some form of relatively stable political cooperation among the major capitalist powers. If such cooperation for the purpose of smoothly managing the world economy developed, one could expect a flowering of supranational regulations. The important question is whether the conditions exist for the development of the kind of political cooperation necessary for the joint management of the world economy.

Reform through joint management

Reform through joint management would mean that several of the strongest capitalist nations would have to agree to manage the world economy collectively and carry out the reforms described earlier. They would jointly play the role performed by a hegemonic power in earlier periods, but they would have to do so with a higher level of responsibility and with new skills appropriate to the more complex problems of the contemporary world economy. While it is impossible to predict whether this kind of joint management will evolve, it is possible to analyze the major obstacles from the point of view of the United States, Western Europe, and Japan.

The United States

... I have argued that the breakdown of the postwar monetary order was rooted in the inability of the United States both to pursue its global aims and to live within the rules of international monetary behavior it had earlier devised. Joint management, however, would necessarily mean the development of a new set of rules that the United States would be expected to obey. It seems very likely that the conflict between the pursuit of US global aims and the "rules of the game" would re-emerge, especially because the partners in joint management have an interest in rules that place serious constraints on US economic freedom. In short, it seems extremely likely that joint management would force the United States at least in certain periods, to accept some combination of global and domestic retrenchment. Global retrenchment means a reduction in the cost of public and private US international activities, while domestic retrenchment means a willingness to accept more stringent anti-inflationary actions, including higher levels of unemployment. Since both forms of forced retrenchment can be hazardous, it would seem that US policy-makers have good reason to avoid the constraints that joint management would most probably involve.

The danger of global retrenchment in a period of intensifying international competition is that it could further worsen the international economic position of the United States, forcing continually more serious retreats, in a kind of snowballing effect. A cutback in US over-seas political and military presence could cause US-based firms to lose economic opportunities to foreign-based firms. The loss of major con-struction contracts and control or access to lucrative raw materials could hurt the profits of US-based firms and lead to higher prices of US raw material imports. Similarly, limitations on the ability of US firms to continue their overseas growth by exporting capital from the United States could result in a relative strengthening of foreign-based multina-tionals. Again, this would be most costly in competition for raw mater-ials, construction projects, and sales of heavy equipment, but it might also damage the ability of US firms abroad to compete profitably in other manufactured goods.

In addition to strengthening the relative position of Western European and Japanese capitalists, American retrenchment might also mean a strengthened position for the socialist bloc and for the revolu-tionary and nationalist forces in the underdeveloped world. If US retrenchment is not matched by a complementary extension of polit-ical and military efforts by Western Europe and Japan, there would be increased opportunities for countries to opt out of the capitalist world economy. Underdeveloped countries that did not move that far would still have greatly increased bargaining power in relation to the devel-oped capitalist countries. And as long as Japan and Western Europe did not fill the political vacuum left by retreating US power, China and the USSR would increase their own bargaining power in relation to both the developed and underdeveloped world.

These risks involved in retrenchment compound the difficulties facing a state apparatus that would have to design a strategy for imper-ial retreat that combines maximum balance-of-payments savings with minimum damage to the US international position. If the state were free to pursue the most rational strategy, the job would be merely difficult, but the state must formulate its policies in the context of pres-sures by a variety of powerful interest groups, many of which are strongly represented in the state apparatus itself. For example, the deci-sion to reduce the American political, military, and foreign-aid pres-ence in a country where a handful of US multinationals have investments would be strongly contested by those firms and by a lobby of people with strong political, cultural, and economic ties to that par-ticular country. It is difficult for the government to resist this kind of pressure simply on the grounds that it is attempting to pursue the most efficient and economic global policy. Just as the extension of US power internationally was orchestrated through a series of crises, so it would seem that its retreat might be accomplished only through a series of crises that make the need for retrenchment painfully obvious. In short, it would require a powerful counterpressure for the state to be willing or able to sacrifice the interests of those firms that would stand to lose from a retreat from a particular area.[15]

If global retrenchment seems too costly, American policy-makers could respond to foreign pressure by relying on more intense domestic retrenchment. However, domestic retrenchment has serious costs of its own, because unemployment and lower rates of economic growth create a multitude of new problems. Even without joint management, the United States already suffers from levels of unemployment that are substantially higher than those in other developed capitalist countries. And unemployment rates among the urban black population are usually about twice the rate for the whole nation. While it is true that the social and political response by blacks and others to the high levels of unemployment in the 1974–75 recession was remarkably mild, domestic retrenchment could well require that, in certain periods of balance-of-payments difficulties, the United States would have to tolerate unemployment rates substantially above the 8–9 per cent range. Furthermore, any US administration would be foolish to anticipate that the quiescent response to the high levels of unemployment in 1974–75 will become a permanent feature of the political landscape. It is far more likely that future administrations will be under very strong domestic pressure to bring unemployment back down to the 4–5 per cent range. In that context, pressure from abroad for domestic retrenchment would be politically explosive.

The other problem is that domestic retrenchment, with its slower rates of economic growth, could easily heighten the inflationary pressure that results from labor's struggle to defend and expand its share of the total product. In sum, externally imposed economic discipline would increase the likelihood that the United States would follow the British pattern of economic stop–go. Brief periods of inadequate and inflationary economic growth would alternate with periods of high unemployment, and the economy's underlying problems would only worsen. The greatest danger for US policy-makers in such a pattern is the possibility that, as in Britain, the consequences of stop–go would be intensification of class conflict and radicalization of the labor movement. Because of this risk and because of the dangers involved in international retrenchment, it is of considerable advantage to the United States to avoid the constraints on its action implicit in joint management. The United States is likely to acquiesce in a system of joint management that would probably entail substantial sacrifices only if Western Europe and Japan could apply convincing pressure.

Western Europe and Japan

The relation of Western Europe and Japan to joint management is complex. While their governments and strongest firms have much to gain from coordinated management of the world economy and the consequent American retrenchment, there is likely to be strong domestic resistance to the expanded international role required by joint management. The use of economic resources for expanded political–military roles and the adoption of the style of global powers will generate domestic conflicts. Yet this expanded political–military role is necessary, first to convince the United States to accept joint management, and then to make a jointly managed system work. To complicate matters further, the struggle by Japan and Western Europe for an expanded international role occurs in the context of military and economic dependence on the United States. This dependence can be manipulated by the United States to discourage pressures by the Europeans and Japanese for concessions on economic management.

The most immediate gain for Western Europe and Japan from joint management would be greater ease in domestic economic management. Limits on American ability to export its deficits and its inflation would help reduce the inflationary pressure elsewhere. Agreement with the United States on new rules for adjustment would help depoliticize the adjustment process and would make the control of inflation easier. Similarly, cooperation would reduce the risk of major currency crises, competitive devaluations, or international debt crises. The process of economic integration in Europe could then proceed without the disruption of periodic currency crises,[16] and Europe and Japan could be surer that their dollar holdings would eventually be redeemed for real resources. Western European and Japanese capitalists would also gain from the extension of their home countries' political influence and the retreat of US power. They would be in a better position to win construction contracts and raw-materials concessions abroad, and they would be able to extend even further the geographical range of their investments. Limitations on capital exports from the United States would decrease the threat of takeovers and competitive investments by US multinationals. And joint management would probably mean that the international capital market would become less biased toward US firms, so that Japanese and Western European firms would be better able to borrow to finance their own expansion.

Despite these advantages, the obstacles to this kind of extension of power are formidable. For Western Europe the issue is tightly inter-twined with the prospects for economic and political integration. For Japan, the issue is closely knit with the legacy of the Second World War and the popular reactions against a militaristic and aggressive foreign policy. In both cases, the strength of left-wing political forces at home operates as a double limitation on an ambitious foreign policy. The Left tends to oppose the expansion of international political–military commitments out of anti-imperialist and anti-militarist motiv-ations. At the same time, demands by the Left and by the labor move-ment for higher wages and increased social spending make it difficult to free resources for international purposes. Strong domestic pressures can make it difficult for a nation to operate in the international sphere – fulfilling such obligations as providing credit to other countries or honoring military commitments – with the consistency expected of a major power.

For Western Europe the pursuit of a coherent international policy depends either on the further development of a supranational author-ity or on the emergence of a cohesive alliance among its most powerful nations, West Germany and France. The first development is problem-atic for the near future for many of the same reasons that make the emergency of international economic management unlikely – most fundamentally, the reluctance of states to cede sovereignty over crucial economic policy decisions. The latter development is more likely, but there is the continuing possibility that an alliance can be shattered by international conflicts of interest or by domestic pressures that block agreement on critical issues. But without a reasonably stable alliance at the center, the European nations would be left to formulate independ-ent foreign policies. Only Germany, acting independently, could make a claim to joint partnership, but it would be difficult for her to make that claim credible. Given the present political alignments within Germany, the exercise of independent political power on a global basis would place a real strain on available resources.

Japan would also find it difficult to make a claim to global joint part-nership if Western Europe as a region did not participate in the effort. But even under the most ideal circumstances, it is uncertain whether domestic resistance to a greatly expanded international role for Japan would be overcome. The rapid pace of Japan's post-Second World War industrial growth has left a huge backlog of social demands that might interfere with an expanded world role. More significantly, the strength of the opposition to militarism in Japan could preclude the rapid expansion of political–military influence that would have to be a condition for gaining and sustaining a jointly managed world economy. A country whose military forces are constitutionally defined as "Self-Defense Forces" has trouble establishing its credibility as a reliable world power.[17]

Western Europe and Japan can also be dissuaded by the United States from pressing too hard for an effective global partnership. As long as joint management is seen by the United States as an undesirable alternative, the United States can attempt to play on internal division in and between Western Europe and Japan to block an effective challenge. In Western Europe, this can be accomplished by a divide-and-conquer policy that attempts to prevent the emergence of a unified EEC. The United States can also use the threats of withdrawing military protection and of heightened economic conflict to counter European and Japanese pressures. An overly aggressive use of these threats could backfire, because it might result in strengthening the impulse in Western Europe and Japan toward a more independent policy. However, the point remains that internal divisions, lack of adequate economic resources, and American counterpressures will make it difficult for Western Europe and Japan to press successfully for joint management of the world economy despite the advantages to them of such a regime.

The unreformed future

I have tried to show that neither of the frequently cited paths to international monetary reform is likely to produce results in the foreseeable future. Yet I have also argued that the need for reform is critical if the system is to function. If international monetary reform is both necessary and unlikely, it follows that the international monetary system will suffer severe and chronic crises in the years ahead. Such a prediction, however, does not imply that there will be an international financial crisis on the scale of the Great Depression of the 1930s. While that possibility is no longer unimaginable, the resources available for crisis management are formidable enough for an economic collapse to be avoided under most circumstances.[18]

The common interest among the major capitalist nations in avoiding an international economic collapse is strong enough so that ad hoc measures can be found for dealing with almost all crisis situations. This makes it possible for the international monetary system to survive for some time despite its fundamental weaknesses. It is even possible to imagine that ad hoc cooperation among the major capitalist nations could quickly undo the damage if an international financial collapse unfolded before governments could act to halt it. If, for example, a series of major bankruptcies led to an international financial panic similar to the one in 1931 that forced Germany to adopt exchange controls, it might be still possible for governments to intervene to provide financing for international trade. Such intervention, combined with measures to save the banking system, could prevent the collapse from leading to a rapid decline in business activity internationally.

This type of crisis management can be extraordinarily effective if the major nations are willing to put aside their differences long enough to rescue the international economy. If, however, one or more nations attempt to extract concessions from the others as a condition for coop-eration in efforts at crisis management, serious problems can arise. When the nation holding out for concessions is indispensable to an effective rescue, and when other nations are unwilling to grant the concessions, effective crisis management can be blocked. This could mean that the negotiations dragged on past the deadline for effective action, or simply that efforts at crisis management were abandoned.[19] In either event, the consequence could be that a potentially manage-able crisis escalates out of control, leading to a collapse of international trade and global deflation. Obviously, such an outcome would be dam-aging to all nations, including those that blocked effective action ini-tially, so it is unlikely that a group of national policy-makers would take such an intransigent stance lightly. I would argue that they would take such a risk only when they perceived a fundamental threat to their nation's political stability. If, for example, a regime was being challenged by powerful domestic opposition movements of the Left or of the Right, its policy-makers might feel that the regime's survival depended on gaining certain concessions internationally, such as the freedom to reduce unemployment despite adverse balance-of-payments effects. In such a case, national policy-makers might consider that the burden of causing an international economic collapse would fall on those nations that were too shortsighted to grant the concessions nec-essary for national stability.

At present, few governments of major capitalist powers face serious threats from dangerously disloyal opposition movements. The threat posed in Italy and France by the Communist party's insistence on its right to play a role in the government is hardly enough to justify dis-ruptive international actions by Italian or French policy-makers. The danger in these cases is minimal, because these parties have pledged themselves to parliamentary methods and there is little likelihood that they will act to dismantle the structures of Italian or French capitalism. However, far more threatening movements might arise in these nations and in others if present economic conditions continue. High levels of unemployment and inflation can strengthen radical political movements of the Left and of the Right that are unwilling to respect established institutional structures in their eagerness to respond to economic and social problems. Such movements could force national policy-makers to change the way they negotiate internationally, with the consequence of destroying the minimal level of international co-operation required for effective global crisis management.[20]

It is here that the major effects of the present international monetary system might be felt. The unreformed international monetary system heightens advanced capitalism's tendency toward stagflation – the co-existence of high unemployment and high inflation. It does this in part because of the vicious circle described before; almost all measures of balance-of-payments adjustment can serve to intensify inflationary pressures. The present system also works to transmit inflationary pressures from one nation to another, even to nations that have already reduced their levels of economic activity. But the more intense the inflationary pressures, the worse the trade-off between inflation and unemployment. So policy-makers must worry in periods of relatively low inflation that a reduction in unemployment might dangerously accelerate inflation, and they must be willing to impose even more severe unemployment in periods of high inflation.

As the problem of stagflation worsens, governments will be forced to resort to politically unpopular policies, such as prolonged high unemployment and reductions in government services. These measures can generate mass support for opposition movements that challenge the political and economic status quo. Such threats to national political order can work to undermine international economic order, and by doing so they can heighten the possibility of even more disruptive international economic developments. Further international disruptions would be likely to create more economic havoc internally, which would also strengthen the hand of the domestic opposition movements, and so on. It is through this kind of complex pattern that the present international economic order is likely gradually to self-destruct: domestic political responses to the problem of stagflation – a problem that has been exacerbated by the international monetary system – will effectively destroy the conditions for the international economic cooperation that is essential for the system's continued survival.

Alternatives

In the meantime, however, a number of political alternatives are open to nations that perceive the mounting costs of continued participation in the existing international monetary system. All these alternatives involve a sharp break with liberal economic principles, because they use extensive government intervention to insulate the domestic economy from the pressures of the world economy. In the near future, these alternatives are most likely to be advocated by those opposition movements that arise to protest the consequences of stagflation. But if international monetary reform continues to prove illusory and the domestic costs of the present system mount, all nations will have to face these alternatives. Even if only one major nation chose to opt out of the present system, it would have a major impact on the others.

While the range of actual policy devices that can be used to insulate economies from international market pressures is almost unlimited, the alternatives that use such devices systematically can be reduced to a number of "ideal types."[21] It is not possible here to fill in the political dynamics and class forces involved in each of the ideal types, but I will attempt to outline schematically the major dimensions of these political alternatives.

The first alternative is actually much less feasible now than it was in the 1930s and 1940s. This is the idea of national capitalism, by which I mean a system that leaves ownership of the means of production in private hands while almost all international economic transactions are organized by the state. Foreign trade would be controlled by the state and the outflow of capital would be severely restricted. However, if the government of a developed capitalist nation attempted to impose this solution, presumably as a response to severe domestic disruptions caused by the world market, it would immediately come into conflict with all the multinational corporations operating within its borders. These corporations would be unable to function within a national capitalist system, and we could expect to see ferocious opposition on their part. If the government refused to back down, it is likely that the economy would be severely disrupted by the multinationals. For the government to stand its ground, it would probably have to take direct control of large sectors of the domestic economy and mobilize popular support. It seems most likely that victory in the conflict with the multinationals would lead quickly to full socialization of the domestic economy, because the government and its supporters would have lost patience with the prerogatives of private capital. If, on the other hand, the multinationals were victorious, the society would likely return to liberal capitalist principles.

If the national capitalist form of insulation is no longer viable, that still leaves two other ideal types from the 1930s and 1940s: fascism and socialism. While it is naive to anticipate a form of fascism identical with its earlier incarnations, the basic outlines of Nazi economic policy in the pre-Second World War period remain a viable, but temporary, solution to the problems facing developed capitalist nations today. In the fascist form of insulation, the nation does not close itself off from international transactions, but it uses the state to organize those trans-actions to maximize the national wealth with little regard for the "rules of the game" of liberal capitalism. The state works closely with the nation's most powerful firms to boost exports, expand access to cheap foreign raw materials, and increase the return of profits from overseas operations. This might be combined with strict controls on other capital flows and restrictions on foreign multinationals operating within the nation's boundaries. Those measures are backed by an aggressive foreign policy that makes full use of military and political threats to intimidate weaker nations. A large share of the nation's resources is devoted to military purposes, and a garrison society that represses dissent is constructed on the grounds of severe external threats.

The logic of this solution is that the problem of stagflation would be resolved by military spending and direct government intervention to control wage levels. The control of wages would require a direct assault on the trade union movement, which could be justified by the external crisis. At the same time, the aggressive foreign economic policy could help relieve internal pressures by providing resources to appease certain sectors of the population. While this neofascist form of insula-tion would require a sharp break with current policies and an increased danger of war, it still remains a possibility, because it provides immedi-ate solutions to a number of interlocking problems. In other words, the danger of fascism cannot be lightly dismissed, because it provides measures to resolve temporarily the contradictions created by liberal capitalism.

Another response to these contradictions is the final form of insula-tion, the socialist solution. Socialism eliminates the problems created by national capitalism because it combines strict governmental control over all international transactions with socialization of the domestic economy. It does not require the aggressive foreign economic policies of fascism, because the radical reorganization of the domestic economy can bring the national economy closer to self-sufficiency. Socialism can exist in more authoritarian or in more democratic forms, but all forms would employ centralized control over international transactions with the criteria for decision-making based on a comprehensive economic plan designed to optimize certain goals. Authoritarian and democratic socialism would differ in the ways in which the goals and techniques of the economic plan would be formulated. In authoritarian forms, the political elites have broad opportunities to direct the planning process in their own favor. In a democratic form of socialism, popular participation in the decision-making process could work to assure a close fit between the plan and the actual needs of the population.

The ideal of socialism has been that humanity would one day be able collectively and consciously to control economic processes, rather than remain subject to the whims of uncontrollable natural and market forces. The struggle by the United States to restore an open world economy in the period after the Second World War has created a world system in which those market forces increasingly conflict with the welfare of the world's population. If our goal today is the improvement of human welfare, this requires subordinating market forces to conscious human will, but there are profound dangers if that will is exercised predominantly by new or existing elites. Only democratic socialism holds the promise of fulfilling the historic goal of conscious and collective control of the economy.

Notes

1. I am arguing that inflation is the visible manifestation of the contradictions of advanced capitalism, in the same way that periodic economic crises were the indication of contradictions in classical capitalism. This means that there is no single cause of inflation, but it can be traced in a variety of ways to the contradiction of private appropriation of socially created value. This view of inflation draws on Andrew Glyn and Bob Sutcliffe, *Capitalism in Crisis* (New York: Pantheon, 1972); James O'Connor, *The Fiscal Crisis of the State* (New York: St Martin's Press, 1973); Jacob Morris, "The Crisis of Inflation," *Monthly Review*, 25 (September 1973), pp. 1–22.
2. This was the problem with Britain's stop–go policies.
3. These problems are analyzed in Richard N. Cooper, *The Economics of Interdependence* (New York: McGraw-Hill, 1968), especially pp. 139–47.
4. See, for example, Fred Block and David Plotke, "Food Prices," *Socialist Revolution* 16 (July–August 1973), pp. 89–98.
5. See *Wall Street Journal* (September 23, 1975) (Arthur Laffer).
6. Germany has been the most important low-inflation country using these arrangements in recent years. See William Pollard Wadbrook, *West German Balance-of-Payments Policy* (New York: Praeger, 1972).

7. "Since restoration of international balance typically calls for a decline in total expenditures, attempts to preserve real income (and expenditure) will frustrate the currency depreciation, higher wages will lead to higher prices leading to further currency depreciation, and so on in an endless cycle." (Cooper, *The Economics of Interdependence, op. cit.*, p. 233)

   See also *Wall Street Journal* (January 10, 1974) (Arthur Laffer).

8. For an analysis of the inflationary consequences of recent floating rates, see John Hewson and Eisuke Sakakibara, *The Eurocurrency Markets and Their Implications* (Lexington, Mass.: D. C. Heath, 1975), Chapter 5.

9. Eric Chalmers, *International Interest Rate War* (London: Macmillan, 1972), documents the way in which countries raised their interest rates competitively during the 1960s. This kind of interest-rate competition has serious inflationary consequences.

10. For example, further efforts by Third World countries to improve their position within the world economy will involve renewed strains on the developed economies and the international financial structure. It is quite possible also that some underdeveloped nations will be forced to repudiate some of their foreign debts, which could have a devastating impact on international finance.

11. The coordination I am describing would have to go far beyond the rather limited cooperation developed within the OECD, the Group of Ten, and the Bank for International Settlements. It would also have to be far more extensive and elaborate than the types of coordination agreed on at the Rambouillet Summit. *New York Times* (November 19 and 23, 1975).

12. The belief that the flowering of the multinationals can overcome the tensions between nation states is a modern version of the argument made before the First World War by Kautsky. Kautsky argued that the increasing interpenetration of capital across national boundaries created a kind of "ultraimperialism" that would make national conflicts fade into insignificance given the shared interests of international capital. Lenin polemicized against Kautsky's position on the grounds that uneven development would assure that any particular divisions of the spoils would sooner or later prove unsatisfactory to some imperialist powers, and a period of renewed conflict would ensue to revise the international arrangements. Kautsky, "Ultraimperialism" [1914], *New Left Review*, 59 (1970), pp. 41–6; V. I. Lenin, *Imperialism: The Highest Stage of Capitalism* (New York: International Publishers, [1917] 1939). A number of recent writers have taken the development of the multinationals as evidence that the Kautskian position has finally been vindicated; the grounds for intercapitalist conflict have been eliminated. See Stephen Hymer and Robert Rowthorn, "Multinational Corporations and International Oligopoly: The Non-American Challenge," in C. P. Kindleberger (ed.), *The International Corporation* (Cambridge, Mass.: MIT Press, 1970), pp. 57–91; Martin Nicolaus, "The Universal Contradiction," *New Left Review*, 59 (1970), pp. 3–19. My argument is much closer to the position of Lenin and of Ernest Mandel, *Europe Versus America?* (London: New Left Books, 1970). The key empirical issue, however, is the degree to which present international corporations derive critical political and military support from the government of their home country.

13. The ideology of multinationals being above politics is described in Richard J. Barnet and Ronald E. Müller, *Global Reach* (New York: Simon & Schuster, 1974), pp. 56–64. The multinational utopia is effectively critiqued in David Calleo and Benjamin M. Rowland, *America and the World Political Economy* (Bloomington: Indiana University Press, 1973), pp. 186–91.

14. Barnet and Müller, *Global Reach, op. cit.*, pp. 72–104. This support extends both to emergency actions, such as defense against expropriation, and the day-to-day operations of forcing foreign governments not to discriminate against a particular firm. Examples of these latter forms of influence appear occasionally in the business press. For one involving a firm that has been outspoken in its anti-nationalism, see *Wall Street Journal* (October 16, 1975).

15. The extended period during which Britain retreated from a global role would seem to indicate the difficulties in a policy of retrenchment. In fact, Britain's retreats were forced on it by a series of sterling crises. See Susan Strange, *Sterling and British Policy* (London: Oxford University Press, 1971).

16. The fluctuations in exchange rates have been a significant obstacle to the development of closer economic integration in Western Europe, see Arthur I. Bloomfield, "The Historical Setting," in Lawrence B. Krause and Walter S. Salant (eds), *European Monetary Unification* (Washington, DC: Brookings, 1973), pp. 1–30.

17. The intensity of Japanese antimilitarism is discussed in Robert E. Osgood, *The Weary and the Wary: United States and Japanese Security Policies in Transition* (Baltimore: Johns Hopkins University Press, 1972), pp. 19–23.

18. What has changed since the 1930s is that it is now recognized that governments have the capacity to restore some reasonable level of economic activity without radically altering the economic system. That this is widely understood makes it unlikely that a modern depression would last as long as the depression of the 1930s.

19. This is what happened in the German financial crisis of 1931 when France held out for political concessions as the price of cooperation in rescuing the mark.

20. In my view, it is unlikely that the critical decision to refuse to cooperate in crisis-management would be made by a country such as Iran or Saudi Arabia. These nations, despite their oil wealth, lack the muscle to take disruptive action, particularly because they are so heavily dependent on the world market. Even if they did take such action, a united front of the developed countries would be sufficient to manage the crisis. In short, a crisis that began with underdeveloped nations could escalate out of control only if it occurred simultaneously with a major division among the major developed nations.

21. These "types" are the same ones that Polanyi described as responses to the depression of the 1930s: Karl Polanyi, *The Great Transformation* [1944] (Boston: Beacon Press, 1957), pp. 237–48.

18
American Society Since the Golden Age of Capitalism (1987)[*]

Joseph Bensman and Arthur J. Vidich

The period from the end of the Second World War to 1965 has been called the Golden Age of Western Capitalism. By Western capitalism we mean the capitalism of the United States, Western Europe, and Japan. During that period, capitalism had reconstituted itself and solved the internal and external problems brought about by the Great Depression and by Fascism and Nazism.

Since 1965 these countries have experienced economic, political and social crises, including a crisis of legitimacy. These crises are characterized by unemployment, inflation, and the collapse of the international economic system. In part these crises were brought about by the failure of the international monetary system established after the Second World War and its inability to deal with such problems as inflation and the oil crisis. But in addition, the crisis has expressed itself in a failure to recapitalize American industry to sustain efficient industrial production and in new demands placed upon the economic system by previously unfavored groups. Previous successes in the Golden Age caused both rising expectations and a new democratic sense that all groups should experience a share in the prosperity of the Golden Age including the expectation of previously deprived groups that they make up for their past deprivation.

The failure to meet these expectations led, in the 1960s and 1970s, to a decline of civility, anomic riots and segmental political explosions. Modern western capitalism has thus become politically less stable, subject to wide and often unpredictable sources of disturbance, violence, bombings and riots generated by often short-lived, relatively

---

* From *American Society: The Welfare State and Beyond* (South Hadley, Mass.: Bergin & Garvey, 1987), pp. 313–36.

small political, ideological, religious, ethnic and nationalistic movements and fads.

This synoptic summary outlines political phenomena of the late 1960s and early 1970s; but to understand these phenomena more fully one would first have to understand the Golden Age of the post-war period. ...

The post-Second World War expansion and prosperity was to a large extent underwritten by United States governmental deficit funding and monetary and taxation policies which subsidized not only the industrial expansion that guaranteed new markets but created and expanded new occupational classes. These new classes were in the service industries, especially governmental, in education, and in white collar managerial occupations. The expansion of these categories which were primarily absorbed as lower and middle level bureaucrats has led further to an expansion of leisure and culture and the industries designed to service them. The increase in white collar, service, managerial, administrative, and professional occupations far exceeded the declines in employment in basic industries and agriculture and unemployment as a problem appeared to be solved.

This expansion, from the standpoint of western capitalism as a whole, was not only American, but involved the economic and political penetration of American institutions into all areas of the world, but especially among the Western European nations and other industrialized areas, excluding Russia and China. Similar processes of expansion occurred in all of these countries partly as the result of loan and aid programs. But such expansion appears to be part of a generalized process that seems to have occurred with some leads and lags at different levels in various areas of the entire world, excluding only China and Albania. It is difficult to determine whether American expansion was the cause of these worldwide trends, but one can say with some degree of certainty that where this expansion occurred its effects in any one country reinforced similar effects in other countries. Thus relatively continuous and stable expansion occurred at economic, political and cultural levels in the western capitalist world during the period from 1945–1965.

The overall expansion in the United States that was almost without interruption for 20 years led first to a sense of new opportunities for previously unfavored groups such as blacks, youth, working classes, and new immigrants, and in the cases of older working class groups, especially ethnic working classes and their children, the realization of new opportunities. For the older generation of industrial workers, the new opportunities were seen as a symbol of arrival and acceptance. In spite of the Great Depression, America had redeemed much of its promise by giving them steady work at relatively high wages, seniority in unionized plants, and consumer's durables such as home ownership, automobiles, television, and home appliances. This has been called people's capitalism. For their children, those entering young adulthood in the 1960s, these new opportunities were increasingly taken for granted because they had been reared in an environment of prosperity. Thus for them the prosperity was seen as the basis for making further demands on the "system."

Of course, the rising expectations that were a result of the expansion and prosperity were not evenly spread across the national class structure or the society. Regional, national and international variations occurred. What can be said at most is that those groups who in their own life time experienced the sense of opportunity earliest in point of time, age, and generation stabilized their expectations earliest and tended to use that stabilized standard as a floor from which to make further demands. Thus the achievement of "success" tended to "pacify" the older working class who realized in their own lifetimes more material property than they had expected, and to dissatisfy both their children and other groups who either took that success for granted – and did not regard it as success – or entered the economic scene too late to participate in the affluence of the Golden Age.

A major aspect of the Golden Age at its economic and institutional level was that it was the product of both conscious and unstated agreements among the various *organized* political and economic segments of society. Those agreements were that the respective parties to them would practice restraint on their demands on the system, would respect each other's "rights" and would not attack the system as a whole. It meant that organized labor would not make excessive wage demands upon industry, that industry would not make excessive price demands upon the public, and that government through tax and monetary policy would provide a basic expansive economic framework and would referee the economic demands of all parties by jawboning, mediation, and defining and enforcing price and wage guidelines. In accepting this overall framework, the various parties to the agreements accepted the legitimacy of the new forms of Keynesian state capitalism.

Less organized groups in the society such as the middle classes, farmers, youth, and to a much less extent minority groups were "bought off" by favorable agricultural, educational and social welfare policies.

Yet by 1968, the system had begun to collapse and its collapse was made manifest by 1970, reaching extreme proportions in the economic decline of 1972–1973. By this time in the United States an annual inflation rate of 12 per cent and an unemployment rate reaching its high point ... seemed to signal the collapse of the Keynesian system of state capitalism. Radical critics saw this as a new failure of capitalism, the long deferred crises or contradiction of capitalism, or as a failure of the Keynesian solution to the contradiction of capitalism. Even those who had no ideological interest in seeing capitalism collapse, began to doubt whether the patchwork, Keynesian pragmatism constructed by Franklin Roosevelt and maintained and expanded by Truman, Eisenhower, Kennedy, and especially Johnson could continue to work.

Some academicians, segments of middle class youth, blacks, and Spanish-speaking radical groups began even earlier in the 1960s to reject a political–economic system which had been engineered partly for them without their consent by an establishment that appeared to control the system. At present it is even fashionable to predict the end of the system, capitalism, and even western civilization. Prophets of despair who are not necessarily Marxists become the profiteers of doom, even if that doom is to arrive a hundred years or more in the future.

The question of whether the collapse of Keynesian state capitalism is permanent is perhaps the most profound question of our times. If it has collapsed, the consequences may be too far reaching and frightful to contemplate by all but committed romantic radicals, for the collapse would be more than a collapse of an economic and political arrangement, and could be, as viewed by some, the collapse of western civilization itself.

Whether in fact the system is collapsing or whether its recurring crises are merely re-adjustments of the western world system is the problem that now faces the United States only two centuries after the founding of the Republic and the publication of *The Wealth of Nations*.

We will first analyze in some detail more of the dynamics of the western system in order to trace out some additional causes of its apparent failure.

Sources of strain in Keynesian state capitalism

The system of relatively full employment which was a consequence of Keynesian institutional arrangements caused, by its very nature, a gradual and continuous wage and price inflation. Relatively full employment has always resulted in pressures to raise wages, and high levels of consumption result in pressure on prices. Through the entire period of the 1950s and 1960s continuous rises in prices at about a 3 per cent level were part of the consequence of the sustained prosperity, even when pressures for prices and wage increases were restrained by the implicit and explicit agreements upon which rests the political basis of the Keynesian political economy.

Increased levels of inflation were a product of the Vietnam war when military budgets of [$]25–35 billion were met by deficit spending rather than by new taxation, causing higher demand and prices than would otherwise have occurred. Moreover, the Vietnam war led large numbers of youth and ultimately the liberal middle classes to become disenchanted with or to reject the political framework which previously had supported them in their educational aspirations and lifestyles. At the same time, the continuing inflation caused substantial segments of the business community to question not only the Vietnam war but also the terms of the political and economic agreements they had made with organized labor and the administrators of wage–price guidelines. Throughout the 1960s a substantial segment of the business community began to inquire into the level of unemployment that would be appropriate to control inflation and produce a disciplined labor force. The estimates ranged from $1^1/_2$ per cent early in the period to 3–4 per cent by the mid 1960s.

When Richard Nixon became President the proposals to create a reserve pool of unemployment in order to lessen wage pressures and to diminish demand could be turned into policy directives. During President Nixon's first term the primary device used to control inflation and induce the necessary unemployment was monetary policy. Interest rates were raised with the hope that such increases in capital costs would limit expansion and thus halt inflation. Whether in fact these policies worked is difficult to estimate. Certainly unemployment increased, but the rate of inflation also increased. Moreover, it is not easy to ascertain whether the rate of inflation would have had an ever-greater increase without such policies, but one can be sure that increased interest costs were inflationary with regard to short-term investment. Investors with short-term capital hoped that the increased capital costs would be absorbed by even greater rates of inflation. If the inflation rate was greater than the interest rate, inflation would then pay off the increased capital costs at a profit. Long-term investment at a 10 per cent interest rate on money borrowed especially in plants which required long periods of time to construct (such as an atomic energy plant which might require 7–9 years to build) would make the costs prohibitive. Yet the effect of cutting expansion in these areas was not necessarily deflationary in the long run because high interest costs so incurred would discourage other production by making investment capital less available in areas where increased production would take off the market the expendable income that was in itself inflationary. The productivity that could result from lower interest rates would result in lower costs and would create the additional commodities that would absorb the excess expendable income and eliminate excess unmet demands as a source of inflationary pressure.

In the late 1960s the expectation by businessmen of still higher interest rates resulted in a flow of capital into Western Europe and a decline in long-term capital investments in heavy industry in the United States. Businessmen were followed in making foreign investments by institutional investors and money managers who saw opportunities for quick profits in European and Japanese money markets because of a continuing decline in the value of the dollar relative to other currencies. The already existing large stock of dollars in international markets which had accumulated throughout the period 1945–1965 were increased too by these new exports of business capital and resulted in a further decline of the value of the dollar. In addition hopes of even higher interest rates resulted in competitive investing in commercial paper with little or no productive result, and a rise in the cost of government borrowing especially for municipalities and state governments. By 1970, the outward flow of capital was so great that American exports were no longer competitive on the world's markets and the United States had accumulated embarrassingly large trade deficits which were the result in part of high levels of imports encouraged by domestic inflation. This forced a de facto devaluation of the American dollar which was the basis of the international monetary system. It further forced a formal devaluation by President Nixon in 1970 which tended to increase American domestic prices, encourage American exports and thus caused further inflation within the United States.

Both the inflation (whatever its causes) and President Nixon's electoral victory in 1972 ended the implicit political and economic agreements that constituted the basis of the Golden Age of American Capitalism. Prior to 1968, Democratic administrations and even the Eastern Republican establishment tended to restrain themselves with respect to increasing prices and taking a positive attitude towards labor. The small margin of the Republican victory in 1968 meant that an overall change in policy could not be conspicuously undertaken. In fact, President Nixon was careful to announce, "I am a Keynesian," at the same time that he began to subvert the agreements that were the basis of a Keynesian political economy. But while President Nixon maintained the rhetoric and the substance of Keynesian policy, he drastically changed the direction of that policy to favor certain segments of the business class, especially those on the outer rim. When businessmen recognized this shift in orientation and realized that the administration was favorable to their economic demands they felt free to increase prices without the restraints of wage–price guidelines. The Nixon administration subverted price and wage controls by eliminating limits on the price of raw materials, and on profits and dividends. This policy of leaky controls invited successive price increases, made mockery of the 5 per cent statutory ceilings on wages and prices, and subjected only labor to its restraints. One can speculate that the wage–price control legislation was designed to fail. In part the approval for price increases was purchased by political contributions; in part businessmen may have understood that their past contributions assured a lack of interference with a policy of price inflation whether such policies were the result of explicit agreements or not.

From 1970 onwards, at increasing levels raids upon the consumer were organized first by smaller and later by big business. These raids were expressed in raising prices of milk, sugar, grains, meat, coffee, and soy beans. In part, some of these raids were the product of natural disasters in producing areas which, however, became a source of unusual profits for processors, distributors, and retailers. Others were the result of economic mismanagement as in the case of the sale of American grain to Russia and China – although some of the mismanagement must be seen as part of a public relations effort designed to further detente and to deflect attention away from Nixon's growing domestic problems.

The precipitating events of the depression of 1973–1974 were twofold: (1) the oil crisis and (2) the automobile price increases of 1973 and 1974. The oil crisis perhaps reflects the end product of a series of bungled attempts by American oil companies to avoid paying corporation taxes in the United States. To avoid domestic taxes the oil consortia arranged to have the oil producing countries change the label of what previously had been royalties into taxes: taxes to be paid to foreign governments could be subtracted from taxes to be paid to the government of the United States. In order to make this change, it was first necessary for the oil drilling companies to work out a uniform pricing and taxing scale among the oil producing countries. This meant that the previously disorganized and often hostile oil producing countries had to be organized, and it was undoubtedly the organizing genius of the American oil companies and the American State Department that made OPEC possible. This organizational achievement together with the withdrawal of the British Navy from the Persian Gulf and Indian Ocean made the Arabian Gulf states autonomous and permitted a unity among the Arab states which they had until then never been able to achieve. The first result of this unity was the expropriation of higher and higher per centages of the ownership of the oil drilling countries. The next [was], after the Arab–Israel war of 1973, the oil embargo followed by a ten-fold increase in oil prices. The oil companies themselves compounded the problem by withholding delivery of in-shipment oil for American markets at the time of the crisis, creating further shortages that justified still larger price increases. Part of the strategy behind such withholding may have been the desire to raise the price of domestic oil and to de-regulate the natural gases. In these aspects then the action of the oil companies was another raid against the American consumer. The OPEC countries in following a policy of restriction of output, cartelization of production, and managed prices were pursuing a similar policy, though their methods resembled more the methods of the Standard Oil companies of the first decade of the 20th century. They had learned this lesson too from American monopoly capitalism.

From another point of view, the lesson of the oil crisis is that the Keynesian system is an international system which involves a policy of mutual self-restraint on the part of all of its participants, international as well as domestic. The OPEC countries as part of that international system, like the oil companies and an increasing part of American domestic and international corporations, rejected the restraint of a Keynesian system.

The immediate effect of the politics of oil was to fuel inflation not only in the direct costs of heating and transportation but in the total petrochemical industry that contributes to the cost of agricultural products, plastics, and the industrial uses of energy.

The automobile companies exceeded the greed of the raw materials producers by raising prices 8 per cent in 1973 and 11 per cent in 1974. But unlike foods, the purchase of an automobile is postponable, and the immediate effect of increases in automobile prices of almost $2,000 per car was a drastic decline in automobile production and large-scale unemployment in the automobile and related industries.

This occurred at almost the same time that oil companies used the oil crisis as a screen for the consolidation and rationalization of the retail sales of gasoline. This entailed the elimination of independent gasoline retailers and single pump chain outlets in many rural parts of the country where these had existed since the 1920s and 1930s.

By 1973, unemployment had reached the level of 8.7 per cent and inflation an annual level of 12 per cent. In 1986 unemployment hovers a round 7 per cent and a non-inflationary equilibrium has been reached at much higher levels of prices, but not wages. This equilibrium, however, is threatened by large trade imbalances and the high carrying costs of the national debt.

Social and political aspects of economic strains

This historical overview of economic policy does not account for political changes which preceded and to a large extent helped to explain the economic changes. The reaction to the Vietnam war and the revolution of rising expectations among minority groups which in part was a product of court decisions, the civil rights legislation of the early 1960s, and the war on poverty, caused a backlash in the election of 1968 which was expressed in more intensified form in the election of 1972.

It is difficult to determine whether President Nixon's response to students and urban riots in the 1968–1972 period was purely a calculated attempt to profit from the anxieties of the American middle class concerning the cultural and political revolution of the time or whether honest political righteousness was the dominant factor in the dirty tricks, Watergate crisis. Certainly a great many of President Nixon's house staff defended their crimes on the basis that only a Nixon victory in 1972 could save the United States from subversion or revolution. The two sets of motivations could have operated separately as apparently they did, and neither of these motives appeared to conflict with a determined policy of President Nixon to reward contributors or extort contributions in exchange for actual or implicit rights to raid both the treasury and the consumer.

But Watergate was more than either political righteousness or campaign politics, for it violated the very basis for legitimacy underpinning much of the American political system. The notion that government is responsible to its own laws has been a cardinal principle in American society no matter how often it has been dishonored in practice. It has been the basis for the cry "Turn the rascals out" from the time of ... the defalcations of Sherman Adams and General Vaughan. But even given the negative reactions by large segments of the American middle and working classes to the youth and black rebellions of the late 1960s, the American public had a vast reluctance to turn the then most recent rascal out. Only the Saturday night massacre, the firing of Archibald Cox, and the resignation of Elliot Richardson produced a constitutional crisis which, in turn, was intensified by the televising of the Ervin hearings and the publication of the tapes. Perhaps President Nixon's obscenity and the cold, calculating nature of his contempt for his subordinates, colleagues, and the public was enough to produce the demand for impeachment and to force his resignation.

But the basic data about dirty tricks, the Watergate and Ellsberg break-ins, political favors for campaign contributions, as well as assaults on the press and political opposition were widely known, but not documented by public hearings, before the election of 1972. The Democratic congress, the general public, and even Nixon supporters were not impelled toward taking action against the President until the continuously unfolding pattern of public exposure left these groups no other choice than to press for impeachment or forced resignation. Prior to the Saturday night massacre, the public was led by the belief that can be summarized as "Say it ain't so, Joe." No one wanted to believe that the President could be so despicable; or if he was, no one in office wanted to be the first to say so. In part, the refusal to accept the increasingly documented charges against President Nixon and his administration was based upon the acceptance by some groups of the argument that strong measures were necessary to repress the youth and black rebellions. Other groups were prone to accept the Nixon political strategy as part of the cost for favorable social and economic policies, and of possible international gains.

In short, Nixon in his economic and social policy was meeting the basic desires of a large part of the middle and upper classes, including their desire to curb some of the effects of the rise in expectations of youth and minority groups. But, in addition, President Nixon's policy of repression of youthful demonstrations against the Vietnam war, of the new moralities of rampant drugs, sexuality, dropping out and communalism, the rhetoric of black liberation, urban disorder and crime in the streets also were the source of anxieties for the lower middle and ethnic working classes as well as almost all classes in the rural fringes in the South and Southwest and in the small town heartland of mid-America.

Certainly, the anxieties of these groups could be catered to by cut-backs of poverty and welfare programs and of support to university education and the withdrawal of federal funds from cities with high densities of minority ethnic groups, especially in the industrial and Democratic northeast. Moreover, the expression of these anxieties and aggressiveness toward those groups who appeared to provoke the anxi-eties could be expressed in cuts in budgets of those programs that appeared to subsidize and support them. As a result, taxes could be cut and the incomes of favored groups maintained in a time of rising prices and budgetary squeezes by cutting expenditures on those who were regarded as socially, economically, or morally useless or danger-ous. Thus the righteousness generated by hostility to the disturbers of the American dream as it was experienced by those who supported Nixon could be used in justifying economic policies which the embat-tled lower middle, middle and upper classes would support anyway. They could put all their rotten eggs in one basket.

The anxieties exposed by the black and youth rebellions permitted political attacks on the press, the liberal establishment, on congres-sional autonomy and on a federal bureaucracy which was largely a hold-over from the eight preceding years of Democratic administra-tions. President Nixon thus attempted to make these anxieties the basis of a total policy that would undermine all opposition to whatever poli-cies he happened to support at the moment, but especially the opposi-tion to the East Asian war that he had pledged to end.

The resignation of President Nixon solved for that moment the prob-lems of political corruption and political legitimation. President Ford's emphasis on clean politics and on fair political tactics seemed initially to obscure all other issues including the issues of inflation, stagnation and the rising demands for political benefits by minority groups, blacks, environmentalists, and the exponents of the new cultural poli-tics such as women, homosexuals, and lesbians.

President Ford may well have been an accidental president or, if one wishes to see it so, the political fall-out of Watergate. In terms of econ-omic policy, he presented a substantially different approach from that of President Nixon. Nixon appeared primarily to be attempting to corrupt and deflect the Keynesian state system in order to reward polit-ical supporters of a new political establishment he was in the process of creating. President Ford, if one accepted both his political statements and his congressional record, appeared to be fundamentally opposed to the very idea of a Keynesian political economy. His rhetoric was that of deregulation and dismemberment of the bureaucratic governmental establishment, of support of the individualistic entrepreneur no matter how little the individual exists as an economic force and how greatly the corporation so exists, and of budget and tax cutting to provide discretionary income disposal for those groups thus freed from taxes and regulatory controls. To be sure his apparent natural inclinations were supported and encouraged by the apparently stronger rhetorical individualism of Ronald Reagan. Both appealed to those groups who felt they were overconstrained by the Keynesian political formula and both go back to a political rhetoric which was expressed in recent times only by Senator Goldwater in 1964 and by Alf Landon in 1936. Yet, it is not political tradition, by itself, that determines policy, for the inflation of the mid-1960s has to some extent affected everyone. The problem emerges is: who is to bear the cost of inflation?

The major issue in American society since at least 1970 is to find some group other than one's own on which to displace these costs. Cuts in taxes, especially income and corporate taxes, place the increasing costs of inflation in the hands of others than those who have the greatest income. The addition of regressive taxes, especially social security taxes, increases the burden on those who have the least income. Cuts in welfare payments, of course, have hurt the "unworthy" poor and especially those unworthy poor who have made their poverty the basis for political demands. The termination of poverty programs has hurt the blacks and Spanish minorities who have dared to make their presence felt and who are "collectively" reputedly "responsible" for violence in the streets. At the same time increased budgets have been allocated to law enforcement agencies and institutions. Cuts in educational expenditures for students and research programs have disadvantaged working and middle class youth and their professors while research funds have been made increasingly available to applied sciences and to industry. To the extent that educational programs may be encouraged, they are designed to facilitate career education when unemployment makes careers more difficult to find.

Cut-backs in aid to the cities have the effect of penalizing all of the above groups, but especially the ethnic minorities who increasingly reside in the city. The suburbs and exurbs which are populated primarily by middle classes are largely exempt from such cuts. And these latter groups are likely to support such cuts justifying their support on the grounds of the law-abiding character and righteousness of the suburban and exurban way of life.

In the meantime, the cities have had to bear the burden of increased welfare payments caused by earlier migration from rural areas, and of maintaining the urban commercial and cultural facilities and services for commuters and tourists. They have had to absorb the rising wage costs of the urban civil service that partially maintains and supports the less favored groups mentioned above.

These cut-backs of urban services and urban welfare constitute a reversal of Keynesian fiscal policy of the Golden Age wherein the expansion of service industries and employment was one of the chief objectives of Keynesian economic policy. In addition the high interest rates designed to curb inflation have represented an increasing set of costs to municipal and state governments which, as a result, have been forced to further cut benefits to those groups that would otherwise have been supported by traditional Keynesianism.

American society in the Golden Age was a society based on continuous expansion, and part of that expansion was produced by deficit financing with the expectation that a continuously rising gross national product would cover the costs of borrowed capital. So long as gross national product rose, the method of financing would succeed. The recession of 1973–1974 made this policy unworkable and produced an urban crisis as municipal and state costs continued to rise because the earlier commitments were long-term ones and government income declined as a result of the downturn in gross national product. The cities, especially those in the Northeast, were forced to refinance high interest rate debt at a time of declining tax bases and revenues. The decline in part has been generated by a long-term flight of middle classes to suburbs and a shift of industry to the suburbs which in part were financed or supported by federal highway and tax policy. As a result cities, up to now only in the Northeast, are increasingly forced to cut services and employment in major areas of municipal social programs and services at a time when mass employment in other segments of industry has not yet reabsorbed previous unemployment created in other sectors by industrial cutbacks in the period 1972–1974.

In part the decline of cities in the Northeast is caused by a flight of industry and jobs to the "sunbelt." The expansion in the latter area is partly the result of federal support of defense industries, and partly a result of the flight of industry to less unionized parts of the country and to places where lower levels of economic development have resulted in low taxes and the willingness of underdeveloped areas to assume part of the initial costs of such development.

Societal trends in an economy of scarcity

Whether these fiscal and moral crises are a permanent part of American life is yet to be assayed. Energy prices are not likely to return to pre-

1973 prices, though their major inflationary effects have already been absorbed in present price structures. At the same time, the industrial world is still vulnerable to the same kinds of economic warfare and price uncertainty of that earlier period. The exploitation of new energy sources, whether oil fields in Alaska, the North Sea, Mexico, Korea, etc., do not as yet guarantee energy independence let alone lower prices since these areas are being explored and developed in the expectation that present or higher prices will prevail. The exploitation of American coal reserves has not proceeded at a rate sufficient to assure freedom from dependence on imported oil, and atomic energy appears to be a victim of high interest rates and the lack of the ability of engineers to solve the major technical problems necessary for competitively efficient production, not to mention problems of safety and waste disposal. Solar energy so far appears to be a public relations solution to the energy problem.

The effect of the fiscal crisis of the cities has not yet been felt in its full intensity and in the extent of its full diffusion throughout the country.

The most resistant indicator of a return to previous economic levels has been unemployment levels which since late 1974 have remained at between $9\frac{1}{2}$ and 8 per cent and which have dropped only slowly and in small decrements over the past twelve years.

Other economic consequences of a declining rate of expansion are still to be felt. Throughout the 1950s and 1960s the educational establishment has been geared to producing an increasing proportion of the total population for college entrance and the achievement of baccalaureate and higher degrees. The assumption behind this expansion was that of a continuous expansion in the service segments of the society which was to be financed primarily by government. It was also supported by the expansion of the white collar and bureaucratic structure of industry. However, by the late 1960s the number of white collar, bureaucratic, administrative, managerial and technical jobs appeared to have become stabilized. Even as this stabilization was occurring, the educational system and the expectations of youth were premised on the assumption that the same rate of expansion would continue. Since the early 1970s educational institutions have been turning out degree holders for whom there are proportionately fewer and fewer jobs at the level for which the students are presumably prepared. The educational planners and youth have solved this problem by preparing students for taking jobs for which less and less preparation is necessary. Thus the college educated population increasingly takes jobs that previously did not require degrees, and degree holders work in marginal jobs, combinations of part-time jobs, arts and crafts, street vending jobs, are unemployed, or try to stay in college while waiting for jobs to become available.

The short-run effects of the new scarcity are curious and contradictory. The experience of scarcity is a new experience for most youth in the United States. The twenty-year revolution of rising expectations has been reversed by a decline in actual opportunity. In the short run youth has become desperate to get into the economic system before further declines in opportunity occur. This has tended to defuse the youth rebellion: an increasingly large per centage of youth attempt to become square and meet square occupational demands by minimal conformance. Because of these economic realities, youth increasingly express their dissatisfaction through forms of personal and cultural expression. While dress and tonsorial styles have become increasingly subdued in relation to the demands of the square market, the demands have been modified by employers because of their own habituation to the wearing of more extreme styles. Youth dissatisfaction thus takes the form of non-work related personal and cultural consumption. Hence, the smoking of pot becomes more and more acceptable though there appears to be a decline in hallucinogenic and hard drugs. These concessions and modifications have been a concession to the reality of the market place.

At another level non-conformance is expressed in new forms of sexual arrangements including open living together on the part of large numbers, grouping in urban and rural households, network systems of sexuality and commensalism, overt lesbian families, and out of the closet homosexuality and same-sex marriages.

At the other extreme there are whole new systems of religious commitment and affiliation. These include attachment to new combinations of theology, mysticism, asceticism, communalism derived from Buddhism, Hinduism, primitive Christianity, early Judaism and Mohammadanism. In addition there has been a revival and expansion of earlier Anabaptist traditions as expressed in Jehovah's Witnesses, Seventh Day Adventists, Southern Baptists, and other Protestant traditions exemplified by such figures as Oral Roberts, Billy Graham, and the Reverend Moon. At a more secular level are the whole range of quasi-religions including Scientology, Transcendental Meditation, co-counseling, psychological groupies, Erhard seminar training, and encounter grouping. At a still more secular level are Kung-fu, Karate, and other forms of physical fitness perfectionisms.

All of these forms of religion are not to be taken as simple aberrations and deviations. They represent at the most intimate and fundamental levels a rejection of rational industrial society, but this rejection does not constitute a direct political confrontation. They permit believers to live simultaneously within and outside the society by segmenting their public and private lives. They represent a more radical alternative to mass media consumption which attempts to accomplish the same purposes though managed from above and lived vicariously. At the personal and cultural levels these alternative life styles may well represent a radical rejection of the whole tradition of western society without particularly attacking its organizational or political structure. This change could well be a profound break with our past and appears to be independent of immediate fluctuations of the business cycle.

The new disenchantment

The prospects of long-term permanent unemployment of large segments of youth and blacks after a period of (a) rising expectations or (b) a desperate desire to "get back in" may have more disturbing implications. If it appears that it is impossible to get back in, then a sizeable segment of both black and new middle class populations may find it difficult to make ideological and cultural compromises with the system. A long-term prospect for American and Western society is that a permanently disaffected group may exist in the midst of an imperfectly stabilized neo-Keynesian society.

In urban areas this may mean a return to urban violence, greater growth of upper class ghettos to complement the existing lower class ghettos, and patterns of residential segregation and fortification which deny the existence of the city as an entity.

At the national and international scene, organized small scale adventurism appears to be a permanent way of life for some disaffected youth and some racial, minority, and ethnic groups. The level of organization and size of such groups may be so low, however, that a solution to the damage these groups cause may not exist. Sporadic violence, bombings, assassinations, and terrorism come to be accepted as part of the permanent cost of living in industrial society.

The problems in the underdeveloped world will undoubtedly be worse. There, problems of political instability will compete with problems of starvation, famine, genocide, and large-scale organized political extremism. The Western world could try to survive by making itself into a fortress hoping to isolate itself from the problems of the under-developed world, but not from its resources.

Whether the domestic and international problems of the United States and western society are solvable is an open question, but a pre-condition for an approach to their solution depends upon maintaining high levels of employment and productivity within a world of decreasing natural resources and increasing competition for them. It would appear that they might be solvable only if approached from a world-wide perspective, which seems even more dubious. But again, if they can be solved, they can only be solved when the underdeveloped world is given and is prepared to receive the benefits and the procedures of western technology and the constraints that accompany them. All but a few nations of the world are committed to industrialization and to the world credit system and cannot reverse their course. To be successful in this venture means the development of stable systems of production and distribution within an orderly and pacific political order, the development of narrow occupational, craft and administrative skills necessary to the industrial organization of society, the acquisition of motivational and consumption patterns that permit the accumulation of capital, the efficient utilization of capital provided by the capital-rich nations in the form of loans and aid, and the development of fiscal and monetary policies to protect themselves from domestic and foreign expropriation of their internal accumulation.

At present, the acquisition of these productive institutions and social characteristics has occurred in only a few of the developing nations. In part the image of western "consumerism," the attractiveness of industrial consumer goods ranging from trash and junk to consumer durables, is more visible than the production habits, motivation, and discipline necessary to generate that consumerism. Western society achieved "consumerism" after decades and even centuries of primitive and secondary modes of capital accumulation. The new, developing, societies see the attractiveness of consumerism without being able to see the sacrifices that capitalism previously had imposed upon its own societies (though they have seen the sacrifices capitalism imposed upon colonial society). They would like to acquire the apparent fruits of industrialism without knowing how to generate the capital that produces those fruits.

The intense, immediate demand in the developing societies for industrially produced consumer goods, hampers the accumulation of capital. The desire to enjoy those goods, especially by the upper classes and political elites, inhibits the development of a social character geared to the acquisition of skills, and long-term planning which are the pre-conditions for industrialization. Only those underdeveloped countries that are rich in petroleum, fossil fuels and minerals for which there is a high international demand have the opportunity to acquire the capital and modern technology without the sacrifices associated with primitive capital accumulation. Only these countries can reach sophisticated levels of consumerism for significant numbers of their populations in relatively short periods of time.

Governments engaged in modernization thus are forced to use draconian measures to inhibit consumption among the masses, while they provide vast opportunities and little restraint to the entrepreneurial classes. But world-wide pressures for immediate personal gratification are so great that policies of repressive austerity are only partially successful even when politically possible.

The industrialized western nations face problems of maintaining systems of positive economic and political motivation. The achievement of affluence among its new middle classes has tended to erode the incentives for mobility, for discipline, for achievement, and for long-term personal planning. It has, in short, weakened if not made obsolete the Protestant Ethic. In the short run, the new scarcity has reinvoked the discipline for mobility among large parts of the middle classes but may embitter the new lower class ethnic aspirants who are denied opportunity after the desire to achieve economic and political mobility has been aroused in them. In the long run, the new scarcity may embitter substantial portions of the new middle classes and the rising ethnics who for different reasons may be frozen out of a productive role in the economy.

New forms of cleavage appear to be emerging in western society. On one side there is a dominant segment of population committed to the industrial structure of that society. This industrially committed segment is itself continuously sub-divided into small segments at various skill, occupational, industrial, managerial, and income levels. The committed segment may range from semi-skilled workers to the managerial and financial upper classes. But this group is cut-off from a sub-proletariat which is denied economic opportunity as well as the chance to acquire the skills, motivation, and education to enter the industrially committed sectors of society.

This scarcity-induced exclusion from the fruits of consumer society cannot be anything other than a source for continuous protest, disruption, and lawlessness for some groups. Such lawlessness exists more frequently and continuously at a personal level than at a political level;

and such lawlessness serves to reinforce the boundaries between the committed and uncommitted segments of the society. Disease, poverty, alcoholism, vice, and a whole host of symptoms of despair and personal and social disorganization accompany lawlessness as the characteristics of scarcity induced and enforced exclusion.

A third major segment into which western society seems to subdivide itself is the "counter culture." Originating in the middle classes, segments of youth voluntarily segregate themselves from the committed world or drop out because the new scarcity may impose intellectual, academic, and personality demands upon them that are too severe for them to bear. At the same time because of the scarcity, "society" cannot or is unwilling to guarantee that the sacrifices necessary for commitment will be rewarded. In the 1960s a ready-made cultural frame for dropping-out was constructed. Now the counterculture includes ever-expanding cults, "ideologies," organizational forms, experimentation for the achievement of personal salvation outside the system, and adventuristic political assaults on the system. The counter culture is so varied, so unorganized and disorganized that it constitutes no major threat to the system, even though it appears to be a stable feature of western societies.

The only imaginable threat to the system posed by the disenfranchised subproletariat and the counter culture would be if its numbers were so large or its ethics were so pervasive that it destroyed the motivational schema that makes the committed industrial sector possible. The new scarcity seems to prevent such a possibility. Scarcity reinforces the motivation of the haves, as it strengthens the opposite motivation of the have-nots.

The "culture" of the counter culture also permeates the life styles of those who are occupationally committed to the industrial establishment. Dress and tonsorial styles, sexual experimentation and new forms of sexuality, the use of marijuana (though not LSD), attraction to new forms of art, the multi-media, high and low porn and new forms of music have become chic and stylized among large segments of the "occupationally committed" at increasingly wider ranges of the occupational and age structures.

These "counter-cultural" elements become increasingly integrated into the "normal" culture, but a separation of cultural styles occurs at the level of work. Commitment to the industrial structure is increasingly confined to the place of work. It includes the acquisition, display, and exercise of skill, craftsmanship, and dedication to [the] occupational task at hand. The private life with its acceptance of life-style elements that previously might have been characterized as countercultural is rigidly separated from the work life of the individual.

Such a division of life into two spheres is facilitated by a greater permissiveness by employers of work-unrelated deviancy. Employers increasingly do not inquire into the non-work life of their employees.

At the same time, the attractiveness of the personal styles of the counter culture and the difficulty of maintaining a divided life continuously thrusts members of the industrially committed middle classes into the total world of the counter culture. The counter culture as a distinct, isolated segment of western society is thus fed by the young who are unable or unwilling to compete in the square world of commitment, and by those who have competed, often successfully, but who are unwilling or unable to maintain a divided life.

The separation of western society into three major distinct sectors appears to be a permanent feature of that society. The development of the counter culture is one of the major products of the Golden Age of affluence. Affluence appears to have raised the level of idealism among scions of the middle classes to the point where a commitment to industrial society could not gratify that idealism. The new scarcity appears to have stabilized the counter culture and is likely to make it permanent. It does so because when scarcity produces increased competitiveness for education, jobs, and for self-discipline and personal achievement, the on-going counter culture provides new sets of culturally sanctioned alternatives for withdrawal from that society.

Scarcity also provides the basis for the increased segmentation and isolation of ethnic and racial groups and other subproletariats, but it does so in new ways. Because the new scarcity follows a period of rising expectations, heightened political aspirations and governmental sponsored mobility, the sense of failure and despair may be greater among these groups than would otherwise be expected.

American society has traditionally maintained a partially open society by providing at least the promise and often the actuality of opportunity. In part this was due to cheap land and natural resources much of which was made available from the public domain. In part the process of industrialization itself provided opportunities for the domestic lower classes and successive waves of European immigrants. In addition, substantial opportunities were provided by governmental fiscal and taxation policy. In the Golden Age extensive opportunity was provided by fiscal, budgetary, and tax policies. The new scarcity began in the recession of 1972, but was foreshadowed in 1968 by a switch in the beneficiaries of these federal budgetary policies. In 1986, the focus of federal policy appears to reserve the benefits of the economic system for those who have already arrived and to place the burden of the cost of inflation and unemployment on wage workers and those who have not arrived. This is a historic reversal of traditional federal policy, including not only that of President Johnson's 1965 policy to end poverty, but also a much older policy of the United States to provide opportunity to all but the slaves.

In the post-Golden Age this reversal serves to seal-off and make permanent the boundaries between the three major cultural and social segments of American and western societies. Downward mobility between the segments is always possible. Upward mobility within each segment is also possible, but upward mobility across the segments is increasingly denied and frustrated by current social policies.

If the traditional virtues of an open society are to be maintained a drastic reversal of social policy is necessary. But maintaining mobility and economic expansion will be increasingly difficult in a world where limitations of natural resources including energy and mineral and fossil fuels and even land are becoming increasingly apparent.

In the underdeveloped world all of the above problems occur at more extreme levels. Governmental policy may be less important as a barrier to opportunity than the almost insurmountable problems of developing societies to mobilize human energy, to achieve discipline, and to efficiently utilize capital.

Such barriers to development as noted may be less important to a few countries like Brazil, Iran and Saudi Arabia where the abundance of natural resources may provide the basis for the accumulation of capital without the rigors of primitive accumulation of capital, and with greater margins of safety for a more slowly developing industrially motivated labor force.

By and large, the underdeveloped world faces the prospect of a much smaller industrially committed labor force than in the west and a very much larger sub-proletariat. The uncommitted intelligentsia may be small in relation to the total population but relatively large in comparison to the committed industrial classes.

If civilization is defined as the possibility for increasingly larger segments of the population to achieve not only economic well-being but the prospect of realizing their potentials by the escape from misery, the prospects are indeed bleak.

In some societies the bleakness seems to be due to difficulties that are inherent in their history and situations. In other countries, like the United States, the difficulties are willed. The desire to achieve and maintain affluence at the expense of others becomes the basis for social policy, and produces an economically, culturally, and socially closed world.

19

The Multinational Corporations and International Production (1987)*

Robert Gilpin

Since the end of the Second World War no aspect of international political economy has generated more controversy than the global expansion of multinational corporations.[1] Some consider these powerful corporations to be a boon to mankind, superseding the nation-state, diffusing technology and economic growth to developing countries, and interlocking national economies into an expanding and beneficial interdependence. Others view them as imperialistic predators, exploiting all for the sake of the corporate few while creating a web of political dependence and economic underdevelopment.[2] A few experts have even predicted, in more exuberant moments, that by the end of the century several dozen immense corporations would virtually control the world economy.[3]

A simple working definition of a multinational corporation is a firm that owns and manages economic units in two or more countries. Most frequently, it entails foreign direct investment by a corporation and the ownership of economic units (services, extractive industries, or manufacturing plants) in several countries. Such direct investment (in contrast to portfolio investment) means the extension of managerial control across national boundaries. The international operation of these corporations is consistent with liberalism but is directly counter to the doctrine of economic nationalism and to the views of countries committed to socialism and state intervention in the economy.

---

*   From *The Political Economy of International Relations* (Princeton: Princeton University Press, 1987), pp. 231–38, 252–62.

Both hopes and fears about multinational corporations are well founded. Many multinationals are extremely powerful institutions and possess resources far in excess of most of the member-states of the United Nations. These corporations have continued to grow in importance. Total worldwide foreign direct investment was about half a trillion dollars in 1981.[4] The scope of operations and extent of the territory over which some multinational corporations range are more expansive geographically than any empire that has ever existed. They have integrated the world economy more extensively than ever in the past, and they have taken global economic interdependence beyond the realms of trade and money into the area of industrial production. This internationalization of production impinges significantly on national economies.

Although the domination of the world economy by multinational corporations seemed assured in the 1960s, an event took place in 1973 that profoundly challenged and altered their seemingly invincible position in the world economy. The oil embargo by OPEC and the subsequent massive rise in the price of petroleum demonstrated that nation-states had not lost their capacity for counterattack. Within a relatively short period of time, the gigantic oil companies – previously the quintessential international corporations – had had many of their foreign subsidiaries nationalized and had become subservient to states earlier considered powerless and servile. World history records few equivalent redistributions of wealth and power in such a short period.

Subsequently, another significant change took place. Although some of the oldest and most successful multinational corporations are non-American, US corporations had dominated the scene throughout the 1960s and into the next decade. After the mid-1970s, however, their preeminence was challenged and, in some cases, surpassed not only by European and Japanese corporations but also by the multinationals of such newly industrializing countries as Brazil, India, and South Korea.[5] Resurgence of the nation-state and the emergence of powerful non-American corporations made the picture far more complex by the mid-1980s than it had been. This shift to the "New Multinationalism" will be discussed below.

The nature of the multinational

What are the distinguishing characteristics of a multinational corporation [MNC]? An MNC tends to be an oligopolistic corporation in which ownership, management, production, and sales activities extend over several national jurisdictions. It is comprised of a head office in one country with a cluster of subsidiaries in other countries. The principal objective of the corporation is to secure the least costly production of goods for world markets; this goal may be achieved through acquiring the most efficient locations for production facilities or obtaining taxation concessions from host governments.

Multinational corporations have a large pool of managerial talent, financial assets, and technical resources, and they run their gigantic operations with a coordinated global strategy. The multinational attempts to expand and perpetuate its market position through vertical integration and centralization of corporate decision making. IBM, Exxon, General Motors, Mitsui, Toyota, Fiat, and Nestlé are typical examples. Until the last quarter of this century, the two most prominent types of foreign investment were manufacturing investments in developed OECD economies and extractive industry investments, especially petroleum, in the less developed world. In later decades services have also been more and more dominated by the multinationals.

Foreign direct investment is generally an integral part of the global corporate strategy for firms operating in oligopolistic markets.[6] Whereas traditional portfolio investment is driven by differential rates of return among national economies, foreign direct investment is determined by the growth and competitive strategies of the oligopolistic corporations. Although the former has most frequently been concentrated in government loans and infrastructure types of investment, direct investment tends to be sector-specific and is usually based on the existence of some competitive advantage over local firms, advantages that the corporation wishes to exploit or preserve. As this type of investment creates economic relations of an integrative nature and involves the corporation in the internal economic affairs of a country, it has become extremely controversial.

In the 1960s, foreign direct investment experienced a metamorphosis for several reasons: the compression of time and space due to improvements in transportation and communications, government policies favorable to the multinational corporations, and the supportive international environment provided by American power and economic leadership. American corporations, wanting to maintain access to a relatively closed yet growing market, began to make massive investments in Western Europe largely as a response to the formation of the European Common Market and the subsequent erection of a common external tariff. Direct investments by American corporations searching for petroleum and other resources also expanded in the

Middle East and elsewhere. Subsequently, European, Japanese, and other corporations began to emulate the Americans until by the mid-1980s corporations of many nationalities reached into all parts of the globe.[7]

As these corporations increased in importance, economists and others endeavored to explain this novel phenomenon. Initially, the two available types of explanation were those of international capital movements and international trade. Capital movement explanations accounted for foreign investment simply on the basis of higher rates of return abroad, which was adequate to explain portfolio but not direct investment; traditional trade theory had little to contribute and largely ignored the subject. It became obvious that a new theory was required, and early efforts focused on the significance of trade barriers, exchange rates, and favorable public policies. They also stressed the importance of technological developments, such as the jet airplane and satellites, that reduced the costs of transportation and communication. There was also a growing emphasis on the role of oligopolistic competition.

This eclectic approach was intended to incorporate the many different motives for and types of foreign direct investment. In time, however, economists began to set forth more general explanations. ... An abbreviated consideration of this theoretical effort helps to underscore the significance of the emergence of the multinationals for the political economy of international relations.

Although a unified theory that explains all cases of foreign direct investment has yet to be developed, the principal factor explaining the multinational corporation is the increasing importance of oligopolistic competition as one of the preeminent features of the contemporary world market economy.[8] Foreign production has become a vital component in the integrated global strategies of the multinational corporations that now dominate the international economy. Thus, the same developments that have transformed the international trading system,[9] also account for the multinational corporations. Their global dominance is due to the increased importance of economies of scale, monopoly advantage, and barriers to entry in a particular economic sector. Multinationals have been able, through their trade and foreign production strategies, to take advantage of the relatively more open world economy produced by the several rounds of trade negotiations.

Two theories stand out among those that emphasize the oligopolistic nature of these corporations. The first is "product cycle theory," developed principally by Raymond Vernon[10] and subsequently elaborated by other economists. The second and more recent variant is the "industrial organization theory of vertical integration."[11] The product cycle theory applies best to foreign direct investment in manufacturing, the early overseas expansion of American corporations, and to what is called "horizontally integrated" investment, that is, the establishment of plants to make the same or similar goods everywhere. The more general industrial organization theory, on the other hand, applies best to the New Multinationalism and to the increased importance of "vertically integrated" investment, that is, the production of outputs in some plants that serve as inputs for other plants of the firm. This production of components or intermediate goods has been greatly extended through contracting and joint ventures. Although many multinationals engage in both types of foreign investment or variations of these arrangements, the distinction is important in understanding corporate behavior and its effects.[12]

Product cycle theory, though it does not capture all important aspects of trade and investment, does incorporate some of the most important elements: the development and diffusion of industrial technology as a major determinant of the evolution of the international economy, the increasing role of the multinational corporation, and its integration of international trade and production. The theory is well suited for explaining American foreign investment in the 1960s and the reason why this investment generated intense hostility not only abroad but also from American labor. According to this view, the patterns of international trade and investment in industrial goods are largely determined by the emergence, growth, and maturation of new technologies and industries. The theory maintains that every technology or product evolves through three phases in its life history: (a) the introductory or innovative phase, (b) the maturing or process-development phase, and (c) the standardized or mature phase. During each of these phases, different types of economics have a comparative advantage in the production of the product or its components. The evolution of the technology, its diffusion from economy to economy, and the corresponding shift in comparative advantage among national economies explain both the patterns of trade and the location of international production.[13]

The first phase of the product cycle tends to be located in the most advanced industrial country or countries, such as Great Britain in the nineteenth century, the United States in the early postwar period, and Japan to an increasing extent in the late twentieth century. Oligopolistic corporations in these countries have a comparative advantage in the development of new products and industrial processes due to the large home market (demand) and to the resources devoted to innovative activities (supply). During the initial phase, the corporations of the most advanced economy or economies enjoy a monopolistic position, primarily because of their technology.

As foreign demand for their product rises, the corporations at first export to other markets. In time, however, the growth of foreign demand, the diffusion of the technology to potential foreign competitors, and rising trade barriers make foreign production of the good both feasible and necessary. During this second or maturing phase, manufacturing processes continue to improve and the locus of production tends to shift to other advanced countries. Eventually, in the third stage of the cycle, the standardization of manufacturing processes makes it possible to shift the location of production to less developed countries, especially to the newly industrializing nations, whose comparative advantage is their lower wage rates; from these export platforms either the product itself or component parts are shipped to world markets. Such intrafirm trade has become a prominent feature of the contemporary world economy.

Although the product cycle existed in some form in both the late nineteenth and early twentieth centuries, since the end of the Second World War several important changes have taken place in its operation. The rates of technological innovation and diffusion have dramatically accelerated; modern research and development activities and communications have enhanced both the competitive importance of innovations and their more rapid diffusion to competitors throughout the global economic system. International production has become an important ingredient in corporate strategies as oligopolistic corporations increasingly try to maintain their monopolistic position and market access through foreign direct investment. Finally, the combination of highly standardized products and production techniques with the existence of relatively cheap labor has made the NICs significant sources of industrial products and components. The consequent acceleration of shifts in comparative advantage and of changes in the location of international production have made both international trade and foreign investment highly dynamic.[14]

In brief, product cycle theory helps account for a number of the important features of the contemporary world economy: the significance of the multinational corporation and oligopolistic competition, the role of the development and diffusion of industrial technology as major determinants of trade and the global location of economic activities, and the integration of trade and foreign production in corporate strategy. These developments have stimulated both home and host governments to utilize industrial and other policies to make these powerful institutions serve what each perceives to be its own national interest.

The limitations of product cycle theory led to a concerted effort to develop a more general and inclusive theory of the multinational corporation and foreign direct investment. This industrial organization theory of vertical integration combines both industrial organization and international economic theory; it begins with the modern theory of the firm and transfers it to the international economy. Its central ideas, which can be noted here only briefly, help explain the New Multinationalism and the contemporary role of the multinationals.

The industrial organization approach began with the recognition that the "costs of doing business abroad" involve other costs to the firm than simply exporting from its home plants. Therefore, the firm must possess some "compensating advantage" or "firm-specific advantage," such as technical expertise, managerial skills, or economies of scale that enable it to obtain monopoly rents from its operations in other countries:

> These unique assets, built essentially in the home market, were transferrable abroad at low cost, implicitly through internal markets, and provided the ability to compete successfully with host country firms.[15]

This basic approach, first developed by Stephen Hymer and Charles Kindleberger, has been greatly extended by drawing upon the theory of industrial organization.[16]

The expansion and success of this vertical form of multinational enterprise have involved three factors. The first has been the internalization or vertical integration of the various stages of the business, primarily to reduce transaction costs. The firms have tried to bring all facets of the productive process, such as the sources and transfer prices of raw materials and intermediate products, within the confines of the corporation and under their control. The second is the production and exploitation of technical knowledge; because of the increasing cost of research and development, the firm endeavors to appropriate the results of its R & D and to retain a monopoly as long as possible. The third is the opportunity to expand abroad made possible by improvements in communications and transportation. The same factors that led to the domination of national economies by large oligopolistic corporations are transforming the international economy. The result of this evolution has been a complex and sophisticated international corporate structure.

The strategy of the vertically integrated multinational is to place the various stages of production in different locations throughout the globe. A primary motivation of foreign direct investment is to take advantage of lower costs of production, local tax benefits, and, especially in the case of American firms, US tariff schedules that encourage foreign production of component parts. The result of this internationalization of the production process has been the rapid expansion of intrafirm trade. A substantial fraction of global trade has become the import and export of components and intermediate goods rather than the trade of final products associated with more conventional trade theory.

In addition to the other motives analyzed above, the multinational corporation also attempts to erect barriers to entry through its foreign investments. In oligopolistic industries where economies of scale and home demand are important factors in international competitiveness, the firm invests in many economies in order to thwart the emergence of foreign rivals. In this endeavor it is frequently assisted by the industrial and trade policies of its home government. Thus, this element of the multinational's global strategy is the firm's counterpart of the tactic of "industrial preemption."[17]

As with international trade, the transfer by the multinational corporation of the domestic system of industrial organization to the international realm has had significant economic and political consequences. The fact that foreign direct investment and the internationalization of production has taken place in a politically divided international system of competitive nation-states raises major political problems. It has opened the possibility of home states utilizing and manipulating the multinationals in order to achieve foreign policy and other objectives. Important sectors of labor in the home country regard foreign direct investment as a threat to their interests. And host states fear that the penetration of their economics by the multinationals has been detrimental to their economic, political, and other interests. ...

The new multinationalism

Observers with varying points of view have been proved wrong in their predictions for the multinational corporations. Multinationals have neither superseded the nation-state nor gone the way of the East India

Company.[18] Both state and corporation have proven themselves to be remarkably resourceful and versatile in dealing with one another. The efforts of the United Nations, the OECD, and regional organizations to impose an international code of regulations on corporations have not succeeded, nor have American efforts to implement regulations restricting the behavior of host governments toward the multinationals.[19] The international investment regime is being fashioned by negotiations among individual corporations, home governments, and host governments rather than according to universal regulations or complete freedom of corporate action. The result of this interaction is a complex and contradictory pattern of relations between multinationals and governments that, barring a major catastrophe, could last indefinitely into the future, a future that will necessarily be different from the past in several critically important particulars.

First and most important, a slowdown in the rate of growth of the aggregate level of foreign direct investment appears to have taken place due to decreased rates of economic growth and increased political uncertainties around the world. Simultaneously, the competition among both developed and less developed countries for capital and technology has intensified. Developed countries, beset by high unemployment (with the major exception of Japan), compete more vigorously to attract investment. LDCs have opened their doors wider to the multinationals in the 1980s because of the effects of world recession, the experience of the global debt crisis, and the decreasing availability of other forms of capital or means of acquiring technology.[20] Although the economic improvement of many less developed countries and the increased competition among multinationals have strengthened the bargaining position of certain LDC governments, the direction of investment has tipped more toward the advanced countries. As pointed out earlier, it is significant that the United States has not only continued to be the largest home country but has also become the largest host country.

The less developed countries have become more and more differentiated in their ability to attract foreign investment. Rising political and economic uncertainty has altered the business environment and caused the multinationals to diversify their investment, especially within the developed economies.[21] The Iranian revolution, the growing number of socialist governments, and the confiscation of corporate assets have made corporations wary of making large long-term commitments in the less developed world. The investment there has tended to be increasingly concentrated in the few countries, such as

South Korea, Mexico, Taiwan, the Philippines, Singapore, Hong Kong, and Brazil, whose economies emphasize export-led growth, possess pools of inexpensive skilled labor, or have large and expanding internal markets. These investments have been primarily in services and manufacturing to serve foreign or local markets rather than the extractive investments of the past. Bankers' growing reluctance to make loans to over-indebted LDCs has led to greatly increased competition among these countries for direct investment. These tendencies have accentuated the pattern of uneven development among the less developed countries and have led bypassed countries to make the paradoxical charge that the refusal of the corporations to invest in them is a new form of capitalist imperialism.

Within this overall setting, certain interrelated trends can be discerned: (1) the increasing importance of "vertical," as opposed to "horizontal," foreign direct investment, (2) the expansion of intercorporate alliances across national boundaries, and (3) the increasing importance of off-shore production and sourcing of components and intermediate goods. Multinationals have been encouraged to diversify their production of components and products among the NICs as nontariff barriers have developed within the advanced countries. These developments, which became more prominent in the late 1970s, are together transforming the international trading and investment regime.[22]

As has already been noted, horizontal investment involves the replication abroad of some aspects of a firm's domestic operations, and vertical investment occurs when a firm invests abroad in activities that (1) provide inputs for the home production process or (2) use the output of home plants. That is, vertical foreign direct investment entails the fragmentation of the production process and the location throughout the world of various stages of component production and final assembly of components. This fragmentation is intended to achieve economies of scale, to take advantage of cost differences of different locales, and to exploit favorable government policies such as tariff codes that provide for duty-free entry of semifinished products or of goods assembled abroad from components produced domestically. The development and increased specialization of branch plants has led to the spectacular rise of intrafirm or corporate-administered trade discussed earlier. By one reckoning, this form of trade accounts for approximately 60 per cent of American imports.[23]

The shift from wholly owned subsidiaries abroad to joint ventures and other forms of intercorporate alliances has been accelerated by a number of political, economic, and technological factors: (1) access to a market frequently requires a domestic partner; (2) the rapid pace and cost of technology necessitates that even large corporations spread the risk; (3) the huge capital requirements of operating globally and in all major markets; (4) for American firms, the loss of technological leadership in many fields; and (5) for Japanese firms, to forestall protectionism. Thus, for example, General Motors is reported to have approximately thirty alliances with other corporations.[24]

The global rationalization of international production has accorded increasing importance to alliances between the multinationals and overseas suppliers of products and components. At the core of many if not most of these arrangements are Japanese suppliers in automobiles, electronics, and advanced technologies. Japan supplies something like 40 per cent of American component parts in electronics, automobiles, and other sectors. The role of the newly industrializing countries in this internationalization of production is also rapidly expanding.[25] Through such mechanisms as joint ventures, contractual arrangements, or the establishment of wholly owned subsidiaries, American and other multinationals are transferring more advanced technology to the NICs and entering into cooperative arrangements with an expanding number of countries like Mexico, Taiwan, and South Korea.

By combining the productive technology and global marketing organizations of the corporations with the low-wage skilled labor of the NICs, both the firms and the NICs can increase their competitive strength in world markets. For example, American and Korean firms are forging ties in a typical balance-of-power fashion to counter the rising ascendancy of Japanese firms in computer chips.[26] The rise of the yen and the tying of the Korean currency to the dollar have encouraged this alliance. It should be particularly interesting to observe developments in mainland China, where the Communist government has created special manufacturing zones to tap the technology of the corporations and to produce exports for overseas markets.

In effect, a shortcutting of the traditional product cycle has occurred. Whereas in the past the locus of comparative advantage and the production of goods shifted from the United States to the other advanced countries and eventually to the newly industrializing countries, in the late 1980s the initial production of a good or component may take place in the NIC itself; assembly of the finished product may occur in the advanced economy. This obviously benefits the MNCs and the NICs, but it is deeply resented by large sections of labor in the United States and Western Europe.

Interfirm alliances and cooperation, arrangements that are frequently sanctioned and promoted by national governments, have also become increasingly important.[27] The escalating cost of technological development, the importance of economies of scale, and the spread of the New Protectionism have made participation in the three major markets of the world – the United States, Western Europe, and Japan – a necessity for multinational corporations; this in turn has most frequently necessitated acquisition of a local partner.[28] The result is that the multinationals are invading one another's home markets and new practices are evolving.[29] The new United Motor Manufacturing Company established in 1983 by those two powerful rivals, General Motors and Toyota, to produce subcompact cars in the United States is the most noteworthy example. As *Business Week* (July 21, 1986) observed, complex corporate alliances are increasingly important.[30]

These developments foretell the end of the old multinationalism. The day is past when corporations of the United States and a few other developed countries could operate freely in and even dominate the host economies and when foreign direct investment meant the ownership and control of wholly owned subsidiaries. Instead, a great variety of negotiated arrangements have been put in place: cross-licensing of technology among corporations of different nationalities, joint ventures, orderly marketing agreements, secondary sourcing, off-shore production of components, and crosscutting equity ownership. In the developed countries the General Motors-Toyota alliance is undoubtedly a harbinger of things to come. In the developing world the corporations see the LDCs less as pliable exporters of raw materials and more as expanding local markets and industrial partners or even potential rivals. Thus, the relatively simple models of both liberal and dependency theorists are becoming outmoded in the final quarter of the century.

These developments are also changing attitudes and policies in both the less developed and developed countries. The former have become more receptive to the multinationals but are also pursuing policies to shift the terms of investment in their favor. The responses of the developed countries – which will be vital in determining the ultimate success of this new multinationalism – are more problematic. In the United States, Western Europe, and Japan, debate is just beginning between the gainers and the losers from these changes. Both states and corporations are girding for battle in a global market where national and corporate strategies as much as traditional factors of comparative advantage will greatly influence the outcome of economic competition.

Attitudes in the United States toward foreign investment, as noted earlier, began to change in the 1970s and 1980s. Although opinion has continued to favor the multinationals, questioning of foreign direct investment has increased considerably, especially in those sections of the country most concerned about the decline of traditional industries and plagued by high levels of unemployment. Responding to changing pressures, American corporations have taken modest steps to restrict foreign production and to export abroad from domestic plants. The United States has also tried to increase its share of world investment and the benefits from foreign direct investment by the firms of other countries. Through the threat of local content legislation and protectionist barriers, efforts have been made to encourage Japanese and other corporations to locate future investments in the United States. In effect, the United States is moving to reverse the flow of global investment in the direction of greater investment in the United States itself.

In the early 1980s, however, the overvalued dollar, high wage rates, and the high cost of capital along with other factors accelerated the movement abroad of industrial production and the expansion of offshore procurement. The powerful tendency toward vertical foreign direct investment and increased reliance on importing components led *Business Week* to worry that the American economy was becoming merely an assembler of foreign-produced components and American firms becoming "hollow corporations" whose primary task had become to assemble or distribute imported goods.[31] For example, the "American" automobile has almost disappeared and is largely an assemblage of imported components.[32] Or, to take another example, $625 of the $860 manufacturing cost of that marvel of American ingenuity, the IBM PC, was incurred overseas by subsidiaries of American multinationals ($230) and by foreign firms ($395). In brief, the United States, it was feared, was being transformed from a manufacturing to mainly a distribution economy.

Many Americans became concerned over the loss of manufacturing jobs and its income distribution effects. Capital, it is pointed out, benefits from overseas investment as does foreign labor, but domestic labor loses from the outflow of capital unless it somehow compensated.[33] The Reagan Administration, because the thrust of its policies was away from the notion that the government should aid the losers and develop adjustment policies to assist injured businesses and workers, encouraged the spread of protectionist pressures.

A longer-term worry was the so-called boomerang effect. Critics charged that in the short run increased reliance on subcontracting and imported components might make sense as a means of meeting foreign competition, but that the importation of these goods was further weakening American manufactures and accelerating the diffusion of American technology and expertise to potential foreign competitors. In the early postwar era, the American strategy of following the product cycle meant that mature goods for which the United States no longer had a comparative advantage were produced abroad; by the 1980s, American multinationals were more and more manufacturing their newest products abroad and importing them into the United States. In the long term, such a strategy of increased dependence on foreign components manufacturers would intensify competitive pressures on the American economy. In this fashion, the New Multinationalism has raised a host of opportunities and challenges that the United States must address.

The West Europeans during the 1980s have not yet come to terms with the New Multinationalism. Although significant differences exist among the Europeans, varying from Great Britain's privatization of the economy to French nationalization, some major trends are discernible. The Continental economy has been increasingly closed to imports of goods produced elsewhere, especially those from Japan and the NICs. Meanwhile, cooperative efforts by European firms with American and Japanese corporations such as joint ventures and technology licensing have been encouraged in order to close the growing technology gap between Europe and the other advanced economies. As the Common Market has increased its barriers to imports, foreign multinationals have had to invest in Europe or at least to share their technology in order to gain access to the relatively closed European market.

Government intervention in the economy through outright nationalization, government participation, and government initiation of joint development projects such as the Airbus has increased. A considerable fraction of the private sector in Western Europe has been nationalized. Seeking to emulate the Japanese "capitalist developmental state," a term coined by Chalmers Johnson,[34] or simply to create employment, one European government after another has taken over key sectors of the corporate economy. Through rationalizing and concentrating their industries, the Europeans are attempting to create corporate "champions" that will compete with American and Japanese multinationals in European and overseas markets. These European corporations are being fashioned into instruments of an emergent industrial policy that is contributing to the growing regionalization of the world political economy.

Undoubtedly the most significant development of the early 1980s was the increasing multinationalization of the Japanese economy. Although much less advanced than the global role of American and European corporations, the expansion abroad of Japanese multinationals in the 1980s has been truly remarkable. Still quantitatively small in 1985 by American or European standards, it was of increasing significance, especially in the United States.[35] Although only about 7 per cent of total world foreign direct investment, it was highly concentrated in basic industries and in the increasingly important high-tech and service sectors.[36] As *Business Week* (July 14, 1986) pointed out, the Japanese were building an industrial empire inside the American economy itself.

The traditional Japanese emphasis on exporting from home plants and investing overseas primarily in extractive industries began to give way in the mid-1970s. Responding to the energy crisis and rising labor costs at home, Japanese firms initially invested in the LDCs to acquire energy-embodied semiprocessed goods and to transfer production abroad to other Asian countries in those industries in which Japan no longer had a comparative advantage; indeed, even in the mid-1980s most Japanese foreign direct investment is in Asia.[37] The goods produced abroad in these low-technology industries have been for local consumption or for export to third economies. There has been little boomerang effect, that is, little export of the goods back to Japan itself.

Subsequently, the erection of trade barriers and the appreciation of the yen in the mid-1980s caused the Japanese to accelerate foreign production in the developed country for which the product was destined. This type of foreign direct investment has become especially important for the American and, to a lesser extent, the West European market. Whereas Japanese direct investment in the United States and Canada for the period 1951–1972 totaled only $303 million, by 1984 Japanese direct investment in the United States had reached $16.5 billion; in Western Europe the amount was $1.1 billion.[38] In the 1980s American and European foreign direct investment was motivated primarily by declining comparative advantage at home; Japanese foreign investment in the other advanced economies has been almost entirely intended to get around trade barriers raised against its extraordinarily efficient corporations. In effect, these Japanese companies have been forced against their own will to become multinationals.[39]

Japanese foreign direct investment has been generally "pro-trade" and designed to complement its overall economic strategy. Through corporate and state cooperation it facilitates exports to foreign markets and ensures access to resources and particular imports. It has also been strongly motivated by the desire to avoid trade friction and to prevent the rise of protectionist barriers abroad. Japan has viewed foreign investment principally as an instrument to maintain and expand its role in the emergent world economy.

The penetration of the American and, to a lesser extent, the West European economies by Japanese multinationals is transforming the relationships of the advanced countries.[40] Through the establishment of wholly owned subsidiaries, the purchase of participation in foreign and especially American firms, and the establishment of joint ventures in such areas as automobiles, steel, and electronics, Japanese investments have rapidly evolved from areas of simple fabrication, assembly, and the production of light components to heavy high-technology production requiring economies of scale. By the mid-1980s Japanese automobile corporations manufacturing in the United States had become, as a group, one of the four major producers of automobiles within the country. The extraordinary pace of the increase of Japanese investment in the United States, the range of products involved, and the transplantation into the American economy of Japan's unexcelled comparative advantage in new manufacturing techniques has begun to have a profound effect on the American economy and to give rise to deep anxieties. Governor Richard D. Lamm of Colorado has spoken of "economic colonialism" by the Japanese.[41]

At this writing the consequences of the transfer of the full spectrum of Japanese competitive dynamism into the American market are highly speculative but nonetheless significant. In the first place, trade barriers against Japanese imports have had the paradoxical effect of intensifying competition within the American economy itself as Japanese corporations have jumped the barriers and established manufacturing operations in the United States. Second, American trade barriers and the growth of Japanese-American corporate cooperation may displace and have a detrimental impact on European and NIC sales in the United States, unless the latter two pursue a similar course. And, third, important groups in the United States are responding negatively to Japanese "take-overs" in the American economy, especially in the sensitive high-technology industries; they are exhibiting all the fears manifested earlier in Western Europe and the less developed countries regarding American multinationals. The outcome of these conflicting developments in the Nichibei economy will affect not only the future of the US economy but also the shape of the international political economy.

Conclusion

The multinational corporation and international production reflect a world in which capital and technology have become increasingly mobile while labor has remained relatively immobile. Continuous changes in comparative advantage among national economies, advances in modern transportation and communications, and favorable government policies encourage corporations to locate their production facilities in the most advantageous locations around the globe. Some of these advantages include the existence of pools of low-cost skilled labor, proximity to markets, and tax advantages. The result of this internationalization of industrial production has been the creation of a complex web of interlocking relationships among nation-states and the world's giant corporations.

The economic and political consequences of international production and the formation of economic alliances across national boundaries have become matters of controversy and speculation. These developments raise the classic issues debated by liberals, Marxists, and nationalists over the stability of international capitalism. Do these transnational alliances represent a transcendence of the "law of uneven development," or are they merely temporary alliances that will dissolve with the continuing uneven development of national economies?[42]

In the tradition of nineteenth-century liberals who extolled trade as a force for peace, some writers believe that the sharing of production by states and corporations of different nationalities creates bonds of mutual interest that counter and moderate the historic tendency for the uneven development of national economies to give rise to economic conflict. If corporations of declining economies are able to continue as industrial producers through foreign direct investment, it is argued, they will be less apt to resist the rise of new industrial powers. Thus some predict that the multinationals and their political allies will defend the liberal world economy and resist the forces of economic nationalism.[43]

Other observers of "the internationalization of production," following the Leninist and nationalist traditions, are more skeptical and believe that these state and corporate alliances could fragment the world economy into rival blocs and economic groupings. For example, these transnational alliances do not solve the surplus capacity problem, the question of who will produce what, or the issue of how the losers will be compensated. If these matters are not resolved, skeptics believe that the New Multinationalism could create a world in which the corporations and their allies would engage in what former West German Chancellor Helmut Schmidt called in 1974 "the struggle for the global product." This may be an apt phrase to characterize the New Multinationalism.

Whether Kautsky's or Lenin's predictions regarding the possibilities of intracapitalist economic cooperation and conflict will eventually prove correct remains to be seen. What can be said in the mid-1980s is that the stability of the world market economy depends ultimately upon the quality of leadership (hegemonic or pluralistic), a solution of the adjustment problem, and the creation of international norms that both increase global economic stability and guarantee states an adequate degree of economic autonomy.[44]

At the least, the increased mobility of capital and the increasingly arbitrary nature of comparative advantage have given rise to intensified international competition for investment. Through tax policies, the erection of trade barriers, and even the creation of a skilled and disciplined labor force (e.g., Taiwan), governments attempt to attract corporate investments and influence the international location of economic activities. The multinationals of different countries compete for access to these economies, thereby giving the host states some bargaining leverage regarding the terms of the investment.

The result of these developments is a complex pattern of relationships among corporations, home governments, and host countries that has increasingly politicized foreign investment both at home and abroad. Through individual actions and in alliance with one another, each actor attempts to enhance its own position. To the extent that one government wrings concessions from corporations, it triggers counterpressures in other countries. As host governments attempt to transform the terms of investment in their favor, they create concern at home over trade imbalances, lost jobs, and "run-away" plants. Thus, groups and states attempt to manipulate corporations for their own particularistic interests.

Governments and corporations are having to come to terms with a vastly altered international environment in which the location of the world's economic activities and the terms on which foreign direct investment take place have become of vital importance. Which countries will possess which industries, and who will reap the benefits?

Answers will be determined partially by the interplay of market forces as corporations seek out the least costly sites for their production, but these issues will also be determined by the power and interests of the several participants themselves as they compete for individual advantage.

Notes

1. Although many types of firms operate internationally, the multinational corporation is the most important because of its effects on the integration of national economies.
2. An excellent collection of representative pieces on the mutlinational corporation is George Modelski (ed.), *Transnational Corporations and the World Order* (San Francisco: W. H. Freeman, 1979).
3. Some sections of this chapter have been adapted from Robert Gilpin, *US Power and the Multinational Corporation: The Political Economy of Foreign Direct Investment* (New York: Basic Books, 1975) and other writings.
4. US Dept. of Commerce, *International Direct Investment: Global Trends and the US Role* (Washington: US Government Printing Office, 1984), p. 1.
5. *The Economist* (July 13, 1983), pp. 55–6.
6. Richard E. Caves, *Multinational Corporation and Economic Analysis* (New York: Cambridge University Press, 1982).
7. Mira Wilkins, "The History of European Multinationals – A New Look," (1986), unpublished and "Japanese Multinational Enterprise before 1914," (1986), unpublished, discuss the relatively unknown early history of European and Japanese multinational corporations.
8. Henry K. Kierzkowski (ed.), *Monopolistic Competition and International Trade* (Oxford: Clarendon, 1984).
9. *Editor's Note:* As discussed in Chapter 5 of *The Political Economy of International Relations, op. cit.,* "The Politics of International Trade," pp. 171–230.
10. Raymond Vernon, "International Investment and International Trade in the Product Cycle," *Quarterly Journal of Economics,* 80 (1966), pp. 190–207.
11. Paul R. Krugman, "Economies of Scale, Imperfect Competition, and Trade: An Exposition," (1981), p. 8, unpublished.
12. See Caves, *Multinational Corporations, op. cit..*
13. Seev Hirsch, *Location of Industry and International Competitiveness* (Oxford: Clarendon, 1967).
14. Marina v. N. Whitman, *International Trade and Investment: Two Perspectives, Essays in International Finance,* 143, International Finance Section, Department of Economics, Princeton University (1981), pp. 12–13, discusses the example of the changing world automobile industry.
15. Mark Casson (ed.), *The Growth of International Business* (London: George Allen & Unwin, 1983), p. 38.
16. Caves, *Multinational Corporations, op.cit.,* and Casson, *The Growth of International Business, op. cit.,* are excellent discussions of this approach.
17. As discussed in *The Political Economy of International Relations, op. cit.,* Chapter 5.

18. I must confess that in my earlier writings I was much too pessimistic regarding the possibility of American multinationals adjusting to changes in the world situation. The slowing-down of American investment abroad and the increase in foreign direct investment in the United States undercut many of my earlier concerns. On the other hand, the MNCs must now function in a highly restricted political environment and the nature of the MNC operations has changed importantly with the rise of what I call the New Multinationalism.

19. Stephen D. Krasner, *Structural Conflict: The Third World against Global Liberalism* (Berkeley: University of California Press, 1985), Chapter 7.

20. *The Economist* (February 19, 1983), pp. 86–7.

21. Whitman, *International Trade and Investment, op. cit.*, p. 14.

22. Susan Strange, "Protectionism and World Politics," *International Organization*, 39 (1985), pp. 233–59.

23. John Gerard Ruggie, "Political Structure and Change in the International Economic Order: The North-South Dimension," in Ruggie (ed.), *The Antinomies of Interdependence: National Welfare and the International Division of Labor* (New York: Columbia University Press, 1983), p. 475.

24. *The New York Times* (August 6, 1986), p. D2.

25. Joseph Grunwald and Kenneth Flamm, *The Global Factory: Foreign Assembly in International Trade* (Washington, DC: The Brookings Institution, 1985).

26. *The New York Times* (July 15, 1985), p. D1.

27. Whitman, *International Trade and Investment, op. cit.*, p. 14.

28. Kenichi Ohmae, *Triad Power: The Coming Shape of Global Competition* (New York: Free Press, 1985).

29. *The Economist* (February 11, 1984), p. 63.

30. Ohmae, *Triad Power, op. cit.*, provides a very good review of these developments.

31. *Business Week* (March 11, 1985), p. 60, (March 3, 1986).

32. *The New York Times* (August 10, 1985), p. 31.

33. Paul Samuelson, "International Trade for a Rich Country," Business and Financial Conditions, *The Morgan Guaranty Survey* (July) (New York: Morgan Guaranty Trust Company, 1972), p. 10.

34. Chalmers Johnson, *MITI and the Japanese Miracle: The Growth of Industrial Policy, 1923–1975* (Stanford: Stanford University Press, 1982), p. viii.

35. *The New York Times* (August 9, 1986), p. 1.

36. *The Economist* (February 19, 1983), p. 87.

37. James C. Abegglen and George Stalk, Jr., *Kaisha – The Japanese Corporation* (New York: Basic Books, 1985), pp. 244–59.

38. Kiyohiko Fukushima, "Japan's Real Trade Policy," *Foreign Policy*, 59 (1985), pp. 23–4.

39. Bruce Nussbaum, *The World After Oil: The Shifting Axis of Power and Wealth* (New York: Simon & Schuster, 1983), p. 246.

40. The relationship of American and Japanese multinationals is older than is generally appreciated; Marina v. N. Whitman, "American-Japanese Direct Foreign Investment Relationships, 1930–1951," *Business History Review*, 56 (1982), pp. 497–518.

41. *The New York Times* (September 16, 1985), p. 139.

42. Robert O. Keohane, *After Hegemony: Cooperation and Discord in the World Political Economy* (Princeton: Princeton University Press, 1984), pp. 43–4) analyzes this increasingly important issue.
43. Guatam Sen, *The Military Origins of Industrialization and International Trade Rivalry* (New York: St Martin's Press, 1984), pp. 241–5.
44. For a consideration of these issues, see *The Political Economy of International Relations*, *op. cit.*, Chapter 10, "The Emergent International Economic Order," pp. 364–408.

20
The New Global Economy: Problems and Prospects (1990)*

Gerald K. Helleiner

The international economy is in a precarious state. Recovery from the longest and most severe recession since the 1930s has been geographically unbalanced, uncertain in its durability and limited in its capacity to overcome continuing fundamental economic imbalances. Victory over inflation in the industrialized countries has been purchased at heavy cost – in terms of high unemployment, savagely depressed commodity prices, and, in the USA, an unsustainable overvaluation of the currency. Few believe that these remedies have permanently or adequately overcome the problem. A massive overhang of questionable debt (both domestic and international) saps confidence in the financial system and limits its capacity to encourage productive new investment upon which sound recovery depends. The manifest failure of macroeconomic policy coordination among the major Western powers – with the US budget deficit and the consequent unbalanced monetary-fiscal policy mix, which is usually cast as the principal villain – is a further source of anxiety. International trade and investment, though now rising again, remain threatened by protectionist pressures unprecedented in their ferocity in the past 50 years. High unemployment, rapid technological change, and limited willingness or capacity to countenance necessary structural changes seem likely both to limit growth and to buttress protectionist sentiment in the Organization for Economic Cooperation and Development (OECD) and particularly in Europe, at least until the end of the century. Meanwhile, in the developing countries, and particularly in Africa and Latin America, the cost of the major external shocks of the past decade continue to be paid.

* From *The New Global Economy and Developing Countries: Essays in International Economics and Development* (Brookfield, VT: Edward Elgar, 1990), pp. 20–32.

Collapsed raw material prices, increased prices for inputs, and unusually high real interest rates have necessitated sharp cuts in real wages and farm incomes. In Africa successive droughts have made a bad situation tragically much worse, resulting once again, in C. P. Snow's "ultimate obscenity": rich people sitting in the comfort of their living rooms watching others starve on color television. Unfortunately, Sub-Saharan African *per capita* incomes are likely to continue to decline for the next 10 years and it will be longer still before the depreciating and inadequate infrastructure of roads, equipment, buildings – including schools and hospitals – will be on a stable growth path once again.

To the outside observer of what Barbara Ward has called Spaceship Earth – the proverbial Martian – the global economy would certainly seem to be malfunctioning in major ways: severe macroeconomic imbalances, major and seemingly unnecessary inefficiencies and grotesque inequities. But what would surely strike our Martian friends as oddest of all is our apparent failure to grasp the undoubted fact that the "global economy" has now arrived.

The world has changed in truly fundamental ways since the burst of international institution-building that followed the chaos of the Great Depression and the Second World War. The most important changes are usually summarized in the word "interdependence," which has already become something of a cliché in the rhetoric of international meetings. Yet we have not sufficiently incorporated it in either our analytical models or our politics.

It was the very success of the world economy in the 1950s and 1960s that brought major changes in its make-up. Revolutionary changes in transport and communications systems, liberalized trading arrangements, the relaxation of foreign exchange controls in most of the industrialized market economies, and other impulses, generated growth in international exchange of goods, services and capital that far outstripped growth in production. Increased interdependence or, as some would have it, "interrelatedness" was obviously associated with important benefits to individual nations. But it also left national economies much more vulnerable to exogenous influences originating in other parts of the world economy. In particular, domestic incomes and employment became more vulnerable to other countries' trading and industrial policies. International capital flows limited national governments' control over domestic monetary affairs and exchange rates. In some instances, international labor flows also generated new domestic tensions.

The new interdependence or interrelatedness of nations is thus multidimensional. It is not merely, or even primarily, a matter of international trade although the proportion of exports in overall economic activity has risen dramatically since the Second World War – that of the USA has doubled during the past 15 years, and the world's trade interdependence appears now to have reached levels beyond those of the period prior to the First World War, or any period since.

The most significant new element in international exchange is in the capital account of the balance of payments. Billions of dollars of short- and medium-term funds are "sloshing" about the world's major money and capital markets, wreaking havoc with prospects for independent macroeconomic management and stable exchange rates. Open economy macroeconomics has now displaced most earlier textbook theorizing about closed economies. (The only closed economy now is that of the planet – and we forget, at our peril, that the global closed-economy "multiplier" is larger than that which applies to economies with import leakages.) But we do not yet have a firm handle on the substitutability of different kinds of financial assets in different countries and denominated in different currencies, or on how national or global stabilization objectives can be reconciled with the new capital market interdependences, or on the benefits and costs of such proposed remedies as controls over capital movements, regulation of Eurocurrency markets, and the operation of an international lender of last resort.

Labor markets, too, exhibit new interdependence, particularly for the higher skills. Recruitment is now conducted worldwide in many occupations and transnational firms, and domestic labor market segmentation – by age, sex, race, language, and so on – is frequently greater than that found in consequence of national borders.

And employment, trade, investment, and financial issues and policies are themselves linked, one with another, in ways that are much more significant today than they once were. Certainly, trade questions can no longer be considered in splendid isolation from monetary and financial ones. What sense can it make to conduct discussions and negotiations on the servicing of Mexican or Brazilian debt in one institution, while the trading circumstances that may make it possible, or impossible, for them to generate the necessary foreign exchange to service them is discussed in another? The payment of their interest depends on their achievement of trade surpluses. Since there are clear political limits to the degree to which their imports can continue to be restrained via austerity programmes, their exports have to expand. One can, and must, expect increasing Latin market penetration in the North in those products – mainly manufactured – in which they have some comparative advantage. Can these matters be explained to the Northern advocates of anti-dumping duties, countervailing duties, customs slow-downs, quotas and voluntary export restraints? Continuing protectionist measures will guarantee financial disaster! To put it another way, easier financial terms and increased flows for debtor nations will make it easier for workers in our import-competing industries and for advocates of liberal trade policies.

Similarly, US monetary and fiscal policies are today inextricably intertwined with its trading policies. The story is well known – large budget deficits (amounting to a significant proportion of the world's total supply of savings) generating, with current monetary policies, high interest rates; these high interest rates and the prospect of low inflation generating capital inflow to the USA and an appreciated dollar; dollar appreciation, in turn, generating record US trade deficits and unprecedented pressure for protectionism.

The link between trade and direct foreign investment is also a matter of increasing importance as investment decision-making is increasingly globalized. The traditional conceptions of international trade – buttressed by 200 years of economic theorizing – have probably taken us just about as far as we can go with them. Rather than thinking of the micro-level problems of world trade in terms of international trade – that is, as trade between nations – it is time to think of them in terms of global industrial organization.

What is at issue, industry by industry, is the location of new investment, and the incentives to locate in different places, not just policies relating to trade after production begins! Tomorrow's trade is the product of today's investment decisions. The big actors in global industrial organization – in investment and in trade – are governments and transnational firms. Governments now regularly take over, or bail out, large firms, offer a variety of incentives (and sometimes disincentives) to both investment and trade, and develop industrial policies and adjustment policies with varying degrees of success.

Transnationals have internalized and, to some degree, cartelized large proportions of their global trading activity. In the automobile industry, General Motors, Ford, and Chrysler each team up with Japanese auto firms and each US firm seeks to influence the interfirm disposition of quotas for the entry of "their" Japanese products to the US market. Much of international trade is consequently already "managed" – by both governments and firms.

It seems likely that future international consultations in steel, automobiles, wheat flour, textiles, and so on will take place between governments and transnational firms in sectorally specialized committees that are, in effect, negotiating global industrial policy. Adam Smith, in 1776, in *The Wealth of Nations*, pointed out the risks of such arrangements within nations: "People of the same trade seldom meet together, even for merriment and diversion, but the conversation ends in a conspiracy against the public, or in some contrivance to raise prices."

International anti-trust is still in its infancy!

Other markets are also increasingly analyzed in global and holistic fashion. The world's interlinked food production and distribution system is a matter of increasing concern as modern communications make the wealthy and well-fed more aware than ever before of the horrors of famine, and generate new political pressures to respond, if not to endemic poverty and malnutrition, at least to intolerable short-term crises. Global market structure and demand prospects in the food sector will inevitably be subject to closer scrutiny than before. On one potentially contentious matter the evidence now seems to be clear – that countries successfully increasing their food (and other agricultural) production simultaneously increase their food imports out of their consequent rising incomes. North American farmers have nothing to fear from efforts to expand Third World agriculture.

In the period following the Second World War, arrangements for political cooperation among sovereign States on matters of economic policy were unable to keep up with the rapid pace of effective economic integration. Trade and capital flows created new and durable private and micro-level links between economies that ran far ahead of intergovernmental macro-level ones. At the same time the economic successes of the industrialized countries other than the USA and many of the developing countries created a much more multipolar world. Political decisions on matters of economic policy that could have wide international ramifications, even if made for purely domestic reasons, were now made in a much wider variety of geographic locations, in a much more decentralized manner. The world economy thus evolved in such a way as to increase both the breadth and the depth of international economic interdependence while, simultaneously, the required political mechanisms for the joint pursuit of previously agreed global economic objectives became ever more complex. The existing multilateral institutions struggled to adapt to the needs of changing world political and economic realities, but their efforts were sometimes flawed and not always very enthusiastically encouraged by national governments.

To this emerging system, already under stress, were then added the major shocks of the 1970s – two major oil price shocks, global price inflation, and two severe recessions. The 1970s also saw rising rates of unemployment in the industrialized countries, and slower overall global growth. These shocks and trends created further strains not only in the world economy but also in the system of multilateral economic cooperation. New problems, new contexts, within which old objectives had to be pursued, and powerful new actors – both governmental and private – further complicated international efforts to restore previous levels of economic performance and overall order.

Ultimately more serious than any of the problems of the international economy so far mentioned (it is still an international one in law, even if a single global one in fact) is the crisis of credibility in the major multinational (global) economic institutions: notably the GATT in trade, the World Bank, and International Monetary Fund (IMF) in finance, and the various other economic institutions of the United Nations family. The central intergovernmental pillars of the post-Second World War international economic system are over 40 years old, old enough to be experiencing the usual pains of mid-life – reduced capacity to interact with, and understand (let alone influence), the rapidly changing world around them, a feeling that they are misunderstood, nostalgia for the wonderful years of their youth, creeping arteriosclerosis, and other debilitating concomitants of age. Can one reasonably expect that the current creaking institutional machinery will get the world safely through the next 40 years?

The reasons for erosion of confidence and credibility in the traditional forms and institutions of multilateral cooperation are many and various. The great impulse to international cooperation provided by the depression of the 1930s and the Second World War has long since faded away. The economic difficulties plaguing rich and poor countries in more recent years have tended to make them turn inwards, neglecting the international and collective dimensions of the depressed state of the world economy. Some of the most powerful countries, notably the USA, seem to be turning away from previous commitments to multilateralism, and increasingly pursue their interests through bilateral channels. Nor have the international agencies themselves always responded or adapted well to the enormous, almost revolutionary, changes in world conditions that have occurred in the 40 years of their existence or to more recent economic pressures; instead political stalemates and bureaucratization frequently combine to produce a prolifer-ation of irrelevant meetings and reports, to which governments pay less and less attention as they seek to grapple, under heavy pressure, with the realities of an unstable and uncertain world.

The original purposes of the multilateral economic institutions are nowhere in dispute. Efforts at international cooperation in the early postwar years were blessed by a widely shared vision of solidarity and peaceful cooperation in a shrinking world. The General Agreement of Tariffs and Trade (GATT), the World Bank, and IMF sought to encour-age a liberal and non-discriminatory world – of stability, order, and justice in economic affairs – a necessary concomitant of the wider noble aspirations of the founders of the United Nations. It is true that the founding membership did not include large numbers of subse-quently independent developing countries, and that the Great Powers exercised dominant influence over their original make-up. But the developing countries later joined in large numbers. In this context, international development came to be seen as a joint and collective responsibility of the international community, even if achievement of agreement on the details of the mandate inevitably involved contro-versy over national and international responsibilities. Similarly, in later years, a new awareness of the ecological threats to mankind as a whole gave fresh impetus to joint international action to protect the atmos-phere, the oceans, and biological resources.

Although, today, there is not the unusual vision and determination that characterized the early days of the United Nations, diplomats and statesmen still universally acknowledge the fact of international interdependence and express their belief in effective international economic arrangements that encourage economic growth, macro-economic stability, and development of the poorer parts of the globe. The requirement that a system of independent sovereign states have rules governing national governments' international policies, and cooperative responses to problems of trading and macroeconomic policy, is still universally recognized. "Beggar-thy-neighbour" policies for dealing with domestic economic difficulties, they agree, must still be minimized. Sudden and unexpected policy lurches, with their potential for disruption, ill-considered reaction, and cumulative down-ward spirals, must be prevented. International crises must be jointly defused and those most vulnerable buffered against their deleterious effects. And agreed means for developing, in an equitable and efficient manner, the global commons – the oceans, space and environment – must be found.

As I have emphasized, the "international" economy has, to a significant extent, now become a single global economy; and events and developments in one of its parts have ramifications throughout the system. International trade, international monetary arrangements, and international development finance are all matters on which a degree of intergovernmental consensus is absolutely essential for a healthy global economy. It is undoubtedly recognized now, as it was in 1944, that, in principle, it is in each national government's interest to support such an international consensus.

Yet where are we, in fact?

In trade, the most fundamental principle of GATT – non-discrimination, unconditional most-favoured-nation treatment for all – is today routinely flouted in practice. The Multifibre Arrangement in textiles and clothing specifically and formally authorizes discrimination against low-income (low-cost) countries and, although that Arrangement, and also its predecessors, were originally temporary measures, they have discriminated for nearly 30 years. Now a host of ad hoc industry-specific and firm-specific deals have made further encroachments upon the non-discrimination principle, and frequently on the aspiration toward maximum transparency as well. So-called "voluntary export restraints" and "orderly marketing agreements," industrial policies, export subsidies, and countervailing measures, are increasingly deployed selectively to discourage the most efficient and the least capable of retaliation. While some still praise the sheer survival capacity of the GATT system, increasing numbers foresee the prospect of continuing disintegration of rules and norms, and the growth of trade disorder. Desperate efforts to re-energize the GATT in the Uruguay Round still risk foundering over (mainly North–South) disagreement as to whether the unfinished business of the past should take priority over widening aspirations in investment, agriculture, services, and intellectual property – of particular interest to the USA – for the GATT'S future. If they fail, the USA threatens reversion to bilateral (that is, discriminatory) trade deals with individual allies. Despair over the prospect of further progress within the fully multilateral trading arrangements of the past and the continued growth of discriminatory and ad hoc protectionist policy instruments have driven some, including the Canadian government, towards advocacy of special (discriminatory) trade arrangements. The interest of a middle-sized trade-dependent economy like Canada resides overwhelmingly in the strengthening of multilateral rules and dispute settlement mechanisms rather than in bilateral arrangements. The Canadian approach to the

USA is a measure of official perceptions of the sad state of the multilateral trading machinery.

In international finance, despite the IMF's admirable and much publicized leadership role in efforts to move through successive international debt crises without undue damage to the global financial system in the early 1980s, its power to perform the functions for which it was established has been weakening. The fact is that the IMF was effectively residualized as a manager of world liquidity during the 1970s. With the resumption of international commercial bank lending, all but the lowest-income, and by definition the least commercially creditworthy, countries became able to finance temporary balance-of-payments problems with greater speed, in larger amounts, and with less "hassle" over conditions, via the private banks rather than the IMF. This largely demand-determined alternative supply of international liquidity legitimized the declining capacity of the IMF to perform its traditional role as a source of liquidity and surveillance. Its overall resources were not expanded at anything like the rate at which the value of international transactions was growing, let alone at rates sufficient to respond to the fact that these transactions had become subject to much larger relative shocks than at any time since the 1930s. The resultant privatization of international liquidity creation, predictably, proved highly unstable and inequitable. The banks cut back their international lending during the latest recession – at the very time when a socially oriented liquidity system would have expanded it. Moreover, privatization meant that the poorest countries acquired considerably smaller shares of overall liquidity expansion than was planned for them in the original Bretton Woods arrangements. The international liquidity shortages that resulted in those countries particularly hard hit by the recession, notably the developing countries, have generated acute hardship and an uncalled-for degree of austerity. Ad hoc responses to these countries' liquidity shortages have included continued debt rescheduling on the part of banks and governments, and growing resort to various forms of counter-trade, such as barter, that does not rely upon traditional forms of international financing. These solutions are far from ideal and remain extremely fragile; and the IMF is no longer in a position to significantly influence global macroeconomic management.

The World Bank was created in an effort to ensure that long-term development finance would flow in adequate volume to those parts of the globe where the returns were high but, because of international and other imperfections, market incentives were unlikely to generate the socially desirable levels of flow. It was, and is, essentially an intermediary between private capital markets and developing country borrowers. Despite its triple-A credit rating and a long list of available high-return programmes and projects awaiting financing, its borrowing (and therefore lending) is today being limited because of inadequate expansion of its capital base. The US government, seeing the resurrection of international capital markets, apparently believes that there is no longer so much need for the World Bank's intermediation, despite the fact that the private banks and capital markets are manifestly failing to lend in adequate amounts themselves. Nor is direct foreign investment, despite much talk, picking up the slack. The soft-loan arm of the World Bank, the International Development Association, and the International Fund for Agricultural Development – all with remarkably good records of financing productive activities in low-income developing countries – have at the same time experienced even more severe cutbacks in their lending activities in consequence of reduced governmental support. The previous intergovernmental consensus about the need to assist development processes in the Third World and to buffer the most vulnerable against shocks not of their own making seems to be breaking down or may even be in full retreat, although popular response to African famines suggests that Northern electorates may still care.

Governments have responded to the pressures of the past decade in ways they have seen to be politically supportable and economically effective over a relatively short time horizon. In recent years, neither the international implications of domestic measures nor the possible longer-run detrimental effects of actions apparently beneficial in the short term have typically carried much domestic political weight. Macroeconomic policies and sector- or industry-specific measures have been undertaken unilaterally, bilaterally, or among small groups of cooperating countries, regardless of wider multilateral forums or agreements. The larger and more powerful the country, the greater its capacity for effective pursuit of its own objectives in disregard of international feedback effects. The most adversely affected by the increasing resort to unilateral, bilateral and small group action, and the decline of multilateralism are undoubtedly the middle-sized and smaller countries. In this, the interests of Canada, the smaller European countries and the developing countries are as one. But all countries are bound to lose from a failure to agree and abide by fully multilateral arrangements for the stabilization and development of the world economy.

The Northern public mood remains overwhelmingly myopic concerning the global economic prospect. Typical responses to the new global economy thus far are frequently reactive and negative ones. Far from responding to its challenges, we often seem to be trying to turn back the clock – to return to less "dependent" modes, to insulate ourselves from unfavorable external influences, to off load upon non-voting foreigners as many of our domestic problems as we dare. Along that route – travelled also in the interwar years – lies, of course, the potential for international economic disaster. Where each national government thinks only of its own immediate interest there is risk of mutual injury, cumulative downward spirals, and international anarchy.

The multilateral economic institutions that bolstered world economic progress in the 1960s are, today, at best, "dead in the water." Many would say they are actually slowly sinking.

What, then, are the essential requirements for multilateral economic cooperation – to encourage more predictable and equitable functioning of the world economy? The primary objective must be to establish or reestablish norms and rules, particularly in trade and in finance, which reduce the prospect of sudden and socially counterproductive policy change. The most fundamental principles that such rules should embody are the traditional ones of non-discrimination and uniformity of treatment. In order to be effective, the details of such rules have to be credible and accepted by all: at present there is widespread perception that they are flouted with impunity by rich countries, both in trade and in finance, and that they are applied with vigorously to the weaker and poorer states. Only if the strong are seen to be ready to subject their policies to the same international scrutiny and discipline as the rest can such rules effectively contribute to multilateral cooperation.

There must also be effective forums for dialogue and information exchange among countries whose approaches and policies may operate at cross-purposes. Present arrangements are widely considered to be unsatisfactory, particularly by developing and smaller countries which tend to be left out of the larger countries' informal networks.

Additionally, and quite distinct from the need for forums for dialogue, is the need for an effective machinery for multilateral negotiation when the time for multilateral negotiation of specific issues arises. Much international economic negotiation is inherently bilateral, but bilateral approaches do not encompass the full range of current global needs. Effective multilateral machinery is required not only for the normal ongoing process of negotiation of international economic issues as they arise – rule construction, dispute settlements and so on – but, more particularly, for the management of major international economic crisis and conflicts.

There must also be intensified efforts to resolve the continued problems in the relationships between powerful multilateral institutions, particularly the financial ones, and their smaller members. In the case of conflicts between a government and the international monetary and financial institutions with regard to the appropriate conduct of national economic policy, there should be opportunities for some kind of hearing or appeal. Procedures for transparent hearings or appeals for smaller countries considering themselves wronged or ill-treated by multilateral institutions would lend the latter credibility and acceptance where their record of objectivity is now significantly in question.

But these are generalities. There are serious negotiations underway today in the GATT; and there are concrete proposals afloat for the launching of extended discussions and negotiations over the future of the international monetary and financial system. The USA ostensibly accords top priority to the GATT round. The developing countries place heaviest priority instead on discussions of the Bretton Woods financial system. Trade, investment and finance are integrally linked, and the multilateral institutions that deal with them all are weakening at the very time when their strengthening would seem more appropriate. Surely some compromises can be found, to permit urgently needed multilateral economic cooperation to be strengthened in response to the new global needs? The vision of effective multilateral economic cooperation, based on concrete need, that drove sovereign states in the 1940s must somehow be rekindled in the more complex and more dangerous circumstances of the 1990s. The risks of failure to achieve it have become very high. Today, as in that earlier period of institution-building, the interest of small and middle-sized powers is particularly clear; and their potential role, as builders of bridges across ideological and political chasms, should not be underestimated. It is time, in the spirit of the original architects of the Bretton Woods institutions, and with the same overall noble aspirations for the new global (rather than the old international) economy, to launch a major fully multilateral review and reconstruction of our global economic institutions. The major agenda items should include:

(a) macroeconomic policy surveillance and coordination, crisis management, and the exchange rate régime;

(b) international liquidity and the role of the IMF;
(c) development finance and the role of the World Bank;
(d) the trade and investment régime.[1]

Perhaps these suggestions are still too much to hope for. At a minimum, however, we must now come to terms, both analytically and politically, with the new global economy and the interrelatedness of nations within it. Analytically, we must develop the tools of global macroeconomic analysis and measurement, while we improve understanding of the new multidimensional interrelatedness that has rendered the traditional assumptions of international economic theorizing obsolete. Patterns of global investment, global market structures and global market segmentation phenomena must be carefully analysed by economic analysts of a more micro-orientation, in much the same way as they currently approach these issues within nations. Here are rich new research agendas for analysts of vision.

And, politically, we must condition ourselves to think more globally, both in terms of longer time horizons and in terms of wider fields of vision. Whether we wish to do so or not, such thought will increasingly be forced upon us by the continued spatial shrinking of our planet and its concomitant new national interrelatedness. It is better to prepare for it, carefully and dispassionately, in order to avoid the shocks, surprises, and possibly costly policy lurches that could otherwise accompany belated learning processes. We must review both the meaning of national sovereignty in a world of deepened mutual interdependence and the adequacy of our current international economic (and other) institutions for the effective pursuit of global interests. As in the past, we may only come to a full realization of new needs through painful experience. Perhaps disorder in the global economy must increase before political attitudes can change. I pray not. It should surely not be necessary to wait for events to carry the world still further backward before setting out to plan and construct a more satisfactory global future.

Note

1. For a detailed exposition of these issues see the report of the group I chaired for Commonwealth Finance Ministers, *Towards a New Bretton Woods* (London: The Commonwealth Secretariat, 1984).

21

Capitalisms in Conflict? The United States, Europe, and Japan in the Post-Cold War World (1995)[*]

Barbara Stallings and Wolfgang Streeck

The end of the cold war and the disappearance of socialism as a major political–economic force opened the way for important changes in the capitalist world. These changes were of at least two types. On the one hand, the cessation of cold war hostilities between the United States and the Soviet Union downgraded the role of military in favor of economic power. This shift, in turn, increased the international standing of Europe and Japan at the expense of the United States, since the former are much stronger economically than militarily. On the other hand, the disappearance of socialism as an economic system focused attention on the differences among models of capitalism. In the 1990s, much more heed is being paid to variations in the ways of doing business in the United States, Europe, and Japan. While neither of these trends is totally new, the changed international panorama since the fall of the Berlin Wall greatly increased their salience.

For theorists and practitioners alike, a major question concerns the characteristics of the post-cold war international political economy. At the macrostructural level, debate centers on whether the emerging system will be a multilateral, interdependent one, with close cooperation among capitalist powers, or a regionalized one consisting of trade and investment "blocs" in North America, Europe, and Asia. Our argu-

---

[*] From Barbara Stallings (ed.), *Global Change, Regional Response: The New International Context of Development* (New York: Cambridge University Press, 1995), pp. 67–72. The authors thank Phil Ruder and Akira Suzuki for research assistance. *Editor's Note*: This selection does not include quantitative analysis focusing on oil trade and investment flows which is part of the original chapter.

ment is that both of these processes are happening and will continue to do so. This simultaneity, which we call "nonhegemonic interdependence," results in an unstable situation. The participants respond by trying to improve their own positions in the global economy, by convincing their competitors to degrade theirs, or by creating new rules and institutions to contain conflict.

This chapter analyzes these emerging relationships among major capitalist powers. It presents the two main positions in the structural debate and then moves to "test" the two arguments by looking at some ... qualitative data on relations among the three centers of capitalism ..., examin[ing] behavior within international organizations, especially the General Agreement on Tariffs and Trade (GATT) and the World Bank. Next we briefly sketch out what we think are the main differences among the three versions of modern capitalism and place them in the context of global economic conflict and cooperation. Finally, in line with the overall goals of the volume, the chapter concludes with some hypotheses on the implications for the third world of changing relations among capitalist powers.

Debates on the structure of capitalism

Debate on the structure of capitalism has arisen repeatedly when major political and economic changes have occurred in the world. Thus, the antecedents of the current controversy can be traced back at least to the early years of the twentieth century, when they arose out of the "scramble for colonies" among European nations and the hypothesized causes of the First World War. The primary protagonists at that time were Marxists, especially Lenin and Kautsky. Lenin argued that strong rivalry (ultimately resulting in war) was the natural relationship among nations, while Kautsky suggested that a form of "ultraimperialism" was a possible alternative.

As the war began, Kautsky, the leading figure in the German Social Democratic Party, published an article in which he suggested that the exhausting effects of the war might lead to a "holy alliance of the imperialists."[1] His reasoning was that the capitalist economy was seriously threatened from two quarters: opposition was growing among the more developed colonial nations, and the working class in the industrial nations was also protesting against increased taxes to support wars. A possible solution, according to Kautsky, was an alliance of industrial nations to jointly exploit the rest of the world.

Lenin wrote shortly afterward to attack Kautsky's position, arguing that the real tendency was for cartels to be formed within countries, but for competition to take place between them.[2] Subsequently, the cartels would divide the world among themselves. While agreeing that alliances might be formed, Lenin believed they would be only temporary since strength, which forms the basis of the division of territory, changes unevenly among the participants. Those who grow more rapidly will pull out of the alliance and go to war to increase their share.

Fifty years later, as US hegemony began to decline just as that of Britain did in the years leading up to World War I, conflicts among advanced capitalist countries began to reemerge, and a similar debate arose with respect to the United States and Western Europe. In this second round, many of the same questions and arguments were heard. Was the basic character of relations among advanced capitalist nations unity or rivalry? Who was the primary enemy – other capitalist nations or "outsiders" (i.e., socialist countries and socialist groups in peripheral nations)?

There was an additional dimension, however, in terms of the role of the United States. While there were a few analysts who spoke of a Kautskian type of alliance, where nations voluntarily cooperated, the dominant version of the unity hypothesis in the 1960s was represented by those believing that US hegemony would not only continue but perhaps become even stronger in the future. Based on their alleged superiority, deriving from their greater size and access to technology, US firms were expected to subordinate European capital. US military superiority would also be an asset, creating a unified capitalist world under the hegemony of the United States; contradictions between nations would become increasingly insignificant.[3]

Arguing that the previous position greatly exaggerated US power was a group of European analysts.[4] They pointed out that the size advantage of US firms was being rapidly eliminated by mergers in Europe, and that Europe's lower wages could provide an advantage in export competition. In addition, they predicted that European governments would come to the defense of their firms, leading to increased contradictions within the capitalist world. The emergence of a supranational European state would put Europe on an equal footing with the United States.

As the old bipolar system broke down in the 1990s, the same debates surfaced once again. International political economists have put forward two main answers to the question of how the new system will work. One group of analysts argues that the new world order is best characterized as a single global system superimposed upon individual nation-states, which are themselves losing importance. Other analysts find the world breaking up into three blocs centered on the United States, Japan, and Europe (or perhaps Germany). The resulting political–economic zones are said to be further differentiated as to the models or "styles" of capitalism prevailing there.

In a provocative recent analysis, whose sponsors describe it as "explod[ing] the myth that the world is moving inexorably into regions and exclusive trading blocs," Albert Fishlow and Stephan Haggard argue that globalism is the more likely outcome.[5] Echoing the debates of the 1960s, they give particular weight to the role of the United States as a global actor – a member of several regions simultaneously – which is projected to militate against regionalism. The authors provide data to show that interregional trade between the United States and Asia, and Asia and Europe, is growing as fast as intraregional trade. Turning to investment, they argue that even more than with trade, interregional flows dominate those within regions. "There is thus reason to expect that capital mobility can provide an escape valve from the trend toward 'degenerate regionalism.'"[6]

On the political side, they are dubious that regional integration can be successfully constructed without strong economic underpinnings. Preferences and barriers alone, if the "natural" economic links do not exist, are probably doomed to failure. As examples, they point to failed attempts to construct regional or subregional groups in Africa and Latin America. Moreover, there may also be barriers to increasing political types of integration. Historically based tensions in the Asian area have thus far impeded attempts to institutionalize the increased economic interactions. Such tensions seem to have been submerged for the moment in the Western Hemisphere as Latin American governments express great interest in the American Free Trade Area that has been proposed as a successor to the North American Free Trade Agreement (NAFTA), but they may well reappear.

Coming from a different theoretical position as a world-systems analyst and using historical data to make his case, Bruce Cumings also argues that a "trilateral regime of cooperation and free trade" is likely to develop "with the three great markets of each region underpinning and stabilizing intercapitalist rivalry in the world system."[7] Comparing the post-cold war period with the hundred-year peace (1815–1914) described by Polanyi, Cumings says that "today, as in the 19th century, we find several great powers of roughly equivalent weight with a stronger interest in creating wealth than in accumulating power."[8] Germany and Japan, he argues, have left their militarist pasts behind them and have "had their democratic revolutions, even if it took the Second World War to get them."[9] Under these structural circumstances, trilateral cooperation, such as that put forward under the Carter administration, would unite Washington, Tokyo, and Berlin to preside over a boom period for the advanced industrial world. The boom would be fueled by new technologies and new markets in Central Europe and East Asia.

Lester Thurow is perhaps the best known of the analysts who foresee the world turning toward regional blocs. The basis of Thurow's argument is that "the GATT–Bretton Woods trading system is dead."[10] The postwar multilateral system died, he says, as the normal result of its great success. While the logical next step would be another Bretton Woods conference to write new rules for the world economy, this is politically impossible without a hegemonic power. Consequently, the new rules will be written by those who control the largest market: in this case, Europe. The type of rules to emerge will be "managed trade" and "quasi-trading blocs"; the blocs will be centered on the European Union (led by Germany), Japan, and the United States. Countries within blocs will get special privileges not offered to others.

Relations among these quasi-blocs, according to Thurow, will center on a new kind of competition. While competition in the second half of the twentieth century involved "niche competition," where different countries or groups of countries specialized in different activities, the twenty-first century will witness "head-to-head competition." In the latter, all want the same industries – for example, microelectronics, biotechnology, telecommunications, computers, robotics – because these are the leading sectors that produce high-wage, high-skill jobs. With niche competition, all players can win; head-to-head competition produces many losers.

Among the reasons that losers will emerge in the new system are the differences among types of capitalism practiced in the blocs. Thurow identifies two basic types: Anglo–Saxon and German–Japanese; more subtle differences are found between the latter two:

> America and Britain trumpet individualistic values: the brilliant entrepreneur, Nobel Prize winners, large wage differentials, individual responsibility for skills, easy to fire and easy to quit, profit maximization, and hostile mergers and takeovers – their hero is the Lone Ranger. In contrast, Germany and Japan trumpet communitarian

values: business groups, social responsibility for skills, teamwork, firm loyalty, industry strategies, and active industrial policies that promote growth. Anglo–Saxon firms are profit maximizers; Japanese business firms play a game that might better be known as "strategic conquest." Americans believe in "consumer economics;" Japanese believe in "producer economics."[11]

Thurow clearly believes that the German–Japanese style of capitalism is superior in the context of the late twentieth and early twenty-first centuries. Without changes in US policy – similar in kind if not in degree to those proposed by the Clinton administration – the prognosis is clearly for the United States to fall further and further behind.

Models of capitalism: between conflict and cooperation

The analytical challenge, we suggest, is to understand the dynamics of nonhegemonic interdependence among three capitalist centers with their own heterogeneous socioeconomic characteristics. Nonhegemonic interdependence entails simultaneous conflict as well as cooperation in global economic relations, and probably steady oscillation between the two. Differences in internal structures constitute sources of competitive advantage and disadvantage in the international economy. These structural differences can also be used as instruments of political protection from the social dislocations caused by international and domestic markets, in effect turning domestic characteristics into a subject of international politics and potentially, conflict.

As has been said, with the end of the cold war, advanced capitalism is increasingly viewed, not as one economic system, but as a family of subsystems of considerable diversity.[12] Three types of capitalism are commonly distinguished, represented by the three leading centers of economic activity: the (Anglo–)American, the continental–Western European, and the Japanese versions. To the extent that the United States, the European Union, and Japan are regarded as potential hegemons of regional blocs, it is assumed that the domestic structures of other, geographically proximate bloc members will be more or less similar to those of the respective hegemonic powers. Still, each bloc is itself internally heterogeneous – although arguably less so than the global system – and thus replicates internally some of the problems of the "management of diversity" that exist between blocs. This applies in particular to Western Europe, but there are also important differences among the United States, Canada, and Mexico, which contributed to the tensions over NAFTA, and among the countries regarded as follow-ing an East Asian extension of the Japanese model.

The growing interest in capitalist diversity is a response to differ-ences in national economic performance in the 1970s and 1980s, which appeared hard to explain in strictly economic terms. Since Britain and the United States lagged in performance, most of the growing literature on the subject is aimed at identifying features of the socioeconomic systems of their main competitors, Germany and Japan, which could account for their economic ascendancy and the relative decline of Anglo–American capitalism.[13] Theories of capitalist diversity focus on differences among leading market economies in both institu-tional structures and cultural orientations – from government indus-trial policies to "work ethic" and "trust" – which may explain why some countries fared better than others in the increasingly dynamic and competitive technological and economic environment of the period. We will briefly summarize the three models as they are typi-cally portrayed and then explore how the differences among them may interact with the external relations among the three interdependent capitalist blocs.

Japanese capitalism has been described as significantly different from received Anglo–American models of capitalist economy, especially with respect to the way markets – for labor, capital, and final products – are embedded in social and political institutions and relations. In one version of the model, the state bureaucracy plays the central role in the governance of Japanese capitalism, suspending or deploying competi-tive markets in the service of national economic and political objec-tives.[14] In other accounts, it is a highly cohesive and disciplined civil society, structured by strong premodern institutions and orientations, which is easy to mobilize for collective action and protects Japanese capitalism from the dysfunctions of possessive individualism, excessive competition, and noncooperative, particularistic rationality.[15]

Either way, the result is described as a capitalist economy function-ing on the basis of robust long-term commitments of resources and loyalties and supported by densely integrated primary social structures, which provide large firms with lasting commitments to work, as well as high legitimacy for authority and hierarchy. Moreover, it appears that the Japanese state or Japanese society, or both, have a capacity to contain inequality, thereby protecting social cohesion, as well as effec-tively suppress disobedience and discontent – a puzzling combination that leads Western observers alternatively to describe the Japanese system as based on both coercion and consensus.

The Anglo–American model, by comparison, expects high economic performance from socially and politically unregulated market transactions and from unconstrained choices of rational, self-seeking individuals unencumbered by preeconomic social ties. Its basic operating principles are those of nineteenth-century laissez-faire liberalism and neoclassical economics, with their emphasis on individual liberty and the formal rationality of monadic actors pursuing exogenous preferences.[16]

The key to productivity and competitiveness in the Anglo–American model is "flexibility": the capacity of private economic actors to change their commitments rapidly as external conditions shift, to invest and divest as they see fit, and to enter and exit at their discretion. Economic institutions must be designed to facilitate this; for example, market access must be easy, labor markets must be open, and capital markets must be efficient. Also, for private individuals to be able to pursue their perceived interests independently, and for markets to be allocatively efficient, state intervention must be limited to guaranteeing the essential conditions of free markets; commitments of resources must be reversible in the short term; and organizational or social loyalties must not interfere with individuals' pursuit of market advantage. While in the Japanese model the emphasis is on commitment, the Anglo–American system prefers flexibility.[17]

It is more difficult to sketch out a Western European type of capitalism. In part, this is because Europe is internally much more heterogeneous than the United States or Japan. Note that the European Union includes Britain, which is in many respects more similar to the United States than to continental Europe. It also includes Greece and Portugal, which are, for all practical purposes, developing countries. Even France and Germany, the two major EU powers, are very different political economies. Internal diversity, for example, in the regulation of labor markets or in national institutions of monetary policy making, is at the root of the present frictions holding up the further integration of the European Union. In fact, those who refer to a Western European model of capitalism often mean the largest and most powerful European country, Germany, somehow making the problematic assumption that its socioeconomic institutions will eventually spread to all of Western Europe through the European Union or other channels.

Like Japan, the "European" model is typically described as sustained by strong social controls and commitments that favor long-term orientations and suppress preferences for short-term liquidity.[18] But in Europe, such "rigidity" is sustained, not primarily by cultural norms of discipline and obedience, but in large part by politically constructed and democratically legitimated public institutions, which serve as substitutes for traditional loyalties and inherited primary group integration. To this extent, the European model is not halfway between the United States and Japan, but represents a separate "social democratic" type of advanced capitalism in its own right.

In particular, "trust," long-term cooperation, and acceptance of collective objectives in the European model are based on social, industrial, and political citizenship rights. Together, these constitute a highly developed welfare state securing a high floor of provision for each citizen, as well as institutionalized rights of individuals and organized groups to participation and voice in the polity and at the workplace, making exit less necessary for expressing discontent. The traditional acceptance of authority and cultural identification of large corporate organizations with village or family-like communities, as prevail in Japan, are replaced with politically negotiated social compacts in a "bargained economy." Institutional arrangements that impose and enforce a high floor of social standards on the economy both require and, ideally, give rise to a high-wage economy that relies on developed human capital and professional, participatory work motivations for a production pattern geared toward quality-competitive markets for diversified goods and services.[19]

The belief that there may be inherent performance differences among the Anglo-American free-market, Japanese socially integrated, and European politically bargained models of capitalism reflects the catching up of Germany and Japan with the United States in the 1970s and 1980s, the associated long-term decline in the value of the dollar, persistent trade imbalances, and the failure of the US manufacturing sector to upgrade its products and restructure its production to take advantage of new flexible technologies and more differentiated global markets. While it is difficult to relate divergent performance to specific institutional features of the three models, at the center of the debate is the observation that both the Japanese and the continental–Western European economies display various kinds of social and institutional rigidities, that is, arrangements that, in one way or other, contain, condition, or control the operation of free markets.

While in the received wisdom of neoclassical economic theory and Anglo–American capitalist practice these rigidities should obstruct competitive performance, declining US competitiveness gave rise to the suspicion that they may in fact be essential for it. Correspondingly, attention began to focus on the possible price in economic efficiency of what was increasingly seen as excessive flexibility, mobility, and individual rationality in Anglo–American free-market capitalism. Indeed, as close investigation of both Japanese and German production systems found them to be highly flexible on a wide range of crucial dimensions (such as product turnover or worker redeployment), discussions of the economic consequences of the institutional differences among the three models of capitalism increasingly centered on the question of which society provides its economy with the most productive combination of rigidities and flexibilities.[20] Exactly which institutions are needed to defend economic efficiency against the detrimental effects of excessive market flexibility is not entirely clear; candidates include the Asian family, the MITI bureaucracy in Japan, workplace training, German codetermination, and many others.[21]

The claim that socially supported "flexible rigidities" are essential for good economic performance is not uncontested. Defenders of the Anglo–American model argue that institutional rigidities give rise to competitive advantage only insofar as they grant unfair privileges to some market participants at the expense of others and of overall allocative efficiency.[22] Examples include Japanese capital markets and corporate governance, which make it almost impossible for outside investors to acquire control over a Japanese company, or the European Charter of Fundamental Social Rights for Workers, which is suspected by US observers as laying the foundation for protectionist trade policies to defend high European labor standards. It is at this point that the debate over the comparative advantage of different institutional variants of capitalism intersects with the discussion of the maintenance of cooperative external relations among capitalist systems.

As yet, the nature of nonhegemonic interdependence among different models of capitalism, and the questions it poses for global economic coordination and governance, are not well understood. To the extent that differences in internal characteristics give rise to divergent economic performance, trade and monetary imbalances among the three models can be assumed to be endemic, resulting among other things in periodic monetary crises and recurrent pressures for realignment of currencies. As exchange rate adjustments redistribute competitive advantage, they are often difficult to accomplish cooperatively and may be undertaken unilaterally with national or bloc "sovereignty" over monetary matters deployed as a weapon in international economic rivalry.

In particular, regional trading blocs representing different versions of advanced capitalism will seek refuge in coordination within blocs if coordination between blocs is not possible, or is possible only on terms that are deemed, nationally or internationally, unacceptable. In this sense, blocs that are relatively homogeneous internally represent partial solutions to global coordination problems, internalizing some of the externalities that are created by an internationalized economy, while leaving others to be negotiated among a reduced number of larger and more powerful entities.[23]

Just as they are moving between conflict and cooperation, heterogeneous societies under global interdependence are exposed to simultaneous pressures for divergence and convergence.[24] For example, international free trade places a variety of pressures on interdependent domestic regimes to become more similar to each other, while it also mobilizes powerful domestic constituencies in defense of national institutions as sources of competitive advantage or political protection. Less successful systems that cannot escape from free trade find themselves searching for ways to improve their competitiveness, above all by the assimilation of international "best practice." Today, this mode of adjustment is facilitated by the rapid global diffusion of information and DFI in "transplants," which makes superior production systems easily observable in lagging recipient countries.

Still, there seem to be narrow limits to convergence as a response to declining competitive position. To the extent that superior economic practices are rooted in their home country's social institutions and cultural values, recipient countries may be unable to adapt them in other than a marginal way. For example, even if MITI-style industrial policy was undeniably a source of international competitive advantage, it is hard to see how the US Department of Commerce could ever become a US MITI. Similarly, while German vocational training may have enabled German manufacturing to master successfully the restructuring of the past two decades, it cannot easily be grafted onto US social structure and culture. And, even where international best practice is not incompatible with a declining country's social fabric or cultural identity, its introduction may be opposed by strong interest groups that would be negatively affected by it. If their resistance cannot be broken, convergence will not occur, regardless of the resulting competitive disadvantage.

A country that is unable to converge toward a superior model may try to employ political or military power to make the latter converge on itself, eliminating international imbalances in performance by imposing its own – less competitive – practices on its competitor. An example of this would be the Structural Impediments Initiative, initiated by the Bush administration in an attempt to make possible continued free trade with Japan. Threatening loss of access to its domestic market, the United States tried to convince Japan to help reduce the US trade deficit by making major changes in its domestic economic institutions, including an expansion of consumer credit to lower the national savings rate, a greater role for stock markets, and more reliance in industrial procurement on spot markets as opposed to long-term contracting among related firms. Refusing to give up what they, and many others, regarded as sources of competitive advantage, the Japanese suggested seeking convergence on best rather than second-best practice, urging the United States to increase its savings and investment rate, improve its educational system, and train its workers better. Little came of the initiative, and it is hard to see how it could. Disagreement among the parties is fundamental: what from the perspective of one model is superior economic practice, an exclusively domestic concern, is restraint of trade and protectionism for the other, in breach of international codes of good conduct.

Just as little, if not less, is to be expected from a third possible mode of convergence: the construction of an international regime in which system competition would be embedded and partially suspended, prohibiting participants in free trade from seeking advantage by undercutting a set of common social standards. Such a regime existed by and large in the postwar world of globally organized capitalism, in which central aspects of domestic labor regimes were taken out of international competition, and labor-inclusive industrial relations systems, with extensive social policies, free collective bargaining, and political responsibility for the maintenance of full employment were de facto conditions of admission to international free trade.[25]

Today such restraints on regime competition at the expense of social protection of workers have mostly disappeared. Defection from the joint standards of the postwar period began with the nonadversarial reorganization of the Japanese industrial relations system in the early 1960s, and continued with the deunionization of the US economy in the 1970s and 1980s and the final abandonment of the New Deal in the past decade, when income inequality rose dramatically and real incomes of about half of the workforce declined. Being the last holdout of postwar labor-inclusive industrial pluralism and adversarialism, Western Europe now is faced with the question of how it can sustain its social democratic domestic arrangements and still compete with Japan and the United States, where social expenditures are low and working time is longer. This question was behind the "Eurosclerosis" debate in the early 1980s. It is also in the background of present, not very successful, attempts in the European Union to attach a labor-inclusive "social dimension" to the internal market – an effort that, as has been mentioned, US observers see as a first step toward trade protectionism.[26]

The obstacles to convergence being what they are, continued diversity and conflict among the three variants of capitalism are highly likely. At the same time, each system's stake in continuing exchange and cooperation will probably remain high, ensuring that conflict will be accompanied by and embedded in efforts at cooperation. In special cases, competitive pressures may elicit constructive domestic responses that upgrade competitiveness without upsetting domestic balances and provide social protection through superior productive performance – as in Germany and, to some extent, in Japan during the 1970s and 1980s. But inevitably this will lead to calls from less lucky competitors for changes either in the internal structures of successful systems, or in the international arrangements under which they were successful. Pacts between systems to manage competition cooperatively will be tried at times, but given profound institutional divergence and widely different views of what is a legitimate subject of international politics and what belongs to a sovereign country's domestic affairs, there will always be strong temptations to defect in the pursuit of unilateral advantage. Rather than pursuing this subject further here, we will now turn to an exploration of how the specific mix of conflict and cooperation that results from the differences among the three leading models of capitalism reflects on the developing world.

Implications for third world development

Three initial questions arise with respect to the relevance of the differences among the three central capitalist models for economic development on the periphery: (1) To what extent can the several models of capitalism be exported to other countries? (2) Do the triad members, in their struggle for influence in the developing world, want or have to export their versions of capitalism to "client countries" in order to ensure access and control for themselves? (3) Do the models differ in their capacity to help countries develop economically?

On the surface, the Anglo–American model would appear easy to export, given that all it seems to require is the destruction of institutions and traditions that prevent the emergence of "free" markets. As the Central and Eastern European experience is beginning to show, however, even free markets are not a "state of nature," as assumed in economic theory, but depend on complicated legal and social conditions. Market creation requires institution building of an extent that comes unexpected to free-market enthusiasts informed by standard economics. For example, the development of an efficient administrative infrastructure, the establishment of private property rights and of institutions for trading such rights, and the building of effective hierarchical management control in private firms are all necessary prerequisites.

This does not mean that the more visible institutionalized Japanese or continental–Western European models are easier to export. Quite the contrary, it would appear that the Japanese path depends on a combination between a strong or even authoritarian state with high, normatively based cohesion in civil society. European-style capitalism requires a developed system of citizenship combined with and blending into a residual supply of economic and social traditionalism. Both sets of conditions are even more difficult to create intentionally than a free market, unless there are favorable circumstances that supply them, as it were, by accident. An interesting point for our analysis is the degree to which past geographic (and therefore historical–cultural) links within regimes provide these prerequisites.

Concerning the second question, it is far from clear to what extent and under what conditions hegemony of one country over another requires that the domestic institutions of the weaker country mirror those of the stronger one. This is an important question for future research. It would appear that a free-market and free-trade economy like that of the United States would depend comparatively strongly on other countries adopting the same principles. This might explain the Structural Impediments Initiative and other pressures for convergence placed by the United States on Japan.

The Japanese, by contrast, might be quite comfortable with free-market conditions in countries to which they want access. At the same time, they may also prefer such countries to be more like themselves if this means that they will be more difficult for rivals to penetrate. The European Union, of course, must be strongly interested in exporting its labor and environmental standards to Eastern Europe. But, apart from this, given the Union's lack of a common foreign policy capacity – the main countries, especially Britain and France, insisting on maintaining their traditional national zones of influence – it is hard to see where the question of a common European hegemony and its domestic preconditions in developing countries might arise in the first place.

As to the relative performance of the three models with respect to economic development, we have seen that rival claims have been put forward about the superiority of a "Japanese" or "Asian" path to development over the type of free-market policies advocated by the United States and the IFIs. No claims, as far as we are aware, have been made for the superiority of a "European" model, perhaps above all because it is not quite clear what this model is.[27] If we look at some empirical evidence on the question of performance in developing countries, it seems clear that the dominant trend over recent decades, accentuated by the 1980s, is growing differentiation. The question concerns the relationship between such differentiation and a particular region's insertion in the international political economy.

The differentiation is captured at the most general level by the notion that the 1980s were a "lost decade" – a decline in *per capita* income to levels not seen since the early 1970s or even the 1960s – for Africa and Latin America, while the Asian countries grew very rapidly. Indeed, the superior performance of the Asian countries over a long period has been most notable. The star performer was Japan itself, but [a] World Bank study ... demonstrates that all eight of the Asian countries it studied have performed well above their counterparts in other regions.[28] The 1980s exacerbated this trend: *per capita* income in East Asian developing countries grew by an average of 7 per cent per year, while *per capita* income shrank in Africa and Latin America.

Over this same period, developing countries as a whole saw their share of world resources fall, but Asian countries have generally been the exception. Take market access, for example. Developing Asia's share of world exports rose in the 1980s from 8 to 13 per cent, while those of Latin America and Africa fell from 9 to 6 per cent.[29] At least some of this difference can be attributed to Japanese firms, especially the trading companies, incorporating Asian labor and raw materials into their exports. Also, while their worldwide share of financial flows fell, Asia was the only developing region that maintained access to the private capital markets.[30] At the opposite extreme, Sub-Saharan Africa has been marginalized almost completely from private capital flows and has to rely on shrinking amounts of foreign aid. Again, Japanese capital, both public and private, was crucial in providing the Asian advantage.

Two important questions, then, come out of this chapter in terms of economic development. Does association with a particular part of the triad skew the development chances of third world countries or regions? And, if so, what are the processes behind any positive or negative effects? Three basic hypotheses seem worthy of investigation. First, differential access to investment and other financial resources might influence possibilities for development in the third world. Second, incorporation into trade/investment networks or lack thereof might skew changes for success. Third, the influence of models of capitalism might be among the most important aspects of regional location.[31]

Notes

1. Karl Kautsky, "Ultra-Imperialism," *New Left Review*, 59 (January–February 1970 [1914]), pp. 3–18, at 46.
2. V. I. Lenin, *Imperialism: The Highest Stage of Capitalism* (New York: International Publishers, 1939 [1917]).
3. This type of argument was put forward in the 1960s by both the Marxist Left and more mainstream economists and policy makers on both sides of the Atlantic. See, e.g., Harry Magdoff and Paul Sweezy, "Notes on the MNC," Parts 1 and 2, *Monthly Review*, 21(5) (October 1969), pp. 1–13, and 21 (6) (November 1969), pp. 1–13; Gaston Defferre, "De Gaulle and After," *Foreign Affairs*, 44(3) (April 1966), pp. 436–45; Anthony Eden, "The Burden of Leadership," *Foreign Affairs*, 44(2) (January 1966), pp. 229–38.
4. The case for an independent Europe was also put forward by advocates of many political positions, although their conclusions varied. Some saw more conflictual relations developing as a result of a united Europe. See, e.g., Ernest Mandel, *Europe versus America?* (London: New Left Books, 1970), and Bob Rowthorn, "Imperialism in the 1970s: Unity or Rivalry?" *New Left Review*, 69 (September–October 1971), pp. 31–54. Others saw a unified Europe as necessary for the EC to participate in an interdependent Atlantic Alliance. See e.g., Michael Stewart, "Britain, Europe and the Alliance," *Foreign Affairs*, 48(4) (July 1970), pp. 643–59; Walter Scheel, "Europe on the Move," *Foreign Policy*, 4 (Fall 1971), pp. 62–76; Zbigniew Brzezinski, "America and Europe," *Foreign Affairs*, 49(1) (October 1970), pp. 11–30.
5. Albert Fishlow and Stephan Haggard, *The United States and the Regionalisation of the World Economy* (Paris: OECD Development Centre, 1992). The quotation is from the back cover of the publication.
6. Ibid., p. 19.
7. Bruce Cumings, "Trilateralism and the New World Order," *World Policy Journal*, 7(2) (Spring 1991), pp. 195–222, at pp. 211–12.
8. Ibid., p. 203.
9. Ibid., p. 204.
10. Lester Thurow, *Head to Head: The Coming Economic Battle among Japan, Europe, and America* (New York: Morrow, 1992), p. 65.
11. Ibid., p. 32. A similar argument is presented in Jeffrey Garten, *A Cold Peace: America, Japan, Germany, and the Struggle for Supremacy* (New York: Times Books, 1992).
12. In addition to authors referred to earlier in this chapter (Thurow and Garten), see Michel Albert, *Capitalisme contre capitalisme* (Paris: Seuil, 1991); Ronald Dore, "Japanese Capitalism, Anglo–Saxon Capitalism: How Will the Darwinian Contest Turn Out?," Occasional Paper, 4, Centre for Economic

Performance, London School of Economics, 1992; and Jeffrey Hart, *Rival Capitalisms: International Competitiveness in the United States, Japan, and Western Europe* (Ithaca: Cornell University Press, 1992).

13. On declining US competitiveness, see, e.g., Michael L. Dertouzos, R. K. Lester and R. M. Solow, *Made in America: Regaining the Protective Edge* (Cambridge, Mass.: MIT Press 1989); Michael E. Porter, *The Competitive Advantage of Nations* (New York: Free Press 1990); and Stephen Cohen and John Zysman, *Manufacturing Matters: The Myth of the Post-Industrial Economy* (New York: Basic Books, 1987).

14. Chalmers Johnson, *MITI and the Japanese Miracle: The Growth of Japanese Industrial Policy, 1925–1975* (Stanford: Stanford University Press, 1982).

15. See Ronald Dore, *Taking Japan Seriously: A Confucian Perspective on Leading Economic Issues* (Stanford: Stanford University Press, 1987), and David Friedman, *The Misunderstood Miracle: Industrial Development and Political Change in Japan* (Ithaca: Cornell University Press, 1988).

16. Neoclassical theorists are often accused of having generalized the defining properties of one type of capitalist economy, turning them into universally applicable prescriptions. In particular, markets are conceived in this model not as expedient sociopolitical constructs, but as a state of nature preceding all other social institutions, as the natural right of individuals inherently disposed to "truck and barter." The locus classicus for a critical review is Karl Polanyi, "The Economy as Instituted Process," in G. Dalton (ed.), *Primitive, Archaic, and Modern Economies: Essays of Karl Polanyi* (Boston: Beacon, 1968), pp. 139–74.

17. This is the conceptual core of Ronald Dore and Wolfgang Streeck's ongoing project, "Varieties of Capitalism: Economic Institutions in the United States, United Kingdom, Japan, and Germany."

18. Many authors, including Thurow and Albert, find similarities between the Japanese and the European, or German, models of advanced capitalism, contrasting both Japan and continental Western Europe (Albert's "Rhenish" version of capitalism) with the United States and, to some extent, Britain.

19. See Peter J. Katzenstein (ed.), *Industry and Politics in West Germany: Towards the Third Republic* (Ithaca: Cornell University Press, 1989).

20. Ronald Dore, *Flexible Rigidities: Industrial Policy and Structural Adjustment in the Japanese Economy, 1970–80* (Stanford: Stanford University Press, 1986).

21. Lowell Turner, *Democracy at Work: Changing World Markets and the Future of Labor Unions* (Ithaca: Cornell University Press, 1991).

22. See, e.g., Dennis J. Encarnation, *Rivals beyond Trade: America versus Japan in Global Competition* (Ithaca: Cornell University Press, 1992).

23. An example is the European Monetary System, which was devised by France and West Germany in the late 1970s as a protection against the vagaries of the dollar and the use by the US government of the dollar exchange rate in the service of US domestic and international policy objectives.

24. J. Rogers Hollingsworth and Wolfgang Streeck, "Countries and Sectors: Concluding Remarks on Performance, Convergence and Competitiveness," in J. Rogers Hollingsworth, Philippe C. Schmitter and Wolfgang Streeck (eds), *Governing Capitalist Economies* (New York: Oxford University Press, 1993), pp. 270–300.

25. It is important to remember that the social democratic labor-capital settle-ment, which lasted for the first two decades after the war, was enforced by the United States as the hegemonic power of the capitalist world, not least to ensure that the burdens the New Deal had imposed on its domestic economy would have to be carried by its competitors as well. Another intention was to stabilize parliamentary democracy throughout the Western world against both communist and fascist alternatives and as a condition of political and military cohesion under US leadership.

26. Wolfgang Streeck, "National Diversity. Regime Competition and Institutional Deadlock: Problems in a European Industrial Relations System," *Journal of Public Policy*, 12(4) (1993), pp. 301–30.

27. European unions certainly claim that high labor standards are in the long run beneficial to developing countries, and this message is also heard from the International Labour Organisation. There are doubts, however, whether this is accepted even by an EU country like Spain, which is led by a Socialist government. In any case, the German "social market economy" is only rarely offered as an export article, and it has recently been found difficult to export even from West to East Germany.

28. World Bank, *The Asian Miracle: Economic Growth and Public Policy* (Washington, DC: World Bank, 1993).

29. IMF, *Balance of Payments Yearbook*, Part 2, 1987 and 1993.

30. *Editor's Note*: See Stephany Griffith-Jones and Barbara Stallings, "New Global Financial Trends: Implications for Development," in *Global Change, Regional Response, op. cit.*, pp. 143–73.

31. *Editor's Note*: See Barbara Stallings. "The New International Context of Development," in *Global Change, Regional Response, op. cit.*, pp. 349–87.

Epilog[*]

Harry F. Dahms

As the contributions of this volume suggest in different ways, in order for economic activity to become the center of social life in western and non-western societies, two developments had to occur first. Industrialization had to reach the level of economic organization at which the modern corporation became the dominant social institution. In addition, beyond insuring social and political stability, the function of democratic government had to be redefined to include an active responsibility for sustaining a socio–political environment directly conducive to economic growth and development (see Adams, Offe, and Cohen and Zysman, Chapters 10, 12, 14 in this volume). These two developments set the stage for an unprecedented level of cooperation between governments and economic organizations. Without the new "political economy" of managerial capitalism (see Chandler, Chapter 1 in this volume), it would not have been possible for economic definitions of value to replace the non-economic forms of value that once determined the importance of a multiplicity of contexts and realms of human activity and forms of social life.

The corporate form of economic organization appears to be superior to other forms of economic organization not just because it reduces economic contingencies that might threaten economic efficiency and organizational planning. In addition, by gaining greater control over the contingencies resulting from social, political, and cultural changes, conditions and processes – especially the threat of labor struggles – the modern corporation to varying degrees reduced a multiplicity of undesirable "utility costs." Corporations are the organizational strategy par excellence for economic decision-makers to control extra-economic conditions and noneconomic forces that might threaten profit opportunities. In this respect, the modern corporation indeed fulfills much of western democratic societies' economic planning function – as claimed by John Kenneth Galbraith (Chapter 9 in this volume), with

---

[*]   Written for this volume.

variations in degree between countries. In doing so the corporation alleviates pressures on the administrative state that increase the ability of the latter to sustain favorable business conditions.

Assuming that large economic organizations and their interests are among the driving forces determining the direction of social, societal, and civilizational change in today's world, how do they contribute to or facilitate the reconfiguration of the three institutional pillars of *modern* society – business, labor, and government? Under conditions of globalization, the meaning and nature of markets is undergoing transformations. So is the social, political, and economic role and relevance of the labor movement, and the composition of the working classes in different parts of the world. Some argue, finally, that along with the transformation of markets and the disappearance of labor unions, nation-states and their governments also are undergoing fundamental change both in status and function. What kind of economic exchange mechanisms, work force, and political systems are compatible with and conducive to the interests of transnational corporations in "world capitalism"?

The largest economic organizations represent unprecedented levels of organization and control, allowing them to exercise extreme forms of planning – at a time when concern with the threat of economic planning is in decline. This dissipating concern with planning may well be a consequence of the collapse of European socialism, and the westernization of China. Yet during the final decade of the twentieth century, the largest merger wave ever was underway, with the world's largest company created in one week, only to be superseded within a short period of time by the next merger achieving yet another superlative of some form or other – setting another "world record" which, in turn, was likely to fall within a matter of months or weeks. It appears that the collapse of "actually existing socialism" in Eastern Europe set the stage for a leap in the degree of planning exercised by national, multinational and transnational corporations that no other form of economic organization, nor any national government, can achieve, and afford to ignore. It also appears that in the West, the end of socialism caused public concern about the "threat of planning" to dissipate, thus providing large corporations with opportunities to engage in levels of concentration and planning that might have been impossible as long as our thinking about economic matters was framed in terms of market vs. planning, as exemplified by Aron (Chapter 4 in this volume).

Yet to what end have these levels of organization, control, and planning been achieved? At a time when networks replace markets, organized labor continues to lose ground, and the future of the nation-state itself is in doubt, we seem to have lost any sense of purpose for whose realization the technological achievements, organizational mastery, and vast amounts of wealth have been accomplished.

The answer, paradoxically, may lie in the shift from industrial manufacturing to big business in the sense of *big finance* – a shift that continues unabated. At its basis is a trend in capitalism as a system that is increasingly conducive to profit-making as a purpose in itself, rather than oriented toward production, and socially beneficial economizing. It is only since the close of the twentieth century that we are in the position to recognize just how much capitalism has moved beyond the principles of industrialism, and only now can we begin to speculate about the possible implications resulting therefrom. Most of all, we must wonder whether "globalization" will further amplify the *financialist* orientation in contemporary capitalism, or whether it will engender a "return to basics," i.e., to capitalist production and wealth creation as a means to enhance all of humanity's economic well-being. Though it is likely that globalization will be characterized by both of these trends, among others, we must ask whether too much of an emphasis on financialism, if unchecked and unrestrained, might from some point onward undermine further economic development and growth. It is certainly possible, after all, that governments of the most advanced capitalist societies will permit their financial sectors, by default or intent, to define economic priorities, to identify feasible corporate strategies, and to shape the relationship between business, labor and government at the national level. At such a time, national economies centered increasingly around their respective financial sectors might engender the formation of an international financial order that lacks the solid foundation of its material counterpart – industrial production driven by efficiency considerations – as well as a secure institutional infrastructure. Under such conditions, financial capitalism may imperil continued economic growth and development, and forestall well into the future any hope for attaining a more rational, reliable, and reasonable relationship between business, labor, and government, and – by implication – between the economy, society, and the state.

Virtual capitalism?

By the end of the twentieth century, it was no longer deniable that the twentieth century – not the nineteenth century – was the truly capitalist century. In 1848, Karl Marx and Friedrich Engels famously, and ambivalently, praised the achievements of the bourgeoisie and pointed to the downside of the social order built upon the capitalist mode of production.[1] Today, we have even more reason to celebrate the histori- cally unprecedented achievements of modern capitalism, after yet another century and a half of economic, political, and social "progress." Who would want to question that the attained achieve- ments went far beyond the dreams of most who lived during the early decades of the 20th century?[2] On the other hand, the fears of those who were concerned that the powers unleashed by industrialism would threaten the future of human civilization, were confirmed as well: examples include the devastation of cultures due to the increasing homogenization of forms of life and coexistence, the effects of indus- trialization on the global climate, the proliferation of endangered animal and plant species, and a decline in the quality of life that cannot be measured economically.[3] As Marx and Engels predicted would likely happen, we are in a difficult position to clearly identify the exact price human civilization has been paying for

> a constantly expanding market for its products [that] chases the bourgeoisie over the whole surface of the globe. It must nestle every- where, settle everywhere, establish connexions everywhere ... [T]hrough its exploitation of the world-market [it has] given a cos- mopolitan character to production and consumption in every country ... [and] drawn from under the feet of industry the national ground on which it stood. ... The bourgeoisie, by the rapid improve- ment of all instruments of production, by the immensely facilitated means of communication, draws all, even the most barbarian nations, into civilization... It compels all nations, on pain of extinc- tion, to adopt the bourgeois mode of production; it compels them to introduce what it calls civilization into their midst, i.e., to become bourgeois themselves. In one word, it creates a world after its own image.[4]

It is becoming ever more apparent why Marx referred to the social world of the nineteenth century in terms of bourgeois society, not "capitalism." It most certainly was the former: during the nineteenth century, the capitalist promise of a different future was very much in conflict with other sources of order: aristocratic, traditional, democra- tic, and socialist, among many others. Paradoxically, it may be more appropriate to think of the present in terms of capital*ism* as a social formation (most notably in the United States), than of societies at an earlier point in time, or stage of development. At no other time have business interests been more universally accepted; at no other time has there been more of a consensus (if tenuous) about the primacy of economic concerns and imperatives. Decision-makers in politics and society must first heed the economic prospects of any project, policy, and plan, before they can concern themselves with social, political and cultural matters. Indeed, due to its almost exclusive status as a commonly shared, all-embracing world interpretation in the West, "capitalism" appears to be a more appropriate designation of the current state of affairs than at any earlier point in history: there is little left capable of resisting its appeal as an organizing principle and a basis of power, and whatever remains that does not succumb altogether operates according to, in support of, or at the mercy of capitalist principles.[5]

At no time have we been closer to a social formation where capital and capital transfers have played a more central role for a multitude of social, political, and cultural decision-making processes. The trend has been, and continues to be, for the "capitalist" (i.e., financial) aspect of market economies to become ever more self-sustaining. Finance capitalism, as described by Veblen, Hilferding, and others, was an emerging economic order *within* industrial capitalism that grew increasingly detached from manufacturing and its orientation toward increasing productivity and efficiency. While industrial capitalism sought to draw legitimacy from its purported advancement of the general well-being of society, finance capitalism is not burdened with such concerns.

Contrary to conventional wisdom, therefore, it was not during the nineteenth century that capitalism became fully recognizable, but during the twentieth century. Accordingly, each of the five transformations described and analyzed in this volume might have pointed away from capitalism; yet in the end, they did not engender developments that resulted in qualitative changes beyond capitalist economy or society. Instead, as is apparent today, the five transformations in different ways solidified and stabilized the organization and operation of an economic system that is in constant danger of undermining its very social, cultural, political, and financial foundations.

Over the course of the twentieth century, the financial sector of advanced capitalist economies grew steadily. Many of the financial successes and especially the failures of the 1980s and 1990s (such as the savings and loan debacle, the derivatives scandals, and the crisis over hedge funds, as well as most especially the Asian crisis) were due to the growing orientation within the business communities of advanced capitalist societies, toward profits *independently* from productivity. Both Veblen's and Fligstein's chapters (2 and 16 in this volume) rightly characterize the prevailing model of corporate control in terms of this financial orientation – the *financial* definition of corporate control. The implications of this definition of organizational control are vast and far-reaching, and directly related to the nature of the social, political, cultural, and economic consequences resulting from globalization. In particular, controlling the international monetary order that emerged over the course of the twentieth century proved to be an especially daunting challenge (see especially Chapters 6 and 17 in this volume, by Kindleberger and Block, respectively), one that the most advanced societies are not likely to meet within the near future.

The US economy remains the single most important pillar of world capitalism. Yet there is no single American model of capitalism *per se* – in fact, there are several models of American capitalism, specific to different sectors of the industry and economy. On the other hand, there cannot be any doubt that the financial concept of organizational control has been gaining momentum especially in the American economy. The type of economic orientation that corresponds to this financial definition of corporate control is short-term, profit-oriented, anti-social, anti-government, anti-competition, and anti-production, and its most conspicuous manifestation is the *virtual corporation*.[6]

In a sense, the virtual corporation is the most extreme and most apparent manifestation of the trend currently underway: to make money on the basis of simulating, and manipulating the *appearance* of, productivity and efficiency. At this point, however, the virtual corporation is but a sign of things to come. For now, virtual corporations highlight rather than embody the trend which the western economies as a whole are following: the growing casino economy[7] at the center of advanced capitalism, oriented toward profits rather than productivity. If the virtual corporation were to become the "most important economic and social organization" in western capitalist societies, capitalism may yet emerge in pure form: the total rule of Capital. However, it is rather unlikely that the virtual corporation can attain such a status. For capitalism needs the front of productivity and efficiency in order to sustain the semblance of legitimacy and the motivational foundations of a work ethic that insures that the not-so-productive few will continue to obtain vast profits at the expense of the many who do the work of manufacturing products and providing services. Nor is it necessary for the virtual corporation to become central for the underlying features of the kind of capitalist orientation it represents to become discernable. At its core, the casino economy is both meaningless and dangerous, as it lacks strong material foundations, has few structure-enhancing properties, is a constant threat to economic stability, and benefits a minute group of people. In effect, derivatives, hedge funds, virtual corporations, and the like, all point toward a stage of capitalism where the Protestant ethic is more and more an obstacle to profit-making. The discrepancy between the latter as the motivational basis for work and employment, and the principles of decision-making in large corporations steadily is growing wider.

Purely capitalistic (i.e. exclusively profit-oriented) corporations are but the tip of an iceberg that betrays more and more the operation and purpose of the global economy. At this stage, the link between profits, production, and the "social good" is becoming increasingly tenuous. The relationship between the economic system, government, and their societal context, clearly no longer can be understood along such lines alone. Though "society" certainly does benefit from existing socio-economic and political arrangements, the fact that it does benefit, appears to conceal the degree to which economic progress, productivity, and efficiency no longer account for capitalism's continued prevalence.

The best indicator for this condition is the volume of money transactions that has become the primary, and purest form of profit-making. The capabilities created by computers regarding the continuous invention and re-invention of monetary instruments to attract more and more money from institutional investors, in the form of hedge funds, derivatives, and certainly many more instances of similar provenance to come – side bets of many different types that promise to generate quick profits which, in some cases, are truly fantastic – introduce into markets an added instability under the guise of reducing risks. This capability can be put to uses, 24 hours a day, 7 days a week: decisions are being made on the basis of movements of money that perfect the exploitation of the tiniest edge for a few days, hours, or less. However, these transactions have practically no tangible equivalents, nor is there any necessary link between profits made this way, and the increasing productivity of the economies and the sectors of industry involved. At the same time, a financial collapse would leave economies in shambles, because they are turning into fronts for profits in finance, not vice versa – a reversal in the order of things that brings us closer still to pure capitalism. It may not be surprising, therefore, that the virtual corporation has its monetary counterpart: *virtual money.*[8]

Globalization: beyond markets, labor, and democracy?

The dominant feature of emerging world capitalism under the aegis of globalization appears to be its free-wheeling nature. Despite the emphasis corporate and political decision-makers have placed on control and organization, it is apparent that increases of the latter are not bound to benefit societies in the form of greater stability, security, and predictability of the economic process, production and distribution. In fact, the exact opposite seems to be the case: increases in the degree to which politics, culture, and society are being controlled and steered by large corporate structures and national governments as their political corollaries, appear to be most conducive to the interests of the competitive needs of multinational and transnational corporations. Accordingly, the heightened control and organization of social forces benefits the purposes of corporations that have a vested interest in making sure that the economic process will not become and – perhaps more importantly – will not *appear* to become, more stable and reliable.

Under such conditions, how can social scientists avoid providing analyses and proposals that solidify the existing order, and limit the variety of possible trajectories of future development? In closing, I will argue that the most crucial task for social scientists may be to put forth rigorous assessments of what has changed, of the transformations that have occurred as they are manifest in the changed meaning of key concepts we employ to analyze the existing economic order. In a second step, social scientists may help to engender debates at the societal level, about the relationship between the changes western capitalist societies have undergone, and the values that guide our daily conduct, our ways of viewing the world, and the means we have at our disposal to make sense out of the world in which we live – which should shape the direction of future socio–economic developments. Unless social scientists contribute to reassessments of how prevailing norms and values in western societies can be reconciled with existing forms of organization and strategies for solving a multiplicity of problems at all levels of social organization, the promise of modernity – to gain an adequate understanding of the defining features of advanced societies as the basis for socially reasonable solutions – may be squandered for a long time to come.

Of central relevance is the tension between forms of economic organization that grow to such magnitudes that they can compete with, pressure, and coerce national governments to comply with their strategic plans and choices. We need to reassess the validity and viabil-

ity of basic analytical and descriptive categories employed by economists and social scientists over the course of the twentieth century, to
understand the transformations that have occurred – market, labor,
and nation-state. How do these concepts still apply, and to what
degree do they enable us to understand the world in which we live?

Beyond the market society: networks in the information age

It has been one of the truisms of economic thinking that the market
principle is the most desirable mechanism to insure continuous division of labor, economic growth, development, and via competition,
increasing productivity and efficiency. Yet to what degree is this presumption still feasible, for analytical purposes and as the basis of economic policies? Do production, distribution, and exchange in all
"markets" (especially in commodity, labor, and capital markets) still
follow, or in turn advance the principle of competition? It certainly
would be overstating the point to assert that at this time, there are no
markets left that follow and advance competition. Yet at the same
time, the mere fact that the market principle works in some cases, may
serve as an excuse not to recognize that the economic process can no
longer be explained in terms of the logic of markets.

Toward the end of the twentieth century, according to Robert
Kaplan,

> the 200 largest corporations employ[ed] less than three fourths of
> one per cent of the world's work force, [but] they account[ed] for
> 28 per cent of world economic activity. The 500 largest corporations
> account[ed] for 70 per cent of world trade.[9]

Even if we consider that such estimates are imprecise, they highlight
the problematic nature of referring to the self-regulating market mechanism as a meaningful analytical and descriptive category for social-
scientific analysis. Continued usage of the category of "market," and
the suggestion that in fact we work in market economies and live in
market societies, becomes highly problematic as soon as we critically
examine the basic presuppositions of our analyses. Some argue that the
market has altogether disappeared, which is merely overstating a
clearly identifiable trend.

While we may be inclined to interpret tendencies that point beyond,
or away from, the market as a central, empirically viable category, as
the final verdict about its lost analytical utility, we must recognise the
simultaneity of multiple – if contradictory – principles. In part, the
tension between concepts and facts is due to the continued orientation

of production, distribution and exchange toward actually existing markets with suppliers and customers – while the principle according to which the economic process functions at the macro-level no longer is primarily related to market mechanisms.

Despite the current resurgence of neo-liberal ideas, and the return of economic policies oriented toward laissez-faire, this return occurs under conditions that are radically different not just from the world of the 19th century, but even from the times when laissez-faire first came under scrutiny by economic and social analysts during the 1920s (see Keynes and Polanyi, Chapters 5 and 7 in this volume). Under the radically changed conditions governed by network-based, transnational corporations, it would seem, the category of "market" needs to be replaced by the category of "network" operating according to the principle of "concentration without centralization."[10]

This shift from markets to networks necessitates a major reorientation in our perspective on social and economic analysis, as well as on economic and social policy. It also draws attention to the need to differentiate countervailing trends at different levels of social and economic organization. In the age of computers, with information as an emerging and increasingly more important factor, means, and infrastructure of production, the basic concepts of economic (and related sociological) analysis are in need of fundamental reconsideration. We need to recognize that the transnational corporation may become the dominant form of economic organization, and, following Berle and Means (Chapter 3 in this volume), the most important form of social organization. To be sure, it will not be the *only* form of economic organization; and its predominance may be contingent on the existence of smaller units that fulfill a variety of indispensable functions transnationals cannot fulfill.

The *nature of control*, not the condition of organized capitalism (see Schumpeter, Chapter 8 in this volume, for different models) as such, or of "monopoly capitalism," is at issue here. If we continue to adhere to ideas and values that may have been feasible during the nineteenth century, the negative consequences could be far-reaching indeed. Moving beyond those ideas, on the other hand, appears to be among the gravest challenges. Markets no doubt continue to exist as trade and exchange, production and distribution, supply and demand determine economic activity and decision-making in some form and to some degree. On the other hand, whether markets ever were "free" is an altogether different question.[11]

What, then, is the significance of the current revival of neo-liberalism? In which sense does it resemble earlier manifestations of laissez-faire? How is it related to predominant forms of organization? In what sense is the issue of freedom of transaction, and of contract to work, still meaningful, after the shift from manufacturing to services? Furthermore, what is the nature of planning (see Jordan, Chapter 11 in this volume)? With what effects, under what circumstances? How are markets possible under network conditions? What implications result for the kind of society we live in? To what degree do acclamations of the glory of capitalism still make sense?[12]

Beyond work: downsizing labor

The centrality of industrial work to life in modern society has shaped prevailing notions of what kinds of theories of capitalist societies are needed for its understanding, and the kinds of policies at our disposal for solving an array of societies' problems. The shift from manufacturing to services opened the door to a major reorientation in the role of work in modern post-industrial society. The combination of Fordism and Taylorism generated the greatest and longest period of industrial growth and economic expansion. The most industrially and economically advanced societies reached a level of wealth, productivity, technological development, and organizational skill that prepared the rationalization of industrial production, leading to vast reductions of the manufacturing work force. As a result, a manufacturing sector oriented toward mass markets and centered around the assembly line, moved into a service-based, "post-Fordist" age.[13] However, Taylorism remained, and was continually refined further.[14] Business leaders recognized the shift from a manufacturing-based economy, with high union membership, skilled, well-paid jobs, to a service economy, as an opportunity to launch the final strike against organized labor. Since the mid-1970s, deindustrialization has been accompanied by a continuous decline in union membership, especially in the United States, along with a steady erosion in benefits, job security, and quality jobs.[15] This trend gained momentum during the late 1980s' period of downsizing, the shift to "lean production" and "just-in-time" production principles. However, as David Gordon has shown, downsizing hit the remaining manufacturing base and the productive workforce to a far greater extent than the managerial hierarchies.[16] Some have argued that the shift from manufacturing to a service-based economy entails nothing less than a sustained offensive to eliminate organized labor altogether, even though work remains that need to be done. The shift from a unionized to an increasingly temporary workforce in the service-based economy would be entirely consistent with this offensive

– cloaked in the mantle of competition-driven "economic" imperatives (see Bluestone and Harrison, and Kolko, Chapters 13 and 15 in this volume).

A growing literature addresses the declining need for skilled workers not just in the manufacturing sector, but also in the service sector.[17] There is an on-going debate in Europe about establishing a guaranteed minimum income, in response to advanced economies becoming ever more productive and efficient, requiring and supplying less and less work to be done.[18] In certain respects, we are returning to earlier debates addressing what is to be done if, after an extended period of economic growth, the amount of necessary work at the national (or at the global) level falls far short of the available workforce in advanced economies. Do capitalist societies have the capacity to redistribute work at the societal level?[19]

Beyond the nation-state: downsizing democratic government

An emerging literature dedicated to determining the role of national governments under conditions of multinational and transnational capitalism has concluded that the status and role of the third pillar of modern capitalist societies – the nation-state – is undergoing a major transformation as well. Like the first two pillars, the re-definition of the function of the nation-state appears to be imminent, to the point where some suggest that its disappearance is becoming more likely – either to be supplanted by the formation of post-national economies (see Stallings and Streeck, Chapter 21 in this volume), or replaced by supra-national corporate structures and organizations, e.g., the "network state".[20] While these assessments may be premature – especially given that in the case of impending economic crises at the global scale, only nation-states provide the mechanisms to respond to it, and to sustain social and political stability necessary for recovery – the trend is clear. Even the most well organized industrial sectors will not be able to insure social and political stability, but a world dominated and divided by large corporations is no longer unimaginable. A world fully dominated by corporations would have eradicated the need for nation-states, or forced the latter to merge with large corporations to the point where their respective boundaries, interests, and strategies become indistinguishable. Just as it is in the interest of large corporations to reduce competition, and to undermine organized labor, so too is it in their interest to reduce the degree to which governments are responsive to democratic will-formation and the ability of democratic constituencies to express their discontent with economic developments.[21]

If corporations succeed at undermining the power of nation-states, they also reduce the threat of democracy as a principle that is directly opposed to the principle of hierarchical, patriarchal corporate control: bureaucracy.[22]

In concrete terms, the actual disappearance of nation-state and national governments is unlikely. A profound redefinition of their function and power, on the other hand, is not. Many multinational corporations (see Gilpin, Chapter 19 in this volume) are far better organized, and enjoy far wider reach, than a growing number of nation-states around the globe, especially in the Third World and the countries of the former Soviet hemisphere. Multinational and transnational corporations usually do not have the power to directly compel national governments to comply with their demands; however, they do have the power to rewrite the rules of the game of international competition. The greater the sphere of influence of large corporations, the greater the need of nation-states to compete with each other in the interest of attracting business operations, by providing a conducive business, production, and labor-supply environment. In addition, the role of national governments is being redefined regarding the need to fulfill functions they had to fulfill during the Cold War, such as providing a social welfare net. With the collapse of "actually existing European socialism," there appears to be less of a need to provide such a net, in the absence of the competition of social systems that was the Cold War. While the people in western societies appear to be more willing to accept cuts in social services, business corporations are far less willing to fund them. In addition, economic and political decision-makers appear to sense that in the absence of the former conflict between East and West, reducing the welfare state will not threaten social and political stability.

The economic planning function has shifted almost completely from the national interest to private interests – states have continually lost more of their ability to define national economic agendas, especially in terms of specifying the social purpose of economic production, desirable production, and benefits derived from the kind of services that are supplied by economic organizations. National governments and modern societies react to developments in the economic sphere, rather than the economic sphere reacting to definitions of political purpose and socially desirable goods and services.

Furthermore, we may wonder whether during an economic downturn, business organizations will be more capable of confronting challenges than they were during the 1930s. Since they do not appear to be willing to secure profits and business conditions in the larger social, political, historical and global framework, they do not prepare for the consequences resulting from possible economic slow-downs (see Bensman and Vidich, Chapter 18 in this volume), in ways that would enable them to move beyond narrow definitions of profitability, short-term successes, and the minimization of social investment. Finally, there is no real willingness to consider constructive implications of global cooperation and interest (see Helleiner, Chapter 20 in this volume), although there is a new organizational body for mediating global national and economic interests, the World Trade Organization (WTO), founded in 1995.

The future of capitalism

Given the apparent success of American capitalism under the aegis of globalization, a growing number of national governments feel compelled get "on board" sooner rather than later. Yet can we be certain that American economic success derives from its factual economic superiority over alternative forms of economic organization in other capitalist societies, such as Japan and Germany? Considering the differences between existing economic infrastructures in capitalist societies, in what ways can we relate the patterns of success in one society to the possibility of similar successes in other, presumably comparable societies? The conditions for, and the foundations of economic success in the US, Japan, and Germany, for instance, in many ways are so different that their compatibility needs to be continually redetermined. Their respective constellations of business, labor and government are characterized by such tremendous differences that comparative analysis cannot start out from the assumption that one economic theory, and one analytical framework, can apply equally well for each individual case. In fact, by presuming that one approach should apply equally to all capitalist economies – and by predetermining the design of the approach accordingly – we risk superimposing a reference frame that is likely to *prevent* us from recognizing crucial differences. In this light, attempts to replicate American economic and financial success in other societies, without first identifying the comparative advantages and disadvantages of their respective capitalist systems, may turn out to be quite perilous for the achievement of economic and financial success in the latter.

Near the close of the twentieth century, Thomas Shapiro wrote that the

> changes we are seeing in [American] society during the 1990s – stagnating living standards, increasing poverty, a precarious middle class, and a growing gap between rich and poor – are probably the result of the specific way that economic restructuring is taking place in the United States.[23]

Those eager to replicate the "American model" of globalization, however contrived, in other parts of the world, should consider that the comparable success of this "model" may derive not only from the economic superiority of its business organizations, but from their superior social and political "control" over the work force and the population at large. Viewed along such lines, globalization may be a promise for American capitalism, enabling it to perfect further the patterns of organizational control toward sustaining and enhancing profit opportunities. Yet, depending on the specific features of other capitalisms, globalization may constitute a major threat to other nations' existing competitive advantages, whose foundations are being undermined by the conviction that the "American model" is above all an economic model. We should contemplate that the American model instead may be a form of social, cultural, and political organization geared towards maximizing control; and that the implementation of similar strategies in other capitalist societies may not be possible, or possible only at great social and political costs – given the organizational and cultural foundations of their respective economic systems. As a mechanism of implementing decisions that is fundamentally hierarchical, paternalistic, and bureaucratic, control may be the form of social organization characteristic of social systems that are not willing or capable of *solving* a multiplicity of social, political, economic, and cultural problems, and admitting the prevalence of fundamental contradictions in the social structure, to consider what it would take for such problems to be *resolved* once and for all.

Notes

1. "The bourgeoisie, historically, has played a most revolutionary part ... [It] cannot exist without constantly revolutionizing the instruments of production, and thereby the relations of production, and with them the whole relations of society ... The bourgeoisie, during its rule of scarce one hundred years, has created more massive and more colossal productive forces than have preceding generations together. Subjection of Nature's forces to man, machinery, application of chemistry to industry and agriculture, steam-

navigation, railways, electric telegraphs, clearing of whole continents for cultivation, canalization of rivers, whole populations conjured out of the ground – what earlier century had even a presentiment that such productive forces slumbered in the lap of social labor? ... All that is solid melts into air, all that is holy is profaned, and man is at last compelled to face with sober senses, his real conditions of life, and his relations with his kind." (Karl Marx and Friedrich Engels, *Manifesto of the Communist Party* [1848], in Robert C. Tucker (ed.), *The Marx-Engels Reader*, 2nd edn, New York: W. W. Norton, 1978, pp. 469–500; here, pp. 475–7).

2. Examples could be drawn from political, social, and economic philosophy and theory, as well as from political ideology, literature, art, and film. Consider especially the variety of contributions to the emerging genre of science fiction, which more or less noticeably related to the social, political, and economic conditions during the early decades of the century.

3. See especially Ulrich Beck, *Risk Society. Toward a New Modernity* (London: Sage, 1992).

4. Tucker (ed.), *Marx-Engels Reader, op.cit.*, pp. 476–7.

5. See Giovanni Arrighi, *The Long Twentieth Century: Money, Power, and the Origins of Our Times* (New York: Verso, 1994), e.g. p. 214; also William Greider, *One World, Ready or Not. The Manic Logic of Global Capitalism* (New York: Simon & Schuster, 1997), *passim*.

6. See, e.g. William H. Davidow and Michael S. Malone, *The Virtual Corporation. Structuring and Revitalizing the Corporation for the 21st Century* (New York: HarperCollins, 1992).

7. Susan Strange, *Casino Capitalism* (New York: Basil Blackwell, 1986).

8. See especially Elinor Harris Solomon, *Virtual Money. Understanding Power and Risks of Money's High Speed Journey into Electronic Space* (New York: Oxford University Press, 1997).

9. Robert D. Kaplan, "The Future of Democracy," *Atlantic Monthly*, 280(6) (December 1997), pp. 55–80; here, p. 71.

10. E.g. Bennett Harrison, *Lean and Mean. The Changing Landscape of Corporate Power in the Age of Flexibility* (New York: Guilford Press, 1994 [1997 edn]), esp. pp. 8–12; Manuel Castells, *The Rise of Network Society*, Vol. 1 of *The Information Age: Economy, Society and Culture* (Malden, Mass.: Blackwell, 1996).

11. See especially William Lazonick, *Business Organization and the Myth of the Market Economy* (Cambridge: Cambridge University Press, 1991); also Robert Kuttner, *The End of Laissez-Faire. National Purpose and the Global Economy after the Cold War* (New York: Alfred A. Knopf, 1991); and Ravi Batra, *The Myth of Free Trade. A Plan for America's Economic Revival* (New York: Charles Scribner's Sons, 1993).

12. For instructive examples for such acclamations, see Arthur Seldon, *Capitalism* (Cambridge, Mass.: Blackwell, 1990); and George Reisman's monumental *Capitalism. A Treatise on Economics* (Ottawa, Ill.: Jameson Books, 1996).

13. On the need for the development of a sophisticated critical theory of post-Fordism, see Robert J. Antonio and Alessandro Bonanno, "Post-Fordism in the United States: The Poverty of Market-Centered Democracy," *Current Perspectives in Social Theory*, 16 (1996), pp. 3–32; David Harvey, *The Condition of Postmodernity. An Enquiry into the Origin of Cultural Change* (Cambridge, Mass.: Blackwell, 1990). For a similar perspective on deindustrialization, see Ben Agger, "The Dialectic of Deindustrialization: An Essay

on Advanced Capitalism," in John Forester (ed.), *Critical Theory and Public Life* (Cambridge, Mass.: MIT Press, 1985), pp. 3–21.

14. Stephen P. Waring, *Taylorism Transformed. Scientific Management Theory since 1945* (Chapel Hill, NC: University of North Carolina Press, 1991).

15. See Bruce Western, *Between Class and Market. Postwar Unionization in the Capitalist Democracies* (Princeton: Princeton University Press, 1997).

16. David M. Gordon, *Fat and Mean. The Corporate Squeeze of Working Americans and the Myth of Managerial "Downsizing"* (New York: Free Press, 1996). The work's second chapter, "The Bureaucratic Burden" (pp. 33–60), for instance, shows how downsizing has hit the productive work force much harder than the supervisory and managerial positions, whose share in non-farm, non-governmental sector in the United States adds up to at least twice the size of most other industrialized nations.

17. Especially Jeremy Rifkin, *The End of Work. The Decline in the Global Labor Force and the Dawn of the Post-Market Era* (New York: Tarcher/Putnam, 1995).

18. Philippe van Parijs is the leading social scientist in this tradition; see *Marxism Recycled* (Cambridge: Cambridge University Press, 1993); *Real Freedom For All. What (If Anything) Can Justify Capitalism?* (Oxford: Clarendon Press, 1995); and the edited volume, *Arguing for Basic Income: Ethical Foundations for a Radical Reform* (New York: Verso, 1992). See also Robert van der Veen, and Philippe van Parijs, "A Capitalist Road to Communism," *Theory and Society*, 15(5) (1986), Bill Jordan, *The State. Authority and Autonomy* (New York: Blackwell, 1985), esp. pp. 285–348; and Claus Offe, Ulrich Mückenberger and Ilona Ostner, "A Basic Income Guaranteed by the State: A Need of the Moment in Social Policy," in Offe, *Modernity and the State: East, West* (Cambridge, Mass.: MIT Press, 1996).

19. Marx addressed this issue at what came to be the end of *Capital*, Vol. 3, in his distinction between the realm of necessity and the realm of freedom: Robert C. Tucker (ed.), *The Marx–Engels Reader*, 2nd edn (New York: W. W. Norton, 1978), pp. 439–41. John Maynard Keynes also took up this problem, in his 1930 article, "Economic Possibilities For Our Grandchildren," *Essays in Persuasion*, Vol. IX of *The Collected Writings of John Maynard Keynes* (London: Macmillan, 1972), pp. 321–32.

20. See Manuel Castells, "A Powerless State?," in *The Power of Identity*, Vol. II of *The Information Age: Economy, Society and Culture* (Malden, Mass.: Blackwell, 1997), pp. 243–308. See also Susan Strange, *The Retreat of the State. The Diffusion of Power in the World Economy* (Cambridge: Cambridge University Press, 1996); Kenichi Ohmae, *The End of the Nation-State. The Rise of Regional Economies* (New York: Free Press, 1995); Jean-Marie Guéhenno, *The End of the Nation-State*, trans. Victoria Elliott (Minneapolis: University of Minnesota Press, 1994).

21. See Noam Chomsky, *Power and Prospects: Reflections on Human Nature and the Social Order* (Boston: South End Press, 1996), pp. 73–74.

22. See especially Heidi Hartmann, "Capitalism, Patriarchy, and Job Segregation by Sex," *Signs: Journal of Women in Culture and Society*, 1(3), Part 2 (1976). On the tension between democracy and bureaucracy more generally, see David Beetham, *Bureaucracy* 2nd ed. (Minneapolis: University of Minnesota Press, 1996).

23. Thomas Shapiro (ed.), *Great Divides. Readings in Social Inequality in the United States* (Mountain View, Cal.: Mayfield, 1998), p. 1.

Acknowledgments

First and foremost, I wish to thank the series editors, Robert Jackall and Arthur J. Vidich, for their inspiration, continued encouragement and support, and for important suggestions made at crucial points especially in the process of selecting the most suitable contributions from a field of research that is vast and inexhaustable. I also would like to thank Richard Swedberg, Larry Isaac, Lawrence Hazelrigg, and John Myles for their willingness to discuss specific issues at various stages in the selection and writing process. Special thanks to Paul Lipold, a promising graduate student of political economy in FSU's sociology department, who followed the development of this volume from its inception, provided advice and expressed impressions regarding the suitability of specific selections (frequently functioning as the targeted reader's voice), and who helped in a variety of ways. Finally, I also thank Kimberly Barton for making sure that over the course of several years, the project remained on my list of priorities; Daniel Harrison and John Farnum for reading and commenting on various versions of the introduction and epilog; and several cohorts of undergraduate students who enrolled in my course, *Sociology of Business, Labor, and Government.*

The editor and publishers acknowledge with appreciation permission from the following to reproduce copyright material:

The MIT Press, for Alfred D. Chandler, Jr., "The Role of Business in the United States: A Historical Survey," in Eli Goldston, Herbert C. Morton and G. Neal Ryland (eds), *The American Business Corporation: New Perspectives on Profit and Purpose* (Cambridge, Mass.: MIT Press, 1972), pp. 39–56.

Esther J. Baran, for Thorstein Veblen, "The Industrial System of the New Order," in *Absentee Ownership and Business Enterprise in Recent Times* (New York: B.W. Huebsch, 1923), pp. 229–50.

Prentice-Hall, Inc., for Adolph A. Berle, Jr. and Gardiner C. Means, "The Concentration of Economic Power," in *The Modern Corporation and Private Property* (New York: Macmillan, 1932), pp. 18–19, 24–7, 28–33, 35, 40–6, 356–7.

Weidenfeld & Nicolson, for Raymond Aron, "Industrial Society," in *18 Lectures on Industrial Society* (London: Weidenfeld & Nicolson, 1961), pp. 73–84.

The Royal Economic Society, for John Maynard Keynes, "The End of Laissez-Faire" (1926), in *Essays in Persuasion* (New York: W. W. Norton and London: Macmillan, 1963), pp. 358–73.

Charles P. Kindleberger, for "An Explanation of the 1929 Depression," in *The World in Depression 1929–1939* (Berkeley: University of California Press, 1973), pp. 291–307.

Commentary, for Karl Polanyi, "Our Obsolete Market Mentality," in *Commentary*, 3 (February 1947), pp. 109–17. © 1947 by the American Jewish Committee

Joseph A. Schumpeter, for "Capitalism in the Postwar World," in Seymour E. Harris (ed.), *Postwar Economic Problems* (New York: McGraw-Hill, 1943), pp. 113–26.

Houghton Mifflin Publishers, for John Kenneth Galbraith, "The Technostructure," "The Industrial System and the State I," and "The Industrial System and the State II," in *The New Industrial State* (Boston: Houghton Mifflin, 1967), pp. 70–1, 296–306, 308–17.

American Economic Review, for Walter Adams, "The Military–Industrial Complex and the New Industrial State," *American Economic Review* (*Papers and Proceedings*), 58(2) (1968), pp. 652–65.

Bill Jordan, for "Planning, Corporatism, and the Capitalist State," *The State. Authority and Autonomy* (Oxford: Blackwell, 1985), pp. 219–37.

Claus Offe and John Keane, for Claus Offe, "Some Contradictions of the Modern Welfare State," *Contradictions of the Welfare State*, trans. John Keane (Cambridge, Mass.: MIT Press, 1984), pp. 147–61.

Barry Bluestone and Bennett Harrison, for "Closed Plants, Lost Jobs," *The Deindustrialization of America* (New York: Basic Books, 1982), pp. 25–29, 31–6, 37–8, 39–43, 44–8.

Basic Books, for Stephen S. Cohen and John Zysman, "Toward a Policy Agenda for Competitiveness," *Manufacturing Matters: The Myth of the Post-Industrial Economy* (New York: Basic Books, 1987), pp. 220–4, 242–3.

Joyce Kolko, for "Restructuring and the Working Class," in *Restructuring the World Economy* (New York: Pantheon, 1988), pp. 305–24, 327, 329–31, 343–45.

Harvard University Press, for Neil Fligstein, "The Social Construction of Efficiency," in *The Transformation of Corporate Control* (Cambridge, Mass: Harvard University Press, 1990), pp. 295–314.

University of California Press, for Fred L. Block, "The International Monetary Order in Crisis," in *The Origins of International Economic Disorder: A Study of United States International Monetary Policy from World War II to the Present* (Berkeley: University of California Press, 1977), pp. 203–25.

Marilyn Bensman and Arthur J. Vidich, for Joseph Bensman and Arthur J. Vidich, "American Society Since the Golden Age of Capitalism," in *American Society: The Welfare State and Beyond* (South Hadley, Mass.: Bergin & Garvey, 1987), pp. 313–36.

Princeton University Press, for Robert Gilpin, "The Multinational Corporations and International Production," in *The Political Economy of International Relations* (Princeton: Princeton University Press, 1987), pp. 231–8, 252–62.

Gerald K. Helleiner, for "The New Global Economy: Problems and Prospects," in *The New Global Economy and the Developing Countries: Essays in International Economics and Development* (Brookfield, VT: Edward Elgar, 1990), pp. 20–32.

Cambridge University Press, for Barbara Stallings and Wolfgang Streeck, "Capitalisms in Conflict? The United States, Europe, and Japan in the Post-Cold War World," in Barbara Stallings (ed.), *Global Change, Regional Response: The New International Context of Development* (New York: Cambridge University Press, 1995), pp. 67–72, 87–99.

Notes on the Contributors

Note: The following list does not cite the books from which the chapters in this volume are taken.

Walter Adams (1922–98) was Distinguished University Professor of Economics and former president of Michigan State University. He co-authored several works with James W. Brock, including *The Bigness Complex: Industry, Labor, and Government in the American Economy* (1986); *Dangerous Pursuits: Mergers and Acquisitions in the Age of Wall Street* (1989); *Antitrust Economics on Trial: A Dialogue on the New Laissez-Faire* (1991); and *Adam Smith goes to Moscow: A Dialogue on Radical Reform* (1993).

Raymond Aron (1905–83) was one of the foremost French sociologists and historians of the twentieth century. He taught at the University of Toulouse, the Ecole Nationale d'Administration, the Sorbonne, and at the Collège de France. His many books include *The Opium of the Intellectuals* (1962); *Main Currents in Sociological Thought* (1965); *Peace and War: A Theory of International Relations* (1966); *The Industrial Society: Three Essays on Ideology and Development* (1967); *Democracy and Totalitarianism* (1968); *Progress and Disillusion: The Dialectics of Modern Society* (1968); *Essay on Freedom* (1970); *The Imperial Republic: The United States and the World, 1945–1973* (1974); and *In Defense of Decadent Europe* (1977).

Joseph Bensman (1922–86) was Professor of Sociology at the City University of New York and a Lecturer at the New School for Social Research. His works include *Dollars and Sense: Ideology, Ethics and the Meaning of Work in Profit and Non-Profit Organizations* (1967); *Craft and Consciousness: Occupational Technique and the Development of World*

Images (1973) and *Between Public and Private: Lost Boundaries of the Self* (1979) – both co-authored with Robert Lilienfeld; and *Small Town in Mass Society* (1st edn, 1958; co-authored with Arthur J. Vidich).

Adolf A. Berle, Jr. (1895–1971) was a Professor of Law at Columbia University, Assistant Secretary of State during the Roosevelt Administration, and US Ambassador to Brazil. His works include *Studies in the Law of Corporation Finance* (1928); *Liquid Claims and National Wealth* (1934; with Victoria J. Pederson); *New Directions in the New World* (1940); *The 20th Century Capitalist Revolution* (1954); *Economic Power and the Free Society* (1957); *Tides of Crisis. A Primer of Foreign Relations* (1957); *Power Without Poverty. A New Development in American Political Economy* (1959); *The American Economic Republic* (1963); *Power* (1969); and *Navigating the Rapids, 1918–1971* (1973).

Fred L. Block is Professor of Sociology at the University of California, Davis. He is the author of *Revising State Theory: Essays in Politics and Postindustrialism* (1987); *Postindustrial Possibilities: A Critique of Economic Discourse* (1990); *The Vampire State: And Other Myths and Fallacies About the US Economy* (1996); co-author of *The Mean Season: The Attack on the Welfare State* (1987) and he has published articles in recent years in *Monthly Review*, *Political Science Quarterly*, *Politics and Society*, and *World Policy Journal*.

Barry Bluestone is Frank L. Boyden Professor of Political Economy at the University of Massachusetts, Boston, and a senior fellow at its John W. McCormack Institute of Public Affairs. His publications include *Capital and Communities: The Causes and Consequences of Private Disinvestment* (1980; with Bennett Harrison); *Aircraft Industry Dynamics: An Analysis of Competition, Capital, and Labor* (1981; with Peter Jordan and Mark Sullivan); *The Great U-Turn: Corporate Restructuring and the Polarizing of America* (1988; with Bennett Harrison); and *Negotiating the Future: A Labor Perspective on American Business* (1992; with Irving Bluestone).

Alfred D. Chandler, Jr. is Isidor Strauss Professor of Business History, Emeritus, at Harvard Business School and author of many articles and books, including *Strategy and Structure* (1962); *The Visible Hand. The Managerial Revolution in American Business* (1977) – for which he received the Pulitzer and Bancroft Prizes; *The Essential Alfred Chandler. Essays Toward a Historical Theory of Big Business* (1988; edited by

Thomas K. McGraw); and *Scale and Scope. The Dynamics of Industrial Capitalism* (1990). He co-edited *Managerial Hierarchies* (1980; with Herman Daems); *Big Business and the Wealth of Nations* (1997; with Franco Amatori and Takashi Hikino); and *The Dynamic Firm: The Role of Technology, Strategy, Organization, and Regions* (1998; with Peter Hagstrom and Orjan Solvell).

Stephen S. Cohen is Professor of Planning at the University of California, Berkeley, and Co-Director of the Berkeley Roundtable on International Economy (BRIE). His works include *Modern Capitalist Planning: The French Model* (1977); and *France in the Troubled World Economy* (1982; with Peter A. Gourevitch).

Harry F. Dahms is Associate Professor of Sociology at Florida State University in Tallahassee; he also taught at the Center for European and North American Studies, University of Göttingen. He has published articles on Schumpeter's social theory and on Weberian Marxism (both in *Sociological Theory*), on reification and on the early Frankfurt School's critique of political economy (both in *Current Perspectives in Social Theory*), as well as in *Soziale Welt* and *International Journal of Politics, Culture, and Society*. Currently, he is revising a manuscript on Schumpeter's theory of entrepreneurship which will be published by the University of Minnesota Press.

Neil Fligstein is Professor and former Chair of the Department of Sociology at the University of California, Berkeley. He has published *Going North, Migration of Blacks and Whites From the South, 1900–1950* (1981); and *Markets, Politics, and Globalization* (1997); he regularly contributes to *American Journal of Sociology*, and *American Sociological Review*, and he has published articles in recent years in *The American Behavioral Scientist* and *Annual Review of Sociology*.

John Kenneth Galbraith is Professor Emeritus at Harvard University. He also taught at Princeton, held several government posts during the Second World War, was an advisor to President John F. Kennedy and US Ambassador to India. Among his many works are *American Capitalism: The Concept of Countervailing Power* (1951); *The Great Crash, 1929* (1955); *The Affluent Society* (1958); *Economic Development* (1964); *Voice of the Poor: Essays in Economic and Political Persuasion* (1983); *The Anatomy of Power* (1983); *Economics in Perspective* (1987); *The Culture of Contentment* (1992); *A Journey Through Economic Time: A Firsthand View* (1994); and *The Good Society: The Humane Agenda* (1996).

Robert Gilpin is Dwight D. Eisenhower Professor of International Affairs at the Woodrow Wilson School of Princeton University. His works include *American Scientists and Nuclear Weapons Policy* (1962); *Scientists and National Policy Making* (1964); *France in the Age of the Scientific State* (1968); *Technology, Economic Growth, and International Competitiveness* (1975); *US Power and the Multinational Corporation* (1975); and *War and Change in World Politics* (1981).

Bennett Harrison is Professor of Urban Political Economy at the Milan Graduate School of Management and Urban Policy of the New School for Social Research, and affiliated member of the Department of Economics. In addition to dozens of articles, his recent works include *Capital and Communities: The Causes and Consequences of Private Disinvestment* (1980; with Barry Bluestone); *The Great U-Turn: Corporate Restructuring and the Polarizing of America* (1988; with Barry Bluestone); *Lean and Mean: The Changing Landscape of Corporate Power in the Age of Flexibility* (1994; rev. ed. 1997); and *Workforce Development Networks: Community-Based Organizations and Regional Alliances* (1998; with Marcus Weiss).

Gerald K. Helleiner is Professor of Economics at the University of Toronto; he is the author of *International Economic Disorder: Essays in North-South Relations* (1981); and the editor of *The Other Side of International Development Policy* (1990); *Trade-Policy, Industrialization, and Development: New Perspectives* (1992); *From Adjustment to Development in Africa: Conflict, Controversy, Consensus?* (1994; with G. A. Cornia); *Manufacturing for Export in the Developing World: Problems and Possibilities* (1995); *Poverty, Prosperity, and the World Economy* (1995; co-editor); and *The International Monetary and Financial System: Developing Country Perspectives* (1996).

Bill Jordan is Reader in Social Studies at the University of Exeter; his works include *Freedom and the Welfare State* (1976); *Automatic Poverty* (1981); *Rethinking Welfare* (1987); *The Common Good: Citizenship, Morality, and Self-Interest* (1989); *Social Work in an Unjust Society* (1990); and *A Theory of Poverty and Social Exclusion* (1996); he has co-authored *Trapped in Poverty?* (1992); and he co-edited *Creative Social Work* (1979; with David Brandon); and *The Political Dimensions of Social Work* (1983; with Nigel Parton).

John Maynard Keynes (1883–46) was probably the single most influential economic theorist of the twentieth century. He held various government posts (UK), and taught at Cambridge University. His works include *Economic Consequences of the Peace* (1919); *Monetary Reform* (1924); *Laissez-Faire and Communism* (1926); *A Treatise on Money* (1930); *Essays in Biography* (1933); and *The General Theory of Employment, Interest and Money* (1936). The Royal Economic Society's edition of *The Collected Writings of John Maynard Keynes* (1971–9) comprises 31 volumes.

Charles P. Kindleberger, one of the world's foremost economic historians, is Ford International Professor of International Economics, Emeritus, at the Massachusetts Institute of Technology, and the author and editor of dozens of books, including, more recently, *America in the World Economy* (1977); *Multinational Excursions* (1984); *The International Economic Order: Essays on Financial Crisis and International Public Goods* (1988); *Life of an Economist: An Autobiography* (1991); *Mariners and Markets* (1992); *The World Economy and National Finance in Historical Perspective* (1995); *Manias, Panics, and Crashes: A History of Financial Crises* (1996); and *World Economic Primacy: 1500–1990* (1996).

Joyce Kolko is the author of *America and the Crisis of World Capitalism* (1974), and, with Gabriel Kolko, *The Limits of Power: The World and United States Foreign Policy, 1945–1954* (1972). She lives in Amsterdam and is now completing a study of *Global Capitalism: Convergence and Consensus*.

Gardiner C. Means (1896–1988) was Economic Advisor on Finance to Roosevelt's Secretary of Agriculture, Director in a section of the National Resources Committee, and Associate Director of Research for the Committee for Economic Development. For the US National Resources Committee, he directed and edited *The Structure of the American Economy* (2 vols, 1939–40); he authored *Pricing Power and the Public Interest* (1962); *The Corporate Revolution in America: Economic Reality vs. Economic Theory* (1962); and *A Monetary Theory of Employment* (1994); and he co-authored *The Roots of Inflation: The International Crisis* (1975).

Claus Offe is Professor of Political Science at Humboldt University, Berlin, and taught as Theodor Heuss Professor of Sociology at the Graduate Faculty of the New School for Social Research. Previously, he was Director of the Center for Social Policy at the University of Bremen, and Professor of Political Science and Sociology at Bremen and the University of Bielefeld. His works include *Disorganized Capitalism*.

Contemporary Transformations of Work and Politics (1985); *Beyond Employment: Time, Work, and the Informal Economy* (1992; co-edited with Rolf G. Heinze); *Modernity and the State. East, West* (1996); *Varieties of Transition: The East European and East German Experience* (1997); and *Institutional Design in Post-Communist Societies: Rebuilding the Ship at Sea* (1998; co-authored with Jon Elster and Ulrich K. Preuss).

Karl Polanyi (1886–1964) was an economic anthropologist, a Hungarian political leader, and Professor of Economics at Columbia University. His publications include the classic, *The Great Transformation* (1944); *Christianity and the Social Revolution* (1935; co-edited with John Lewis and Donald K. Kitchin); *Trade and Markets in the Early Empires* (1957; co-authored); *Dahomey and the Slave Trade* (1966); as well as *The Livelihood of Man* (1977; ed. by Harry W. Pearson), along with many articles.

Joseph A. Schumpeter (1883–1950), one of the foremost political economist of the first half of the twentieth century, taught at the Universities of Czernowitz, Graz, Bonn, Columbia, Tokyo, and at Harvard. Along with most of his articles, his books have been translated into many languages, *The Theory of Economic Development* (1911; rev. ed. 1926; Eng. ed.: 1934); *Business Cycles* (1939; 2 vols); *Capitalism, Socialism, and Democracy* (1942); *Essays* (1951); *Ten Great Economists from Marx to Keynes* (1951); *Economic Doctrine and Method* (1954); *History of Economic Analysis* (1954); and numerous collections of his writings.

Barbara Stallings is Director of the Economic Development Division of the UN Economic Commission for Latin America and the Caribbean in Santiago, Chile, and former Director of the Global Studies Research Program at the University of Wisconsin, Madison, from where she is on leave. Aside from many articles, she is the author of *Class Conflict and Economic Development in Chile, 1958–1973* (1978); and *Banker to the Third World: Latin America and US Capital Markets, 1900–1986* (1987); and the co-editor of *Debt and Democracy in Latin America* (1989; with Robert Kaufman); and *Japan, the United States, and Latin America: Toward a Trilateral Relationship Within the Western Hemisphere* (1993; with Gabriel Szekely).

Wolfgang Streeck is Director of the Max Planck Institute for Social Research in Cologne and Honorary Professor at Humboldt University, Berlin. He was Professor of Sociology at the University of Wisconsin,

Madison, and he has taught in Florence, Warwick, Madrid, and Milano. His recent publications include *Social Institutions and Economic Performance: Studies in Industrial Relations in Advanced Capitalist Economies* (1992); *Governing Capitalist Economies: Performance and Control of Economic Sectors* (1994; co-edited with J. Rogers Hollingsworth and Philippe C. Schmitter); and *Work Councils: Consultation, Representation, and Cooperation in Industrial Relations* (1995; co-edited with Joel Rogers).

Thorstein Veblen (1857–1929) was an institutionalist economist and the foremost critic of big business capitalism in America. He taught at the Universities of Chicago and Missouri, at Stanford and at the New School in New York. His books include *The Theory of the Leisure Class* (1899); *The Theory of Business Enterprise. An Economic Study of Institutions* (1904); *The Instinct of Workmanship and the State of the Industrial Arts* (1914); *Imperial Germany and the Industrial Revolution* (1915); *The Higher Learning in America: A Memorandum on the Conduct of Universities by Business Men* (1918); *The Vested Interests and the State of the Industrial Arts* (1919); and *The Engineers and the Price* (1921).

Arthur J. Vidich is Senior Lecturer and Professor Emeritus of Sociology and Anthropology at the Graduate Faculty, New School for Social Research. He is the author of *Small Town in Mass Society* (1st edn, 1958; with Joseph Bensman); *The Political Impact of Colonial Administration* (1980); and co-author of *American Sociology: Worldly Rejections of Religion and Their Directions* (1985; with Stanford M. Lyman); editor of *Reflections on Community Studies* (1964); and *The New Middle Classes: Life-Styles, Status Claims and Political Orientations* (1995); and co-editor of *Conflict and Control: Challenge to Legitimacy of Modern Governments* (1979; with Ronald M. Glassman) and *Social Order and the Public Philosophy* (1988; with Stanford M. Lyman).

John Zysman is Professor of Political Science at the University of California, Berkeley, and Co-Director of the Berkeley Roundtable on International Economy (BRIE). He is the author of *Political Strategies for Industrial Order: State, Market, and Industry in France* (1977); and *The Highest Stakes: The Economic Foundations of the Next Security System* (1992); and co-editor of *American Industry in International Competition: Government Policies and Corporate Strategies* (1983; with Laura Tyson); *The Dynamics of Trade and Employment* (1988; with Laura D'Andrea Tyson and William T. Dickens); and *Politics and Productivity: The Real Story of Why Japan Works* (1989; with Laura D'Andrea Tyson and Chalmers Johnson).

Index of Names

Hart, Gary, US Senator 196
Hart, Jeffrey 414n12
Hayek, Friedrich 149, 220n10, 220n11
Held, David 30n39
Heilbroner, Robert 26n1
Helleiner, Gerald K. 17, 385ff, 429
Henderson, Hubert 131, 136n19
Hershey, Robert D. 256n19
Herskovits, M. J. 150n3
Hewson, John 340n8
Hickson, David J. 30n36
Hilferding, Rudolf 4, 27n6, 420
Hirsch, Seev 382n13
Hobbes, Thomas 6, 105
Holland, Stuart 212, 221n20
Hollingsworth, J. Rogers 414n24
Holloway, J. 221n16
Hoover, Herbert Clark, US President 123, 126, 128, 131, 135n4
Hubert, Don 30n39
Hughes, Charles E. 126
Hughes, Jonathan 28n22
Hume, David 101ff, 148
Huskisson, Thomas 104
Hymer, Stephen 340n12

Illich, Ivan 233

Jacoby, Henry 27n8
Jacquemin, Alexis P. 313n10
Jenny, F. 314n18
Jessop, Bob 221n16, 221n17
Johnson, Chalmers 377, 383n34, 414n14
Johnson, Lyndon B., US President 345, 362
Johnson, Samuel 103, 198
Joll, C. L. 313n5
Jordan, Bill 16, 201ff, 426, 432n18
Josephson, Matthew 28n22

Kaldor, Nicolas 204, 220n4
Kalecki, Michal 204, 220n5
Kaplan, Robert D. 431n9
Katzenstein, Peter 414n19
Kautsky, Karl 340n12, 381, 399f, 413n1
Kaysen, Carl 183n6

Kennedy, John F., US President 345
Keohane, Robert O. 384n42
Keynes, John Maynard 13ff, 29n31, 101ff, 121, 126, 131f, 155, 203, 214, 425, 432n19
Kierzkowski, Henry K. 382n8
Kimball, Linda M. 272n5
Kindleberger, Charles 12, 121ff, 215, 221n27, 370, 421
Kolko, Gabriel 275, 295n2
Kolko, Joyce 16, 274ff, 427
Kono, Toyohiro 314n20, 314n24
Kozol, Jonathan 273n7
Krasner, Stephen D. 383n19
Krugman, Paul R. 26n2, 382n11
Kuttner, Robert 431n11

Laffer, Arthur 339n5, 340n7
Lamm, Richard D. 379
Lamont, Thomas 126
Landon, Alf 353
Lary, Hal 123
Lazonick, William 431n11
Lembruch, G. 220n2
Lenin, Vladimir I. 152, 340n12, 380f, 399f, 413n2
Leontief, Wassily 192
Leslie, Cliff 106
Lester, R. K. 414n13
Lewis, Arthur 132
Lipset, Seymour Martin 28n20
Locke, John 6, 101ff, 105, 118n1
Lodge, Henry Cabot 126
Loeb, E. M. 150n2
Longstreth, Frank 221n23

MacLennan, Carol 255n9
Magdoff, Harry 413n3
Maine, Henry 145
Mair, L. P. 150n1
Malinowski, Bronislaw 142, 150n5
Malone, Michael S. 431n6
Malthus, Thomas 104, 106f
Marshall, Alfred 109, 112
Marshall, Ray 265
Marshall, T. H. 30n37
Martineau, Harriet 105, 107

Index of Subjects